Creativity:
Its Educational Implications

COMPILED BY

JOHN CURTIS GOWAN

Professor of Education
San Fernando Valley State College
Northridge, California

GEORGE D. DEMOS

Dean of Students
California State College
Long Beach, California

E. PAUL TORRANCE

Professor of Education
University of Georgia
Athens, Georgia

JOHN WILEY & SONS, INC.   *New York · London · Sydney*

Contributing Authors

MARY JANE ASCHNER   Formerly Professor of Education, Boston University, Boston, Mass.

KENNETH R. BEITTEL   Professor of Art, Pennsylvania State University, University Park, Pa.

CATHERINE B. BRUCH   Consultant, Los Angeles County Schools, Los Angeles, Calif.

ROBERT C. BURKHART   Professor of Art, Pennsylvania State University, University Park, Pa.

GEORGE D. DEMOS   Dean of Students, California State College, Long Beach, Long Beach, Calif.

LORETTA N. FRETWELL   Professor of Education, Eastern Washington State College, Cheney, Wash.

EDWARD C. FRIERSON   Professor of Education, George Peabody Teachers College, Nashville, Tenn.

JAMES J. GALLAGHER   Professor of Education, University of Illinois, Urbana, Ill.

JOHN CURTIS GOWAN   Professor, San Fernando Valley State College, Northridge, Calif.

J. P. GUILFORD   Professor of Psychology, University of Southern California, Los Angeles, Calif.

RALPH J. HALLMAN   Professor of Psychology, Pasadena City College, Pasadena, Calif.

ROLAND B. LEWIS   Professor of Education, Eastern Washington State College, Cheney, Wash.

DONALD W. MACKINNON   Institute of Personality Assessment and Research, University of California, Berkeley, Berkeley, Calif.

JUDITH L. MCELVAIN   Professor of Education, Eastern Washington State College, Cheney, Wash.

WILLIAM B. MICHAEL   Professor of Education, University of California, Santa Barbara, Santa Barbara, Calif.

R. E. MYERS   Research Assistant, Bureau of Educational Research, University of Minnesota, Minneapolis, Minn.

SIDNEY J. PARNES Professor of Psychology, University of Buffalo, Buffalo, N. Y.

MARVIN A. RAPP Dean, University of New York, Albany, N. Y.

LOUIS J. RUBIN Associate Professor of Education, San Fernando Valley State College, Northridge, Calif.

HERBERT A. SIMON Professor and Dean of Graduate School of Industrial Administration, Carnegie Institute of Technology, Pittsburgh, Pa.

LEONARD STEINBERG Assistant Professor, Department of Guidance, California State College at Los Angeles, Los Angeles, Calif.

BEN B. STRASSER Elementary Science Consultant, Los Angeles County Schools, Los Angeles, Calif.

J. RICHARD SUCHMAN Associate Professor of Education, U.S. Office of Education, University of Illinois, Urbana, Ill.

C. W. TAYLOR Professor of Psychology, University of Utah, Salt Lake City, Utah

ALISON THORNE Housewife, Logan, Utah

E. PAUL TORRANCE Professor of Education, University of Georgia, Athens, Georgia

W. J. WALKER Instructor, Mexico Academy, Mexico, N. Y.

FRANK E. WILLIAMS Research Associate, Bureau of Educational Research, University of Utah, Salt Lake City, Utah

KAORU YAMAMOTO Professor of Special Education, Kent State University, Kent, Ohio

WAYNE S. ZIMMERMAN Test Officer, California State College at Los Angeles, Los Angeles, Calif.

Preface

A spring of fresh water is a nuisance when it first issues from the ground, producing only mud and mire. It cannot be stopped by cement or earth fill; its flow will continue to seep around the edges. But when the spring is given a protective and delimiting margin, and a channel is provided for its stream, it becomes a source of joy. The same is true of creativity.

This book represents a first attempt to help educators transform the muddy beginnings of creativity into a flowing stream in the children they teach and counsel. The spring of creativity exists in all children, but in most the flow has been blocked. Like the spring, creativity is at times destructive, and the young child creates and destroys almost in the same breath. The child may feel guilty over what he has created, for it may not be understood, accepted, or valued by others. Or he may be depressed or remorseful after creative effort, or even frightened by the uncovering of this aspect of his being. For one or all of these reasons, he may decide to cement in the spring rather than to cultivate it. The social problem is to obtain the benefits of creativity without its destructive results.

What kinds of teachers and counselors are best able to help children restore the creative potential? This large question assumes that there is some kind of relationship between teacher personality, teacher classroom behavior, and pupil gain in creativity. As research has indicated, this relationship, if it exists, is far more complex than simple cause-and-effect. It also involves more than just knowledge about curriculum, as some of the readings will demonstrate. That children need supportive guidance for creative performance is a thesis which each of the editors has previously enunciated. Recent research also hints that effective teaching behaviors fostering creativity include energy, courage, wisdom, patience, and originality. But neither this book nor others to come can do more for educators than point the way and help them to make a start.

If you would know more about creativity, look within a child or within yourself. Clean out and edge the spring, and when the surface is very tranquil, look deep into the water below. The little flecks of sand at the bottom will barely move, but they will whisper things you will not find in books. It is this attention to inner detail which brings insight. Whitman in his preface to the first edition of *Leaves of Grass* said: "We are all great poets, but only the greatest poets know it." We are all potentially creative, but only those who have become creative realize it. One of the best ways to cultivate our own creativity is to help children cultivate theirs.

Acknowledgments

An undertaking of this magnitude requires the cooperation of a large number of persons, only a few of whom can be mentioned here. First, of course, come the efforts of the various contributors whose graciousness in allowing their articles to be republished is acknowledged with thanks. To their respective publishers, whose credits are given on the first page of each article, we also extend our thanks for permission to use copyrighted material. Editor Ann Isaacs of the *Gifted Child Quarterly* is singled out for special gratitude for allowing two of her editorial assistants to draw so freely from that journal. Likewise special thanks go to the Charles C Thomas Company of Springfield, Illinois for allowing us to abstract the introduction from a chapter on creativity in Gowan and Demos: *The Education and Guidance of the Ablest*.

The editors also wish to thank Ruth Kranhouse for help in manuscript preparation. We also wish to thank our respective wives for their forbearance.

J. C. G., G. D. D., *and* E. P. T.

February, 1967

Table of Contents

Creativity:
Its Educational Implications

Introduction

George D. Demos and John C. Gowan

OF ALL THE POWERS OF MAN, THAT OF CREATIVITY SEEMS MOST UNIQUE. The generally accepted custom among the ancients was to ascribe divine origin, inspiration or direction to any great creative work. Even the aspects of initiation and selection which are universally found in creative function appear somewhat mysterious.

To create, the mind must withdraw upon itself for a time, to focus its forces, and then project an individualized image of itself onto an external medium. Psychologically this introspection and "focusing" takes the form of a heightened awareness of the peripheral asymmetries in a situation, and a subtle settling into consciousness of concepts at the boundaries of rationality or in the unconscious. It is understandable, then, that the time of creation is a "tender time" when man wishes to draw apart from his fellow men—whether up the mountain, into the desert, or away to his own source of solitude—but almost always into a silence. Creative withdrawal and return, as Toynbee has pointed out, is as characteristic of creative acts of groups as of individuals.

Because creativity is a word which has recently been taken over by science from religion, it is almost impossible to discover it in a dictionary or encyclopedia more than a decade old. It is a new concept, recently attributed to the personality of man, and still fraught with some mystical connotations. For this reason it is necessary to be especially careful in attempting to define it, and to distinguish between creativity and other similar intellectual functions, as well as to note possible different varieties of creativity.

Bronowski (1958:59) distinguishes among discovery, invention, and creation by pointing out that Columbus discovered the West, Bell invented the telephone, and Shakespeare created *Othello*. A fact is discovered, and a theory is invented, but only a masterpiece is created—for creation must engage the whole mind.

Definitions of creativity in terms of *traits* have gradually given way to definitions of creativity in terms of *process*. For example, Stein

I

(Taylor 1955:171) states: Three of the basic assumptions underlying our approach to the problems of creativity are as follows:

1. Creativity is the resultant process that occurs within the individual. In general one tends to judge the creativity of others in terms of "product" that they have produced, or stated differently, in terms of the "distances" between what they have produced and the status of the field before they come on the scene. Such an orientation causes us to overlook the fact that creativity is a process. It is a process of hypothesis formation, hypothesis testing, and the communication of results.
2. Creativity is the resultant process of social transaction. Individuals affect and are affected by the environments in which they live. They do not interact with their environments without changes occurring in both directions.
3. For purposes of empirical research our definition of creativity is as follows: Creativity is that process which results in "a novel work that is accepted as tenable to useful or satisfying by a group at some point in time."

Despite the fact that popular stereotype sometimes confuses the creative genius with the emotionally disturbed, there is ample evidence that character integration and emotional stability provide a necessary steady platform for the subtle awarenesses which make creative functioning possible. Indeed the steadying perspective which withdrawal from the world gives to most of us when we are about to try to become creative, has been noted since the time of the ancient Greeks.

Maslow is particularly clarifying in this regard (1962:127–37). He points out that we tend to think of creativity in terms of products, and that we also judge creativity (as we do achievement) in terms of stereotypes. For example, we assume that any artist must be more creative than any cook. He distinguished "special-talent" creativeness from "self-actualizing" creativeness. The former is a result of high abilities in special fields, and ordinarily restricts production to those fields; it is also relatively independent of mental health. The latter, springing much more directly from the personality, shows itself as an effect of positive mental health and appears as creative flexibility and free energy to accomplish the ordinary affairs of life in a creative way. He further states that to the extent that creativity involves the processes of construction and unification of synthesis, it depends upon character integration in the person. He feels that self-actualizing creatives are less fearful than others, less fearful of other people and less fearful of themselves. They are more self-accepting and this makes it possible for them to perceive and accept reality to a greater degree.

MacKinnon (1963) feels that the creative person is typical of many who make up for what they lack in verbal intellectual giftedness with a high level of energy, a kind of cognitive flexibility which enables them to keep attacking a problem with a variety of techniques from a variety of angles; and being confident of their ultimate success, they persevere until they arrive at a creative solution. This kind of person should remind us that creative giftedness is not necessarily equated with high verbal intelligence.

The last decade has been characterized by an unusual amount of interest in the genesis of creativity in individuals and in the characteristics of creative people. While this research has often been concerned with scientific creativity, there has been a refreshing willingness to notice the artistic and humanistic components as well.

Taylor (1959) suggests that creativity and giftedness (in the academic sense) may be two different sets of parameters for investigation, and that our attempts to broaden the concept of giftedness to include creativity may ultimately break down. He notes that the ordinary intelligence test covers only a very few of the several mental factors isolated by Guilford (1959), and feels that its lack of factor breadth disqualifies it as a predictor of achievement, let alone creativity.

In describing the creative person, Taylor (1963) also notes the importance of divergent thinking, especially in production of ideas, fluencies, flexibility, and originality. Humor, fantasy, and playfulness with ideas are also among the characteristics of the truly creative person. Other traits mentioned include curiosity, manipulation, questioning ability, and restructuring of ideas. Personality characteristics mentioned are autonomy, independence, femininity of interests, dominance, self-assertion, self-acceptance, resourcefulness, radicalness, and complexity of personality.

The Institute of Personality Assessment and Research (IPAR) at the University of California, Berkeley, through the leadership of MacKinnon and Barron, has made assessment studies of creative leaders in various scientific and cultural fields through interview and questionnaire techniques. MacKinnon (1962, 1963) has summarized the characteristics of creative persons as follows: They are intelligent, original, independent in thought and action, open to experience both of the inner self and the outer world, intuitive, esthetically sensitive and free from crippling restraints. They also have high energy level, a persistent commitment to creative endeavor, and a strong sense of destiny which includes a degree of resoluteness and a measure of egotism.

In order to summarize much diverse research into the characteristics of creativity, materials can be grouped under three headings as follows:

The creative person is able to tolerate conceptual ambiguity: he is not made anxious by configural disorder, but sees in it a clue to a higher synthesis.

Barron (1958:155) reported on his investigations of creativity by studying ways in which creative persons differed from others in their responses to order and disorder. He found that the creatives tolerated disorder better and were more able to find unity in disorder in drawings than were others. Discriminating test items for subjects who previously had shown marked independence of judgment indicated that they were more open to innovation and less disturbed by surface imbalance. Inspection of the items also reveals a high degree of intraceptiveness and rejection of authoritarian tendencies.

Barron also indicated some consensus among social scientists in the feeling that psychological health is important for creativity. Commonly mentioned factors included: (1) accuracy of reality perception, (2) stable somatic and psychosomatic conditions, (3) absence of hostility and anxiety, capacity for friendly and cooperative relationships with others, (5) spontaneity and warmth, (6) social responsibility. He noted, however, that a number of the creative men of history were afflicted with some type of psychological difficulty, and suggested that it is not so much the presence or absence of psychopathology as the way it is handled that marks the creative.

From such considerations Barron (Taylor 1955:164) developed five hypotheses with regard to creative persons: (1) that they prefer complexity and some degree of apparent imbalance in phenomena, (2) that they are more complex psychodynamically and have greater personal scope, (3) that they are more independent in their judgment, (4) that they are more self-assertive and dominant, and (5) that they reject suppression as a mechanism for the control of impulse.

Creative people have a great fund of free energy. This free energy often seems to result from a high degree of psychological health.

One of the concomitants of creativity that has been mentioned by various authorities is the possession of much free energy. The source of this energy seems to come from within the person and is the effective release of his aptitudes as a result of good mental health.

Obviously, since not all potential creators are in perfect mental health, one way to make them more creative is to ameliorate their psychological climate. This can be done by reducing anxiety, allowing for a feeling of worth and well-being, and by extending the boundaries of security. Thus, counseling and psychotherapy can be effective tools in enhancing creativity.

Since anxiety can be raised even in a normal individual by the lonely, unorthodox and apparent irrational, unconventional or tabooed quality of creative work, it takes courage to face the hostile and dubious crowd with a new theory or work of art, and courage is a necessary component of the creative worker's character. Socrates was put to death for his beliefs, Einstein risked professional ruin with his theory of relativity, Freud was reviled, Darwin considered an enemy of Christianity, and Galileo imprisoned and forced to recant. The ability to handle large amounts of anxiety without losing creative thrust or psychological health is an important consideration.

Creativity appears to be enhanced by the predisposing, focusing or constricting of interests and attention. This channeling occurs first in the child as a result of parental pressures and relationships: it is forwarded or retarded by the environmental stimulation of school, and it is finally refined and directed to its target by the self-motivation of early successes.

Roe (Taylor, 1957:102 ff.) for example, traces the genesis of creative scientists from the casual acceptance of a child by his parents. She feels that broad occupational interests develop from the same nexus. She finds that it is difficult to get free flowing creativity from a child who has been overprotected. In her studies of physical scientists she found that they (in contrast to artists) did not need to make a fuss, and had a free and easy way of creating. She suspects that there are many potential creative scientists in the lower socioeconomic levels where there is more casual acceptance of a child by his parents.

The efforts of educators to augment the creative output of their students rests on three assumptions: (1) that everyone has some measure of creative ability, (2) that such abilities as the individual possesses are capable of being developed by practice, and (3) that such training is a proper function of the school.

We may note that if creativity is an aptitude factor of intelligence it may be theoretically impossible to augment it significantly. Since much of education, however, consists of the enhancing of special aptitudes, one may be justified in asking how this particular aptitude is best promoted. Since creativity depends *par excellence* on its newness, novelty, strangeness and difference, it is a somewhat difficult process to say how we shall prepare children for it—other than giving them a good general background and sound mental health, and not stifling their creative drives.

This educational problem of producing achievement and productivity without sacrificing originality and creativity is a serious and enlarging educational issue, for which there is no immediate and ready answer. American public education must face this issue squarely in the coming decade.

The instructor's role in furthering the student's creativity is a protective and nurturing one. Briefly, it appears to consist of the following steps or phases:

1. *Inspiration:* This means the kind of teaching and general relationships which inspire the student to learn; in some cases to please and emulate the instructor, or, of equal importance, the freedom to verbally disagree.
2. *Stimulation:* Enclosed in the content of the curriculum should be stimulating, new and exciting experiences. It is also the far-off in time and space, the realistic, the unusual, the novel, intraceptive and unhackneyed.
3. *Amelioration:* Students cannot create without inspiration and stimulation, and they will not create without the ameliorating influence of a warm, safe and permissive atmosphere. They need a zone of psychological safety out of which they can step to explore the world but to which they can return quickly when frightened or disturbed by their discoveries. The time of creation is a tender time. Professors can help by rewarding initial efforts and by not negatively reinforcing creativity, however crude, by harsh criticism. Lastly, and most vital, is a general atmosphere of warmth and even affection. All of us, and especially the young, tend to create things for those we love.
4. *Direction:* The instructor needs to be in a position to direct developing talent to an area and a level where it will be most effective. While this is properly a guidance function, it is something which the able teacher can handle.
5. *Encouragement and development:* The final aspect of the instructor's role is the encouragement of the developing capacities into a practical channel. Some of this will take the form of constructive technical criticism when the student is ready for it. Some of it will take the form of referral to competent authorities, to books, or other nonpersonal resources.

In conclusion, we in education have a tremendous responsibility to become more effective in bringing a larger portion of our students through the educative process untrammeled and in possession of their full potential. May we become more successful at this most vital task!

y shouldn't over-pro-ed however see p. 5

REFERENCES

Barron, F. "The Disposition Towards Originality." *Conference on Identification of Creative Scientific Talent* (Taylor, C. W. ed.) Salt Lake City, Utah: Univ. of Utah Press. 156–170. 1955.

Barron, F. "The Psychology of Imagination." *Scientific American.* 199:3:150–170. 1958.

Bronowski, J. "The Creative Process." *Scientific American.* 199:3:58–66. 1958.

MacKinnon, D. W. "Personality Correlates of Creativity." (Mimeo.) A paper presented at the Second Conference on Productive Thinking, National Education Association, Washington, D. C., May 2–4, 1963.

MacKinnon, D. W. "What Makes a Person Creative?" *Saturday Review.* 45:6:15–17 ff. Feb. 10, 1962.

Maslow, A. H. *Towards A Psychology of Being.* Princeton, N. J.: D. Van Nostrand. 1962.

Taylor, C. W. (Prin. Investigator.) *The Identification of Creative Scientific Talent.* Salt Lake City, Utah: Univ. of Utah Press. 1955, 1957, 1959.

Taylor, C. W. "A Tentative Description of the Creative Individual." (Mimeo.) Univ. of Utah. 1959.

Taylor, C. W. and Barron, F. (Editors.) *Scientific Creativity: Its Recognition and Development.* New York: John Wiley and Sons. Feb. 1963.

CHAPTER ONE

General Considerations

What Makes a Gifted Child Creative?
—Four Theories

John Curtis Gowan

RESEARCH INDICATES RATHER DEFINITELY THAT WHEREAS INTELLIGENCE and creativity are highly correlated below about 120 I.Q., above that figure they are nearly independent variables. If this is so, factors which produce creative gifted children must be different from factors which produce non-creative gifted children. It is our task to examine four theories as to the nature of these causes.

I: THE STRUCTURE OF INTELLECT THEORY

Guilford declares that creativity consists of a number of closely related factors of intellect in the divergent thinking slab of the structure of intellect model (see figure). Particularly important in this slab is the chimney formed by the intersection of semantic contents with divergent thinking production. This chimney of factors contains those we usually stereotype as "verbal creativity," including ideational fluency, spontaneous flexibility, associational fluency, and originality. Under this theory, creative gifted children are those with high endowments in these factors; whereas non-creative gifted children have their high endowments elsewhere.

As long as we believed that intelligence was fixed and unidimensional, the role of experience in facilitating its development was very limited. But if intelligence is multidimensional and partly environmental, then the role of experience becomes important indeed. The stimulation of

REPRINTED by permission of the Author and *Gifted Child Quarterly*, 9:3–6, Spring, 1965.

potential factors of intellect may in some ways be regarded as similar to the refinement of athletic finesse through development and facilitation of aiming abilities and eye-hand coordination. To say so is not to resurrect the old ghost of formal discipline, but to infer that research has made us more sophisticated regarding the differing properties of the factors of intellect. The transfer capabilities of the cognition of semantic units (verbal comprehension) may be slight, whereas those of the evaluation of semantic implications (problem sensitivity) may be sizeable. If we reduce the structure of intellect cube to the two dimensions of operations and products (see figure), we find that ease transfer is not the only variable that changes from "top left" (verbal comprehension) to "bottom right" (problem sensitivity). Other notable differences which also have important educational implications include the ease with which the factor ability is retained under stress, anxiety, or authoritarianism. There is also a developmental aspect in the young child's facility with factors at the "top left" as a necessary prelude toward his developing facility with those at the "bottom right."

II: CREATIVITY AS SOUND MENTAL HEALTH

This view of creativity, which owes much to Maslow, sees creativity in terms of complete character integration or lack of barriers between the conscious mind and its preconscious areas. The ability to "regress in the service of the ego," retrieve material from the preconscious, and return with it to the world of reality is a vital aspect of creative production, as Thurstone and others have noted. The result of such full-functioning is, of course, self-actualization in the Maslovian sense.

Such considerations suggest that the ability to handle the more complex factors of the structure of intellect model depend, not only on the result of a rich curriculum stimulation, but also on the improvement of emotional and ego strength on the part of the child. It takes longer to hold in tension a problem which has many answers (or none), than it does one which can be quickly solved convergently. The anxious child, however bright, may not be psychologically capable of the stress involved.

While it is incumbent upon the child to develop emergent synthesizing abilities at higher actualizing levels, it is incumbent upon society to see that his prior needs are satiated to the extent that he can devote his energies to intellectual tasks. The child who is hungry is too concerned with his hunger to learn. The child who is insecure about love and safety needs is too preoccupied to apply himself. The child whose social difficulties blunt his learning propensities is also operating at a lower hierarchial level.

Gifted children who have these problems are often able to "get by" while operating at a very low level of efficiency. But only when these primitive levels are satisfied can we expect bright children to perform at their cognitive best. Consequently a corollary of cognitive stimulation in the classroom is guidance which frees able children for the full-functioning in more complex intellectual areas. Ego strength and a healthy self-concept are part of the stock-in-trade which the child needs to operate in a world of reality. We can condition a psychotic, but to educate a child properly in the wide-spectrum of the structure of intellect model requires attention to his mental health as well as to his cognitive competence.

III: THE OPPOSITE OF AUTHORITARIANISM

Somewhat akin to the previous theory is the concept of creativity as the opposite of authoritarianism. The compartmentalization, stereotyping and anti-intraception of the authoritarian personality prevents creative functioning. Hence the degree to which we have been tarnished with authoritarian practice diminishes our creative potential, and narrows the possible avenues of creative endeavor. Investigations with the California Psychological Inventory, for example, show that flexibility (creativity) and tolerance (lack of authoritarianism) are well correlated. This view of creativity, like the previous, suggests that children can be helped to preserve their creativity by non-authoritarian attitudes on the part of parents and teachers, especially by not having negative evaluations put upon their initial efforts. The importance of the child's being first the recipient of, and later the producer of sound (rather than pejorative) evaluations is a most important adjunct to his becoming productively creative. For this kind of evaluation is the way in which creative fantasy becomes bonded to useful reality. Like sistole and diastole, they are the complementary components of "effective surprise." It may be worth a slight discursion to see why this is so.

In economics, the entrepreneur who has risk capital also has 1) a reasonably safe financial position from which to operate, 2) some excess capital which he values, but which he is willing to risk on a situation which he can partly control, and 3) some know-how or sophistication in the operation he proposes to prosecute, which, in his mind at least, increase his prbability of gain over that of chance expectancy.

The Semantic Contents Slab of the Guilford Structure of Intellect
(The three other slabs, are figural (F), symbolic (S), and behavioral (B).).

Operations	Cognition	Memory	Convergent production	Divergent production	Evaluation
1st Letter	O	M	N	D	E
3rd Letter U Units	CMU Verbal comprehension: To know meanings of words.	MMU Memory for ideas: To retrieve memorized ideas.	NMU Concept meaning: To discover an idea subsuming several given ideas.	DMU Ideational fluency: To produce many ideas.	EMU Idea selection: To judge which idea most meets a criterion.
C Classes	CMC Conceptual classes: To see common attributes of groups of ideas.		NMC Semantic classifying: To sort ideas into meaningful classes.	DMC Spontaneous flexibility: To generate many classes subsumed under an idea.	EMC Idea classification: To select ideas best subsuming several ideas.
R Relations	CMR Semantic relations: To see relations between ideas.	MMR Associational memory: To retrieve memorized associations.	NMR Semantic correlating: To produce an idea related to another in a specified way.	DMR Associational fluency: To produce manipulations having an idea in common.	EMR Semantic relation selection: To select best relationship.

	C	M	N	D	E
S Systems	CMS General reasoning: To see basic relationships in a problem.	MMS Memory for complex ideas: To recall the complex interrelations of ideas.	NMS Semantic patterning: To generate a system from several ideas.	DMS Expressional fluency: To produce many sets of ideas.	EMS Experimental evaluation: To judge which elements are congruent and consistent.
T Transformations	CMT Penetration: To see affects of a change of interpretation.		NMT Semantic redefining: To produce a change of interpretation or emphasis in ideas.	DMT Originality: To produce "effective surprise."	EMT Judgment: To choose best interpretation in terms of meaning.
I Implications	CMI Conceptual foresight: To foresee consequences or implications.		NMI Deduction: To deduce a statement of results from a set of ideas.	DMI Semantic elaborating: To produce many details elaborating an idea.	EMI Problem sensitivity: To explicate concern or uncertainty.

He is encouraged by a) past success, b) ready-money and credit, and c) a climate which favors this kind of operation.

In education the "reasonable adventurer" has 1) a safe psychological base from which to venture, and to which to return, 2) some excess capital in the form of energy, prestige, ideas, which he is willing to risk, and 3) some sophistication in the "strategies" game. Like the entrepreneur, he is encouraged by a) past success, b) the availability of prestige and status (if you lose it on a bad guess, you get it back again), and c) a climate that encourages curiosity.

It is perfectly obvious that teachers have a great deal to do with a child's past successes, the availability of prestige, the control of authoritarianism, the type of evaluations, and the climate which encourages risk-taking in search of creativity. Oftentimes they subtly discourage children completely in such a search by leveling off the classroom, keeping a tight control on available prestige, and similar actions, so that the child may fear to make any guess, since it may lose him something which is irretrievable. The teacher can also discourage creativity through reasonable risk-taking by teaching toward convergent thinking exclusively, emphasizing memory processes, and by keeping the authoritarian level high. The only kind of risk taking which develops in such an atmosphere is the unrealistic risk-taking of the predelinquent, in which risk-taking is divorced from its probable consequences.

But the development of such attitudes of realistic risk-taking in search for ideas on the part of students does not depend alone on the avoidance of authoritarian tendencies on the part of the teacher. It also encompasses careful counseling efforts to parry the crushing effects of anxiety on creativity. It involves the education of curiosity as a respectable emotion. It requires the development of risk-capital in the form of ideas and strategies with which to experiment. If we are going to take responsibility for the impact of emotional and cultural factors on productive thinking (and we shall probably not get much creativity out of children unless we do), we must take a lot more responsibility for the guidance aspects of the child's emotional development than we have. We must come to see that even for the gifted child, a stimulating curriculum experience requires increased supportive guidance, since it increases the motivation of the child to deal at higher levels with the problems presented, and this higher level of operation requires better mental health for such full-functioning.

The process of reducing experience from James' "Blooming, buzzing confusion" to a world of mostly-manageable, and mostly understandable events is what education is all about. If we are successful, we gradually improve from a situation where to risk is to lose everything through commission, and to block is to lose everything through omission, to a situation where we are willing to risk a little more each time in a game where the odds keep increasingly favoring us. Our anxiety becomes reality-oriented in the sense that we are scared of freeways but able to drive on them, and we habituate ourselves to a strategy of realistic evaluation in an imperfect but generally understandable world.

FUNCTION OF THE CHILD'S OEDIPAL RESPONSE TO THE AFFECTIONAL APPROACH OF THE OPPOSITE-SEXED PARENT THEORY

The above function is a final and somewhat original theory of creativity. According to this theory, boys who were close to their mothers, and girls who were close to their fathers during the period from four to seven will become more creative than others. Such a theory, of course, would explain why there appear to be more creative men than women in the world. The child, at this time, enchanted by the warm affect of the opposite-sexed parent responds to this in the only way he can,—by the creative manipulation of his immediate environment, and by an enlargement of the bridge between his fantasy life and his real world. While this view of creativity has much more consequence for parents than for teachers, it is worth considering.

These four theories of creativity are by no means proved. They are offered here as a brief summary of the state of the art in 1965. All of them have important educational implications, however, and it is time we test them, and if found valid, employ them in the stimulation of creativity in our bright youth. One of the bright spots in creativity research (as opposed to research on intelligence a generation ago) is that we go into it not with the feeling that creativity is fixed and unchangeable (as the I.Q. was once thought to be), but we consider creativity as responsive to environmental stimulation, and therefore dependent upon our educational efforts. May they be forthcoming!

The Necessary and Sufficient
Conditions of Creativity
Ralph J. Hallman

THE PURPOSE OF THIS PAPER IS TO PRESENT A CONCEPTUAL SCHEME FOR systematizing the extensive and diverse research data which this decade has produced in connection with the problem of creativity.

THE STATUS OF THE DATA

The data regarding creativity now exist in the form of random, unrelated insights or as outright disagreements and contradictions. The disorganized state of this evidence prevails largely for two reasons. In the first place, a wide variety of disciplines have investigated the creative process and have tended to emphasize their separate interests. Philosophers, psychologists, scientists, artists, writers, engineers, and businessmen have contributed information, and this information reflects a particular concern. For example, the philosophers tend to discover the grounds for creative productions among the final powers operating in the universe; the psychologists, among the dynamisms of personality functions; the scientists, among the self-regulating forces of protoplasm or of matter; the artists and writers, among the products which they create; the engineers and politicians, among the externally defined needs which they confront; the businessmen and managerial officers, among the interpersonal relations of their organizations.

In the second place, the structure of the creative experience itself is very complex and therefore can accommodate widely diverse approaches. It involves components which are unrelated to each other except in this one circumstance. They bear no necessary relations to each other in the external world, that is, outside the bounds of the creative process. To be sure, the creative act is a single event, a highly integrated movement involving the total organism such that during the experience all boundary lines fade, distinctions blur, and the artist experiences himself as one with his materials and his vision.

REPRINTED by permission of the Author and *Journal of Humanistic Psychology*, 3:1, Spring, 1963.

Yet, the creative act is multifaceted as well. It includes psychological, environmental, cultural, physical, and intellectual aspects. The evidence clusters around one or another of these aspects or around one of the methodological approaches to the problem.

For example, a large body of evidence has accumulated in connection with the effort to identify the particular *personality traits* which make for creativity. The assumption is that the creative process can be fully accounted for by providing an exhaustive list of such traits. The psychiatrist, the clinician, and the factor-analyst have shown great interest in explaining creativeness by means of traits. For example, Guilford's psychometric method has identified in the creative personality such traits as sensitivity to problems, fluency, flexibility, originality, ability to transform meanings, and ability to elaborate (*19*). Fromm speaks of four traits: capacity to be puzzled, ability to concentrate, capacity to accept conflict, and willingness to be reborn every day (*13*). Rogers has a similar list: openness to experience, internal locus of evaluation, and ability to toy with elements (*46*). Maslow has perhaps the most extensive list (*33*); the creative personality, he says, is spontaneous, expressive, effortless, innocent, unfrightened by the unknown or the ambiguous, able to accept tentativeness and uncertainty, able to tolerate bipolarity, able to integrate opposites. The creative person is the healthy, self-actualizing person, Maslow believes. Others who have identified creative traits are Barron (*5*), Meier (*36*), Whiting (*60*), Angyal (*3*), Mooney (*38*), Lowenfeld (*28*), and Hilgard (*23*).

Another body of data has been collected to prove that creativity can be fully explained as a series of *chronological stages*, each stage of which makes its unique contribution to the total process. Wallas (*58*) provides the classical statement of this position, and he has been followed by Patrick (*41*) and Spender (*52*) in connection with creativeness in poetry; Hadamard (*21*) and Poincaré (*42*) in mathematics; Arnold (*4*), Patrick, and Montmasson (*37*) in science. Others who define creativity in terms of serial stages are Ghiselin (*16*), Vinacke (*57*), and Hutchinson (*24*).

A third cluster of evidence surrounds the definition that creative activity involves an interchange of energy among *vertical layers* of psychological systems. Creativeness consists in a shift of psychic levels. Most writers identify two psychological levels and refer to them variously as the primary and secondary processes, the autistic and the reality adjusted, unconscious mechanisms and conscious deliberation, free and bound energies, gestalt-free and articulating tendencies. These writers include Freud, Ehrenzweig (*10*), and Schneider

(48). Maslow adds to these two levels a third one called integration *(30)*. Murray also speaks of three levels, the physical, mental, and superordinate-cultural creations *(39)*. Taylor's list of five levels moves away from the notion that levels are defined as psychic systems: these are the expressive, productive, inventive, innovative, and emergentive *(55)*.

Yet a fourth set of data regards creativeness as *types of thinking* and seeks to distinguish those forms of thinking which are creative from those which are not. It is generally agreed that creative thought consists of certain integrating, synthesizing functions; that it deals with relational form rather than with individual instances; that it discovers new forms which can accommodate past experiences. It involves a real fusion of forms and not merely a juncturing. Spearman refers to creative thinking as the education of correlates *(51)*; Mc-Kellar, as autistic, prelogical, and imaginative *(35)*; Vinacke, as imagination rather than voluntary, rational operations *(57)*; Bartlett, as divergent autistic thinking as distinguished from closed systems *(6)*. Bruner's book *On Knowing* makes the same distinction *(8)*.

A fifth type of evidence consists in the great numbers of *personal reports* from creative artists and scientists which are available. These vary from descriptions of private experiences, as in the case of Nietzsche *(40)*, to public policies as taught by Reynolds *(44)*, and to such heterogeneous collections as the recent one by Ghiselin *(16)*. A complete survey of evidence would need to include such other problems as motivation for creativity, the kinds of creative acts, the concept of genius, and cultural influences.

We can conclude, I believe, that there is some advantage in viewing this valuable but disorganized evidence from the point of view of some conceptual system. The formal structure of such a system would need to reflect the necessary and sufficient conditions of creativity. These criteria would eliminate the less relevant data which have become associated with creativeness, and would unify into a consistent framework the great number of unrelated discoveries which have been made.

I propose, then, that on the basis of evidence now available a tentative statement can be made regarding these conditions. I propose that the creative act can be analyzed into five major components: (1) it is a whole *act*, a unitary instance of behavior; (2) it terminates in the production of *objects* or of forms of living which are distinctive; (3) it evolves out of certain *mental processes*; (4) it co-varies with specific *personality transformations;* and (5) it occurs within a particular kind of *environment*. These may be expressed in abbreviated form as the act, the object, the process, the person, and the environment. A demonstration of the necessary features of each of these factors can employ both descriptive and logical procedures; it can refer to the relevance of empirical evidence, and can infer what grounds are logically necessary in order to explain certain facts.

THE CRITERION OF CONNECTEDNESS

Descriptively, the first criterion can be called the condition of *connectedness*. Observers who have collected evidence about this aspect of creativeness agree that some form of combinatorial activity is requisite to creativity. Logically, a demonstration of this criterion employs the category of *relation* as a principle of explanation. But it may be more meaningful to refer to it as the concept of metaphor. This category isolates the relation of similitude rather than of difference as basic to connectedness. It is implied by the most fundamental characteristic of human creativity, namely, the requirement that man work with materials which he himself has not created. Lacking the omnipotence and omniscience of God, man cannot create out of nothing. He cannot create in the sense of bringing something into being from what previously had no existence. This condition therefore imposes upon him the need to create by *bringing already existing elements into a distinctive relation to each other*. The essence of human creativeness is *relational*, and an analysis of its nature must refer to the connectedness of whatever elements enter into the creative relationship. The analysis must demonstrate that though man does not create the components, he can nevertheless produce *new connections among them*. It must prove that these connections are genuinely original and not simply mechanical. Logically, this means that connectedness comprises relationships which are neither symmetrical nor transitive; that is, the newly created connections as wholes are not equivalent to the parts being connected. Neither side of the equation validly implies the other, for the relationship is neither inferential nor causal; rather, it is metaphoric and transformational.

Let us refer to the research literature for descriptive materials which both logically require this criterion and also provide evidence for its validity. This criterion appears under a variety of names, but it does invariably appear. It is described variously as a combination, composition, configuration, novel relationship, constellation of meanings, new organization, purposive pattern formation, complete relatedness, integration, oneness, fusion, and education of correlates.

All forms of creativity, Bruner says, grow out of a *combinatorial* activity *(8)*, a placing of things in new perspectives. Arnold refers to this criterion as the combining of past experiences into new patterns, into *new configurations* which in some manner satisfy the creator and perhaps society *(4)*. For McKellar, it is a *fusion* of perceptions which have long lain dormant *(35)*; for Gerard, an act of *closure*, a restructuring of the field of perceptual experience *(14)*; for Taylor, the molding of experiences into *organizational patterns* which are new and different; for Poincaré, the production of combinations, of *ordered wholes (42)*; for Kubie, the discovery of *unexpected connections* among things, a fusion produced by the free play of unconscious symbolic processes *(26)*; for Murray, a *compositional* process which results in some new object, experience or image *(39)*; for Rogers, the emergences of novel *relational products*. Ghiselin concludes from his studies of the creative work of artists, scientists, musicians, and writers that the most necessary requirement of creativity is that it present a *new configuration*, a new constellation of meanings which have no specific precedent *(16)*.

These writers may locate connectedness either in the act of perception, in intellect, in personality development, or in the object. But all agree that it is necessary. There is one refinement to this statement: creativity is both a combination of elements into new relations, and a *re*-combining of them. This means that creativity is not merely the capacity to connect elements in a new way, but to transplant these new combinations onto previously unrelated materials. It is the capacity to regard life metaphorically, to experience even orderliness as plastic, to shift intellectual processes from one formal system to another. It is, as Rogers puts it, to remain in process, to discover structure *in* experience instead of imposing structure *upon* experience. Thus, the criterion of connectedness expresses the meaning that creativeness deals largely with relational structures; it implies a fusion of elements into these new structures rather than a mechanical arranging of them; it means that connections are actually produced and are not found.

THE CRITERION OF ORIGINALITY

Descriptively; the second criterion can be called the condition of *originality;* empirical observations identify this quality as being essential to the *products* which have emerged from the creative process. Logically, it requires the category of *singularity* as a principle of explanation, though the psychologist may prefer the term "individuality." This category, I shall argue, specifies four qualities which any item must have if it is to exist as an idiographic, nonclassifiable object, that is, if it is to be genuinely original. These are novelty, unpredictability, uniqueness, and surprise; they refer to the same fundamental characteristic of originality, but from the frames of reference of philosophy, science, art, and psychology respectively.

These four aspects of originality distinguish the authentically creative from the more mechanical arrangements. Logically, this means that they define what is meant by a class of objects as well as by a singular item. The completely idiographic instance logically equates with a class concept, and it functions similarly in syllogistic reasoning. Both the completely original individual and the universal are idiosyncratic and not further classifiable; these four qualities confer this uniqueness.

First, then, novelty means newness, freshness, inventiveness; it is universally recognized by writers in the field as an indispensable quality of originality. Creativity is the fusion of perceptions in a *new* way (McKellar), the capacity to find *new* connections (Kubie), the emergence of *novel* relationships (Rogers), the occurrence of a composition which is *new* (Murray), the disposition to make and recognize *innovations* (Lasswell), an action of mind that produces *new* insights (Gerard), the molding of experiences into *new* organizations (Taylor), the presentation of *new* constellations of meanings (Ghiselin). This meaning has been expressed by Wilson and his co-workers (62) in terms which can be handled more efficiently by the statistical method; these are cleverness, remoteness of association, and uncommonness of response. Guilford briefly considers the possibility that originality may relate more closely to the personality trait of unconventionality than to qualities of newness. That is, he considers whether originality is a function of temperament instead of the objects produced, but he carries this no further than speculation.

Second, originality means unpredictability. This factor refers to the relationship of the created object to other states of affairs in the real world, and asserts that creativeness uncouples such objects from causal connections. It asserts the incompatibility of creativity and causality theory. Generally, philosophic and scientific systems assume orderliness and necessity in the cosmos; they accommodate the concept of originality only with difficulty, for the creation of originals violates necessity and demands freedom. Creativity produces qualities which never existed before and which could never have been predicted on the basis of prior configurations of events. Metaphoric activity intrudes upon logical-causal necessity.

Third, originality means uniqueness. It asserts that every instance of creativeness differs from every other instance, that products which are original have no precedents. Original creations are incomparable, for there is no class of objects to which they can be compared. They are untranslatable, unexampled.

Fourth, originality means surprise. Just as novelty describes the connections that occur in the creative act, unpredictability to the setting of the new creation in the physical environment, and uniqueness to the product when regarded as valuable in its own right, so surprise refers to the psychological effect of novel combinations upon the beholder. Surprise serves as the final test of originality, for without the shock of recognition which *registers* the novel experience, there would be no occasion for individuals to be moved to appreciate or to produce creative works.

The element of surprise has been observed by creative artists and scientists in themselves, by experimental psychologists, and by clinicians. There is general agreement that recognition must be sudden and unexpected in order to achieve fullness of surprise. Fromm holds that the capacity to be aware, to respond freely and spontaneously, reduces tendencies to project and to distort and consequently permits the surprise response (*13*). Schachtel agrees that originality produces emotive shock and that it erupts with suddenness in conditions of unfettered and open encounter with the world (*47*). Getzels and Jackson find that surprise takes the form of unexpected endings to plots, of incongruities, and of humor (*15*). Bruner regards effective surprise as the very essence of creativity itself (*8*).

I shall leave open the question whether originality requires the production of a tangible object. Those who emphasize craftsmanship demand an object; others, as Maslow, believe that creativity can express itself in a style of living.

THE CRITERION OF NONRATIONALITY

Descriptively, the third criterion may be designated as the condition of nonrationality. Even those research workers who are not psychoanalytically oriented agree that certain *unconscious mental processess* are responsible for the metaphoric function of fusing images into new creations. Logically, this criterion depends upon a category of *causality* as a principle of explanation. The psychological version of this process includes references to the primary processes, to motile rather than bound energy, to various stages of creativity, to psychological levels of creativity, or to types of mental processes.

This criterion describes the metaphoric, symbolizing processes which produce new connections. I refer to it as nonrational because the combinatorial activity occurs in the form of unconscious operations; it does not belong to the rational mind, nor is it consciously controlled. Rationality divides and distinguishes; it focuses upon differences. Metaphoric activity unites and relates; it flourishes upon similarities, and transpires among the primary processes. Non-rationality is not merely a condition of novelty; it is a cause. The relationship between such processes as condensation, symbolization, displacement, and neologisms and the production of new connections is a causal one. It is the very nature of unconscious (or preconscious) levels of the mind to function metaphorically. The mechanisms which constitute the unconscious operations make this inevitable. Unless they function, no new connections can occur. Thus, there is an invariant relationship between the two.

The nonrational processes function by imposing upon ideas and images the quality of plasticity. Metaphor gives plasticity to language, and makes poetry possible; it gives plasticity to thinking, and makes scientific inventions possible; it gives plasticity to perceptual forms, and makes art possible. Metaphor disengages our belief attitudes from the conditioning induced by logical inference and presents new belief possibilities. It softens the discursive tendencies of language, and consequently allows new meanings to be fashioned. With the inferential limitations lifted from language and with causal connections uncoupled from objects, these become malleable and therefore make possible new visions, unexpected views of the world and of experience. The nonrational mechanisms which produce these new visions constitute the energy system of creativity, and operate similarly in all creative individuals whether they be scientists, artists, or housewives.

Inspection of the research literature indicates that at least three conceptual schemes have been devised for explaining the creative process. The first conceives of creativity as a sequential *series of stages* of activity, the second as vertical *levels* of psychological functions, and the third as *types* of mental processes. These three schemes agree upon one major fact: that segment or level of the creative process which is invariably associated with the creation of novelty is nonrational. It lies below the surface of consciousness; it resists rational analysis; it dissolves under logical examination.

The classical statement of the theory of stages was first formulated by Wallas in 1926; he identifies four distinct stages and calls them preparation, incubation, illumination, and verification (*58*). The second and third stages actually produce the new connections, the novel relationships, and these transpire in the form of nonrational operations. The incubation stage, for example, consists of spontaneous, uncontrollable events which cluster themselves seemingly in accordance with their own autonomous laws. It involves the relaxation of conscious thinking operations and the inhibition of logical control. Maslow refers to this process as voluntary regression (*31*), Ehrenzweig as surrender of the ego (*10*), and Rogers as openness to experience (*46*). The stage of illumination remains even more of a mystery. Being singular, unpredictable, idiosyncratic, it resists formal description. Writers from Plato to Lu Chi in ancient China to Nietzsche have remarked about the unexplainable nature of inspiration. Patrick has been most diligent in trying to prove the theory of four stages (*41*). Poincaré and Hadamard (*21*) agree that the four stages adequately account for mathematics creations. Arnold (*54*), Patrick, and Montmasson (*37*) discover the same four stages in connection with scientific inventions. Patrick and Spender (*56*) believe that poetic creativeness occurs in sequential stages. Other writers who explain the creative process in this fashion were mentioned above (*57*).

The evidence that nonrationality serves as a necessary condition of creativity becomes more conclusive when it is examined from the point of view that it consists in the interchange of energy among vertical levels of the psyche. This theory accepts the distinction between the primary and the secondary processes, between the unconscious (or preconscious) and conscious functions, between autistic and reality-adjusted thinking, and it asserts that though the actual creative process involves a shift in psychic levels, the shift must always occur in such manner that the metaphoric fusion of elements shall transpire in the unconscious levels and be projected upwards into consciousness. Each level contributes to the creative process. The unconscious supplies the surge and the power, the imagery and the concreteness, the ambiguity and conflict, the actual connectedness. The rational level provides the elaboration, the testing, the gestalts, the socially derived approvals. Again, other writers who have developed this theory are mentioned above.

The third description of the creative process conceives of it in terms of types of mental operations. According to this definition, the creative act is one which combines forms of thought into new relationships. Creative thinking is only one of several kinds of operations included in the higher mental processes; it is usually distinguished from other kinds of thinking largely in terms of its nonrational aspects. As has been mentioned, Guilford, Vinacke, McKellar, Rapaport, Bartlett, and Bruner make this distinction. In every case it is the nonrational, the autistic, the metaphoric, the internally oriented, the spontaneous and involuntary, the integrating, unbound energies which are active in producing new connections. These differ from the conscious, the inhibitory, the rational, controlled, purposive, reality-oriented processes which, to be sure, play their part in creativity; but their function is one of elaboration and testing, not fusing. It is the fantasy-dominated forms of thought which contain clues to mind's creative capacities. These nonrational processes account for the seeming effortlessness and the spontaneity of creative activity; they explain the autonomy, the quality of "otherness," of being visited by a daemon or a voice. They account for connectedness. And they account for the direction which creative movement assumes.

THE CRITERION OF SELF-ACTUALIZATION

Descriptively, the fourth criterion can be called the condition of self-actualization, a pattern of personality growth which clinicians and analysts have studied. Logically, this criterion rests upon the category of *change* as an explanatory principle. Perhaps the psychologist prefers to speak of it in terms of motivation as the energy source for change, and of growth in the direction of psychological health as the goal toward which this energy is directed. This category must account for change as transformation and as transcendence.

This criterion asserts that creativity involves a fundamental change in personality structure, and that this change occurs in the direction of fulfillment. It distinguishes between those personality involvements which remain merely perfunctory and nonproductive and those which prove to be genuinely creative. It distinguishes between energy transformations which are habitual, tension-reducing, and repetitive and those which are tension-organizing, forward-pointing, and growth-oriented. It implies that though all personality change may not terminate in growth, all instances of personality growth are possible grounds for creativeness. It implies that though many forms of energy exchanges may be necessary in order to account for human behavior, only those kinds which eventuate in the realization of potentialities lead to creative acts. Thus, it identifies creativity with self formation, and therefore implies that unless significant transformation occurs in personality during an activity, that activity will fall short of the creative.

This criterion seems to be logically necessary. Personality dynamics can best account for the unique qualities of experiences and of products. It can best serve as the unifying agency for the entire creative process. Since this process in every instance has been analyzed into either discrete stages of activity, or sharply differentiated strata of psychic levels, or into distinct types of mental functions, some explanation must be given as to why such diverse operations mesh so efficiently and move forward in the creative act so effortlessly. A unifying principle is necessary, and the factor of personality-in-motion can serve as this principle.

Empirically, this criterion is supported by the great wealth of data which has been reported. Maslow (*32*) has spoken most forcefully on this theme. He equates creativity with the state of psychological health, and this with the self-actualization process. There is no exception to this rule, he says; creativity is a universal characteristic of self-actualizing people. This form of creativeness reaches beyond special-talent creativeness; it is a fundamental characteristic of human nature. It touches whatever activity the healthy person is engaged in.

This criterion also asserts a connection between motivation and creativity, for the self-actualizing person is characterized by an unusually strong motivational drive. These impulses energize the individual in such manner that he is impelled to act, to express, to perform; and they also produce personality transformations. The creative person, driven by an urge which eventually takes full possession of him, cares less about mundane things, spurns conventional attitudes, rejects security. These drives are pervasive, persistent; they resist deflection. Thus, a large body of literature has accumulated around this problem of motivation of creativity.

The Freudian theory that the creative urge grows out of substitute gratifications for incestuous and parracidal desires experienced during pregenital stages is still widely supported. Oriented to the past, our present responses are conditioned by past experiences; they are a form of tension reduction. Relief of tension both provides pleasure and insures reinforcement. Followers of the Freudian school are Brill (*7*), Engleman (*11*), Deri (*9*), Van der Sterren (*56*), Macalpine (*29*), Weiss (*59*), and Sterba (*54*). A major variation of this theme is that creative motives are efforts to make restitution and atonement for objects and persons destroyed during aggressive fantasies. Segal (*49*), Fairbairn (*12*), Levey (*27*), Grotjahn (*18*), and Sharpe (*50*) concur in this analysis. They agree that creativeness stems from the efforts of the infant to restrain his destructive tendencies. This theory accounts for the urgency and the power which lie behind motivation. Some of Freud's followers reject the view that creative power is an alibi for thwarted sexuality. They associate it with some compensating force; Adler as compensation for organ inferiority (*1*); Rank, for man's mortality and finitude (*43*); Jung, for feelings of finitude as well (*25*).

These writers emphasize creativity as a process of will affirmation, of individuation, of self formation.

Thus, strong motivational drives have important effects upon creative activity. They energize the organism and impel it into creative expression. McClelland (34) describes other effects: motives relate, unify, and integrate the diversity of needs and goals in behavior. They provide organization, orientation, and direction; they introduce directional trends, create need-related imagery, increase interest in future possibilities. We recognize these effects as identical with the metaphoric process. Allport (2) points out the relationship of motives to emotions and asserts that they too serve a unifying, selective function. Further, strong motives sensitize the individual to a greater number and variety of environmental cues, and they push the level of aspiration upward. The highest aspiration involves self-actualization, which constitutes both the goal of life and its motivational wellspring. The theory of motivation as goal seeking completes the analysis of this fourth criterion. In the sense that personality transforms itself in the process of achieving the goal of mature growth, there is established a connection between creativity and self-actualization.

THE CRITERION OF OPENNESS

Descriptively, the fifth and final criterion can be called the condition of *openness*. It designates those characteristics of the environment, both the inner and the outer, the personal and the social, which facilitate the creative person's moving from the actual state of affairs which he is in at a given time toward solutions which are only possible and as yet undetermined. These conditions, or traits, include sensitivity, tolerance of ambiguity, self-acceptance, and spontaneity. Since these are passively rather than actively engaged in the creative process, this criterion may be explained logically within the category of *possibility*. But again, the psychological meaning of this category may best be expressed under the concept of deferment, as distinguished, for example, from closure; of postponement as distinguished from predetermined solutions.

Defined as traits by most psychologists, these conditions are learned and are not aspects of man's inheritance; they are environmental factors. They characterize both the individual and society; they describe such social organizations as schools and families, and they refer to personalities. The term "openness" is meant to encompass all such traits; however, I am proposing that this general category can be further subdivided into four distinguishable but closely related clusters of environmental factors. These are listed in the preceding paragraph. The larger category of openness is borrowed directly from Rogers: "This is the opposite of psychological defensiveness, when to protect the organization of self, certain experiences are prevented from coming into awareness except in disturbed fashion . . . It means lack of rigidity and permeability of boundaries in concepts, beliefs, perceptions, and hypotheses" (*45*).

Sensitivity refers to a state of being aware of things as they really are rather than according to some predetermined set. The creative person is sensitive to the world of objects, to problems, to other people, to gaps in evidence, to unconscious impulses. The following are some of the research workers who agree that sensitivity is a condition for creative work: Angyal (*3*), Fromm (*13*), Mooney (*38*), Guilford (*20*), Stein (*53*), Lowenfeld (*28*), Greenacre (*17*), and Hilgard (*23*).

The ability to tolerate ambiguity is another trait which has been commonly accepted. It is the ability to accept conflict and tension resulting from polarity (*13*), to tolerate inconsistencies and contradictions (*33*), to accept the unknown, to be comfortable with the ambiguous, approximate, uncertain. The creative person can postpone decisions and accept the abeyance as pleasantly challenging. Zilboorg (*63*), Wilson (*61*), and Hart (*22*) concur in this analysis. Flexibility is an extension of the traits of sensitivity and tolerance of ambiguity. These latter traits allow the individual to change and to take advantage of change. Flexibility means being able to toy with elements, to operate without being anchored to rigid forms, to escape traditional solutions, to be playfully serious, to perceive meaning in irrelevancies.

The third set of meanings contained in the criterion of openness points to the need of the creative personality to have a sense of personal destiny and worth which will allow him to accept himself as the source of values. It is obvious that anyone who tolerates uncertainties and conflicts for long must enjoy an anchorage within some value system apart from the conventional order, and this would need to be himself. The forward-pointing search for possibilities which characterizes the creative process implies an acceptance of self as a source of judgment. The new creations exist at first in the future and in tentative form; they exist as possibilities. If they become original creations, they must then take on the values which the individual assigns to them. Since the creative person must speculate, test, modify, postpone completion of his work, he needs to rely upon his own sensitivity for guidance.

Finally, the fourth set of meanings connected with openness relates to spontaneity. This quality gives the creative act the feeling of being free, autonomous, undetermined. It allows creative behavior to be unbound and uncoupled from previous causal conditions. It produces the response of wonder and awe. It is responsible for the quality of freshness, of being born anew every day, of childlike naïveté, of naturalness and simplicity.

SUMMARY

This paper has submitted no new evidence about the creative process. Rather, it has suggested one possible way for organizing in a meaningful way the great amount of material which has already accumulated. It proposes five necessary and sufficient conditions for creativity as a basic framework which can encompass relevant data. These have predictive value. When all five are present, creativeness must of necessity result.

REFERENCES

1. Adler, Alfred. *Problems of Neurosis* (London: Routledge, 1959).
2. Allport, G. W. *Patterns and Growth in Personality* (New York: Holt, Rinehart, and Winston, 1961), p. 198.
3. Angyal, Andras. A Theoretical Model for Personality Studies, in *The Self,* ed., C. E. Moustakas (New York: Harper and Row, 1956), pp. 44–57.
4. Arnold, J. E. Creativity in Engineering, in *Creativity: An Examination of the Creative Process,* ed., P. Smith (New York: Hastings House, 1959), pp. 33–46.
5. Barron, F. Needs for Order and Disorder as Motives in Creative Activity, *The Second Research Conference on the Identification of Creative Scientific Talent,* ed., C. W. Taylor (Salt Lake City: University of Utah Press, 1958), pp. 119–128.
6. Bartlett, Frederick. *Thinking: An Experimental and Social Study* (New York: Basic Books, 1958).
7. Brill, A. A. Poetry as an Oral Outlet, *Psychoanalytic Review,* Vol. 18, No. 4 (Oct., 1931), pp. 357–378.
8. Bruner, Jerome S. *On Knowing* (Cambridge, Mass.: Belknap Press, 1962).
9. Deri, F. On Sublimation, *Psychoanalytic Quarterly,* Vol. 8, No. 3 (1939), pp. 325–334.
10. Ehrenzweig, Anton. *The Psychoanalysis of Artistic Vision and Hearing* (London: Routledge, 1953), p. 193.
11. Engleman, A. A. A Case of Trensexion upon Viewing a Painting, *American Imago,* Vol. 9 (1952), pp. 239–249.
12. Fairbairn, W. R. D. Prolegomena to a Psychology of Art, *British Journal of Psychology,* Vol. 28 (1938), pp. 288–303.
13. Fromm, Erich. The Creative Attitude, in *Creativity and Its Cultivation,* ed., Harold H. Anderson (New York: Harper and Row, 1959), pp. 44–54.
14. Gerard, Ralph W. What is Imagination?, in *Selected Readings on the Learning*

Process, ed., T. L. Harris and W. E. Schwan (New York: Oxford University Press, 1961), pp. 81–89.

15. Getzels, J. W. and Jackson, P. W. *Creativity and Intelligence* (New York: John Wiley and Sons, 1962), p. 37.

16. Ghiselin, Brewster ed., *The Creative Process* (New York: New American Library, 1952), p. 21.

17. Greenacre, P. Childhood of the Artist, in *The Psychoanalytic Study of the Child*, Vol. 12 (New York: International Universities Press, 1957), pp. 47–72.

18. Grotjahn, M. *Beyond Laughter* (New York: McGraw-Hill, 1957).

19. Guilford, J. P. A Psychometric Approach to Creativity, Mimeographed, University of Southern California, Mar., 1962.

20. Guilford, J. P. Traits of Creativity, in *Creativity and Its Cultivation*, pp. 142–161.

21. Hadamard, J. *The Psychology of Invention in the Mathematical Field* (New York: Dover Publications, 1954).

22. Hart, H. H. The Integrative Function in Creativity, *Psychiatric Quarterly*, Vol. 24, No. 1 (1950), pp. 1–16.

23. Hilgard, E. R. Creativity and Problem-Solving, in *Creativity and Its Culvtivation*, pp. 162–180.

24. Hutchinson, E. D. *How to Think Creatively* (Nashville, Tenn.: Abingdon Press, 1949), p. 25.

25. Jung, C. G. *Psychology of the Unconscious*, trans. B. M. Hinkle (New York: Dodd, Mead, 1916), pp. 62–86.

26. Kubie, L. S. *Neurotic Distortion in the Creative Process* (University of Kansas Press, 1958), p. 50.

27. Levey, H. B. A Theory Concerning Free Creation in the Inventive Arts, *Psychiatry*, Vol. 2, No. 2 (May, 1940), pp. 229–231.

28. Lowenfeld, Viktor. Current Research on Creativity, *Journal of the National Education Association*, Vol. 47 (Nov., 1958), pp. 538–540.

29. Macalpine, I. and Hunter, R. Rossini. Piano Pieces for the Primal Scene, *American Imago*, Vol. 9 (1952), pp. 213–219.

30. Maslow, A. H. Creativity in Self-Actualizing People, in *Creativity and Its Cultivation*, pp. 83–95.

31. Maslow, A. H. Emotional Blocks to Creativity, *Journal of Individual Psychology*, Vol. 14 (1958), pp. 51–56.

32. Maslow, A. H. Personality Problems and Personality Growth, in *The Self*, pp. 232–246.

33. Maslow, A. H. *Toward a Psychology of Being* (Princeton, N. J.: D. Van Nostrand, 1962), pp. 129–130.

34. McClelland, D. C. *Personality* (New York: William Sloane, 1951), p. 485.

35. McKellar, Peter. *Imagination and Thinking* (New York: Basic Books, 1957).

36. Meier, N. C. Factors in Artistic Aptitude, *Psychology Monograph*, Vol. 51, No. 5 (1939), pp. 140–158.

37. Montmasson, J. M. *Invention and the Unconscious* (London: K. Paul, French, and Trubner, 1931).

38. Mooney, R. L. Groundwork for Creative Research, in *The Self*, pp. 261–270.

39. Murray, H. A. Vicissitudes of Creativity, in *Creativity and Its Cultivation*, pp. 96–118.

40. Nietzsche, F. Ecce Homo, *The Philosophy of Nietzsche* (New York: Modern Library, 1927), pp. 896–897.

41. Patrick, Catherine. Creative Thought in Artists, *Journal of Psychology*, Vol. 4 (Jan., 1937), pp. 35–73.
42. Poincaré, H. *The Foundations of Science* (New York: Science Press, 1913).
43. Rank, Otto. *Art and the Artist* (New York: Alfred A. Knopf, 1932).
44. Reynolds, Sir Joshua. *Discourses on Art* (Chicago: Packard and Co., 1945), p. 164.
45. Rogers, C. R. *On Becoming A Person* (Boston: Houghton Mifflin Co., 1961), p. 353.
46. Rogers, Carl R. Toward a Theory of Creativity, in *Creativity and Its Cultivation*, pp. 69–82.
47. Schachtel, E. G. *Metamorphoses* (New York: Basic Books, 1959), p. 242.
48. Schneider, D. E. *The Psychoanalyst and the Artist* (New York: Farrar Straus and Giroux, 1950), p. 58.
49. Segal, Hanna. A Psychoanalytic Approach to Aesthetics, *International Journal of Psychoanalysis*, Vol. 33, (1952), pp. 196–207.
50. Sharpe, Ella. Certain Aspects of Sublimation and Delusion, *International Journal of Psychoanalysis*, Vol. 11 (1930), pp. 12–23.
51. Spearman, C. E. *The Creative Mind* (New York: Appleton-Century, 1931), p. 83.
52. Spender, S. The Making of a Poem, *Partisan Review*, Vol. 13, No. 3 (Summer, 1946), pp. 294–308.
53. Stein, M. I. Creativity and Culture, *Journal of Psychology*, Vol. 36 (Oct., 1953), pp. 311–322.
54. Sterba, R. and E. Beethoven and His Nephew, *International Journal of Psychoanalysis*, Vol. 33 (1952), pp. 470–478.
55. Taylor, I. A. The Nature of the Creative Process, in *Creativity: An Examination* . . . , pp. 51–82.
56. Van der Sterren, H. A. The "King Oedipus" of Sophocles, *International Journal of Psychoanalysis*, Vol. 33 (1952), pp. 343–350.
57. Vinacke, W. E. *The Psychology of Thinking* (New York: McGraw-Hill, 1952).
58. Wallas, G. *The Art of Thought* (New York: Franklin Watts, 1926), p. 85.
59. Weiss, J. Cezanne's Technique and Scotophilia, *Psychoanalytic Quarterly*, Vol. 22, No. 3 (1953), pp. 413–418.
60. Whiting, C. S. *Creative Thinking* (New York: Reinhold, 1958).
61. Wilson, R. N. Poetic Creativity, Process, and Personality, *Psychiatry*, Vol. 17, No. 2 (May, 1954), pp. 163–176.
62. Wilson, R. C., et al. The Measurement of Individual Differences in Originality, *Psychological Bulletin*, Vol. 50, No. 5 (Sept., 1953), pp. 262–370.
63. Zilboorg, G. Psychology of the Creative Personality, in *Creativity: An Examination* . . . , pp. 21–32.

Education and Creativity

Sidney J. Parnes

MORE AND MORE RESEARCH PROJECTS HAVE BEEN POINTING UP THE part that education can play in the development of creative efficacy. At the University of Chicago, the studies of J. W. Getzels and P. W. Jackson (2) have found that, among bright students, the most highly creative ones excel in achievement to as great a degree as do the highest IQ students. This has been corroborated by E. Paul Torrance of the University of Minnesota (23).

This finding has kindled interest in creative performance as a criterion in the selection of "gifted" children, a supplement to the traditional criteria of IQ and teacher's preference. (Incidentally, research suggests that highly creative children are often disliked by their teachers, a fact with broad implications for educational thought and practice.) With respect to these traditional criteria, John Holland, director of research at the National Merit Scholarship Corporation, has claimed, "Generally, such measures (as IQ and teacher's preference) are moderately accurate for predicting college grades, but they have little relation to post-college achievement." [1] His organization has now embarked on a study of achievement in a group of boys and girls chosen mainly on the basis of exceptional creative performance.

Elnora Schmadel of the University of Southern California sounds a widely echoed note: ". . . the findings of this study indicate that creative thinking abilities do contribute to currently measured achievement and to measures of desirable achievement" (20). Similarly, Torrance argues that, "Perhaps the most promising area, if we are interested in what can be done to encourage creative talent to unfold, is that of experimentation with teaching procedures which will stimulate students to think independently, to test their ideas, and to communicate them to others" (26).

RESEARCH DEVELOPMENTS

Research on the development of creative behavior has been conducted on an increasing scale ever since the presidential address of

[1] Reported in *Scholastic Teacher*, 12 Oct., 1960.

REPRINTED by permission of the Author and *Teachers College Record*, 64:331-9, 1963.

J. P. Guilford in 1950 to the American Psychological Association. He emphasized the "appalling neglect" of the study of creativity (*6*), indicating that of some 121,000 titles indexed in *Psychological Abstracts* from its beginning until 1950, only 186 were definitely related to the subject of creativity. In the summer of 1958, the Creative Education Foundation published (*15*) the first *Compendium of Research on Creative Imagination*, covering 30 research studies concerned with the identification and development of creative ability. This comprised all recent studies in the field at that time. Then, within approximately 18 months, 30 new research studies were reported and summarized in a second *Compendium*. This also listed 28 additional research projects that had just been started—about double the number apparently under way when the first *Compendium* was compiled.

A new trend was indicated by the nature of the research reported in the later *Compendium*. Until a few years ago, projects dealt mainly with the *identification* of creative talent. About half the studies reported in the second *Compendium* were devoted to the deliberate *development* of creative ability—a far cry from the bare two included in the earlier edition.

At the 1959 University of Utah Research Conference on the Identification of Creative Scientific Talent, a committee was appointed for the first time to report on "The Role of Educational Experience in the Development of Creative Scientific Talent." The committee reported that at least six research projects had indicated that creative productivity can be developed by deliberate procedures (*22*). No research yet reported is inconsistent with this view. Thus, there is a firm basis for the conviction expressed by Guilford in 1952: "Like most behavior, creative activity probably represents to some extent many learned skills. There may be limitations set on these skills by heredity; but I am convinced that through learning one can extend the skills within those limitations" (*7*). In the same vein, Irving Maltzman and his associates at the University of California concluded a group of research studies on originality-training by asserting that the results support the hypothesis that ". . . originality is a learned form of behavior which does not differ in principle from other forms of operant behavior" (*10*).

An illustration of the relevant evidence is the 13-year experience with a course in creative problem-solving at the University of Buffalo.[2] Two research studies have evaluated this creative problem-solving

[2] The 140-page *Instructor's Manual* and 80-page *Student Workbook* for this course are available from the Creative Education Foundation, 1614 Rand Building, Buffalo 3, New York.

course. The first revealed that on five of seven measures of creative ability, the students who had taken the one-semester course were significantly superior to the group of matched control subjects who had not taken the course. The former group also showed significant gain on a scale devised "to assess factors of leadership ability, dominance, persistence, and social initiative" (*12*).

The second study examined the persistence or carry-over effects of the creative problem-solving courses. Results indicated that the improvement in creative productivity persisted for more than eight months after completion of the course (*20*). Criteria used in evaluation of the ideas produced included both uniqueness and usefulness.

Research into the effects of creative problem-solving programs conducted at other institutions has supported the findings (*15, 21*). Presently, the University of Chicago is conducting several research projects on the effects of teaching creative problem-solving governmental and industrial administrators (*8, 9*).

EDUCATIONAL PROGRAMS

Since research has demonstrated that a considerable part of creative behavior is *learned*, courses in creative problem-solving have been multiplying. At the University of Buffalo, the principles and procedures taught in the elective one-semester course have also been used in special programs for groups of students in engineering, law, medicine, education, business, physics, psychology, and ROTC. Similar courses and programs, patterned after those of the University of Buffalo (*16*), have become widespread in educational institutions, in industrial organizations, in the military, and in governmental agencies (*14*).

At Buffalo, students are taught the concepts in Alex F. Osborn's textbook, *Applied Imagination*. The text emphasizes the importance of imagination in all walks of life, the universality of imaginative talent, and the use of creativeness in all stages of problem-solving, from orientation to evaluation.

Perceptual, emotional, and cultural blocks to creative thinking are demonstrated and discussed in the course. Under perceptual blocks are covered such matters as the difficulty in isolating problems, difficulty from narrowing the problem too much, inability to define or isolate attributes, failure to use all the senses in observing. Under cultural and emotional blocks are emphasized the effects of conformity, over-emphasis on competition or cooperation, excessive faith in reason or logic, self-satisfaction, perfectionism, negative outlooks, reliance on authority, and fear of mistakes, failure, or looking foolish.

Early in the course, students learn the principle of deferred judgment. In essence, this principle calls for the deliberate separation of idea-production from evaluation. In other words, during the effort to generate ideas, the judicial process is deliberately suspended; evaluation is deferred in order to allow full play to imagination.

To estimate the efficacy of the deferred-judgment principle as applied to individual idea-production, experimental subjects were given the task of thinking up tentative solutions to assigned problems for periods of five minutes, each student working on an individual (non-group) basis. On one problem, the students operated in the conventional way, concurrently applying evaluation as they tried to think up ideas. On the second problem, they operated in accordance with the deferred-judgment principle, deliberately postponing evaluation. The former method produced an average of 2.5 good ideas. The latter produced an average of 4.3 good ideas, criteria of quality being based on uniqueness and usefulness.

These results indicate that, for this type of creative task, a 72-per-cent better productivity can result from the deliberate deferment of evaluation during the idea-production process, a difference which is highly significant statistically (*13, 18*). This deliberate separation of the creative and judicial functions is emphasized throughout the course.

Within the permissive atmosphere that the principle of deferred judgment provides, students are given practice in attribute-listing (learning to look at problems from a variety of viewpoints). For example, in considering other uses for such an object as a piece of paper, students are taught to look at each attribute of the paper—its whiteness, its four corners, its straight edges, etc. Each of the attributes then suggests a number of possible uses.

CHECK LISTS

Check-list procedures are also encouraged, such as Osborn's check-list of idea-spurring questions. Students are thus taught to process a problem by means of a number of questions: How can we simplify? What combinations can be utilized? What adaptations can be made?

Forced-relationship techniques are similarly covered. For example, after a list of ideas is produced as tentative solutions to a problem, each of these ideas is then artificially related to each other idea on the list in order to force new combinations. Sometimes a somewhat ridiculous idea is taken as a starting point. By connecting the idea with the actual problem, a series of associations is produced, and this often leads in some novel direction towards a new solution of the problem.

Throughout the course, three points are stressed: the importance of taking notes (keeping a record of ideas that come to one at any and all times, rather than only while one is working on a problem), the value of setting deadlines and quotas for production of ideas, and the advantage of setting aside certain times and places for deliberate idea-production. Much opportunity is given for deliberate practice in problem-solving on a variety of problems, including many of those brought in by the students out of their personal experience.

Students are taught to sense problems in their studies, work, and throughout their lives, and to define these problems properly for creative attack. The separation of creative and judicial functions is then practiced in all stages of solution. For example, during analysis, students are taught to list every fact that could be related to the problem. After they have completed this step, they then apply judgment in order to cull out the most important facts. Students next create the longest possible list of questions and sources of additional data that could be useful. Then they go back to the judicial process of selecting the most important questions and sources of data. This procedure continues throughout the final stages of evaluation and presentation of ideas.

When it comes to evaluation, students are taught to develop the longest possible list of criteria by which to evaluate their tentative solutions. They then apply judgment in order to select the most useful ones for the purpose. Thus, the principle of deferred judgment is emphasized, both in individual and in group thinking, in all aspects of the course.

Informal procedures are utilized throughout. Chairs are arranged in a semi-circle in order to encourage the maximum amount of group participation and discussion. The class is often divided into small groups in order to provide practice in team and group collaboration for the production of ideas. Students are given opportunities to serve as leaders of these small groups on various aspects of their own problems as well as on those assigned for practice.

SOME OUTCOMES

In one of a series of studies[3] at the University of Buffalo, the research staff utilized a battery of ten measures which had previously

[3] Single copies of reprints of these reports (*12, 18, 19*) are available from the Creative Education Foundation, 1614 Rand Building, Buffalo 3, New York.

been demonstrated by other investigators to distinguish creative from non-creative persons. These tests were given to students at the beginning and again at the conclusion of three creative problem-solving courses. These students were considered the experimental subjects (*12*). Other students, not taking the creative problem-solving course, were given the same tests at the beginning and end of the semester; they were considered the control subjects. Thus, any comparatively greater gains by the creative problem-solving students could reasonably be attributed to the course.

The experimental and control students were carefully matched for intelligence, age, sex, and time of class. For example, a bright, 20-year-old, female, day-school student in the creative problem-solving course was matched for comparison with a bright, 20-year-old, female, day-school student in another course. All of the students were told that they were participating in an experiment designed to measure changes in their thinking as a result of a semester's work at the University.

Analyses of the results of this phase of the research included these major findings:

1. The creative problem-solving students showed substantial gains in the *quantitative* production of ideas on two tests of idea quantity. Students in the control group showed relatively insignificant gains on these tests.
2. In three tests of the *qualitative* production of ideas, the experimental subjects showed clear superiority over the control group. On a fourth test in this area, the creative problem-solving students showed improvement greater than that shown by the control students, but not sufficiently greater to be regarded as significant. The fifth measure of qualitative production showed no superiority for the creative problem-solving students.
3. Three tests were designed to measure improvement in the personality traits of *dominance, self-control,* and *need to achieve.* The creative problem-solving students gained substantially in dominance as a result of the course, but showed no significant changes in self-control or need to achieve. The dominance scale used is regarded by psychologists as measuring such characteristics as confidence, self-reliance, persuasiveness, initiative, and leadership potential (*4*). Other workers have previously found that dominance is a personality trait associated with creative persons (*15*).

It is significant that dominance was the single personality trait in which the creative problem-solving students showed an increase. This is the particular trait which the course methods were designed explicitly to develop.

Most of the tests designed to measure improvement in quantity and quality of ideas were based on a practical type of creative ability.

Psychologists describe these tests as measuring the factors of originality, sensitivity to problems, spontaneous flexibilty, and ideational fluency. It was on these tests that the students who took the course registered substantial gains.

Two of the tests emphasized a more literary type of creative ability. Students were required to create clever story titles and original plots. On neither of these tests were the gains registered by the students who took the course large enough to indicate superiority over the control students. The test requiring clever story titles, however, showed the greater gain by the course students, and a later experiment showed significant evidence of carry-over effects in this type of creative ability.

UTILITY FOR WHOM?

In general, the creative problem-solving courses were found to be equally helpful to students of low and high initial creative ability, and equally helpful to those with low and high intelligence levels. This finding is in line with Guilford's conclusion that although heredity may place limitations on the skills involved in creative ability, these skills can be extended within those limitations through education.

In general, the older students (aged 23 to 51) in evening classes gained as much from the course as did younger students (aged 17 to 22) in day classes. Likewise, males and females demonstrated equivalent gains.

There is also evidence that when creative efficacy has been developed by education, the improvement endures (*19*). Matched experimental and control subjects were compared on six tests of creative ability. The experimental subjects were students who had completed the creative problem-solving course an average of 18 months prior to the experiment. The control subjects were students *registered* but *uninstructed* in the creative problem-solving course. None of the students had ever before taken the creative-thinking tests.

Course graduates outperformed two separate groups of control subjects on all six measures, including two quantity and four quality tests. All differences were statistically significant in the comparisons with one of the control groups. All but two were significant in comparisons with the second control group.

Incidentally, a popular misconception exists to the effect that the deferment-of-judgment principle is applicable only to group idea-production. The fallaciousness of this impression is demonstrated by the fact that all measurements in the studies at the University of

Buffalo were made on the basis of individual thinking, not on group collaboration.

These studies have produced countless collateral data which have become available as a result of the electronic processing of the information obtained. These data are being put to valuable use. For example, further analyses have been made to discover the proportion of *good* ideas in the first half of a subject's total output of ideas *versus* the last half of his sustained effort. Findings of one such study have shown 78 per cent *more* good ideas to be among those produced in the last half than in the first half. Here, again, qualitative scoring was based on the criteria of uniqueness and usefulness. A subsequent experiment indicated a trend towards *increasingly* greater proportions of good ideas as a subject's total quantity increased. The results of both experiments were found to be statistically significant (*17*).

The above findings support Osborn's theory that in idea-production, quantity leads to quality. The results also seem to concur with William J. J. Gordon's explanation (*3*) of "deferment" in the creative process. He describes deferment as "the capacity to discard the glittering immediate in favor of a shadowy but possibly richer future." The *noncreative* problem-solver gets an idea, sees it as a possible solution to his problem, and settles for that without further ado. The *creative* problem-solver is not satisfied with his first idea. Like the person who invests money to obtain greater rewards later, the creative person foregoes the immediate reward of applying his first idea in expectation of an ultimately better solution (greater reward). A further hypothesis suggested by Osborn's and Gordon's theories is that the *best* idea will come late in the total production period. Experiments are currently being prepared to test this particular hypothesis.

MODIFICATION OF COURSES

In addition to the teaching of creative problem-solving *per se,* there have also been successful projects based on the integration of creative principles and procedures with conventional courses. Two outstanding examples of courses which have thus been modified are Jere Clark's economics course at the University of Chattanooga and Harry Hansen's marketing course at Harvard.

The value of such modifications has been indicated by research on the effectiveness of the similar incorporation of creative principles and procedures into courses in language arts (*24*). Also, a study by Sommers (*21*) reported that mastery of subject matter increased, along with creative ability scores, as a result of weaving creative problem-solving into existing courses.

At the University of Buffalo, pilot research has been conducted with physics students who were given a six-session condensation of the creative problem-solving course. Analysis of the data has indicated that these subjects performed better on creative ability tests than a comparable control group of physics students who had no training in creative problem-solving. Furthermore, on anonymous questionnaires given to the 55 experimental (trained) subjects, 83 per cent expressed the belief that the study of creative problem-solving should be required of physics students and others. Nearly all of the others felt that creative problem-solving should be offered as an elective. Seventy-five per cent indicated a willingness to continue the creative problem-solving sessions for the entire semester.

Several special institutes and workshops have been held regarding the integration of creative problem-solving methodologies with the teaching of other academic subjects. The first was a one-day workshop at the University of Buffalo for teachers of American history. On the West Coast, San Jose State College has taken the lead with an annual five-day Creative Education Institute which offers graduate credit. At this Institute, several hundred teachers devise ways to integrate creative methodologies within their respective subject-matter fields. Frank Williams is in charge of the program.

EDUCATION IN THE FUTURE

In a recent prediction of forthcoming changes in colleges, Paul H. Davis (*1*) states, "In the last one hundred years, the medical profession has changed from folklore to science, from opinions based on hunches to judgments based on controlled experiments. Now the teaching profession is starting a similar transition." One of his predictions is that there will be less emphasis on memory and more on creative thinking.

As we all know, change is bewilderingly rapid in our present nuclear and space age—far more rapid than ever before. The discoveries and innovations of the next 20 years will probably make the previous 100 years seem to have progressed at a snail's pace. Therefore, a person cannot foresee exactly what knowledge he will need five or ten years from now to meet his life's problems. He can, however, develop the attitudes and abilities that will help him meet *any* future problem creatively and inventively.

Furthermore, we receive so much spoon-feeding in our present society in terms of how-to-do-it instructions—in school, at home, and at work—that most of us lack almost any opportunity for being creative. If this is so, we may be developing a society of "sick" people. A. H. Maslow (*11*) postulates that a person who does not have a basic need fulfilled is sick, just as a man is sick who lacks vitamins and minerals. The five basic needs to which Maslow refers are (a) physiological needs, (b) safety needs, (c) love, affection, and belongingness needs, (d) esteem needs, and (e) need for self-actualization.

Maslow emphasizes that the need for self-actualization is a healthy man's prime motivation. Self-actualization means actualizing one's potential, becoming everything one is capable of becoming. Maslow says, "What a man *can* be, he *must* be." Education can help provide for this need by building the environmental turnpikes on which the individual may drive once he has removed the mental governors that restrict his creative ability.

In Carl Rogers's terms, education can help provide the "psychological safety" and "psychological freedom" necessary to the creative individual. This does not mean license for heedless nonconformity. But it does mean complete freedom for nonconformity of *thought*, even if not for nonconformity in behavior. An old adage says, "Give me the courage to change those things that can and should be changed, the strength to accept those things that cannot be changed, and the wisdom to distinguish between the two." This then must be the creed of the creative person.

We still know little about what "creativity" really is. But we do know how to stimulate greater creative behavior in individuals. It is a matter of helping them to release whatever creative potential they possess, like removing the governor from an automobile. The individual's creative ability is frequently so repressed by his education and experience that he cannot even *recognize* his full potential, let alone *realize* it. Once he can be helped to do so, he may attain what Maslow calls "self-actualization."

Education can do much to help the individual achieve this fullest self-realization, whatever his level of native capacity. Many people seem to possess the seeds of creativeness, but the environment fails to provide the proper nourishment for growth. Therefore, these persons never fully live.

Education can provide for "creative calisthenics" to counteract this atrophying of our talents. And just as camping out can be rewarding even though we have homes, creative exercise can be rewarding even though we have access to ready-made solutions. Just as physical education does not take for granted the physical development of our students, likewise creative education must provide deliberately for their creative development. And research does seem to warrant the postulate that the gap between an individual's innate creative talent and his lesser creative output can be narrowed by deliberate education in creative thinking.

In 1948, Carl H. Grabo (*5*) wrote,

"Considering man's hostility to change and innovation . . . it is astonishing that so much of creative and imaginative genius has contrived to leave its impress on the human race. Yet who can doubt that more, habited in weak bodies, blasted early by ignorance and cruelty and superstition, has perished with no record? In our comparatively low civilization, a little is done under favorable circumstances to salvage great talent, to give it opportunity to grow and express itself. Yet how pitifully meager is our salvage and how great the waste! We know that this is so. A more civilized time than ours will strive to develop this, the greatest of all natural resources."

Let's hope that this "more civilized" day is now dawning.

REFERENCES

1. Davis, P. H. Changes are coming in the colleges. *J. higher Educ.,* 1962, *23,* 141–147.
2. Getzels, J. W., & Jackson, P. W. The meaning of "giftedness": An examination of an expanding concept. *Phi Dela Kappan,* 1958, *40,* 75–77.
3. Gordon, W. J. J. Operational approach to creativity. *Harvard Bus. Rev.,* 1956, *34,* 41–51.
4. Gough, H. C. *Manual for the California Psychological Inventory.* Palo Alto, Calif.: Consulting Psychologists Press, 1957.
5. Grabo, C. H. *The creative critic.* Chicago: Univ. Chicago Press, 1948.
6. Guilford, J. P. Creativity. *Amer. Psychologist,* 1950, *9,* 444–454.
7. Guilford, J. P. Some recent findings on thinking abilities and their implications. *Informational Bull.,* 1952, *3,* 48–61.
8. James, B. J. Education for innovative behavior in executives. Research Grant from US Office of Education to University of Chicago, 1960.
9. Livingston, Carolyn W. Unpub. memorandum to Alex F. Osborn, February 10, 1961.
10. Maltzman, I., Simon, S., & Licht, L. The persistence of originality-training effects. Los Angeles: Univ. California, Department of Psychology, Technical Report 4, Prepared under contract Nonr 233 (50) for the Office of Naval Research, August, 1959.
11. Maslow, A. *Motivation and personality.* New York: Harper and Row, 1954.
12. Meadow, A., & Parnes, S. J. Evaluation of training in creative problem-solving. *J. appl. Psychol.,* 1959, *43,* 189–194.
13. Meadow, A., Parnes, S. J., & Reese, M. Influence of brainstorming instructions and problem sequence on a creative problem-solving test. *J. appl. Psychol.,* 1959, *43,* 413–416.

14. Osborn, A. F. Is education becoming more creative? An address given at the Seventh Annual Creative Problem-Solving Institute, Univ. Buffalo, 1961.

15. Parnes, S. J. (Ed.) *Compendiums of research on creative imagination.* Buffalo, New York: Creative Education Foundation, 1958, 1960.

16. Parnes, S. J. *Instructor's manual for semester courses in creative problem-solving.* Buffalo, New York: Creative Education Foundation, 1959.

17. Parnes, S. J. Effects of extended effort in creative problem-solving. *J. educ. Psychol.,* 1961, *52,* 117–122.

18. Parnes, S. J., & Meadow, A. Effects of "brainstorming" instructions on creative problem-solving by trained and untrained subjects. *J. educ. Psychol.,* 1959, *50,* 171–176.

19. Parnes, S. J., & Meadow, A. Evaluation of persistence of effects produced by a creative problem-solving course. *Psychol. Reps.,* 1960, 7, 357–361.

20. Schmadel, Elnora. The relationship of creative thinking abilities to school achievement. Unpublished doctoral dissertation, Univ. South. Calif., 1960.

21. Sommers, W. S. The influence of selected teaching methods on the development of creative thinking. Unpublished doctoral dissertation, Univ. Minnesota, 1961.

22. Taylor, C. W. (Ed.) *Research conference on the identification of creative scientific talent.* Salt Lake City: Univ. Utah Press, 1959.

23. Torrance, E. P. *Explorations in creative thinking in the early school years.* Minneapolis: Bureau of Educational Research, Univ. Minnesota, 1959.

24. Torrance, E. P. *Conditions for creative growth.* Minneapolis: Bureau of Educational Research, Univ. Minnesota, 1960.

25. Torrance, E. P. Status of knowledge concerning education and creative scientific talent. Working paper for a project on the Status of Knowledge about Creative Scientific Talent, directed by Calvin W. Taylor, Univ. Utah, with support by the National Science Foundation, 1961.

Understanding Creativity

Herbert A. Simon

COMBINING THE WORDS "CREATIVITY" AND "THE COMPUTER" IN THE title of this conference is a little bit like combining Beauty and the Beast. A lot of you may wonder how the computer comes into the topic of creativity. My first answer is that a computer, though it is a machine, need not behave in a machine-like manner. The term "machine" usually means to us repetitive, mechanical, inflexible, stereotyped behavior—and clearly that isn't what creative behavior is. But by using computers as flexible symbol-manipulators, not simply as devices for doing speedy arithmetic, we have been able to learn a great deal about human problem-solving; and by simulating that

REPRINTED by permission of the Author and *Carnegie Review* No. 2, 1964–5.

problem-solving on the computer we've been able to use computers to learn about creativity.

But, the question of how the computer was used to do this, how it has been a tool in psychological research on creativity, is the subject of another panel. What I'm going to talk about, ignoring computers for the moment, is what we now know about creativity—about how human beings think creatively. This knowledge in large part is the result of research using computers, but I'm going to leave it to my colleagues to describe the nature of that research.

What do we mean by creativity? When do we call something creative? We call human problem-solving creative to the extent that one or more of the following conditions are satisfied: first, if the product of the thinking has novelty and value either for the thinker or for his society; second, if the thinking is unconventional, in the sense that it requires modification or rejection of previously-accepted ideas. Third, we call thinking creative if it requires high motivation and persistence, taking place either over a considerable span of time or at high intensity. And finally, we tend to call thinking creative if it deals with or solves a problem which, initially, as it was posed, was a vague and ill-defined problem, so that part of the task of the creative thinker was to formulate the problem itself, to give it structure.

Now, in talking here about the nature of creativity, I'm going to proceed on two basic hypotheses. (You may want to question them, or examine whether they are really justified hypotheses, but I'm going to proceed on them in any event.) My first hypothesis is that the creative processes, the processes a person uses when he's doing creative thinking, are indistinguishable from ordinary problem-solving processes. What distinguishes the creative thinker from any person who is solving problems is only the distinctiveness of the product: that his solution is a novel, valuable, unconventional result. The creative thinker uses the same brain cells and uses them in basically the same way as anyone else would in solving problems.

My second hypothesis—and there's a fair amount of evidence to support it—is that the creative process in art and in science are substantially identical, that however much the "two cultures" may be divided in our society—however little scientists may know about the arts or artists about science—the processes they use in their respective fields when they are being creative are basically the same kinds of thinking processes. And I think this basic identity of the creative processes in the various fields of art and science is denied only by people who aren't familiar with both of those fields, who haven't had at least some experience of creativity in both of them, and who are misled by the differences in the products—the difference between a scientific paper on the one hand and a painting on the other, let's say. People are misled by this into thinking that the products, because they're so different, must have been created by entirely different thinking processes. All the evidence, I think, is to the contrary.

Well, what are these processes? How do people go about solving scientific and artistic problems? First of all, we know from our own experiences and from what's been written about the subject, that when we're solving problems a great deal goes on subconsciously—we're not aware of it ourselves, we can't give a complete descriptive account of what we're doing. But there is no evidence that the processes going on *subconsciously* are different in kind from the processes going on *consciously*. And therefore, from the one-seventh of the iceberg that is visible—the part of our thinking that we are conscious of—we can learn a great deal about the part of the iceberg that's below the surface of the water—the subconscious processes that are going on. The main evidence for the identity of processes at the two levels, is that by programming computers to reproduce the kinds of processes that people use consciously in their thinking, and only those processes, we are able to imitate and simulate human problem-solving in a variety of areas. But again my colleagues will have more to say about that.

Now what is involved, what are the processes, whether conscious or subconscious, that go on in problem-solving? *Problem-solving involves selective trial-and-error search in a vast space of possibilities.* In the game of chess, for example—which however complex it might be is certainly simpler than the problems of real life—the number of alternatives that would have to be examined if a person were to look at all the possibilities and then select the best one would be something like ten raised to the 120th power. My mathematician friends assure me this is a very large number: indeed, larger than the number of molecules in the universe. Neither human beings nor computers can look at 10^{120} alternatives. Problem-solving does not involve looking at 10^{120} things; it involves looking at the very small number of things that human beings have time to look at in their thought processes. Thus problem-solving is a *highly selective*, trial-and-error search in an enormous geometrically-branching maze of possibilities. This search generates various possibilities for solutions or partial solutions for the problem that has been posed. After they are generated, these possibilities are tested to see whether they are in fact solutions. We have today considerable evidence in human problem-solving that the numbers of possibilities actually examined in this highly selective search is almost always well under a hundred. Such evidence has been gathered for problems of proving theorems and problems of choosing moves in chess.

In addition to selective trial-and-error search, problem-solving involves abstraction. Abstraction in itself is perhaps a rather vague and abstract term, but I mean something pretty definite by it. By abstraction (or planning, which in this context means about the same thing) I mean taking the original problem-situation, throwing away a good deal of the detail of that situation, arriving thereby at a simplified problem, solving the simplified problem (which, because detail has been omitted is a good deal easier to solve than the original problem), and finally using the solution of the simplified problem, after reinserting the detail, as a guide or plan for the solution of the original problem. In the studies of problem-solving that have been made, we have seen that this kind of abstraction and planning, restructuring or recoding the original problem situation, is one of the very powerful tools of problem-solving that good problem-solvers use effectively. Abstraction aids problem-solving by cutting down the size of that vast maze of possibilities through which the problem-solver must search.

And finally, in addition to selective search, in addition to abstracting and recoding problem situations, problem-solving activity involves searching for and finding patterns. If I were to recite a string of letters—A, BB, CCC, DDDD—and ask you what the next letters were you would immediately reply, I think, with 5 letter E's, EEEEE. Just by hearing me read this string of letters, you discover a simple pattern, going down the letters of the alphabet, and increasing the number of repetitions of each successive letter. This discovery of pattern is a simple example, a very simple example, of behavior that we find universally in problem-solvers; searching in the problem material for various kinds of patterns, and substituting the simple rule that describes the pattern for the complexity of the original problem. It's a kind of behavior that's very prevalent, for example, in listening to and understanding music. The task of the listener is to find patterns in the harmonics and in the melodic line of the tones. His understanding of the music involves hearing these patterns, involves being able to anticipate the patterns in the notes that are still to come. We find these common kinds of processes or activities—selective search, abstracting, pattern-finding—in all sorts of human problem-solving, whether in the sciences or in the arts.

In our particular topic here, Creativity and Creative Problem-

Solving, how do we distinguish routine, ordinary, garden-variety, everyday problem-solving from the kind of problem-solving we value and call creative? There is almost a paradox here, for on the one hand we value creative problem-solving as the best, the finest, the highest form of problem-solving; while on the other hand, if we look closely at the processes that go on when a person is being creative, we find, perhaps, a greater predominance of trial-and-error search in creative problem-solving than we do in everyday routine thinking. Suppose we arrange different kinds of problem-solving along a continuum. On one end of this continuum we put thinking activities that are almost entirely blind search—just trying one thing after another until the right answer is arrived at. At the other end of the continuum we put highly routine thinking, where the problem is so familiar that by simply applying familiar routine, the answer can be arrived at almost effortlessly. Then the kind of professional problem-solving we do every day would lie somewhere between these extremes of blind search on the one hand and routine on the other.

Close to the routine end of the continuum are things that we do habitually and customarily every day—the sorts of things a housewife does when she is preparing dinner, things that she becomes habituated to, because she does them almost daily. One step from this are the kinds of activities that we call professional problem-solving: kinds of problems where a man is able to call on the analytic tools with which his profession provides him—the "tricks of the trade"—so that he can arrive at the solution in a relatively systematic way and without a great deal of search. But by the very nature of his problems —the novelty for which he is seeking—the *creative* problem-solver does not have a specific kit of tools, tailored to the particular problem before him. Hence, to arrive at a solution, he has to engage in far more search, he has to be willing to try many more things, than a person working in a well-defined conventional area of problem-solving, where the tools of his profession show him a systematic and straightforward path to the result. The paradox is that the creative problem-solving process is in many respects less highly organized, less rational or logical, if you like, than is the more routine application of human intelligence to everyday tasks. Hence, the creative kind of problem-solving lies over toward the blind-search end of the continuum.

So much for a very broad description of the problem-solving processes that we see human beings using in general, and the particular forms these processes take when people are trying to be creative. What can we say about the way to be creative? How can we be more creative in our problem-solving activities? What are the conditions under which a person succeeds in producing creative results in his thinking? Obviously, trial-and-error isn't enough: we could work on the problem of relativity, or much less difficult problems than that, all of our lives, just searching at random for solutions, and we probably wouldn't be very surprised if we didn't find them. What has to be added to a willingness to indulge in trial-and-error, if we are to be creative? Must we be smart? Must we be unconventional? Well, of course, both of these are essential. Most creative products in our society that we value are made by people who are more intelligent than the average of the population. However, it would be by no means true to say that the people who score highest on intelligence tests in the population are the ones who do most or all of the creating. There is a correlation, but by no means a perfect correlation, between the intelligence of people and their ability to be creative.

What else is involved? As far as unconventionality is concerned, by definition you have to be different in some respect to be creative. We don't call the result of thinking creative unless it is different, and there is an element of novelty in it. But people who are creative have to be different in this respect also: by definition, only a small fraction of any group of people is going to be among those judged "most creative." By definition, only 1% of all the people in the population are in the top percentile of anything! A creative act then, an invention or any kind of creative product, must go in some respect beyond what a good professional, skilled in the art, could do or would be likely to do. And when we are looking for the conditions of creativity, we're not just looking for the conditions of unconventionality in general, but a particular kind of unconventionality. We are looking for a particular kind of intelligence that allows a person to do things that other professionals who are skilled in the art can't do, or are unlikely to do.

And what are the conditions for this? I would say that you are likely to discover something that is novel and valuable only if one or more of the following conditions—some of which I have already alluded to—are fulfilled. First of all, you can be smarter than other people—but it's immodest to *say* that you are and it's usually unwise to *think* that you are. If, in fact, you have more than your quota of gray matter, that's all to the good, but I think it's very unwise for a professional to depend simply on being more intelligent than other people as a basis for his creativity. It's much safer to suppose that other intelligent people have tackled the same problems that you're going to tackle; and if you turn up novel answers, which other people haven't thought of, it must be because you are using some secret weapon in your attack on the problem that they didn't possess. It's rather unwise to depend solely on your intelligence as that secret weapon.

But what are the other possibilities, the other things that might allow you to arrive at a unique product? First of all, you may have a new problem. Much of the creativity that is exhibited in our world is exhibited in relation to new problems that weren't solved earlier because they weren't posed earlier. Today, for example, there are lots of opportunities to be creative about space travel, because space travel is something that people have only recently considered to be realistically possible. It simply was not in the cards a few years ago. In the history of any field of art or knowledge, a large part of the creativity is exhibited, a large part of the novelty occurs, in very early stages of the development of the field, when the new problems have just been posed.

Another possibility that might allow you to be creative is that you're aware of a new phenomenon, you know some new facts about the world that other people don't yet know. You might have come at those facts in a variety of ways. You might have stumbled over them accidentally. There's a nice word to describe that state of affairs: it's called "serendipity." Serendipity consists in having the good fortune to stumble across important facts that other people have not yet seen. The example of serendipity most often cited is the discovery of the vulcanization of rubber, when Goodyear accidentally dropped some of his materials on a hot stove and noticed that the resulting heated rubber had the properties he was looking for. Now notice two aspects of this example: first of all, it was accidental, Goodyear didn't plan to drop the rubber on the stove; but secondly, the accident happened to a man who was looking for a way to produce rubber, and who had already a great deal of knowledge about the substance he was working with, and about the property he was looking for. Serendipity, the accidental observation of a new phenomenon, almost always happens to a prepared mind, not just to somebody who has thought about the problem for 15 minutes.

Another way in which a person may discover a novel phenomenon is by using a new instrument. When the electron microscope came along, there were possibilities for observing phenomena at the molecular level that had never been observed before, and thereby, being creative in producing new knowledge with this instrument. We could think of many examples in which creativity has consisted of exploiting the potentialities of a new instrument of observation. Another way to see phenomena is by exploring a new country which other people have not yet explored. Until the possibility of space travel had become a reality, we probably were running out of new countries to explore; this is not as good a way of being creative as it was perhaps back in the 15th and 16th centuries.

What are some of the other tools or some of the other secret weapons you might apply in order to be creative and arrive at a novel result? One possibility is to invent or acquire a new analytic tool. It was very difficult before the invention of the calculus to think about the movements of the planets and the stars, and the ways in which the forces that one exerted on another might affect these motions. The task of working through the mathematics was simply too difficult for the human mind. But now any good college sophomore with a course in the calculus can demonstrate that with the inverse square law of gravitational attraction, the moon has to go around the earth in an ellipse. So the calculus was a new analytic tool that enabled Newton and the people who followed him to think through problems that were simply too difficult for the human mind before that time. An analytic tool of comparable power has emerged in our own time. The computer program, and languages specially devised for formulating computer programs, give people who use this analytic tool a way of talking about and thinking about complex phenomena that we simply didn't have before the day of the computer. Hence, people who work with these new languages have opportunities to be creative—to solve problems which couldn't be solved, or which could only be solved with great difficulty, before these languages were available.

Another possible source of creativity, another way in which you might have an advantage over other people in tackling particular problems, would be by being able to draw on a mixture of ideas and cues garnered from different fields of knowledge. If you expose yourself to a variety of disciplines or areas of knowledge, you may be able to put together the ideas you get from these different fields in novel combinations and solve problems that others haven't. Many of the important examples of creativity on record are examples of cases where people have put 2 and 2 together, and where the 2 and 2 came from quite different fields of human knowledge.

Now, the result of being able to apply one or more of these advantages—a superior intelligence, a new problem, some new phenomena that you have observed, a new analytic tool that you possess because you've invented it or gotten it from somebody, or a mixture of cues from different fields—the result of having these techniques available may be that you will remove a barrier to search, you will notice that people have failed to search in the right parts of the problem space, because some kind of tradition has barred out a part of that space; or you will find some new principle of selection, which tells you what part of the space needs exploring, where you should look for the answer to the problem, and as a result you will discover something novel and useful; you will be creative.

I should add at least two items to this account of the conditions of creativity. If we look at examples of creative accomplishments, we can draw from them two quite clear generalizations: First, even with the kinds of tools and equipment I have described, success in solving a difficult problem usually results from a tremendous preoccupation with the problem. There are very few cases where important discoveries have been made by people who haven't had a history of at least 10 years' day-dreaming with the problem, or the problem-area, before they arrived at their discovery. Second, associated with the ability and willingness to stick with a problem for a very long time, to preoccupy oneself with it over months and over years, there has to go a very deep tolerance for ambiguity—an ability to live with a situation, even though the situation doesn't immediately lead to clarity, doesn't immediately lead to a solution of the problem. If a person who finds himself in a big maze of possibilities, a big unstructured problem-space, is overcome with anxiety, if he becomes too eager to find structure in the situation, to find immediate clarity, then he isn't going to be able to preoccupy himself with the problem over a long period of years, to turn it over and over in his mind, to endure that 10 years' day-dreaming. And consequently, he is unlikely to find important creative products.

In my account of the creative process here, and the things I have chosen to mention and to emphasize, I've left out a few of the characteristics of creative problem-solving that are often mentioned in the literature. I don't have space to discuss them at length here, but I would like at least to mention them. A number of people who have described the problem-solving process have said that it goes through the following four general stages: First, preparatory activities —learning a great deal about the problem environment, about the structure of the problem, about things related to the problem that might possibly be relevant and useful. This is sometimes followed by the second step, a period of incubation. There are lots of cases on record where people have worked on a problem for a while, have then put it aside, have thought they were thinking about other things, and then have had a more or less sudden illumination, which is the third stage in this description of the problem-solving process. Perhaps at a time when they were not thinking about the problem at all, these people have suddenly seen where the solution lay, even seen a good deal of the detail of the solution. And illumination, if it occurs, is usually followed by a process of consolidation. The illumination may simply indicate the main lines of the problem solution; then the detail has to be cleared up and the implications of the solution have to be worked out. There has been a great deal of attention to the stages of incubation and sudden illumination following incubation, largely because of the drama of the sudden flash of insight, particularly when it follows a period where the person is not conscious of the fact that he has been working on the problem. As I say, I don't have space here to discuss these phenomena in detail, but I would like to remind you of something I said at the outset of my remarks—that all our evidence indicates that the processes going on during problem-solving, including creative problem-solving, at the *subconscious* level are similar to the processes going on at the *conscious* level. The dramatic flash of insight is probably nothing terribly mysterious, probably nothing terribly miraculous, but simply a shifting of problem-solving activities from a subconscious to a conscious level—not a change in the character or the kinds of those activities.

Well, let me summarize the main things that I have been saying here. First of all, I have been arguing that creative problem-solving is not basically very different from any other kind of problem-solving. In considerable part, developing one's creativity is a matter simply of developing one's problem-solving habits and one's motivation. Secondly, I have been saying, or at least my remarks imply clearly, that creativity is not costless. One reason why a lot of people aren't creative, or aren't more creative than they are, is because they are not willing to pay the price. You are unlikely to be highly creative in significant ways unless several conditions are satisfied. First of all, the creativity must be more important to you than lots of other things you might be doing. It must be more important for you to immerse yourself in the problem, be preoccupied with it, than to attend to other matters. And it will not be possible for a person to immerse himself in a problem-situation unless he is able to tolerate ambiguity, unless he feels comfortable in the face of an unstructured and, as yet, unsolved problem, and can maintain that comfort or at least a reasonably low level of discomfort, over a long period of time. Finally, a person is unlikely to be creative unless he has developed the habit of asking, "What is the question? What is the question I'm trying to answer, and what would a solution look like, if I had one?"

And now it's time, I think, to go back to computers and to the relation between creativity and computers. Since, in my experience in talking about computers, many people seem to think that these terms are antithetical, almost contradictory, and many people seem to be worried about the impact of the computer on our society—seem worried that the computer in some sense threatens man—I'd like to conclude with a statement of my position on this particular issue. And in doing so I'd like to quote something I have written in another place.

The developing capacity of computers to simulate man, and thus both to serve as his substitute and to provide a theory of human mental functions, will change man's conception of his own identity as a species. The definition of man's uniqueness has always formed the kernel of his cosmological and ethical systems. With Copernicus and Galileo, he ceased to be the species located at the center of the universe, attended by sun and stars. With Darwin, he ceased to be the species specially created and specially endowed by God with soul and reason. With Freud, he ceased to be the species whose behavior was governed by conscious, rational mind. As we begin to produce mechanisms that think and learn, he has ceased to be the species uniquely capable of complex, intelligent manipulation of his environment. I am confident that man will, as he has in the past, find a new way of describing his place in the universe—a way that, however different from the present one, will satisfy his needs for dignity and for purpose.

Toward the More Humane Education of Gifted Children

E. Paul Torrance

THE TREATMENT OF THE MENTALLY ILL AND THE EDUCATION OF THE gifted are alike in many ways. Neither has ever been a popular cause. It has always been difficult to elicit either popular or legislative support for the improvement of either. Both have supplied outlets for some of man's needs to pity and to punish. Of the two, the need to punish has perhaps dominated. Both the mentally ill and the gifted

REPRINTED by permission of the Author and *Gifted Child Quarterly*, 7:135–45, 1963. Paper presented to Cincinnati Chapter, National Association for Gifted Children, November 15, 1963.

have been regarded as being mysterious, beyond human understanding, evil and unrighteous. In our retribution, we have resorted to a primitive reaction—punishment. In recent years, realistic accounts of our inhumane treatment of the mentally ill have resulted in increased legislative support for their treatment and perhaps some small increase in public understanding. These gains have by no means ended the inhumane treatment of the mentally ill, but certainly we must admit that tremendous advances have been made.

Frequently, I hear the complaint that there is no emotional appeal involved in proposals to improve the education of the gifted. Having superior potential, gifted children will take care of themselves, I am informed. We are told that the gifted already have more than others, so why should society be concerned about giving them more. We hear such comments as this in spite of our great American dream of a kind of education which will give every child a better chance to become his potentialities. You would think sometimes that this dream must apply to the mentally retarded, but not to the gifted.

I wonder who can be so insensitive as to experience no emotional appeal in some of the stories which come to me of the inhumane treatment of gifted children by hard-working, well-meaning, conscientious parents and teachers. Let me share a few of these with you.

The mother of one gifted thirteen-year-old boy wrote me as follows:

"He is now 13 years old and has had a steadily declining academic record that ended in his being retained in the seventh grade this year. . . . He has a burning *main* interest in electronics and rocks and believe me, his knowledge and interest in these two subjects is great.

"His teachers, principals, and counselors have told me a confusing variety of things (confusing to me anyway). They all agree he is very bright, very bored (daydreams in class constantly), and very withdrawn though not rebellious. Two teachers have told me the school has destroyed his desire to learn. One teacher told me the school cannot help him because the only 'special class' they are informed enough to help are the 'slow' children. Another teacher said to me, 'I'll make him work if I have to break his spirit to do it—and ridiculing and shaming him is the only way with children like him. . . .' Last spring the school counselor and principal decided that flunking him was the only way to make him 'buckle down and work or else.' . . . He can't join the different types of science clubs because he doesn't have a B average—to which the principal urged that he take up football.

"So many doors closed! Where is the spirit of educating and cultivating the child's natural desire to learn—some seed of it is always there, to some extent or another!

"Now, I will tell you of the boy I know, my son. . . . He is an irresponsible scatterbrain—he just can't harness his brain to such unimportant things as taking out the trash when he's hot on the trail of discovering perpetual motion. He *never* daydreams, loves to learn, and is always getting books from the library. He is a hard worker; many times he almost collapses trying to work and experiment late in the night. He has energy enough for ten people. He has an outgoing bubbling personality and a terrific sense of humor. All this he is at home and in the rest of the world *until* he gets to school.

"He speaks of wanting to go to an 'electric college' but says he'll probably quit school when he's 16.

"I feel that he is in a steel box—I think he feels he is too and thinks the only way to be free is get out by quitting.

"How can doors be opened, can you tell me? Can you advise or suggest *anything* that could help?

"Please, don't be too busy to care or answer me. I just don't know where else to turn!"

Who is so callous as to be unmoved by the following poem written by a lonely, gifted nine-year-old girl?

"Loneliness is the stillness in the air,
Rain falling to the ground,
The cold wind whistling through the trees,
The darkness,
The damp, misty air chilling you,
The absence of love.
Loneliness is so many unsaid words."

Who would not be stirred emotionally by the account of the search by Graham's teachers and parents to find some punishment which will fit him. Ten-year-old Graham's mother describes their plight as follows:

"Let me try to list some of the things that are driving his teacher, my husband and me mad . . .

"We have never found a punishment to fit Graham. If placed in a corner, he'd sing. If spanked, he'd howl like we were killing him, yet the minute we left the room the tears would snap off. If sent to his room, he'd simply lay down and go to sleep. Now that he is older, privileges are taken away. They too are taken with no hurt feeling on the surface.

"Graham shows a great capacity for school work when he wants to. He refused to finish addition and subtraction drills at school. It was thought he didn't know the answers. When multiplication was introduced, he surprised everyone by knowing the answers. . . . His teacher reports that he is always raising his hand, walking up to her desk, even trying to instruct the class (fourth grade).

"... I want desperately to understand Graham. I'm sure his home life at the present time is not as happy as it could be. I'm anxious now because I know it will be more difficult as years progress. . . . Please let me know if and where I can get help. Believe me I'm shouting my plea."

The mother of a creatively gifted girl wrote in a similar vein, as follows:

"... I gave her a hard time and spanked her often, figuring she was a very obstinate child. Consequently, she was very nervous and she and I had a pretty horrible relationship. . . ."

Why is it that such hard-working, conscientious, and well-meaning parents, teachers, counselors, and principals treat children in such inhumane ways and obtain such negative results? Why is it that we have today a growing attitude of greater harshness and punitiveness toward children in our society? Why are gifted children so often the special targets of such inhumane treatment?

It is my thesis that the inhumanities which prevail in the education of gifted children are primarily a result of our unwillingness to accept a realistically complex picture of the human mind and personality. In spite of his own complexity, man strives constantly for over-simplifications which lead him into error. I do not know whether this is basic to man's nature or the result of an education that has imbued him with a compulsion to determine the one "right" answer. From the very beginning of our research on giftedness, it has been our dream that we might develop a deeper and more complete understanding of the human mind and personality and their functioning. It is our hope that such understandings will give us the basis for developing a more human kind of education—the kind of education which will give all children (including gifted children) a better chance to become their potentialities.

I would like to try to show how this research is beginning to yield a deeper and more complete understanding of the human mind and personality, and how this understanding can be used in our struggle against the inhumanities caused by an oversimplified view of the functioning of the human mind and personality. It is my hope that in this way we can avoid some of the erroneous and misleading over-simplifications which some of my critics have placed upon our research and my interpretation of it.

I am always shocked to find that someone believes that I:

... favor creative learning *rather* than learning by authority;

... advocate the use of tests of creative talent in identifying the gifted *rather* than tests of intelligence;

. . . emphasize moral courage and honesty *rather* than personal and social maladjustment;

. . . advocate creative thinking and imagination *rather* than the acquisition of knowledge; original answers *rather* than correct ones;

. . . advocate that we reward divergent behavior *rather* than conforming behavior;

. . . believe in providing a responsive environment *rather* than a stimulating one;

. . . recommend that we treat boys and girls alike *rather* than differently; and

. . . encourage chaos and destructiveness *rather* than discipline and order.

In almost every instance, what I have tried to communicate is that the human mind and personality are wonderful and complex and that respect for human values demands that attention be given to both creative learning and learning by authority, to tests of creative thinking as *well* as to tests of intelligence, to moral courage as *well* as to personal and social adjustment, and so on. If you will try to be honest, I believe that you will find that this is possible and that one is not necessarily in conflict with the other, that both kinds of emphasis are not only possible but desirable. Quite briefly I would like to consider each of the dilemmas which critics have tried to construct from what I have reported.

CREATIVE LEARNING AND LEARNING BY AUTHORITY

Recently, a friend visiting in a city in New Jersey, sent me a newspaper clipping from a local newspaper interpreting my NEA pamphlet on "What Research Says to the Teacher about Creativity" (1963a). This newspaper article credited me with advocating the abolition of educational methods which involve teaching by authority. Let us see just what I said in this publication (pp. 12–13).

I did say that, in my opinion, the weight of present evidence indicates that man fundamentally prefers to learn in creative ways— by exploring, manipulating, questioning, experimenting, risking, testing and modifying ideas, and otherwise inquiring. I did not say that it was always good for man to learn creatively. In fact, I cautioned that although the needs underlying learning in creative ways is universal enough to make this way of learning valuable for all children, it should not be regarded as the exclusive method of education or even the exclusive method for any one child. I did insist that many things, though not all, can be learned more effectively and economically in creative ways rather than by authority. I also indicated that many

children who have an especially strong preference for learning creatively, learn a great deal if permitted to use their creative thinking
abilities, and make little educational progress if we insist that they
learn exclusively by authority.

I tried to show how strong human needs are involved in each state
of the process of thinking creatively. If we sense that something is
missing or untrue, tension is aroused. We are uncomfortable and want
to do something to relieve the tension. This makes us want to ask
questions, make guesses, or otherwise inquire. Uncertain as to whether
our guesses are correct, we continue to be uncomfortable. Thus,
we are driven to test our guesses, correct our errors, and modify
our conclusions. Once we discover something, we want to tell someone about it. All of this is why it is so natural for man to want to
learn creatively.

It is also true that man's nature requires that he have anchors in
reality, that he have structure in his environment, and that he have
authorities upon whom he can depend. Just as individuals differ in
the extent to which they prefer to learn creatively, they also differ
in the extent to which they require authorities.

I wish there were time to cite the research evidence and cases of
individuals to show how a failure to accept this complex view of the
learning process leads to inhumane treatment of gifted youngsters.
Perhaps it can help you understand the panic and desolation of
thirteen-year-old Alice when she transferred from elementary school
where she had been permitted to learn both creatively and by authority
to a junior high school where she had to learn primarily by authority.
In elementary school, she achieved a straight "A" record and was
regarded as creative, imaginative, and intelligent by her teachers. Alice's
mother describes the situation as follows:

"She hated junior high almost from the first day. It frightened her. She
complained that she felt lost in it, that it was cold, impersonal. . . . The
teachers are no doubt well-intentioned but they are too overworked to
do anything but get angry, pressure, threaten. These methods have never
worked with her. As a result, she lost interest in her work, lost all her
self-confidence. . . . She has given up her drawing and writing. She says
she can't create or be artistic while she is unhappy about her marks. I
am heartsick about this whole situation because I know she is very bright
and that she has the scholastic potential to do well in college. It would
be a terrible waste of talent and of a good mind for the teachers to give
up on her at this point. I believe I have reason to have faith in her. She
thinks for herself; that's important. On a recent Iowa achievement test,
she averaged at the 95th percentile for the eighth grade (98th percentile
in reading and 99th percentile in vocabulary)."

Here we have a case which is just the opposite of the case of Bob which I have cited many times (Torrance, 1962) to show how a boy who had been considered a hopeless case throughout elementary school and into the ninth grade can regain confidence in himself and begin learning. Bob's English teacher encouraged him to take his tests over the poems and stories they read in class by illustrating them. His sensitive insights about what they had read—insights which he could not express in writing or orally—amazed the other members of the class and brought forth their praise. Soon he became interested in learning how to read, became a much happier and socially better adjusted person.

INTELLIGENCE TESTS AND CREATIVITY TESTS IN IDENTIFYING THE GIFTED

Our work with tests of creative thinking has caused some people to conclude that I advocate the abolition of intelligence tests and the substitution of creative or divergent thinking tests. The truth is that I have continually said that intelligence tests have long been very useful in guiding and assessing mental growth and intellectual potentiality and that they will continue to be useful. I have tried to show why we need to broaden our concept of "giftedness" from that of the "child with the high IQ" to *include also* the highly creative child and *other types*. I have spoken of the importance of giving greater emphasis to the fostering of original work at all levels, making this function at least as important as teaching information.

I have endeavored to present the creative thinking abilities as just one part of our expanded and expanding concept of the human mind and its functioning. Some of the misinterpretation of what I have reported may have come from the accounts of some of our partial replications of the Getzels and Jackson study (1962) in which we have contrasted a group of highly intelligent and less creative children with a group of highly creative but less intelligent children. Some have interpreted this to mean that high intelligence and high creative thinking ability are mutually exclusive, that one cannot be both highly intelligent and highly creative. This is certainly not true. I do not believe that I have ever failed to mention those who are high on both measures. In fact, if we identify a group of children as being either highly intelligent or highly creative, about 30 per cent of them will be both highly intelligent and highly creative.

I believe that these facts do emphasize the need for more serious attention to the individualization of instruction, and to dissuade us from the vain hope of finding the one supreme educational method to which all children will respond. Perhaps the most that we can realistically hope for is to determine what methods are most effective with what types or categories of learners. Many convergent lines of research are beginning to make it clear, that when we change our methods of teaching, or the nature of our instructional materials, that children with different kinds of mental abilities become the star learners and non-learners. This occurs, even when we make no change in the methods and instruments of evaluation. Differences of even greater magnitude occur when we change these. Students who rank highest on a multiple-choice examination requiring recognition and memory may rank near the bottom of their class on an examination requiring decisions, supporting those decisions, and making creative applications of knowledge.

Let us turn now to a few examples of real live, gifted children, and see how our failure to accept a complex view of mental abilities leads to inhumane treatment of gifted children. Ted, who during his junior and senior high school years won eight major national and state awards for creative achievement in science, experienced his share of such inhumanities. It was not until after he entered senior high school that it was discovered that Ted's IQ and his room number had become transposed on his cumulative record during his elementary school years. Ted's mother and his older brother were aware that Ted was being treated as a mentally retarded child. He was always downgraded or ignored by his teachers. He was discouraged from doing whatever he wanted to attempt. Ted's science teacher in junior high school told Ted's brother that Ted had very little potential in science and should not be encouraged in his science interests. A college physics teacher in a nearby college who had been working with Ted, however, maintained that he wished his science majors knew as much about science as Ted did at the time he was in the seventh and eighth grades. It was also at this time that Ted won first place in his area and in the state science fair for his linear accelerator, with which he did biological research. Here is a case where teachers placed reliance upon the reality of the IQ on the cumulative record, rather than the realities of his actual achievement.

Many creatively gifted youngsters suffer inhumane treatment because their teachers refuse to believe that their creative achievements are their own, being blinded either by relatively low IQ's or some type of nonconforming behavior. Such has been the case of Dee, a gifted girl, just finishing junior high school. Her mother describes one such incident as follows:

". . . When I got home from work yesterday, Dee greeted me with tears in her eyes—the history teacher again. This time she did an unforgivable thing. Before the whole class, while pounding on Dee's desk with her hand, she ridiculed Dee by swearing that Dee's homework was not done by her, and that it absolutely was not in her handwriting . . . Dee has the ability to write with either hand. She has done this all her life. It is just as natural for her to switch hands when one gets tired as it is to breathe. The only difference in this instance was a slight change in style. She showed her homework to me while she was preparing it, and asked me how I liked her writing."

There are many kinds of giftedness, however, and whenever we fail to realize this, we are likely to contribute to the inhumane treatment of youngsters who have the potential for outstanding achievement. The case of Mark may prove to be one of this type. At any rate, Mark has always been classed as a "low achiever" and as "not interested in school"—a "no good." His arts and crafts instructor, however, believes that Mark is exceptionally gifted. Mark's mother wrote me as follows:

"The instructor tells us that Mark is an exceptionally talented craftsman, as well an an innovator of original ideas. He has recommended that Mark be sent to art school, and he predicts a promising future for this youngster as an artist or designer. On the other side of the fence, there is his counselor, a man thoroughly sold on verbal and word skills, who can see Mark *only* as a low-achiever . . . His creative abilities and original ideas are recognized only by his arts and crafts instructor, so we are puzzled about what to do. The counselor tells us that the boy tests 'above average' on a standardized IQ test; the art instructor believes, from observation, that Mark is far above average in intelligence."

Such puzzles occur, I maintain, because neither the counselor, nor the art teacher accepts a sufficiently complex view of mental functioning. For a further documentation of cases which illustrate how an over-simplified view of giftedness can lead to an inhumane kind of education for the gifted, I would refer you to Hillel Black's article, "The Scandal of Educational Testing," in the November 9th *Saturday Evening Post*.

MORAL COURAGE AND SOCIAL ADJUSTMENT

On several occasions I have been accused of de-emphasizing the importance of social adjustment. Although this has never been my intent, I have pointed out that what is sometimes perceived as social adjustment may interfere with what I regard as a deeper kind of personal adjustment, a quality we usually talk of in terms of moral courage and honesty. Just as some children who are highly intelligent are not highly creative, some children who are highly adjusted, are not highly moral. In a peer-oriented culture such as ours, it is well to recognize the dangers of giving the greater rewards to those who accept the peer-value system and adjust almost automatically to the immediate group, almost without reference to moral values. The study by Getzels and Jackson (1962) indicated that in certain regards the highly adjusted adolescents are given greater rewards by the school culture than are highly moral adolescents.

In reviewing the Getzels and Jackson study (1963b), I expressed the opinion that their data on high moral standards and high adjustment dramatized one of the most serious defects of many programs of life-adjustment education. I had in mind those programs which stress only good manners, courtesy, conformity, obedience, industry, promptness, positiveness, and agreeableness, to the neglect of courage, independence in judgment, critical thinking, and high morals.

I have stressed the importance of courage and honesty because I believe that any conditioning to the contrary is inimical to creativity and to the development of the full potential of children. I think we must admist that there is much in our homes, schools, churches, and community organizations which conditions for dishonesty and results in the inhumane treatment of children. We find, for example, that parents and teachers in telling what they consider an ideal child, do not assign a place of great importance to courage, honesty, or independence in judgment. In a list of 62 characteristics, courage ranks 30th. In fact, it would appear that teachers in our culture consider it more important that their pupils be courteous than that they be courageous. It is more important that pupils do their work on time, be energetic and industrious, be obedient and popular or well-liked among their peers, be receptive of the ideas of others, be versatile, and be willing to accept the judgments of authorities than to be courageous.

In commenting on the fact that both parents and teachers rate "consideration of others" at the top of the list of characteristics they desire for children, I have always taken pains to state that I, too, place a great deal of value on being considerate of others. I have paused, however, to wonder how truthful we are in some of the things which we call "consideration of others." Some of our friends from other countries tell us that in our desire to appear considerate of them, we promise them things that we have no intention of giving. They tell us that it would be far more considerate if we would be honest rather than polite.

My contention is that we can have for children *both* a higher level of adjustment *and* a higher level of moral strength. Let us pause to examine one example of a gifted junior high school girl, whom we shall call Lena, which exposes some of the torture gifted children suffer when we give the greatest rewards to adjustment—actually coercion or surrender to the will of the teacher. Lena's mother describes the situation as follows:

". . . She is absolutely beside herself with this class in creative writing. She hates her teacher with a purple passion. The woman has a biting tongue, delights in making fun of all her students, all of her criticism is negative, and she has a one-track mind—patriotism. There has not yet been a chance to write anything of their choosing. They have spent the entire year writing essays for her contests. Lena is so sick of her country and the flag and the DAR and RAD, etc., that she is ready to move to Russia.

"Lena finally broke down and wrote one essay to please her. She set out with the intent to write one Mrs. W. would like—"I am the flame of freedom—I burn in the hearts of Americans—I warmed the soldiers at Valley Forge . . . etc. She read it aloud to us, the way Mrs. W. would read it. I almost lost my dinner. However, on THIS, she got an A—very creatively done, the dear lady said. By the next time around, Lena said, 'I won't do that again—it was awful—it wasn't me writing it and I won't be untrue to myself—' So the child is constantly torn between her need to be a creative individual in her own right and this is the thing she talks and thinks about most—being herself, and the need to get a satisfactory grade from Mrs. W."

ACCUMULATION OF KNOWLEDGE AND CREATIVITY

Quite erroneously, some people have interpreted my interest in creative problem-solving activities in the classroom as a de-emphasis upon learning what is known from the past. Nothing could be further from the truth. In my own experiments involving the evaluation of creative ways of learning and in those which I have in any way supervised we have been concerned to see that the experimental methods or materials did not interfere with the achievement of the traditionally measured kinds of achievement. In *none* of these studies have the creative activities interfered with these traditionally measured outcomes. In some of these experiments (Sommers, 1961), students exposed to the experimental creative activities have shown significantly greater gains of the traditional, acquisition-of-knowledge type than their controls.

It would be foolish to ignore the accumulation of past knowledge. It would also be foolish for us to accept it as the final and exclusive truth. In some of my experiments, I have obtained findings which I believe tell us that it is not the amount of information we have that is important in creative problem-solving, but that the attitude we have towards this information makes a difference in how well we are able to use it. How we store information is important. I believe that both the record of my research and my interpretation of the results place me strongly behind the President of my University who made the following statement when he welcomed the 1963 freshmen:

"Welcome into the community of people trying to save what is known and desperately seeking to answer questions my generation could not answer" (Wilson, 1963).

It should be obvious to all that it is impossible to prepare today's school children for all of the demands that they will meet, for all of the changes they will experience. It is utterly foolish to think that we can impart to children all the facts and skills they will need. The information and skills for doing this simply do not exist. It seems to me that the only solution to this overwhelming problem is to develop in today's school children the motivations and skills to continue learning the rest of their lives. I do not see how this can be interpreted as excluding the dissemination of what was known in the past. My plea, especially for gifted children, is that we move out of the shallows, into the depths of learning and experiencing, from the acquisition of knowledge, to doing something with the knowledge that is acquired.

ORIGINAL ANSWERS AND CORRECT ANSWERS

One newspaper columnist (Weider, 1963) attacked me for advocating emphasis on original rather than correct answers. He wrote:

"Torrance, who draws public pay for this work, says questions should be asked which call for original answers—not the "right" one. (Like, if two and two make four, when do they not?)"

My own students know that this does not represent my viewpoint. In a day when it has become an educational sin to ask memory questions on examinations, my students know that I am one teacher who is not afraid to say that there are some facts that are so important and so well established that they should be remembered. These important, firm facts give them anchors against which to evaluate their original answers, and provide them with a source from which to generate original answers. I am simply opposed to exclusive attention to the one *correct answer*. There is a place for both original answers and correct ones.

I think gifted children suffer most when we confuse the acquisition of knowledge, and other types of solid educational achievement with mere conformity. You will recall the case of Ted with his nationally recognized creative achievements in science and his low grades in high school. His scores on the mathematics and science College Board Examinations, however, were outstanding, and his scores in subjects such as English above average. When educational achievement is regarded as a bookkeeping system, attention must be centered upon doing those things which count in the teacher's grade book. Gifted children frequently have more important things to learn and to do. This is reflected in Elizabeth Drews' (1961) comparison of three types of gifted high school students: the creative intellectuals, the high-achieving studious type, and the social leaders. Of these three groups, the creative intellectuals had the lowest teachers' grades but turned in the highest performance on difficult achievement examinations covering a broad range of knowledge. She found that just before examinations, the social leaders were studying and reading for the first time, but reading those things which count in the teachers' grade book. The high-achieving studious individuals were studying as usual and generally studying what they had been assigned. The creative intellectuals, however, were likely to be reading a book on philosophy or a college textbook, activities which have little or no "pay off" in the teachers' grade book.

This confusion of solid achievement with conformity behavior is also reflected in the already mentioned case of Dee. At the time Dee was in the third grade, her teacher reported to her mother that Dee was failing third grade. She explained that she could not understand why, since Dee was intelligent and imaginative. She could stand up in front of the class and tell stories which would grip the attention of the class for hours. In her arithmetic bee, Dee challenged the class' best arithmetic student and beat him soundly, yet Dee was failing third grade.

There just may be something inhumane about the one correct answer approach as it was applied to Bob, once regarded as gifted. Bob was a happy child who wanted to go to school more than anything. Even before he started to school, many people had noted his penetrating questions and conclusions, and generally assumed that he was in the third or fourth grade. Bob's first grade teacher believed in correcting everything that he did. She even corrected and graded his drawings. His mother was saddened when he brought home failing papers, in which he had changed the teacher's dittoed drawing or had added cowboy boots and hats to the drawings that he had been given to color. Apparently Bob was thoroughly confused by this one correct answer approach, and is now suspected as being mentally retarded. He is so energetic and alive at home and produces such clever ideas, that his mother finds it difficult to believe that he is mentally retarded.

DIVERGENT AND CONVERGENT BEHAVIOR

Another frequent misinterpretation that some people in some mysterious manner manage to place on our work is an advocacy of nonconforming behavior with a disregard for conforming behavior. This would be a ridiculous position to take. Successful creative work must usually take place within certain limits of conformity. In groups, conformity to certain values earns for one a kind of license to be nonconforming, usually in productive ways. I think Harold Benjamin's statement on this issue of divergency and conformity reflects my position quite accurately:

"How much uniformity does this society need for safety?

"It needs only that uniformity which the achievement of its greatest goals require. It demands security of life and health for its people. It demands wide opportunities for its people in work and play, in song and prayer. It must provide each individual with maximum aids to the development of his powers to contribute in every way possible to the great goals of his people. . . .

"How much deviation does this society require for progress?

"It requires just as much deviation, just as many uniquely developed peaks of ability, just as much idiosyncrasy as the attainment of its goals will allow and need. All societies are wasteful of the capacities of their people. That society which comes closest to developing every socially useful idiosyncrasy in every one of its members, will make the greatest progress toward its goals" (Benjamin, 1956, pp. 36–37).

In other words, we need and can have both divergency and conformity.

Perhaps the fundamental reason why the creatively gifted child so frequently evokes punishment upon himself and sometimes, pity is that he is divergent—different. Even when he is different in ways which are defined as socially and morally desirable, the divergent characteristic calls forth fear. He may work, or study, too hard and learn more than he should. He may be too honest, too courageous, too altruistic, or too affectionate, as well as too adventurous, too curious, or too determined. Parents do not want their children to be considered different, or unusual, and teachers endeavor to make them conform to behavioral norms, and become socially well-adjusted.

Being different does not seem to bother very young children, but year by year they seem to become increasingly more afraid of being themselves. The awesomeness of being different is well understood by most children by the time they reach the fourth grade. Children have been told this in many ways. My realization of its impact upon children became clearest to me when we asked children to write imaginative stories about animals and people with some divergent characteristic.

Most revealing are the stories about the flying monkey who might be regarded as a symbol of the "gifted child." In the stories of children, the parents of the flying monkey are upset when they learn that their baby monkey can fly. They may send him to another part of the jungle; they do not want him and reject him. They may think that he is mentally ill and take him to a doctor. Or, the mother may have the father give the young monkey "a good talking to" and tell him that the other monkeys will think he is "crazy in the head," if he continues to fly. They tell him that others will fear him and that he will have no friends. They may teach him to hide his wings, or camouflage them so that others will not know that he can fly. Or, they may cut off his wings. He is warned of all kinds of punishment and destruction. It is always the good little monkey who gives up his flying, and other divergent behavior. Even when the monkey's flying ability is used for the good of others, such as obtaining the top bananas for the other monkeys or saving their lives by flying them out of a burning jungle, he may still be ridiculed and punished.

RESPONSIVE AND STIMULATING ENVIRONMENTS

On a number of occasions, I have said that the creative child needs a responsive environment rather than *just* a stimulating one. I did not mean to infer by this that the creative child does not also need stimulation nor that some children might not need a stimulating environment more than a responsive one. I think perhaps my greatest discomfort comes from the interpretation that some people have placed on my use of the term "responsive environment." People frequently ask, "Well, what you mean by a responsive environment is nothing but a *laissez-faire* or permissive environment." What I mean by a responsive environment is quite different from *laissez-faire* and permissiveness. What I have in mind calls for the most alert and sensitive kind of direction and guidance. It means building an atmosphere of receptive listening, relieving the fears of the overtaught and overguided, fending off devastating disparagement and criticism, stirring the sluggish and deepening the superficial, making sure that every sincere effort brings enough satisfaction to assure continued effort, heightening sensory awareness, and keeping alive the zest for learning and thinking.

TREATING BOYS AND GIRLS ALIKE OR DIFFERENTLY

On several occasions I have stated that our misplaced emphasis on sex role differences takes a heavy toll on the creativeness of both boys and girls and causes them to fall far short of their potentialities as human beings. This has been interpreted as meaning that I am advocating that boys and girls be treated alike, that I would make sissies of boys and tomboys of girls. Again, this is far from my intention. What I have been concerned about is the fact that we make taboo or place off limits certain areas of thinking and experiencing for both boys and girls. It seems to me that this reduces unnecessarily the freedom of both boys and girls.

Misplaced emphases on sex differences come into sharpest focus in studies of creative thinking, because creativity, requires both sensitivity or openness, and independence in thinking and judgment. In our society, sensitivity is a feminine virtue while independence is a masculine value. Thus, it is only a divergent personality who maintains both the sensitivity and independence of mind necessary for a high level of creative thinking. I fail to see how sensitivity can really make one less male or how independence of mind can make one less female. Yet there are important differences in the roles which the sexes must play in our society, differences which we would like to preserve.

I think the following excerpts from a letter I received recently from a parent helps us to understand the problem:

"I'm sure you realize that most parents would rather their son be a typical boy, to all outward appearances anyway, than a creative person, especially if as a creative person he would wind up being one/nth less masculine.

"Similarly most parents patiently tolerate the tomboy stages their daughters pass through, just so long, and then begin to quake if the latter don't begin to cast around for a suitable husband, before they get half through their teens. If creativity appears and looms as incompatible with the time-honored behavior of girls, 'To heck with creativity!' is the attitude of parents."

CHAOS AND DISCIPLINE

Perhaps the misinterpretation of my work which has disturbed me most is that creativity leads to lawlessness, delinquency, disorder, and chaos and that I have a disregard for discipline, organization and order. One newspaper columnist, (Weider, 1963), in ridiculing the NEA pamphlet (Torrance 1963a), wrote as follows:

"After all, why stunt a behavior pattern? Come to think of it, a little trespassing, vandalism and some thievery now and then may encourage arson, more rape and a greater frequency of murders.

"How else can a return to savagery be accomplished more quickly? Follow Torrance! No need to fear brainwashing—let's have no brains to wash."

Apparently, this columnist failed to read the following statement which I made in the very pamphlet which he attacked:

". . . It is important that creativity be energized and guided from birth. If it is stifled early, it will only become inactive, if it survives at all. It is true that vigorous creative imagination can survive early stifling and opposition; but if it learns only to act without direction, it becomes dangerous to society and perhaps to civilization."

Although Barron (1963) and others are doubtless correct when they say that highly creative people have a greater tolerance for disorder and complexity than their less creative colleagues, this does not mean that they can tolerate chaos nor that they do not also like order and organization. They can be tolerant of disorder because they have an exceptional capacity to synthesize relatively unrelated and even discordant elements into new combinations and unities. If the disorder or complexity is too great, however, it becomes stressful and even the highly creative mind is unable to function effectively. My point is that order, discipline, organization, guidance, purpose, and direction are necessary, even for creative behavior, and are not incompatible with creativity. The order, discipline, and organization, however, must be flexible enough to permit change and to allow one thing to lead to another.

CONCLUSION

In conclusion, I would like to reiterate my contention that a more humane kind of education for gifted children demands that we adopt a more complex picture of the human mind and personality and that we spend less energy in trying to oversimplify them. In their education and guidance there is a place for:

. . . *both* creative learning and learning by authority
. . . *both* intelligence tests and tests of creative thinking
. . . *both* moral courage and social adjustment

... *both* the mastery of what is known and the creation of new knowledge
... *both* original answers and correct ones
... *both* conforming and nonconforming behavior
... *both* a responsive and a stimulating environment
... *both* a respect for the common humaneness and sex differences of boys and girls
... *both* discipline and creative behavior!

REFERENCES

1. Barron, F. *Creativity and Psychological Health*. Princeton, N. J.: D. Van Nostrand Co., 1963.
2. Benjamin, H. *The Cultivation of Idiosyncracy*. Cambridge, Mass.: Harvard University Press, 1956.
3. Black Hillel. "The Scandal of Educational Testing." *Saturday Evening Post*, November 9, 1963, 72–76.
4. Drews, Elizabeth M. "A Critical Evaluation of Approaches to the Identification of Gifted Students." In. A. Traxler (Ed.) *Measurement in Today's Schools*. Washington, D. C.: American Council on Education, 1961, pp. 47–51.
5. Getzels, J. W. and P. W. Jackson. *Creativity and Intelligence*. New York: Henry Holt and Sons, 1962.
6. Sommers, W. S. "The Influence of Selected Teaching Methods on the Development of Creative Thinking." Doctoral Dissertation. University of Minnesota, 1961.
7. Torrance, E. P. *Guiding Creative Talent*. Englewood Cliffs, N. J.: Prentice-Hall, Inc., 1962.
8. ——— *What Research Says to the Teacher: Creativity*. Washington, D. C.: National Education Association, 1963. (a)
9. ——— "Essay Review: 'Creativity and Intelligence.'" *School Review*, 1963, *71*, 112–115. (b)
10. ——— *Education and the Creative Potential*. Minneapolis: University of Minnesota Press, 1963. (c)
11. Weider, Brayton. "Off the Beat." Corvallis (Oregon) *Gazette Times*, August, 1963.
12. Wilson, O. M. "Welcome to 1963 University of Minnesota Freshmen." Address delivered September 26, 1963, University of Minnesota, Minneapolis, Minn.

Annotated Bibliography

Aschner, Mary Jane and Bish, Charles E., editors. *Productive Thinking in Education*. Washington: The National Education Association, 1965.
   Produced as the valedictory effort of the National Education As-

sociation Project on Academically Talented Students, funded by the Carnegie Corporation, and Directed by Dr. Bish, the book represents the product of two conferences on Productive Thinking. The participants of the conferences in 1960 and 1961 comprised a group of first-line researchers in the area of psychology, and curriculum development. Under the leadership of J. P. Guilford, they included James Gallagher, Richard Suchman, Kenneth Anderson, Louis Fliegier, Jacob Getzels, Miriam Goldberg, O. H. Mowrer, T. E. Newland, M. C. Reynolds, Fred Strodtbeck, Calvin Taylor, Paul Torrance, Virgil Ward, Richard Alpert, David Ausubel, Frank Barron, Nancy Bayley, Ned Bryan, Albert Caron, Elizabeth Drews, Nicholas Hobbs, Esin Kaya, Donald McKinnon, Carson McQuite, Ralph Ojemann, Harry Passow, Irving Sigel, Thelma Thurstone, Walter Waetjen, Elizabeth Wilson, and the Senior editor. The papers in the book are drawn from those presented at the second conference. They are divided into four sections: (1) Intelligence and Its Development, (2) Motivation, Personality and Productive Thinking, (3) Assessment of Productive Thinking, (4) Education for Productive Thinking. Each section has an overview by the editors, three principal papers, followed by commentary by other participants, and then a section on implications for teaching by the editors.

Anderson, H. H. "Creativity and Education." *Association for Higher Education College and University Bulletin* 13: 14; May 1, 1961.

Discusses creativity in education when viewed as closed system and as open system. Creativity is seen both as process and product. The process exists only in the moment of now, the product exists only in the past. Creativity, however, is based on an awareness of the past, a quality of cell structure, a harmonious interaction and a developmental process. "To live creativity is to live truthfully."

Anderson, H. H., editor. *Creativity in Childhood and Adolescence: A Variety of Approaches*. Palo Alto, California: Science and Behavior Books, 1965.

Reports of a conference include: "A Psychometric Approach to Creativity" by J. P. Guilford; "Creativity in Gifted Students and Scientists" by B. R. Snyder, and L. W. Heims; "Creative Possibilities for a Consideration of Creativity" by F. J. Hacker; and "On the Meaning of Creativity" by the editor.

Barron, F. *Creativity and Psychological Health*. Princeton, New Jersey: D. Van Nostrand Co., 1963.

Book of 292 pages includes analyses of the predictive qualities of the Wechsler-Bellevue Intelligence Test, the MMPI, Rohrschach, and the Ethnocentrism Scale in differentiating between the improved and unimproved cases as a result of psychotherapy. Also, describes the development of the Ego Strength Scale derived from the MMPI.

The relationship between artistic creativity and religious belief, transcendental experience, and personal wellsprings of creativity are also examined in a volume which combines theory and research.

Franseth, Jane. "Freeing Capacity to be Creative." *New Insights and the Curriculum*. 1963 Yearbook. (Edited by A. Frazier.) Washington, D. C.: Association for Supervision and Curriculum Development, a department of the National Education Association, 1963.

A somewhat unimaginative review of recent work in creativity by Barron, Guilford, Taylor, Anderson, and others. Good definitions of creativity, but little on specifics of teacher behavior that free youngsters to be creative.

Gallagher, J. J. *Teaching the Gifted Child*. Boston: Allyn and Bacon, 1964.

A valuable general book with a new approach which utilizes concepts from Guilford, Bloom, and others as well as a good deal of research experience from the University of Illinois. Three excellent chapters on curriculum for the gifted: arithmetic, science, and social studies. Other chapters are on creativity, discovery and inquiry training, administration, and personnel.

Getzels, J. W., and Jackson, P. W. *Creativity and Intelligence*. New York: John Wiley and Sons, 1962. (Cf. deMille's review, *Educational and Psychological Measurement* 22: 803–08; 1962.)

Book of 300 pages and 5 chapters explores differences between highly intelligent and highly creative children in a Chicago lab school. A good chapter traces the psychoanalytic theory of creativity. Chapter 4 discusses moral excellence and high adjustment.

Getzels, J. W., and Jackson, P. W. "The Highly Intelligent and the Highly Creative Adolescent: A Summary of Some Research Findings." (pp. 161–72) in Taylor, C. W., and Barron, F., editors. *Scientific Creativity: Its Recognition and Development*. New York: John Wiley and Sons, 1963.

The first study on the differences between the highly creative and the highly intelligent. Both achieved equally well.

Ghiselin, B. "The Creative Process and Its Relation to the Identification of Creative Talent." (pp. 355–64) in Taylor, C. W., and Barron, F., editors. *Scientific Creativity: Its Recognition and Development*. New York: John Wiley and Sons, Inc., 1963a.

Freedom and power in configurative action are important in creativity.

Ghiselin, B. "Ultimate Criteria for Two Levels of Creativity." (pp. 30–43) in Taylor, C. W., and Barron, F., editors. *Scientific Creativity: Its Recognition and Development*. New York: John Wiley and Sons, 1963b.

A discussion of what kinds of acts are truly creative rather than merely resourceful.

Golann, S. E. "Psychological Study of Creativity." *Psychological Bulletin* 60: 548–65; 1963.

In this review of the psychological study of creativity there are four emphases: products, process, measurement, and personality. Three main issues concern questions of: (1) definition and criteria, (2) the process viewed temporally, and (3) necessary personal and environmental conditions. The relationship between creativity and intelligence is discussed to illustrate the need for conceptual reorganization as well as correlational data. We should now be able to utilize personality and stylistic modes as criterion variables and to study how these factors are related at different age levels to behavior that is judged to be creative. This approach holds promise for providing a functional developmental understanding of creativity. (124 references.)

Gordon, W. J. J. Synectics: *The Development of Creative Capacity*. New York: Harper and Row, Publishers, 1961.

"Synectics theory applies to the integration of diverse individuals into a problem-stating, problem-solving group. It is an operational theory for the conscious use of the pre-conscious psychological mechanisms present in man's creative activity." Case histories illustrating the use of synectics' operational mechanisms are provided, together with detailed procedures for organizing and operating synectics groups in industrial contexts. The author's interest in the nature of creative activity culminates in analyses of metaphor and play and their roles in the creative process. (15 page bibliography.)

Gowan, J. C., and Demos, G. D. *The Education and Guidance of the Ablest*. Springfield, Illinois: Charles C Thomas, 1964.

A scholarly and exhaustive review of research on the education of gifted children. Covers history, philosophy, objectives, characteristics, curriculum, guidance, administration, and research. Features of the volume include more research reference (2,000 citations), fuller discussions of objectives, including creativity, more modern treatment of intelligence including the structure of intellect approach, and more emphasis on guidance.

Graubard, S. G., editor. *Daedalus* 94:3, 527–731, Summer, 1965.

This symposium issue is devoted to "Creativity and Learning." The contributors are notable figures, who, however, have not written much previously on the subject. The approach, therefore, tends to be somewhat general. They include: J. B. Wiesner, "Education for Creativity in the Sciences"; D. Hawkins, "The Informed Vision: An Essay on Science Education"; J. Kagan, "Personality and the Learning Process" (mentioned below); L. Eiseley, "Darwin, Coleridge and the Theory of Unconscious Creation"; P. H. Abelson, "Relation of Group Activity to Creativity in Science"; J. D. Brown, "The Development of Creative Teacher-Scholars"; C. W. Wing, Jr., "Student Selection, the Educational Environment and the Cultivation of Talent"; Nevitt Sanford, "The Human Problems Institute and General Education"; and E. P. Torrance, "Scientific Views of Creativity and Factors Affecting its Growth." As can be seen from the various articles, the major orientation is toward science. The article of most value to educators is the Kagan essay on personality and motivational factors, the most relevant parts following: (1) the motive for acceptance and positive evaluation by parents, (2) the motive for differentiation, (3) the motivation to maximize similarity to a desirable model, (4) expectancy of success or failure, (5) anxiety derived from conflicts over learning, (6) preferred modes of dealing with hypotheses or information, and (7) attention and the role of novelty.

Hallman, R. J. "The Commonness of Creativity." *Educational Theory* 13: April 1963a.

Creative capacities (1) exist potentially or actually in every child; (2) are not limited to the very rare talent ascribed to genius; (3) are identifical to those which move the personality in the direction of psychological health; (4) rest on biological processes; and (5) are amenable to environmental influences. Thus, they imply that creativity can serve as a worthy aim of education.

The thesis of this paper is that unless creativity can be established as existing commonly in all children, it can never serve as a proper aim of education. "Writers in the field suggest three possible solutions to the question of range in creative abilities: (1) difference in ability is quantitive, not qualitative; (2) any difference reduces to a matter of latency, as against an overt expression; or (3) the differential tends to disappear when creativity is defined as a way of conducting one's life rather than in terms of the number and kinds of objects one may have produced."

Hallman, R. J. "The Necessary and Sufficient Conditions for Creativity." *Journal of Humanistic Psychology* 3: Spring 1963b.

Lists 5 necessary and sufficient conditions: connectedness, originality, nonrationality, self-actualization, and openness.

McPherson, J. H., and Repucci, L. C. *Creativity Review Vols. I–III.* Midland, Michigan: The Dow Chemical Co. ($3.00), 1962.

Reprint of the first 3 volumes in bound form. Much hard-to-get material, chiefly industrial, available here but without index. Generous reviews of about 100 articles include: Magoun (1940), "The Selection of Men with Creative Ability"; Hutchinson (1949), "How to Think Creatively"; Rogers (1954), "Toward a Theory of Creativity"; Hart (1950), "The Integrative Function in Creativity"; Alfrey, "The Psychology of Invention in Chemistry, Physics and Mathematics"; Rappaport (1951), *Organization and Pathology of Thought;* Ott (1955), "Stimulating Creativity in Research"; Harris *The AC Spark-Plug Test of Creative Ability;* Von Fange, (1954) "The Creative Process in Engineering"; Pye, *Program for Upgrading Research Creativity;* Von Fange (1954), "Creative Sessions in the Creative Process"; Ripley (1953), "Idea Needlers." (An excellent list—JCG.)

Vol. II: Ayres (1955), "Social Attitude Toward Invention"; Tuska (1955), "Increasing Creative Inventiveness"; Maslow (1957), "Emotional Blocks to Creativity"; Pelz, *Social Factors in the Motivation of Engineers and Scientists;* Schutz (1957), "Birds of a Feather Produce Together"; Ryerson and Planty (1960), "Teaching Leadership to Scientists"; Stein, *Stein Research Environment Survey.*

Vol. III: Heist and others (1961), "Personality and Scholarship"; Harris (1960), "The Development and Validation of a Test of Creativity in Engineering"; Bois (1957), *Explorations in Awareness;* Tangerman (1960), "Creativity: A New Appraisal"; Taylor (1960), "Thinking and Creativity"; Barber (1961), "Resistance by Scientists to Scientific Discovery"; Hurt (1961), "Personality Traits of Creative R/D Personnel"; Taylor (1961), "Research Findings on the Characteristics of Scientists."

Osborn, A. F. *The Creative Education Movement (as of 1964).* Buffalo, New York: The Creative Education Foundation (1614 Rand Bldg.), 1964.

Booklet of 48 pages describes research, basic principles, separate courses, institutes, creatively oriented courses, at what age should training begin, creative teaching, group brainstorming, creativity in business, in government, in the free world, creativity as criterion for college admission, the future of creativity.

Osborn, A. F. "Developments in Creative Education." (pp. 19–29) in Parnes, S. J., and Harding, H. F. *A Source Book for Creative Thinking.* New York: Charles Scribner's Sons, 1962.

Address to conference on problem solving by founder of Creative Education Foundation. An excellent overview of subject as of 1960. Discusses brainstorming and other applications.

Parnes, S. J. *Bibliography re Nature and Nurture of Creative Behavior.* Buffalo, New York: The Creative Education Foundation (1614 Rand Bldg.), 1964.

An unannotated bibliography of some 600 items divided into three sections: (1) books and publications; (2) articles; and (3) dissertations.

Parnes, S. J. "Education and Creativity." *Teachers College Record* 64: 331–39; 1963.

Points out that creativity can be improved by various educational experiences. More stimulation of creativity in students is seen as contributing to their better mental health as well as better cognitive functioning.

Parnes, S. J., and Harding, H. F., editors. *A Source Book for Creative Thinking*. New York: Charles Scribner's Sons, 1962.

The most valuable book of readings in Creativity—mainly industrially oriented. Contains 29 selections in 380 pages with several appendices. Readings are organized into sections, but are mainly useful for historical and heuristic significance. Good introductory continuity.

Stein, M. I., and Henze, S. J. *Creativity and the Individual: Summaries of Selected Literature in Psychology and Psychiatry*. New York: The Free Press, 1960.

For criteria of a creative person, subjects were chosen by (1) scores of intelligence tests; (2) number of citatations or lines concerning famous persons in histories or biographies; (3) judgment of professionally qualified people; (4) selection of "eminent" persons; and (5) persons in professions which require creative behavior. Factors motivating the creative are seen as: (a) pregenital drives; (b) defense mechanisms; (c) defense against defenses; (d) insanity; (e) sanity; (f) desire for immortality; (g) need for order; (h) significance of sublimation; and (i) importance of self-actualization.

Taylor, C. W., editor. *Creativity: Progress and Potential*. New York: McGraw-Hill Book Co., 1964a.

Results from three University of Utah research conferences on creativity held in 1955, 1957, and 1959 plus one follow-up conference in 1961. Three main themes: (1) Early Predictors of Creative Potential, (2) Influence of Educational Environment or Situational Factors on Creativity, and (3) Obtaining Measurable Criteria of Creativity. Many recommendations to teachers for fostering creativity, and though the book's major orientation is toward the study of scientific creativity, there is some mention of creativity in other areas.

Taylor, C. W., editor. *Widening Horizons in Creativity*. (Proceedings of 1962 Utah Conference.) New York: John Wiley and Sons, 1964b.

Contents: I. Historical (Toynbee, Thurstone); II. Creative Process Studies (Ghiselin, Mednick, Hyman, Barron, Leary); III. Education and the Development of Creativity (Torrance, Parnes, Drevdahl, Harmon, Jablonski, Brust); IV. Criterion and Prediction Studies (Taylor, Guilford, Holland, Astin, Mullins, Sprecher); V. Creativity in Special Fields, Architects (MacKinnon), Visual Arts (Beittel), Advertising (Elliott), Leadership (Fiedler), Industry (McPherson, Datta).

Taylor, C. W., and Barron, F., editors. *Scientific Creativity: Its Recognition and Development*. New York: John Wiley and Sons, 1963c.

The book is a collection of papers selected from the Proceedings of the First, Second and Third University of Utah Conferences devoted to "The Identification of Creative Scientific Talent" supported by the National Science Foundation. There are 30 contributors whose papers are separately annotated. The emphasis is directed toward creativity as reflected in the activities, personal attributes and working environments of scientists. The last chapter contains an excellent summary of research, followed by a 500-item unannotated bibliography.

Torrance, E. P. "The Creatively Gifted are Cause for Concern. *Gifted Child Quarterly* 5: 79–88; Autumn 1961.

Digest of first chapter in book *Guiding Creative Talent* discusses concerns of education over producing fully functioning creative adults.

Torrance, E. P. "Education and Creativity." (pp. 49–128) in C. W. Taylor, editor *Creativity: Progress and Potential*. New York: McGraw-Hill Book Co., 1964.

A long and well-documented essay on the educational aspects of creativity. Begins with a historical and status review, passes to the Minnesota Tests, and ends with a detailed account of childrens' problems, and suggestions for teachers in the elementary, high school and college levels.

Torrance, E. P. "Explorations in Creative Thinking in the Early School Years: A Progress Report." (pp. 173–83) in Taylor, C. W., and Barron, F., editors. *Scientific Creativity: Its Recognition and Development*. New York: John Wiley and Sons, 1963.

Status report as of 1959 discusses Getzels' and Jackson's experiment, Minnesota Tests of Creativity, and dip in creativity, attempts to increase creative thinking, peer attitudes and Torrance's replication of the high-creative, high-intelligent experiment.

Torrance, E. P. *Guiding Creative Talent*. Englewood Cliffs, New Jersey: Prentice-Hall, 1962.

An original book on teaching and guidance of gifted children. Chapters 1 and 2 are devoted to an introduction to the subject; 3 and 4 to identification of creative children; 5 is a summary of the creative abilities. Chapter 6 describes problems encountered by creative individuals; and 7 tells about problems associated with the repression of creativity. Chapters 8 and 9 discuss guidance in dealing with creative children; and 10 deals with counselor training and administration.

Yamamoto, K. "Role of Creative Thinking and Intelligence in High School Achievement." *Psychological Reports* 14: 783–89; 1964a.

A total of 272 high school students were administered a battery of tests of creative thinking. Lorge-Thorndike Intelligence Test and Iowa Tests of Educational Development. Three groups of "gifted" students were identified in each grade: (1) High Intelligence Group—a group in the upper 20% on IQ but *not* in the upper 20% on creativity; (2)

High Creativity Group—a group in the upper 20% on the test of creativity but *not* in the upper 20% on IQ; and (3) High Intelligence-Creativity Group—a group high on *both* IQ and creativity. Groups 1 and 2 = 26, group 3 = 28. If IQ alone had been used as the basis for identifying "giftedness," about 48% of those in the upper 20% on creativity would have been excluded. When rs between IQ and creativity were computed for each grade, it was found that, except in the 10th grade, coefficients were less than 0.20 and statistically nonsignificant. In the 10th grade, $r = 0.56$ and statistically significant. For all 272 subjects, an r of 0.30 was significant (p = 0.01); rs between IQ and creativity in the 3 "gifted" groups were statistically nonsignificant. There was no difference among these 3 groups on the various achievement measures. No sex difference was found. The findings supported the results of previous studies of Getzels and Jackson (1962) and Torrance (1959).

Yamamoto, K. "Creative Thinking: Some Thoughts and Reflections." *Exceptional Children* 30: 403–10; May 1964b.

Careful review of literature with about 30 citations represents status survey of art and discusses unexplored frontiers.

Yamamoto, K. "Creativity—A Blind Man's Report on the Elephant." *Journal of Counseling Psychology* 12: 428–34, 1965.

Thorough review of the literature points out that the present confused abundance in the study of creativity is the result (1) of different points of departure in definition, (2) differences in assumptions, and (3) differences in research strategies. Holistic and elementaristic approaches are examined.

CHAPTER TWO

Theory and Policy

Some Newer Theoretical Implications
for Creative Learning

John Curtis Gowan

IMPLICATIONS FOR MORE CREATIVE LEARNING IN THE CLASSROOM AS A result of the theoretical models of a number of writers have rapidly accumulated. It seems to be appropriate to bring together a number of these suggestions which have to do with a change in classroom climate and procedures in a direction of more "openness" and more concern over students' mental health. To be sure, able teachers have intuitively been using these procedures for a long time. They were like the person who could find the cat in the dark room. But now that the light is on so that we may all see where the cat is, the rationale for these procedures is understandable. In the space at hand there is room to discuss implications of the contributions of four writers on creativity and mental health: Guilford, Torrance, Barron, and Hollister.

Guilford's Structure of Intellect Model is particularly amenable to interpretations which suggest implications for creative learning. His slab of factor abilities, labeled "divergent production" reflect a whole constellation of factors which are capable of stimulation through classroom experiences. Such verbal abilities in this slab as "ideational fluency" (writing names of things fitting broad classes), "spontaneous flexibility" (listing uncommon uses for a brick), "associational fluency" (writing synonyms for words), "expressional fluency" (constructing a variety of four word sentences using four given initial letters) and "originality" (writing clever titles for a short story) are examples.

REPRINTED by permission of the Author and *Gifted Child Quarterly*, 9:7-8, Spring, 1965.

Secondly, there appears to be a hierarchy of cognitive abilities in their capacity to withstand stress and anxiety. This is indeed the theory of "scatter" on the WISC and other tests. Generally speaking, verbal fluency seems to withstand stress, alcohol, drugs and senility better than numerical or spatial ability, for example. The last ability to be lost by the senile, the schizophrenic, or the drunk is his ability to babble words which have long since lost their meaning. This hierarchy seems related both to the operations and products classification of the Structure of Intellect, with the simpler operations (such as cognition of units) much more stable than the complex categories (such as evaluation of implications). There is, of course, a tendency for teachers to teach the simpler skills to the detriment of the more complex. Since the divergent thinking slab is well up on the scale, it is easy to see that mediocre teaching to somewhat anxious children tends to neglect or to wash out the stimulation of creative aspects of the curriculum.

A third implication of Guilford's work has to do with the knotty problem of underachievement which educators have labored on for a long time without much success. The formulations of Guilford and the experimentation of others have rather clearly shown that creativity is necessary even for conventional achievement. If A and B are equal both in motivation and conventional intelligence, but if B is more creative than A and hence higher in achievement, it will appear that A is an underachiever with respect to B. What counselors have attempted to treat as a deficiency in motivation, may actually be a deficiency in creativity.

While Torrance has made many contributions to the solution of increasing children's creativity, his five suggestions to teachers make an excellent focus for his ideas. First, he says (1961), "Teachers should be respectful of unusual questions." Nothing is more rewarding to a child than to have his questions treated with respect. But for many teachers, this valuing involves placing positive regard on something new or different. Often the generally negative values that teachers place on something that is not "tried and true" prevent them from proper appreciation of children's questions. And the child whose query is rejected feels rejected personally, and soon learns not to ask any others.

Secondly, "Teachers can themselves respect imaginative or unusual ideas." Creative children will often see ideas that the teacher may miss. Besides, teachers cannot stimulate creativity if they are not respectful toward it in the first place. It requires concentration and thoughtfulness to attend carefully enough to an individual child to see the creative potential of the idea he may be expressing rather sketchily.

Thirdly, "Teachers should show children that their ideas have value." Many teachers do not believe that children are capable of valuable ideas, and many children have good ideas and do not pursue them because they do not know how good they are. Whereas some adults (like Columbus) are able to persist with derided and devalued ideas until they can prove them useful, most children need rather immediate reassurance or reinforcement if they are to proceed. The creative teacher finds good things in children to call attention to.

Fourth, "Teachers should provide for periods of non-evaluated practice." Some teachers wish to evaluate everything a child does, not realizing that even the best coaches only evaluate football players during a scrimmage or a game, not every day. We all need time to make mistakes in, time to try out and find out what happens when we do something wrong. There is enough intrinsic motivation in this situation so that teachers should not add penalties to it, otherwise the child may not try at all.

Fifth, says Torrance: "Teachers should tie in evaluation with cause and consequence." Instead of saying, "This is good" and "That is bad" teachers should point out the consequences that this and that lead to, and let children evaluate the goodness or badness of the various results. In this way the teacher can develop the causal thinking which lies at the very foundation of evaluative behavior. We can either condition children to evaluate or we can help them relate their own evaluation to causal thinking. If we want childrens' creativity to be tied to reality, we will teach them to develop causal thinking in their efforts at evaluation.

Some of the hypotheses raised by Barron (1963) about original people have immediate and fruitful educational implications. The first of these statements is that original persons prefer complexity and some degree of apparent imbalance in phenomena. Such a characteristic suggests that teachers should not attempt to structure too highly the experience of these children.

A second hypothesis states that original persons are more independent in their judgments. Evidently they have made more evaluations on their own and have more confidence in them. The development of the child's personal ability to evaluate is one which all teachers should encourage, but which, in fact, many teachers are threatened by.

A third hypothesis states that original persons are more self-assertive and dominant. Their organization of their environment is more complete. This organization and projected leadership needs wise help, not smothering by the teachers. Unfortunately many teachers find such a child stubborn and "bossy," and may condemn him instead of trying to help him to a more socially constructive expression of his characteristics.

A fourth hypothesis is that original persons reject suppression as a mechanism for impulse control. This expression of underlying feeling often gets the creative child into trouble with the teacher who fails to discriminate his constructive non-conformity from the non-constructive non-conformity of the true problem case.

A fifth hypothesis concerns the characteristics of energy, femininity of interests, and general effectiveness of performance found in many original people. Each of these traits involve facilitating adaptations by teachers in providing activities to consume the child's unbounded energy, in emphasizing feminine (verbal) interests, and in rewarding effectively in a wide range of performance, not just in the narrow nexus of grade-getting.

Hollister (1961) of the National Institute of Mental Health is another researcher who has suggested that learning needs to go beyond cognitive memory aspects into more complex areas of analysis, synthesis and evaluation because of the ego-strength thus stimulated. Learnings, particularly those involving cause-effect relationships are far more valuable to the child than those involving mere conditioning, since they help orient him to the world of reality.

Differentiation is a part of learning also promoting the child's mental health and creativity. Fostering discrimination in the growing child between self and others, between reality and fantasy, symbol and reality, subjective and objective, emotions and body-feelings, ideal self and real self, means and ends, concrete and symbolic all help a child to become more mentally healthy and therefore creative. The relationship between mental health and education is not a cause-effect one, but an interactional situation in which each stimulates the other.

Finally, to continue in paraphrase of Hollister, integration of learnings is also desirable for creative performance. Integration allows for a new synthesis of constructs, better and more complete meshing of thoughts, feelings, and time sequences, better ability to cope with and handle process, more complicated mental strategies, and a higher level of adaptation. The end result of the integrative process is to make students more creative, since they are able to bridge wider gaps and to make more complex closures.

Thus, continuing research into characteristics of creative people provides educators with clues to facilitate the development of such persons or at least to avoid smothering their development. We have become aware that these more exotic factors of intellect are much more susceptible to environmental stimulation or deprivation than the more cognitive-memory aspects of intelligence found in most "intelligence tests." We may not want all students to become Thoreaus, but we would do well to encourage the budding Thoreaus in our midst. Indeed, the encouragement and development of the highests reaches of talent in a democracy is the only real alternative in the long run to war, revolution and totalitarianism. The creative students in our school have a tremendous role to play in the history of the future; let us become wiser in giving them the preparation they need in the schools of the present.

REFERENCES

Barron, F. *Creativity and Psychological Health*. Princeton, N. J.: D. Van Nostrand Co. Inc., 1963.

Guilford, J. P. "Creativity: Its Measurement and Development." (pp. 151–68) in Parnes, S. J. and Harding, H. F. *A Source Book for Creative Thinking*. New York: Charles Scribners Sons, 1962.

Hollister, W. G. "Mental Health Considerations in Teaching" (speech at Los Angeles conference, California Association of School Psychologists and Psychometrists), 1961.

Torrance, E. P. "Give the Devil His Dues . . ." *Gifted Child Quarterly*. 5:115–8, Winter, 1961.

Potentiality for Creativity

J. P. Guilford

MEMBERS OF THIS ASSOCIATION ARE NATURALLY AND APPROPRIATELY concerned about the identification of gifted children. If you were involved in public education in my home state of California, the task would be a very simple one. By state law, you would simply select as gifted those children with Stanford-Binet IQs of 130 and above.

In Southern California, where we have a relatively high density of recognized creative people—in architecture, painting, writing, musical composition, and drama, also in the sciences and the technologies— some of us, you may be sure, are not very happy about this situation.

REPRINTED by permission of the Author and *Gifted Child Quarterly*, 6:87–90, 1962.

This is particularly true since it has been shown by Getzels and Jackson (1961) and by Torrance (1959), and others, that many potentially creative children are not as high in IQ as 130.

To this kind of information can be added some results from the Aptitudes Project at the University of Southern California, involving four samples of ninth-grade students of more than 200 each. Letting vocabulary-test scores and reading-comprehension-test scores represent measures of verbal intelligence, we correlated seven such scores with 14 different verbal divergent-production-test scores. The correlations ranged from −.20 to +.52, with a mean of +.18. From scattered information we can derive the hypothesis that the relationship between verbal IQ and creative-test scores is a non-linear one; that below an IQ of 120 in the population the correlation is higher and above an IQ of 120 it is lower. However this may be, selection on the basis of IQ alone will definitely miss many potentially gifted children. If we want to include all the potentially creative children in gifted groups, some very different selection procedures are needed.

SELECTION FOR CREATIVITY

There is sufficient experience with some of the tests of creative abilities to have some confidence in them for discriminating between those with higher and lower creative potential, in certain areas of creativity (Guilford, Merrifield, and Cox, 1961). The research of Getzels and Jackson and of Torrance indicates that high-scoring children in such tests are known for their superior imaginative and productive ways of thinking and writing. The tests used by these investigators, however, are limited in various ways.

In the research on creativity in the Aptitudes Project at USC, we have reached a general conclusion that the abilities in the structure of intellect that seem to have promise as direct contributors to successful creative thinking belong in two major categories. One is the category of divergent production, which includes abilities to generate varieties of information from given information; in other words, multiple responses, all of which are more or less appropriate, in response to a stimulus. In common terminology, the abilities represented are three different kinds of fluency, two kinds of flexibility, and an elaboration ability. The other category is composed of abilities dealing with transformations, that is, redefinitions, revisions, or other kinds of changes of information. This category represents a third kind of flexibility, a freedom from fixedness or from *Gestaltbindung*.

Let us see what all this implies, in comparison with the battery used by Getzels and Jackson for the selection of their highly creative group. In the structure-of-intellect model, there are 24 expected divergent-production abilities, of which 16 are now supported by factor-analytic information. There are 20 expected transformation abilities, of which eight are known. Since four factors are in common to the two categories, where they intersect in the model, the total expected is 40, and the number known is 22. How many of these abilities are represented in the Getzels and Jackson battery of five tests?

As nearly as one can tell from inspection of the tests, which the authors fortunately present in full in their recent book, I should say that four of the divergent-production abilities are represented and three of the transformation abilities, one being in common to the two operation categories. Four of the five tests involve verbal or semantic information or content and one involves figural content.

The aspect of creativity that dominates the battery, therefore, deals with verbal information. We should expect the composite score to predict best creative performances in writing, science, and planning; in other words, in school subjects and vocations in which verbal meanings are the dominant content of thinking. The score should not predict nearly so well, creative performance in the arts (except for writing), in invention of machines, in mathematics, or in interpersonal activity. Artists and inventors deal more with concrete information, such as lines, shapes, colors, and sounds. In mathematics, especially beyond arithmetic, creative thinking involves symbols and their interrelationships. Interpersonal activity is involved in dealing with the behavior of people. We should find it necessary to go beyond semantic tests in predicting success in creative interaction with others. Some of the vocations for which this kind of creativity should be especially important are teaching, psychotherapy, selling, police work, and politics.

IQ tests commonly emphasize abilities in the operation categories of cognition (which is defined in the structure of intellect in a narrower sense than is usual), memory, and convergent production, ignoring divergent production and slighting evaluation abilities, the latter being the basic aspects of critical thinking. As to categories of information, semantic content is very much emphasized, naturally, because verbal concepts are the "coin of the realm" in education. Words are the chief medium of teaching and examining. As to the kinds of *product* of information in the structure of intellect—units, classes, relations, systems, transformations, and implications—IQ tests devote most attention to units, as in vocabulary tests; to relations, as in analogies tests; and to systems, as in arithmetic-reasoning tests. Little attention is given to classes and none to transformations and implications. Transformation abilities were discussed in connection with creative abilities, implication abilities have to do with the everyday operations of prediction, foresight, and deduction, certainly very useful human qualities.

Conferences such as this one imply a recognition of the limitations of IQ tests in selecting gifted children, and a positive recognition of the importance of considering creative abilities in the same connection. But it should not be supposed that by adding a few tests of creative qualities to the few tests entering into IQ scales we have by any means exhausted the whole range of intellectual qualities. I am willing to grant that probably many of the other intellectual abilities may not be very significant in connection with ordinary academic performance, as curriculum and educational procedures are now constituted. It may well be questioned, however, whether the educational regime should not be giving attention to development of some of the intellectual qualities that it is now neglecting and whether those qualities should be involved in teaching and examining the student in some of the present courses of study.

In other words, I am urging that when we go beyond the IQ we go all the way and consider the relevance of all intellectual abilities, in selecting gifted children and in educational processes in general. I welcome the obvious enthusiasm of many educators for creativity. Creativity has become one of the "good" words, as "dynamic" and "reinforcement" have been to many psychologists in recent years. It is good to have enthusiasms, but it is also important to have enthusiasms wisely directed and to see that they are functional in bringing about desirable changes.

To me, the next steps in capitalizing upon the new knowledge concerning creativity and concerning intelligence in general is to re-examine educational objectives, both general and specific, in the light of the new knowledge. The new concepts appear to have natural applications to educational aims and procedures. It should be recognized, of course, that the operational steps of wisely applying those concepts imply a tremendous amount of developmental research. We need to know the relation of all possibly relevant primary abilities, as L. L. Thurstone called them, to all kinds of courses of instruction and to all teaching and learning methods. We need to know whether, as have suggested a number of times before, we may regard the basic abilities as being somewhat generalized skills that can be improved with the right kinds of practice. If we do so, what kinds of practice are needed?

As an example of one kind of developmental research, in the Aptitudes Project we have under way a study of the extent to which each of quite a number of intellectual factors is related to achievement in beginning algebra and in general mathematics at the ninth-grade level. In this study, we have emphasized tests of abilities to deal with symbolic information as well as a smaller number in the semantic area of information. We have started the early stages of a parallel study of basic aptitudes related to achievement in plane geometry at the tenth-grade level. In this connection, figural abilities will be emphasized, also convergent-production abilities and evaluative abilities, in view of the strong logical character of thinking in geometry.

CURRENT SELECTION PROCEDURES

My discussion has wandered a bit from the question of how to select creatively gifted children, but this was intentional in order to emphasize the much broader problem. Although present indications favor divergent-production, and transformation abilities, as the ones most directly involved in creative potential, it can well be said that almost any intellectual ability outside those categories may at some time be a heavy contributor to success in creative production. To be a good, imaginative writer, one must also have a vocabulary of substantial size, a condition that is strongly related to the verbal IQ. To be a good self critic, one must have good evaluative abilities. Viewed in this light, potential for creative production extends to almost all corners of the structure-of-intellect model. Potential for creative types of thinking, depends upon a more limited collection of abilities, but a by-no-means small number of basic abilities. ,

Although about 60 primary intellectual abilities have now been demonstrated, the number of these for which there are available tests is much smaller. More such tests will be forthcoming from our Project, but only as there is confidence in the test forms and in the basic knowledge underlying them.

In the meantime, there is much that teachers and others can do in sizing up children while "waiting for the doctor to come." Many children show unmistakable signs of creative potential in their everyday behavior. One child will make a collection of stones and will classify them for display in some novel way. The science fairs, that appear to be growing in popularity in some places, should be good sources of information, provided the work is the child's own contribution. The children's products, of course, must be interpreted and evaluated as to degree of creativity indicated. When allowed some freedom in art classes (and sometimes even when not), some children show potential for creative performance in that area. From what I have said about the differentiation of abilities as between areas of information, it would be risky to conclude that because a child shows signs of creativity in art he should also be creative in mathematics or in science, or vice versa.

Some of the qualities attributed to the more creative children as reported by Getzels and Jackson and by Torrance could be used as "symptoms," but I should say with some caution. A good number of them in combination should be confirming. The symptoms would more readily indicate the very highly creative child, but might miss others of less potential.

OVERACHIEVERS MAY BE CREATIVE

Some of the so-called overachievers may be in the creative category. When they achieve beyond the level predicted by the IQ, it may be that they are strong in other, non-IQ abilities, but these other abilities need not be in the divergent-production or transformation categories. Alas, some creative youngsters may also be *underachievers*, for lack of recognition and encouragement.

It is reported that the more creative children appreciate humor especially and have some facility in producing humor. As far as we know now, this may be true only of semantic types of creative abilities. A humorless child might still have creative potential in art or mathematics.

Evidently, the creative child is less bound by what we agree to as reality; he is ready to reinterpret it and to change it to suit his purposes. In this sense, he is closer to the brink of insanity than most other children, but not necessarily in any great danger of going over the brink. He does things that appear odd in the context of the behavior of other children. He takes liberties with what he observes and knows. He has a playful attitude toward his experiences. His thinking goes off in unusual directions. He is sometimes referred to as a rebel, but I am inclined to think that this does not apply to all creative children; more likely it applies to those who have felt frustrations because their creativity is not appreciated.

Many more signs could be added but there is not time to mention them; they may be found in the growing literature from continuing research such as that of Torrance. With you, I hope that it will not be too long before good tests have been produced for the various intellectual abilities, ready for experimental use in the educational context.

Let us hope that the enthusiasm now generated in the name of creativity will last and that it can be channeled toward the necessary steps that are needed to achieve a full exploitation of our most precious resource—our human intellect.

REFERENCES

Getzels, J. W. and Jackson, P. W. *Creativity and the Individual.* New York: John Wiley and Sons, 1961.

Guilford, J. P., Merrifield, P. R., and Cox, Anna B. Creative thinking in children at the junior high school levels. *Rep. psychol.* Lab., No. 26. Los Angeles: Univ. Southern California, 1961.

Torrance, E. P., Explorations in creative thinking in the early school years: a progress report. In C. W. Taylor, *The third (1959) University of Utah Research Conference on the identification of creative scientific talent.* Salt Lake City: Univ. of Utah Press, 1959.

Creative Thinking and Conceptual Growth

J. Richard Suchman

THE TERMS "CREATIVE THINKING" AND "CONCEPTUAL GROWTH" MAY have different meanings for different people, so I shall begin my defining them in the sense that they will be used in this paper.

Creative thinking has two defining characteristics. First, it is autonomous; that is, it is neither random nor controlled by some fixed scheme or external agent, but is wholly self-directed. Secondly, it is directed toward the production of a new form—new in the sense that the thinker was not aware of the form before he began the particular line of thought.

Conceptual growth is the expansion, elaboration, or other modification of a conceptual framework to provide meaning for a greater sector of experience. Through conceptual growth, more units of experience become meaningful, and more meaning is found in each unit. It is a step toward a more unified system of ideas at a higher level of abstraction, or toward a broader system of ideas at the same level.

REPRINTED by permission of the Author and *Gifted Child Quarterly,* 6:95-9, Autumn, 1962.

CREATIVE THINKING AND EDUCATION

The question to be considered in this paper is just what role creative thinking has, or can have, in the process of conceptual growth. This question is particularly germane today because educators and psychologists are more concerned than ever with the development of thinking abilities, and because a growing number of experimental curriculum programs are based to some extent on a "discovery method" of teaching. In an age when the knowledge of mankind far exceeds the ability of the individual to keep track of it, much less to retain it, we are beginning to place a new premium on the ability to process information and abstract ideas from it, rather than simply to store it up.

Since Dewey's time we have paid lip service to the teaching of thinking as an educational objective, but in today's classrooms, pupils are still rewarded for how much they retain. The minds of pupils are still treated like little black boxes with informational inputs fed in at one end by the teacher and outputs tested at the other end. And the measure of quality is how well the outputs correspond to the inputs. How many teachers teach with the expectation that they can get more out of a box than they put in? Where I went to school it was automatically assumed that nobody could ever get 100 on a test.

Where creative thinking is used to further conceptual development we have what is usually called the discovery method. The popular idea of this method is that if you let a person have something of a free hand in obtaining and processing data, he will see new relationships, abstract concepts, generalize, and formulate principles, by himself without having these structured for him by somebody else. Hardly any person who has tried to get students to think their way inductively from data to concept would ever claim that all learning can or should take place in this manner, or that it is always the most efficient method when it can be used. But creative thinking has been employed in a wide range of teaching situations with marked success and there are instances where discovery is the only means by which a person can obtain a particular concept.

THE PROCESS OF CONCEPTUAL GROWTH

Bruner's (1958) studies of concept attainment have shown us much about the range of cognitive strategies that people use in solving problems where the solution requires the attainment of a concept. He has shown us that individuals use different strategies depending upon such conditions as the time limitations, the importance of speed, the importance of not making errors, etc. One strategy relies heavily on memory, another on luck, and still another on having lots of time. People are constantly adjusting their strategies of data intake even in the middle of a problem. This is a form of creative thinking, an adaptive flexibility that enables the learner to adjust his patterns of data intake and processing to correspond to his changing cognitive needs.

Inhelder and Piaget (1958) have identified developmental trends in the way that children pursue the casuality of physical events through the manipulation of apparatus. These investigators have also been concerned, like Bruner, with the strategies of concept attainment and particularly the kinds of changes that take place in these strategies as children grow older. They introduce the term operation which stands for a unit of action or thought, a tentative move that is reversible. An operation can be done and undone. They found that about the time the child enters elementary school he begins what is called operational thinking. He stands back from his environment and manipulates it experimentally, performing one operation after another on one part of the environment at a time. He observes the effects of these operations by comparing and relating them to each other. From these comparisons he begins to construct groupings and correspondences which in turn lead to conceptual models of causality. Creative thinking plays a central role in operational thinking as Inhelder and Piaget describe it.

Inhelder and Piaget also introduce two other concepts that help in the analysis of the process of conceptual growth. Assimilation refers to fitting a set of patterned stimuli into one's existing conceptual system. Sometimes percepts must be analyzed or distorted before they can be assimilated. If they cannot be assimilated they remain discrepant and as such are disturbing. They produce tensions. The only recourse one has is to adjust the conceptual system until it accommodates to the discrepant event. In other words, one creates a new conceptual category so that the event can be assimilated. It is only through successive accommodations that conceptual growth can occur. It is hard to imagine accommodation not involving some degree of creative thinking.

It is important to note that both Bruner and Piaget allowed their subjects to operate autonomously in an environment where one could perform operations and obtain a feedback of data immediately. They were able to see that under such conditions individuals over a wide range of ages can expand conceptual structures through self-directed operations.

CREATIVE THINKING IN THE
RESPONSIVE ENVIRONMENT

Two experimental teaching techniques that are currently being developed and tested make extensive use of creative thinking. One is a method devised by O. K. Moore at Yale for teaching pre-school children to read; the other is our Inquiry Training program at Illinois. Moore (1960) allows his subjects to manipulate freely the keys of an electric typewriter. The teacher says the name of each letter the child strikes and of course the child sees each letter as it is imprinted on the paper. No goals are set, no instructions given. Every time a child performs an operation by hitting a letter or a group of letters, he gets a response. When he hits groups of letters that are words, he is given the sound of the whole word. Through this method (which I have drastically oversimplified) three- and four-year-olds learn to read and type incredibly well and very quickly.

The key to Moore's approach is the responsive environment. He gives the learner freedom to operate in his own way, at his own pace, without any extrinsic rewards and pressures. The environment is highly responsive to each action the child performs. Moore opens the door to creative thinking by maximizing the child's autonomy and the feedback data he gets from his operations.

The Inquiry Training method (Suchman, 1961) is a variation on this same idea. Our subjects have mostly been sixth graders and they work in groups. They are shown short motion pictures of physics demonstrations which are designed to puzzle them. To these children the demonstrations are discrepant events. The children are asked to find an explanation of the episode by gathering information through question-asking. They are not permitted to ask for explanations, only data. They must then use the data to piece together their own explanations.

The key elements of this approach are once again the responsive environment and the freedom given the children to operate within it. They may seek assimilation of the problem episode in any way they wish. The data they obtain, the sequence in which they obtain them, and the hypotheses they formulate and test are all selected and used by the children themselves.

As yet we do not have clear evidence regarding the effects of the inquiry method on conceptual growth. There are many other variables that effect learning which we have had difficulty controlling. Furthermore, the exposure to the inquiry method has been brief—one hour a week for twenty-five weeks. Our subjects have been able to learn at least as much through inquiry as through traditional didactic methods.

The effects on motivation were much more marked. The children became quite actively involved in their investigations and maintained a high level of interest and excitement throughout the 25-week period of training. They also became more fluent in their production of questions and more precise and analytical in their probing. There was much less willingness to accept the perceptual whole as valid data. They tended instead to analyze the events and to test the relvance of each variable they could identify. This ability to analyze frees the child from the grip of his Gestalts and permits him to identify variables which can then be isolated and manipulated experimentally. In this manner relationships between variables can be discovered. A conceptual model of casuality can then be constructed and used for explaining, or in Piaget's terms, assimilating the original discrepant event.

CREATIVE THINKING IN A
PROGRAMMED ENVIRONMENT

Creative thinking can also be used in a selective way as part of an otherwise structured teaching program to help the student over certain crucial and difficult conceptual hurdles. The method used by the UICSM Project at Illinois—also known as the Beberman Mathematics Project—is an example of this (Beberman, 1958). They take the position that there is little point in talking about, let us say, the commutative principle unless the pupils have an almost intuitive understanding of just what the principle is. Too often when this is taught through a verbal didactic method the pupils acquire merely a superficial, mechanistic understanding. They know what they have to do to get the answer but they haven't the faintest notion of why. Beberman's method literally engineers the students into discovering the principle themselves.

His classes are given a series of mathematical operations to perform which can be done with simple arithmetic. The problems are arranged in order of increasing difficulty in that the numbers get larger and more difficult to handle arithmetically. However, it is possible to discover a short-cut that simplifies the calculations. By discovering this short-cut the pupil has discovered the commutative principle.

This is quite a different use of creative thinking than the loosely structured responsive environment technique. The learning situation is deliberately contrived to pressure the learner into being creative.

The cognitive strain in each successive problem is greater than in the previous one and gradually builds up to intolerable levels. The necessity to reduce this strain becomes the mother of the invention of short-cuts.

In Bruner's terms, Beberman rigs the payoff matrix in such a way that the children become willing to take risks in trying out new ideas in place of the safer but more laborious method.

The commutative principle doesn't just drop into the child's lap the minute he starts to look for another approach. He works for it. He gets ideas and tries them out. He examines what he has done in previous problems. He is more likely to discover a principle by comparing problems and their solutions than by focusing on only one. Finally, somewhere along the line he notices something he hadn't noticed before and this will lead him to see the principle. But he is more likely to make such a discovery if he invents, experiments and makes comparisons.

SUMMARY

Teaching methods which permit the learner to operate autonomously in the search for new understandings utilize creative thinking to promote concept development. It has been widely observed and reported that children enjoy learning when they can think creatively. Discovery builds the self-esteem of the discoverer, who also develops a sense of autonomy and intellectual potency. According to Hunt (1961) there is intense excitement and pleasure in data processing itself.

But how does creative thinking serve the cognitive processes of learning? Conceptual growth—unless it is mediated entirely through verbal structuring—growth out of transactional episodes between the learner and his environment. The learner gathers data which he tries to assimilate by means of his existing concepts. Where the data cannot be assimilated, he either breaks them down into more basic units that can be assimilated, or he modifies his conceptual structure to accomodate the data. In this way concepts are modified and expanded to make room for discrepant events.

In any act of inquiry the quest for data takes the form of operational sequences. The ordering of these sequences according to a plan or system constitutes a strategy. Bruner found strategy to be a significant variable in his concept attainment experiments. The learner shifts and adjusts these strategies to maximize one or another objective in accordance to the kinds of results that offer the most reward. But the individual learner brings to any problem a unique constellation of abilities and concepts as well as a characteristic approach to concept attainment.

Thus his strategies must suit not only the problem and the kinds of solutions being rewarded, but they must also be attuned to his own individual cognitive and motivational characteristics. He must use the right strategy for him at any given instant. To learn how to do this well he must have freedom to adjust strategies of data collection and processing. Since he cannot be taught a single standard strategy that will work well under all circumstances, he must have a chance to work out his own ideas and discover for himself what works best in each situation. In short, he must have many opportunities to use creative thinking in the process of conceptual growth.

One way to promote the use of creative thinking as an aid to conceptual growth is to make the teacher's role less directive and more responsive, to have the learner focus on a problem, and allow him to gather data freely with the help but not the direction of the teacher. Another way is to present children with problems of data processing that impose so much cognitive strain that the learner tries to invent systems of handling the data more efficiently. If these systems have general validity they must represent some lawful properties of the environment. The discovery of such properties is the fundamental purpose of inquiry.

There are no doubt many other possibilities for facilitating conceptual growth by capitalizing on the creative thinking of the learner. Many of these have been and will continue to be invented by teachers who experiment with teaching techniques. Teachers who do this discover very rapidly what is effective and what is not . . . because there is no environment quite as responsive as a room full of children.

REFERENCES

Beberman, M. *An Emerging Program of Secondary School Mathematics*. Cambridge: Harvard Univ. Press, 1958.

Bruner, J. S., Goodnow, Jacqueline and Austin, George A. *A Study of Thinking*. New York: John Wiley and Sons, 1956.

Hunt, J. McV. *Motivation Inherent in Information Processing and Action*. University of Illinois, Urbana. (Mimeo) 1961.

Inhelder, Barbel and Piaget, Jean. *The Growth of Logical Thinking from Childhood to Adolescence*. New York: Basic Books, 1958.

Moore, O. K. "Orthographic Symbols and the Preschool Child." Proceedings of the Third Minnesota Conference on Gifted Children. Minneapolis, 1960, pp. 91–101.

Suchman, J. Richard. "Inquiry Training: Building Skills for Autonomous Discovery." *Merrill-Palmer Quarterly*, Vol. 7, pp. 147–169. (July 1961).

Must Creative Development
be Left to Chance?

E. Paul Torrance

ONLY A FEW YEARS AGO, IT WAS COMMONLY THOUGHT THAT CREATIVE thinking, the production of new ideas, inventions, and the like had to be left to chance. Indeed many people still think so! Yet, I do not see how any well-informed person can still hold this view. The amazing record of inventions, scientific discoveries, and other creative achievements amassed through creative problem-solving methods (Osborn, 1957), synectics (Gordon, 1961), and bionics (Small, 1962) should convince even the most stubborn skeptics. Experiments involving these deliberate methods of improving creativity have also been rather convincing (Maltzman, 1960; Parnes, 1960; Torrance, 1961). In my own classes and seminars, I have consistently found that these deliberate methods can be taught from the primary grades through the graduate school with the effect that students improve their ability to develop original and useful solutions to problems. In my opinion, the evidence is strong that creativity does not have to be left to chance!

In a similar vein, I have maintained that the development of the creative thinking abilities does not have to be left to chance. Here I find myself in a distinct minority. Indeed, some educators maintain that it would be extremely dangerous to educate children to be creative while they are still children. They maintain that the emphasis must be on conformity, discipline, and fundamentals like the three R's. One educator sought to clinch his argument by saying, "A child has to know the three R's in order to do anything! Isn't it enough that the schools teach him to read, write and figure? Let him dash off on his own errands later; let him specialize in college!" Such a statement, of course, reflects a gross misunderstanding of the nature of creative thinking. The development of the creative thinking abilities is at the very heart of the achievement of even the most fundamental educational objectives, even the acquisition of the three R's. It is certainly not a matter of specialization.

REPRINTED by permission of the Author and *Gifted Child Quarterly*, 6:41–4, Summer, 1962.

For years, students of creative development have observed that five-year olds lose much of their curiosity and excitement about learning, that nine-year olds become greatly concerned about conformity to peer pressures and give up many of their creative activities, that the beginning junior highs show a new kind of concern for conformity to behavioral norms with the consequences that their thinking becomes more obvious, commonplace and safe. In 1930, Andrews published data to document the drop at about age five. Even earlier, the drops at about ages nine and thirteen had been documented and have been further supported in the Minnesota Studies of Creative Thinking (1962).

Those who have commented on the drops in creative thinking ability and creative behavior in general have almost always assumed that these were purely development phenomena. For example, Wilt (1959) observed that creativity may all but take a holiday at about age nine or ten and returns only for a few years after the crisis has passed. She concludes that about all that can be done is to keep open the gates for its return. Rarely, however, has anyone taken a contrary stand. One of these rare individuals, Susan Nichols Pulsifer (1960), has taken such a stand concerning the abandonment of creativity at about age five. She maintains that it is not a natural developmental change but is due to the sharp man-made change which confronts the five-year old and impells him by its rules and regulations.

If our research at the University of Minnesota has contributed anything to thinking about this problem, it has come from my unwillingness to accept the assumption that the severe drops in measured creative thinking ability are purely developmental phenomena which must be accepted as unchangeable. As we entered into our longitudinal studies, it seemed obvious to me that many children needlessly sacrificed their creativity, especially in the fourth grade, and that many of them did not recover it as they continued through school. It also seemed to me that many of our problems of school drop outs, delinquency, and mental illness have their roots in the same forces that cause these drops.

It will certainly take a great deal more research than we now have before very many people will be convinced about this matter. Personally, I consider the accumulated evidence rather convincing. One of the first positive bits of evidence came from my experience in studying the creative development of two fourth-grade classes taught by teachers who are highly successful in establishing creative relationships with their pupils and who give them many opportunities to acquire information and skills in creative ways. There was no fourth-grade slump in these classes, either in measured creative thinking abilities or in participation in creative activities.

A somewhat more convincing line of evidence has come from our studies of the development of the creative thinking abilities in different cultures. As we have obtained results from the administration of our tests of creative thinking in diverse cultures, we have found that the developmental curve takes on a different shape in each culture and that the characteristics of the developmental curve can be explained in terms of the way the culture treats curiosity and creative needs.

For purposes of illustration, let us examine the developmental curves for non-verbal originality in the United States, Western Samoa, Australia, Germany, India, and in United States Negroes. There are no drops in the developmental curve for Samoan subjects. The level of originality begins in the first grade at the lowest level of any of the cultures studied but the growth is continuous from year to year. The second great continuity in development is shown by the U. S. Negro sample, although some of the specific cultural groups in India show curves almost identical to those of the Samoan subjects. Through the fourth grade, German and Australian children seem to show about the same level and pattern of development. Pressures towards standardization and conformity apparently occur quite early and continue for the Australian child but not for the German child. The overall pattern of growth among the children in India is much the same as in the United States, especially in the mission schools and public schools. (Incidentally, the level of the children of India is considerably higher on the verbal than on the non-verbal tasks, while the reverse is true of the United States Negro sample and of the Western Samoan sample.)

Since the development of originality of thinking shows greater continuity in Western Samoa than in any of the other cultures studies, let us look further at these data. Margaret Mead's (1939) pioneering work in the 1920's, reports of modern observers, and our data support a picture of high cultural continuity and suppression of creativity and independence of thought almost from birth and especially during the early years.

According to Mead, "Keep still," "sit still," "keep your mouth shut," and "stop that noise" are thoroughly ingrained into the Samoan child. He is not even permitted to cry. He cannot even experiment with his voice to find out what sounds he can make. The older children have responsibility for disciplining the younger ones so conformity is taught from birth. Even today, Samoan teachers place an unusually high value upon quietness as a desirable characteristic on our "Ideal Pupil Questionnaire." Mead pointed out that Samoans were imitative and reproductive in their crafts rather than creative. Likewise, today we find that Samoan children excel in the craftsmanship of their drawings, when administered the Goodenough Human Drawing Test or Buck's House-Tree-Person Test. Their drawings are reproductive rather than creative. The characteristic MOST valued by Samoan teachers in their pupils is REMEMBERING WELL.

Both Mead and modern observers have stressed the role of the extended family, the participation of all ages in the life of the community, the mixing of all ages even in school, and the like. Mead used these facts and the continuities in regard to sex in explaining why Samoan adolescents did not experience the periods of emotional upset and personality disturbance common among adolescents in the United States. In today's Samoan schools, there is no strict age segregation and a wide range of ages is found in a single grade, especially in the remote government schools.

The characteristics ranked highest by Samoan teachers on the Ideal Pupil Checklists are: remembers well, healthy, and always asking questions. "Always asking questions," however, has quite a different meaning for the Samoan teacher than for the United States teacher. They do not have in mind the searching, inquiring kinds of questions, but the dependency kind of question, "Is this what you want?" "Is this right?" It was even difficult to administer the tests of creative thinking. Samoan pupils continually asked, "Is this all right?" "Is this what you want?" and the like.

Samoan teachers ranked the following characteristics LOWER than did the teachers of other cultures: adventurous, a self-starter, curiosity, determination, energetic, independent in judgment, industrious, self-confident, self-sufficient, sincere, thorough, and versatile. They placed a HIGHER value than did teachers in other cultures on such characteristics as: being a good guesser, competitive, prompt, haughty, physically strong, quiet, and liking to work alone. In general this pattern of values may logically be expected to support cultural continuity and a generally low degree of creativity.

In the remote villages of Samoa, the school is somewhat modified but the culture of the village remains almost untouched. There is little discontinuity even in the schools, however. A number of discontinuities are creeping into the Samoan culture through the more urban mission schools. Many of the taboos introduced by the mission schools are contrary to the traditions of the culture.

These emerging discontinuities are reflected in the developmental curves for creative thinking, if we separate the more urban mission schools from the more remote government schools. Although the degree of originality is lower in the more remote village schools, there is no break in the continuity of development. In the mission schools, there is a higher level of originality but a sizeable drop at about the end of the third grade, very similar to the developmental curves which we find in the United States. Thus, we see the introduction of discontinuities as seeming to be associated with a rise in the level of originality, discontinuity in the development of originality, and personality disturbance. 'Thus, in Western Samoa, the problem of increasing originality seems to be one of introducing discontinuities without producing undue personality disturbance and disruptions in the development of their thinking abilities. In the United States, the problem is the reverse: how to reduce the cultural discontinuities without retarding the creative development. To me, such a feat does not seem impossible. In fact, one of the characteristics of teachers in our studies in the rare kindergarten and fourth grade classes where there are no drops in creativity is their ability to reduce some of the usual cultural discontinuities. Of course, this has usually been done in violation of existing regulations and traditional practices.

DOES A MORE CREATIVE KIND
OF EDUCATION HAVE A CHANCE?

I have argued that creative development does not have to be left to chance and never "just happens." You may now ask, "What chance is there for a more creative kind of education?" "What chance is there that creative development will not continue to be a chance matter?"

In this regard, you can point to past failures of a more creative kind of education to "catch on." Much interesting and valuable research concerning the measurement and development of the creative thinking abilities was reported around the turn of the Century. Apparently this work was almost completely ignored. Again in the 1920's and 1930's there was a resurgance of interest in creative thinking. This interest became lost in the furor created by Progressive Education and was ignored or forgotten. Why should we expect current efforts to be any more successful than those around 1900 and again in the 1920's and 1930's?

While I doubt that I can answer this question satisfactorily, I do think that there are many reasons why we can expect greater success than in the past. The rate of all change is far greater than ever before and we can expect technological changes to be more rapid and adaptations to them more rapid. Far more research is now being done concerning the problem of measuring, developing, and using the creative thinking abilities and our research tools are more powerful than formerly. There is a strong interest in these developments and their communication throughout the United States and in many other countries.

It will not bother me if you are skeptical. This is a healthy attitude. It will bother me, if you do not examine the question honestly in the light of the things you know to be true. After all, in the final analysis, being creative is searching for the truth and living truthfully.

REFERENCES

Andrews, E. G. "The Development of Imagination in the Pre-School Child." *University of Iowa Studies in Character,* 1930, 3(4).

Gordon, W. J. J. *Synectics.* New York: Harper and Row, 1961.

Johnson, R. T. Unpublished Observations on Western Samoan Culture. Bureau of Educational Research, University of Minnesota, 1961.

Maltzman, I. "On the Training of Originality." *Psychological Review,* 1960, 67, 229–242.

Mead, Margaret. *From the South Seas.* New York: William Morrow, 1939.

Osborn, A. F. *Applied Imagination,* New York: Charles Scribner's Sons, 1957.

Parnes, S. J. and A. Meadow. "Evaluation of Effects Produced by a Creative Problem-Solving Course." *Psychological Reports,* 1960, 7, 357–361.

Pulsifier, Susan Nichols. *Minute Magic.* Boston: Chapman & Grimes, 1960.

Small, W. E. Bats, "Porpoises Teach Electronics." *Science News Letter,* June 30, 1962, 81(26), 410–411.

Torrance, E. P. "Priming Creative Thinking in the Primary Grades." *Elementary School Journal,* 1961, 62, 34–41.

Torrance, E. P. *Guiding Creative Talent.* Englewood Cliffs, N. J.: Prentice-Hall, 1962.

Wilt, Miriam E. *Creativity in Elementary School.* New York: Appleton-Century-Crofts, 1959.

Annotated Bibliography

Astin, A. W. "Types of Variables for Creativity Research." (pp. 351–55) in Taylor, C. W., editor. *Widening Horizons in Creativity.* New York: John Wiley and Sons, 1964.

Measures of creativity used by various researchers are viewed as varying along (a) naturalistic vs. manufactured; and (b) degrees of social relevance. Most investigators prefer manufactured variables of low social relevance (tests). The relationship between the type of variable and the methodology (experimental vs. correlational) is discussed.

Bruner, J. S. "The Conditions of Creativity." (pp. 1–30) in Gruber, H. E., and others. *Contemporary Approaches to Creative Thinking.* New York: Atherton Press, 1963.

A "think piece" which proposes that the creative act is "effective surprise"—the production of novelty. Some of the fusing of opposites inherent in such fusion are discussed and illustrated by reference to a creative group.

Guilford, J. P. "Creativity." *American Psychologist* 5: 444–54; 1950. (Cf. "Three Faces of Intellect." *ibid.,* 14: 469–79; 1959; cf. also "The Structure of Intellect." *Psychological Bulletin* 53: 267–93; 1956; cf. also "Factorial Angles to Psychology." *Psychological Review* 68: 1–20; 1961; cf. also "Frontiers in Thinking That Teachers Should Know About." *Reading Teacher* 13: 176–82; 1963a; cf. also "Human Abilities in Education." *California Journal of Instructional Improvement* 1: 3–6; 1958; cf. also "An Informational View of Mind." *Journal of Psychological Research* 6: 1–10; 1962a.)

The definitive article in the development of creativity (additions traced in the later literature). The author sees the more immediate and explorable problem in "creativity" as a double one: (1) How can we discover and (2) promote the development of creative personalities? Here, he emphasizes the factorial concept of personality as leading to a new way of thinking about creativity and creative productivity, where (a) it presents patterns of primary abilities, which can vary with different spheres of creative activity and along which individuals differ in a continuous manner, thus, allowing the nature of these abilities to be studies in people; (b) productivity depends on other primary traits, including interests, attitudes and tempermental variables.

Proposed is: "(1) an exploratory approach to creativity through a complete application of factor analysis which would begin with carefully constructed hypotheses concerning primary abilities and their properties (certain kinds of factors will be found as: sensitivity to problems, ideational fluency, flexibility of set, ideational novelty, synthesizing ability, analyzing ability); (2) these hypotheses lead to the construction of tests of quite novel types, which promise the discovery of new factors. Once these factors describe the domain of creativity we have a basis for the means of selecting individuals with creative potentialities, and know enough concerning the properties of primary abilities to facilitate education to improve and use them." A veritable blueprint of subsequent research.

Guilford, J. P. "Progress in the Discovery of Intellectual Factors." (pp. 261–97) in Taylor, C. W., editor. *Widening Horizons in Creativity.* New York: John Wiley and Sons, 1964.

A general account of progress in "structure-of-intellect" research to 1962 with special emphasis on the factor of divergent production. Contains appendices which make it an unusually good source article for the scholar.

Guilford, J. P. "Factors that Aid and Hinder Creativity." *Teachers College Record* 63: 380–92; February 1962b.
    Discussion of the factors of fluency, flexibility, and originality. Ideational fluency and associational fluency are noted. Spontaneous vs. adaptive flexibility is discussed. Role of quantity of output is mentioned. Sensitivity to problems of the highly creative, and the difference between creativity and high intelligence are also elaborated as are various personality traits often found in creative people.

Guilford, J. P. "Creativity: Its Measurement and Development." (pp. 151–68) in Parnes, S. J., and Harding, H. F. *A Source Book for Creative Thinking.* New York: Charles Scribner's Sons, 1962c.
    Guilford's historic 1950 American Psychological Association address followed by a 1959 exposition of the structure of intellect.

Guilford, J. P. "Potentiality for Creativity." *Gifted Child Quarterly* 6: 87–90; 1962d.
    Divergent thinking and transformation abilities contribute directly to the structure of creative thinking. Included among the former are multiple responses appropriate to stimuli, fluency, flexibility and elaboration abilities; among the latter are redefinition, revision, and freedom from fixedness abilities. Identification of the primary mental abilities inherent in all courses of instruction, moreover, is underway. Algebra and general math courses are cited as examples. Caution is urged in generalizing from a proclivity in one area to another. Also, the signs associated with creativity in the arts may be different from those associated with talent in the sciences.

Hersch, C. "The Cognitive Functioning of the Creative Person: A Development Analysis." *Journal of Projective Techics* 26: 193–200; 1962. (Cf. *Dissertation Abstracts* 18: 296; 1958.)
    Findings support the hypothesis that both relatively mature and primitive processes are more available to the creative individual as compared with non-creative normals. Primitive operations among creators are more adaptive and capable of productive expression while primitive thinking among schizophrenics serves pathological ends.

Kubie, L. S., M.D. *Neurotic Distortion of the Creative Process.* Porter Lecture Series 22. Lawrence: University of Kansas Press, 1958.
    A theory of thinking that causes objects to be seen in new or different ways. Excellent content for those interested in creative teaching.

Leary, T. "The Effects of Test Score Feedback on Creative Performance, and of Drugs on Creative Experience." (pp. 87–111) in Taylor, C. W., editor. *Widening Horizons in Creativity*. New York: John Wiley and Sons, 1964.

An important, disturbing and thought-provoking article which avers that western science concentrates too much on the reality of behavior instead of the reality of consciousness. Sees creativity as one of the many "games" played by our behavior-oriented rules and hence capable of great modification. The real search for creativity should lie within man in his expansion of consciousness which is the only true and adequate source of creativity and which is best stimulated by drugs like psilocybin, accounts of which experiments are given. (Continued research of this type has since made the author highly controversial.)

MacKinnon, D. W. "Identifying and Developing Creativity." *Journal of Secondary Education* 38: 166–74; 1963.

Discusses creativity and its stages. Type 1 creativity is the product of an expression of the inner states. The creator externalizes something of himself into public field. Type 2 creativity is a product unrelated to the creator as a person, such as a patent. Type 3 creativity combines the first two, examples being, architects, performers, musical arrangers. Article concludes by viewing identification of creativity in school and its implications for the teacher and administration.

MacKinnon, D. W. "The Nature and Nurture of Creative Talent." *American Psychologist* 17: 484–95; 1962. (Also [pp. 305–14] in Ripple, R. E. *Readings in Learning and Human Abilities*. New York: Harper and Row, 1964.)

If a person has the minimum of intelligence required for mastery of a field of knowledge, whether he performs creatively or banally in that field will be crucially determined by non-intellective factors. We would do well in the future to pay more attention to the nurturing of non-intellective traits which the author found to be intimately associated with creative talent. Stressed is the openness of the creative person to experience from within and without. This should caution parents and teachers (1) in setting limits; (2) that learning discipline is necessary, but should not be overlearned; (3) there is a time and place for learning; (4) that having learned, they should be used flexibly, not rigidly or impulsively; (5) that there is a danger of prejudging or perceiving if whole areas of experience are excluded from perception; and (6) that new ideas are criticized too soon and too often.

Maslow, A. H. "Creativity in Self-Actualizing People." (pp. 83–95) in Anderson, H. H., editor. *Creativity and Its Cultivation*. New York: Harper and Row, 1959.

Discusses characteristics of self-actualizing persons, peak experiences, primary and secondary form of creativity.

Maslow, A. H. "Emotional Blocks to Creativity." (pp. 93–103) in Parnes, S. J., and Harding H. F. *A Source Book for Creative Thinking*. New York: Charles Scribner's Sons, 1962.

Discusses some of the psychological bases which underlie creativity, and emotional blockages which occur as creativity wells up from the subconscious.

Mednick, S. A., and Mednick, Martha T. "An Associative Interpretation of the Creative Process." (pp. 54–68) in Taylor, C. W., editor. *Widening Horizons in Creativity*. New York: John Wiley and Sons, 1964.

Suggests that creativity consists in forming new combinations of remote associated elements. Describes development of the remote associates test (RAT).

Rogers, C. R. "Towards a Theory of Creativity." (pp. 55–68) in Anderson, H. H., editor. *Creativity and Its Cultivation*. New York: Harper and Row, 1959. (Cf. [pp. 64–72] in Parnes, S. J., and Harding, H. F., editors. *A Source Book for Creative Thinking*. New York: Charles Scribner's Sons, 1962.)

Hypothesizes that those who exhibit openness, internal locus of evaluation, and ability to toy with material will be more creative than controls, and that the group in which the leader allows greater psychological safety and freedom will be more creative than controls.

Rogers, C. R. "Toward a Theory of Creativity." (pp. 347–59) in *On Becoming a Person*. Boston: Houghton Mifflin, 1961. (Cf. also *Review of General Semantics* 11: 249–60; 1964.)

Sets forth a tentative theory of creativity, the nature of the creative act, the conditions under which it occurs and the manner in which it may constructively be fostered. Pointed up are: (1) *The Social Need*, or the price we pay for a lack of creativity; (2) *The Creative Process;* (3) *Motivation for Creativity*, man's tendency to become his potentialities; (4) *Inner Conditions of Constructive Creativity;* (5) *The Creative Act and Its Concomitants;* and (6) *Conditions Fostering Constructive Creativity*.

Ruitenbeck, H. M. *The Creative Imagination* (*Psychoanalysis and the Genius of Inspiration*) Chicago, Ill.: Quadrangle Books, (180 N. Wacker Dr., 60606, $7.50), 1965.

Torrance, E. P. "Essay Review: Creativity and Intelligence." *School Review* 71: 112–15; Summer 1963.

A thoughtful review of Getzels' and Jackson's study which airs many issues about creativity.

CHAPTER THREE

Characteristics

Factors That Aid and Hinder Creativity

J. P. Guilford

IN THE PART OF OUR CURRENT *Zeitgeist* PERTAINING TO PSYCHOLOGY and education, no word has had a more dramatic rise in popularity than "creativity." After generally ignoring the subject, psychologists have come to realize their backwardness in knowledge of this subject. Employers have been asking for more inventive scientists, engineers, and managers. Special courses on how to think creatively have been springing up by the score. Special institutes are being held on the subject. Teachers and educators are asking how they can make courses more stimulating and how they can arouse more productive thinking on the part of students.

The interest is international, as well it might be. The whole world faces two very critical problems—how to feed its exploding population and how to keep the peace. It has been estimated that in the next 20 years we shall need three times the number of scientists and engineers we now have, and they shall have to exercise all the ingenuity of which they are capable. We are reminded by the scriptures, however, that man does not live by bread alone. There is, I think, a very noticeable resurgence of interest in the arts in all their forms. We wish to walk in beauty as well as in peace, freedom, and dignity. There is also good reason to desire increased creativity to achieve aesthetic goals.

INVESTIGATION OF CREATIVITY

My topic suggests that I give most consideration to the abilities and other traits of individuals that make some of them creative and

REPRINTED by permission of the Author and *Teachers College Record*, 65:380–92, 1962.

some not. Knowing these traits should help us to recognize which persons are likely to have the potentialities of becoming creatively productive. The same knowledge should help us in taking steps that should increase creative output in ourselves and in others, and other steps that may remove obstacles in the way of creative productivity. Our primary concern, then, will be the basic facts concerning the nature of creative thinking and of the more creative persons, with reference to the application of this information.

Serious investigation of creativity by psychologists began only in recent years. For centuries the common idea had been that only the exceedingly rare person is genuinely creative and that creativity is a divine gift. As such, it was not to be investigated, or at best, there was little hope of understanding it. Even after Darwin came upon the scene, when creativity came to be regarded as some kind of rare, hereditary blessing, there was still little incentive to attempt to understand it because there was thought to be little that one could do about it. In addition to being very rare, the highly creative person's behavior is sometimes eccentric. This has sometimes branded him as being abnormal and even pathological. Mental pathology was similarly avoided as a subject of study by scientific investigators for a long time.

Creativity became an object of scientific study primarily because of the general interest in individual differences. This approach recognizes that individuals differ psychologically in traits or attributes that can be conceived as continua or dimensions—that there can be varying degrees of a quality possessed by different individuals. This concept was eventually applied to creativity, but in serious ways only about a dozen years ago. This new way of looking at the matter permitted us to think that not only a few peculiarly gifted persons but individuals in general possess some degree of the same creative trait or traits.

This conception has opened the door to many kinds of research. We need no longer study creativity by catching the rare persons who are recognized as having creativity to high degree; a multitude of subjects is now available to investigators. We can discover the various aspects of the phenomenon called "creativity." We can find out the conditions under which creative performance occurs or does not occur.

As in the case of all psychological characteristics that make up personality, we may be forced to recognize that heredity establishes limits of development for an individual. But there is considerable faith among educators that rarely does an individual realize full development in any respect and that there is generally considerable room for improvement. This faith should also be applied to the creative aspects of personality.

BASIC TRAITS AND CREATIVITY

There are a number of approaches to the investigation of the traits or characteristics in which creative individuals are most likely to excel. Some investigators appear to regard the phenomenon of creativity as a single dimension of personality. It is my view that the creative disposition is made up of many components and that its composition depends upon where you find it. Practically all investigators recognize that there are many potentially contributing conditions.

When the problem is approached from the standpoint of individual differences, the most natural scientific technique to apply is that of factor analysis. This is the approach that my associates and I have taken almost exclusively in the Aptitudes Project at the University of Southern California.

According to our original hypotheses (7), we expected to find the more creative individuals to think with greater fluency, with more flexibility, and with greater originality. The tests designed to measure fluency present very simple tasks, and the quantity of output determines the scores. When told to produce a list of items of information of a certain kind, how many responses can the examinee give in a limited time? Quality does not count, but, of course, the responses must be appropriate.

Flexibility in thinking means a *change* of some kind—a change in the meaning, interpretation, or use of something, a change in understanding of the task, a change of strategy in doing the task, or a change in direction of thinking, which may mean a new interpretation of the goal.

There has been some debate concerning the meaning of "originality." In our research and in that of others, originality means the production of unusual, far-fetched, remote, or clever responses. But there are some who say that an idea is not original or novel unless no human being has ever thought of it earlier. This conception is worthless to the scientist because there is no way of knowing that an idea has never existed before. It is somewhat better to say that a novel idea is a new one so far as the particular individual who has it is concerned. But unless we know the individual's past history of thinking, we cannot be sure of meeting this criterion either.

Fortunately, we can resort to empirical signs of novelty in terms of the statistical infrequency of a response among members of a certain population that is culturally relatively homogeneous. This gives us some workable operations for applying the criterion of unusualness. The index of unusualness can therefore be purely objective. As for the far-fetched or remote associations and the clever responses, we have as yet no way to avoid some degree of subjectivity of judgment in assessing test performance to obtain an index of originality.

Another somewhat popular criterion of an original idea is that it is socially useful. Those who deal with practical affairs may be appropriately concerned about this aspect of produced ideas. But such a criterion involves us in values in a way that science cannot deal with directly; hence, the criterion of social usefulness can be quickly dismissed by the psychologist. This does not mean that as a person he is unconcerned about social usefulness. It does mean that as a scientist he cannot afford to be so concerned and so restricted.

FLUENCY FACTORS

We shall now give closer attention to the various factors of fluency, flexibilty, and originality. It turns out that in verbal tests alone there are three differentiated fluency factors (9). Ideational fluency has to do with the rate of generation of a quantity of ideas. The idea produced may be as simple as a single word, as complex as the title for a picture or a story, or as phrases and short sentences that convey unitary thoughts. In a test, we may ask the examinee to list all the things he can think of that are solid, flexible, and colored. He may respond with *cloth, leaf, rose petal, hair, skin, leather,* and so on. Any response that fulfills the specifications is accepted and counts toward the total score. In other tests, we may ask the examinee to list the consequences of a certain action or event, the various uses of an object, or some appropriate titles for a given story. In all such tests, there are strict time limits.

It is easy to see where an operation such as that in tests of ideational fluency fits into problem solving of many kinds. Perhaps a problem situation, when interpreted in a certain way, calls for an object with a certain set of specifications in order to solve it. Once these specifications are realized, the person who can list pertinent possibilities most rapidly could, other things being equal, solve the problem most quickly.

Many a problem calls for a running through of the likely possibilities during the earlier stage of interpreting or structuring it as well as during the stage of finding solutions. This process also probably depends in some degree upon ideational fluency. Of course it is not necessary to run through *all* the logical possibilities in solving a problem. One can ignore the less promising ones. This point will be touched upon later.

Another kind of fluency is called "associational fluency." It pertains to the completion of relationships, in distinction from the factor of ideational fluency, which involves giving ideas that fit a class. As a test of associational fluency, we may ask the examinee to list all the words he can think of that mean the opposite, or nearly the opposite, of the word "good." He may respond with *bad, poor, sinful, defective, awful, terrible,* and so on. This ability is most obviously of use to the creative writer, who wants to find quickly a variety of verbal expressions without having to resort to a thesaurus.

The factor of associational fluency may have more general utility—for example, whenever we apply thinking by analogy as our strategy in solving problems. Thinking of a correlate is the completion of an analogy. Many solutions to new problems are achieved by the practice of thinking by analogy. The success of certain kinds of engineers in their work has been predicted to a small extent by means of a test of associational fluency as found by Saunders (*21, 1956*).

A third kind of fluency is called "expressional fluency." It has to do with the facile construction of sentences. We ask the examinee to write as many four-word sentences as he can, all different, with no word used more than once. We may give the initial letters of the four words, the same four being specified for each sentence—for example, "W_____ c_____ e_____ n_____." To this task, he may reply "We can eat nuts." "Willie comes every night," "Wholesome carrots elevate nations," "Weary cats evade nothing," and so on. You will probably not be surprised when I tell you that in a ninth-grade sample, the girls obtained a higher mean score than the boys.

We do not know yet how much generality to attach to this factor, whether it is limited to tasks such as the writing of sentences or whether it is so broad as to pertain to organizing ideas into systems. If it is as broad as the latter suggestion, it should be of considerable consequence, perhaps in something as important as the trial-and-error development of a scientific theory. The factor has been found significantly related to ratings by psychologists of the creative performances of military officers.[1]

---

[1] From an unpublished study conducted jointly by the Aptitudes Project at the University of Southern California and the Institute for Personality Assessment and Research, University of California, Berkeley.

FLEXIBILITY FACTORS

One type of flexibility we first recognized as "spontaneous flexibility" because the tests that measure it do not even suggest that the examinee be flexible (*5*). Without his knowing it, he can make a good score if he varies his *kinds* of responses. If we tell the examinee to list all the uses he can think of for a common brick, the total number of uses listed is a good score for his status on the factor of ideational fluency. But we also score his performance in terms of the number of times he changes *category* of uses. For example, the person who responds with *build a house, build a school, build a factory*, etc., does not change his class of uses. Another person who responds with *make a paper weight, drive a nail, make baseball bases, throw at a cat, grind up for red powder, make a tombstone for a bird*, etc., changes class with each new response. He shows much more flexibility.

The person who makes a low spontaneous-flexibility score is rigid in the sense that he perseverates within one or a very few classes. As there are several kinds of flexibility in thinking, so there are several kinds of rigidity. When someone tells you that a certain person is rigid, beware of overgeneralization of the term. We do not find in normal (nonpathological) people a very general trait of rigidity vs. flexibility. We find several. This does not say that there are no individuals who are rigid in just about every respect, but the general rule is that they may be rigid in some respects and not in others, at least so far as thinking is concerned.

A new hypothesis may be considered in connection with the factor of spontaneous flexibility. Some advisers on how to think creatively suggest that in starting to solve a new problem, we keep our thinking at a rather high level of abstraction. We think of it first in very general terms. Thus, the person who goes from class to class in the Brick Uses test is operating within the frame of reference of a much broader class within which there are subclasses. A higher level of abstraction may mean thinking in terms of broader classes. This has the effect of broadening the scope of the scanning process in searching for information. Going from one class to another in the Brick Uses test also means considering all the properties of a brick—its weight, its color, its texture, and so on. These are abstractions all lying within the class of the total nature of a brick. This is reminiscent of a stock method of practicing creative thinking, a method known as "attribute listing" and advocated by Crawford (*3*).

A second kind of flexibility has been called "*adaptive* flexibility" for the reason that in tests in which it was first found, the examinee, to succeed, must make changes of some kind—changes in interpretation of the task, in approach or strategy, or in possible solutions. Our current interpretation of the factor of originality is that it is adaptive flexibility in dealing with verbal information.

We have a kind of test, called Plot Titles, in which the examinee is told a very short story and that he is to suggest as many appropriate titles for the story as he can. One of the stories is about a wife who is unable to speak until a specialist performs the appropriate surgery. Then her husband is driven to distraction by her incessant talking until another surgeon eliminates his hearing, when peace is restored in the family.

The number of commonplace titles given to the story may be used as a score for ideational fluency. Such titles include,

A man and his wife
Never satisfied
Medicine triumphs
A man's decisions
Talking and hearing

The number of responses rated as "clever" serves as a score for originality. Such titles are exemplified by

The deaf man and the dumb woman
Happiness through deafness
Operation—peace of mind
Yack, yack, hack

Several other types of tests serve to indicate individual differences in the factor of originality.

ELABORATION

In the course of our investigations of abilities involved in planning (1), we found another kind of ability we have called "elaboration." In one test, given the bare outlines of a plan, the examinee is asked to produce the detailed steps needed to make the plan work. The more details he adds, the better is his score. We believe that the unique feature of this ability is that in tests for it, one item of information leads to another as a kind of extension or completion. In more technical language, we say that the examinee is producing a *variety of implications.*

It was eventually recognized that the abilities of fluency, flexibility (including originality), and elaboration are similar in that the tests of them call for a variety of answers. There is no right or fully determined answer in connection with the information given in the item. There are now parallel tests in which each item *does* have one right answer because it is fully determined by the information given or because there is one conventionally accepted answer. A distinction has therefore been made between *divergent* thinking and *convergent* thinking to represent the two classes of abilities. The abilities of which I have been speaking thus far belong in the divergent-thinking category. Because the individual has to generate his answer or answers, starting from given information, in both categories of abilities, we speak of divergent-*production* factors vs. convergent-*production* factors, respectively.

QUANTITY VS. QUALITY

Several questions arise concerning the relationship of quantity and quality of production. One debated and investigated hypothesis is that "quantity breeds quality." This hypothesis holds that if a person produces a greater total number of ideas, he also produces a greater number of high-quality ideas in a limited time. Another view is that a mental set for quantity is inefficient because if a person spends his time producing a lot of low-quality responses, he cannot produce so many good ones.

There is another aspect of this controversy. When a person is set to give "good" answers, he is applying judgment or evaluation as he goes along. On the one hand, it is believed that an evaluative or critical attitude is generally inhibiting to the flow of ideas, good and poor alike. On the other hand, it is believed that the application of evaluation as one proceeds has a selective effect, holding back the low-quality responses and letting the high-quality responses come through.

The well-known brainstorming technique, attributed to Alex Osborn (*18*) and employed by many others, conforms to the first of these two schools of thought. One of its chief claimed virtues is that the separation of production and evaluation—in other words, suspended judgment—is better procedure. As originally applied, of course, brainstorming has other features, which includes thinking in small groups rather than thinking by individuals in seclusion.

The experimental results bearing upon the issue of suspended judgment are somewhat mixed. Meadow *et al.* (*16*) report that with suspended judgment, the production of "good" answers was a little more than doubled. The problems were to suggest unusual uses for a wire coat hanger and for a broom. The criteria for "good" responses were "unique" and "useful."

In our Aptitudes Project (2), we gave the Plot Titles test with and without the specific instruction to give clever titles. It was expected that the instruction for clever titles would entail more evaluation. The effects of this instruction were shown by a reduction in the number of low-quality responses, an increase in the number of high-quality responses, and a higher average rating of degree of cleverness.

Hyman (*13*) found that his subjects generated 68% more responses under quantity instructions, but that this increase in "good" responses, where "good" meant uncommon and of "high quality," failed to keep pace with the total output. Hyman is probably right when he concludes that quantity may breed quality for some types of problems but not for others. It is also probably true that the *kind* of evaluative attitude applied by the thinker has much to do with the quantity and quality of responses he produces.

Divergent thinking is a matter of scanning one's stored information to find answers to satisfy a special search model. Evaluation comes into the picture in determining whether or not the produced information fits the search model. Relaxed evaluation would permit a broadening of the base of the search, whereas an evaluative attitude with some degree of strictness should narrow the search. In doing so, however, it may lead more efficiently to good answers. This should depend upon the clarity and accuracy of the search model. If the thinker has a good search model, the application of evaluation while he thinks should be helpful.

But if evaluation is of a more vague kind, such as that involving a fear of being unconventional, a fear of thinking socially unacceptable thoughts, or a fear of being wrong, it should be definitely better to suspend judgments based on such criteria. Evaluation incident to an overly strong desire for a quick solution would also be handicapping. But evaluation for the sake of efficient scanning, where there is good strategy in the scanning process, should be beneficial.

Hyman (*13*) has found that a general critical attitude can have rather broad transfer effects in solving problems. A group of engineers, in Hyman's experiment, read some previously given solutions to a certain practical problem under the instruction to list all the good points that they could see in those solutions. A second group was instructed to list all the faults they could see in the same solutions. Later, in solving the same problem and in solving a new one, the uncritical readers suggested solutions of their own that were rated higher on the average than those of the critical group. Thus, very general critical attitudes must be taken into account.

GROUP VS. INDIVIDUAL THINKING

The question of group thinking vs. individual thinking has received a great deal of attention. The virtue claimed for group thinking in brainstorming is that one person stimulates another. In support of this hypothesis, Osborn (*19*) reports that about a third of the ideas produced in group brainstorming are of the "hitchhiking" type. In such a case, one person's idea is based upon another person's idea.

There are results which do not support his hypothesis, however. Taylor *et al.* (*23*) found a larger number of unrepeated ideas produced by individuals working alone than by those working in groups, where both kinds of thinkers were working under the condition of suspended judgment. Taylor points out that the group condition may have the effect of channeling thinking in similar directions, reducing the variety and therefore the quantity of unrepeated ideas.

Perhaps neither the group nor the isolation condition is best under all circumstances or for all individuals. It is quite possible that both can be applied to advantage. The preference of the thinker should have something to do with the choice of condition. A great deal is made of the point that the highly creative person is an independent thinker and that his creation may be a highly personal thing. Torrance (*21*, 1959) found that the more highly creative child (as indicated by his test scores) in a small group often works by himself or is somehow induced by the others to do so.

Whatever the outcome of brainstorming sessions in particular instances, experiments show that courses on creative thinking that are heavily weighted with brainstorming exercises seem to leave the students with beneficial results, and these results have some degree of permanence (*15*, *20*). How much of the improvement to attribute to the brainstorming technique and to which aspects of it the improvement should be attributed are open questions.

CONTEXT OF CREATION

From the discussion thus far, one may conclude that creative performances are to be identified psychologically as a small number of divergent-production operations. Two different qualifications must be introduced. One exception is that two of the factors that we in the Aptitudes Project regarded from the first as being pertinent to creative thinking fall outside the divergent-production group. The other exception is that I have not yet told the whole story regarding the divergent-production factors. I shall make good on the latter omission first.

I have repeatedly stated that the tests on the factors thus far described are *verbal* tests. They pertain to verbally stated information. There are other kinds of information, and the question comes up whether the same person is usually equally creative in handling different kinds of information, material, or content. From our analytical results, we can say that it can happen, but we should rarely expect the same person to be equally capable of creativity in science, in the arts, mathematics, administration, and musical composition. Highly creative individuals in many of these different areas may have outstanding qualities in common, but psychological study indicates that they also have some marked differences.

In the area of divergent-production abilities alone, we find that individuals may be uneven in handling verbal vs. concrete vs. symbolic material. Symbolic material is the kind with which the mathematician deals—numbers and letters. Fluency, flexibility, and elaboration in dealing with concrete (perceived) material are probably of greater importance to the inventor of gadgets, the painter, and the composer, whereas the same kinds of abilities for dealing with verbal material or content are more important for the creative writer and the scientist. In other words, there are parallel abilities for dealing with concrete (or figural) material, symbolic material, and verbally meaningful (or semantic) material.

One of our earlier hypotheses (7) was that the unusually creative person has a high degree of sensitivity to problems. One person notices something wrong or in need of improvement, whereas another fails to observe defects, deficiencies, or errors. The observation of imperfections starts the creative person on his way to creative production. The observation of inadequacy of solutions also keeps the creative thinker at work on his problem (17).

Factor analysis has consistently upheld this hypothesis by finding an ability common to a variety of tests calling for the noticing of defects and deficiencies in such things as common household appliances, social customs, or in solutions to problems. Such an ability, however, seems to fit better in the general category of evaluative factors than it does in that of divergent production.

Not being satisfied with things as they are is a matter of evaluation. We hear a great deal about the "divine discontent" of the creative person. It is said that Thomas A. Edison frequently admonished his workers with the comment, "There must be a better way. Go and find it." The uncreative, in contrast, are often willing to settle for half-way measures and tolerably successful solutions to problems.

Another of our initial hypotheses was that many an invention or new idea is the revision of something that is already known. But the revision is not an obvious one. It takes quite a change in the meaning, interpretation, or use of an object to achieve such an innovation. One of our tests, designed for such an ability, asks which of five objects or their parts could be most reasonably adapted to be used to start a fire when there are available the following items: a fountain pen, an onion, a pocket watch, a light bulb, and a bowling ball. The accepted answer is "pocket watch," since the cover of the watch face could be used as a condensing lens. Since this and other such tests call for one best answer, this factor falls logically in the convergent-production category. The feature that makes a contribution to creativity is that a *transformation* must occur; objects must be redefined. Individuals who are clever at improvising seem to show this kind of ability.

There are other abilities outside the divergent-production category that make some contribution to creative performances in their own ways. We have seen that one of the evaluative abilities—sensitivity to problems—has a function in getting the creative thinker started. Other evaluative abilities should have their uses, whether judgment is suspended or not, in determining whether the products of thinking are good, useful, suitable, adequate, or desirable. If the creator is to finish his job, he will eventually appraise his product, and he will revise it if he feels that revision is called for.

COGNITION AND MEMORY

Thus far I have spoken of three major categories of intellectual factors—abilities of divergent production, convergent production, and evaluation. There are two other major categories—cognitive abilities and memory abilities—all distinguished from those in the first-mentioned categories and from each other. Cognitive abilities have to do with discovery, recognition, or comprehension of information in various forms. Memory abilities have to do with storage or retention of information.

Many people, including some teachers, have for some reason disparaged memory and memory abilities. Some of them, who emphasize the importance of thinking, seem wrongly to believe that good thinking and good memory are incompatible qualities, perhaps even negatively correlated. Actually, good memory contributes to good thinking.

It is not a good, well-stocked memory, as such, that is bad, for even the most creative people have given due credit to stored information. It is the way in which storage is achieved and organized that makes the difference between the graduate who is sometimes described as "merely a walking encyclopedia" and the graduate who has a usable and fruitful fund of information. Memory abilities thus make their indirect but important contribution to creative performance.

The question often arises concerning the relation of creativity to intelligence. In connection with this question, the usual conception of "intelligence" is that which is measured by such tests as the Stanford Binet, the Wechsler scales, or the California Test of Mental Maturity.

In discussing abilities related to creativity, I have referred to them as intellectual factors. It is very doubtful whether these abilities, particularly those in the divergent-production category, are represented to any appreciable degree in standard IQ tests. IQ tests were designed to predict success in school learning, particularly in reading, arithmetic, and the subject-matter or informational courses. But we now know that there are many other kinds of intellectual abilities.

Studies of groups of research scientists and engineers (*22*) show that such groups have high average scores on IQ tests. They would need to have higher-than-average IQs to have passed all their academic hurdles, most of them including the PhD. But only a fraction of these are outstanding for creative performance. But within groups of scientists and engineers, the correlation found between IQ-test scores and creative performance is usually rather low. This is due in part to the restriction of range of IQ within such groups. The evidence seems to indicate that although the qualities in traditional IQ intelligence may be of some help to the creative scientist or engineer, they are by no means sufficient.

The low correlation between creativity and IQ is also found at younger age groups. In high school students, Getzels and Jackson (*21*, 1959) found that if the highest 20% of the subjects on IQ were selected as "gifted," 70% of those who stood in the highest 20% in terms of divergent-thinking tests would have been missed. Torrance (*21*, 1959) has reported a similar finding in the elementary grades. In both instances, it was reported that the teachers knew their high-IQ students better and liked them better. The high-creative without high IQs were often regarded as nuisances, and they were somewhat estranged from other students. Those with both high IQ *and* high creativity were recognized as having unusual but sound ideas, to be good in planning and improvising, and effective in getting attention (*21*, 1959).[2]

---

[2] For systematic treatments of a unified theory of intelligence see references (*8, 11*).

NON-APTITUDE TRAITS

The assessment of traits of temperament, interest, and attitude in connection with creativity has been approached in various ways. One approach has been to find the most outstandingly creative individuals in different professional groups, such as architects, writers, and scientists, and to assess them quite thoroughly by methods that are available. If a creative group differs systematically from the general population or, better, some group outside the profession but matched with it for age, sex, and educational level, it is concluded that this creative group stands apart or is distinguished by the personality trait or traits in question.

There are obvious dangers in drawing conclusions from studies of this kind, unless an appropriate control group has been used. When it is found that creative architects, scientists, mathematicians, and writers alike tend to score highest on theoretical and esthetic interest on the Allport-Vernon-Lindzey *Study of Values*, this may occur just because any high-IQ group would do the same (*14*). When it is found that the creative males tend to score relatively in the direction of femininity on the masculinity-femininity scale of the *Minnesota Multiphasic Personality Inventory* scale, we remember that Terman and Miles (*24*) found that as members of the two sexes are more intelligent and better educated, they respond more alike to test items on masculinity vs. femininity. Nor should it be surprising that the creative groups just mentioned should tend to score high on the Strong *Vocational Interest Blank* scales for architect, psychologist, and author-journalist.

A somewhat better approach is to obtain two samples from the same profession, composed of highly creative and less creative individuals, respectively. The groups can then be compared with respect to various assessed qualities. Sometimes the groups are distinguished on the basis of judgments by their teachers (*4, 12*). In still other studies, subjects of mixed occupations but similar in IQ and educational level have been tested with measures of creative aptitude and of non-aptitude traits (*10*).

NON-APTITUDE DIFFERENCES

We have had to recognize that creative occupational groups share parallel but different exceptional abilities. We should expect the various groups to show some non-aptitude qualities in common and also to show some differences. One difference, for example, has been noted between creative students of art and of science. The more creative art student has been reported to be more of an observer than a participant in what is going on (*12*). The more creative science student is reported to be more of a participant than the less creative student (*6*). Such observations should prevent our generalizing conclusions obtained from one creative group to all other creative groups.

There are many ways in which creative people of many groups are alike, however. There is general agreement that the highly creative person, particularly the original person, is self-confident. Which comes first, originality or self-confidence? It is a little like the old hen-and-the-egg problem. Probably, it works both ways: Originality yields success and hence self-confidence, and self-confidence leads the individual to attempt to solve problems where others would give up. In some instances, self-confidence goes over into conceit, as we have all been aware. Sometimes this is fed by the adulations of admirers. Sometimes it may suggest an underlying hypersensitivity to criticism.

Along with self-confidence, there is usually self-assurance or social boldness. The creative person is especially confident about his own judgment and his own evaluations of his work. He is often described as an independent thinker, which includes having an independent set of values. If he thinks his product is good, he discounts the criticisms of others and may disparage their judgments.

Not only is he more or less independent of other people's judgments, he may be self-sufficient in that he can take people or he can let them alone. He is likely to find ideas more important than people, though he is not necessarily a social recluse. These qualities do not add to his popularity with others, so he is in danger of becoming estranged from his parents, his teachers, and his peers. Contributing to this state of affairs also is a lack of mutual understanding. The creative child and his associates may need special counseling to help smooth over some roughness in interpersonal relationships. This can be done without curbing development along creative lines.

We have found that young men who stand high in one or more kinds of fluency are likely to be somewhat impulsive, cheerful, and relaxed. Those who score high in tests of originality tend to have strong esthetic interests, and they like to indulge in divergent thinking. They do not feel much need for meticulousness or for discipline. Somewhat surprisingly, they show no particular dislike for conventional or socially approved behavior, nor do they show signs of neuroticism.

One of the striking traits found by Getzels and Jackson (*21*, 1959) among high school students who stand high in divergent-thinking tests is a strong sense of humor. This is shown particularly in the kinds of stories they tell in response to pictures. For example, one picture showed a young man working at his desk at six-thirty in the morning. A bright but less creative student wrote the following kind of story: "This young man is very ambitious to get ahead. He comes early every morning to impress his boss so he will be promoted." A more creative student told the following kind of story: "This picture is the office of a firm that manufactures breakfast cereals. It has just found a formula to produce a new kind of cereal that will bend, sag, and sway. The man is a private eye employed by a rival firm to obtain the formula. He thinks he has found it and copies it. It turns out to be the wrong formula, and the competitor's factory blows up."

Such stories usually involve some novel twist or transformation, such as the expression regarding the cereal that will "bend, sag, and sway." Many stories derive their humor from such a source. The person who makes up such stories is exhibiting verbal or semantic transformations, which is a sign that he has a fair degree of the factor of originality. Since this is a semantic ability, and since Getzels and Jackson's tests were verbal, we may well question whether the affiliation of humor and the ability to produce transformations extends to other kinds of content, figural or symbolic. It is probably true, however, that creative painters, composers, and mathematicians also experience a certain amount of enjoyment, if not amusement, in playfulness with their own kinds of materials.

FINAL SUGGESTIONS

Although the temperament and motivational qualities can help us somewhat in identifying potentially creative people, no one of them is a dependable sign, nor would all of them collectively be sufficient. Neither do these qualities help us very much in understanding the nature of the creative processes. On the whole, we have less chance of changing individuals with respect to these qualities in order to increase their creativity, except for changing certain attitudes.

Our chief hope, then, of either identifying the more creative persons or enhancing their creative performances lies with the aptitude factors. If we regard the intellectual factors as distinct but somewhat generalized thinking skills, this statement seems more reasonable. We develop skills by practicing them. The question, then, is one of what kinds of practice can best be applied and under what conditions.

An understanding of the nature of the skills is one of the most important steps either for the teacher or the student. When we know what kind of skill is to be developed, we have a more clearly defined goal toward which to work. Torrance (*21, 1959*) reports that even after 20 minutes of instruction on the nature of divergent-thinking processes, grade-school children showed a clearly observable improvement in performing tasks of this type.

Although special courses on creative thinking have proved beneficial, our whole educational system can be of greater help by giving more attention to this subject. There is abundant opportunity to teach almost any subject in ways that call for productive thinking rather than rote memory. Even the multiplication tables can be taught in ways that give the pupil insight into properties of the number system.

In some experimental courses at the University of Illinois in which mathematics is taught from the lower grades on by what is called a "discovery" method, instead of telling the child the axioms and other principles of mathematics, the teacher lets him discover them for himself by exposing him to appropriate examples. Also at the University of Illinois, science is being taught to children by a discovery method. Some natural phenomenon is demonstrated without explanations to the class, perhaps in motion-picture form. From then on, it is a matter of the students asking questions, with minimum information being given by the teacher, until the student develops his own satisfactory hypothesis.

Education in this country has unfortunately been too much dominated by the learning theory based upon the stimulus-response model of Thorndike, Hull, and Skinner. People, after all, are not rats (with a few exceptions), and they are not pigeons (with similar exceptions). Let us make full use of the human brains that have been granted to us. Let us apply a psychology that recognizes the full range of human intellectual qualities. We must make more complete use of our most precious national resource—the intellectual abilities of our people, including their creative potentialities.

REFERENCES

1. Berger, R. M., Guilford, J. P., & Christensen, P. R. A factor-analytic study of planning abilities. *Psychol. Monogr.*, 1957, 71, (Whole No. 435).
2. Christensen, P. R., Guilford, J. P., & Wilson, R. C. Relations of creative responses to working time and instructions. *J. exp. Psychol.*, 1957, *53*, 82–88.
3. Crawford, R. P. *Techniques of creative thinking.* New York: Hawthorne Books, 1952.
4. Drevdahl, J. E. Factors of importance for creativity. *J. clin. Psychol.*, 1956, *12*, 21–26.

5. Frick, J. W., Guilford, J. P., Christensen, P. R., & Merrifield, P. R. A factor-analytic study of flexibility in thinking. *Educ. psychol. Measmt.*, 1959, *19*, 469–496.

6. Garwood, D. S. Some personality factors related to creativity in young scientists. Unpublished doctoral dissertation, Claremont Graduate School, 1961.

7. Guilford, J. P. Creativity. *Amer. Psychologist*, 1950, *5*, 444–454.

8. Guilford, J. P. Three faces of intellect. *Amer. Psychologist*, 1959, *14*, 469–479.

9. Guilford, J. P., & Christensen, P. R. A factor-analytic study of verbal fluency. *Rep. psychol. Lab.*, No. 17. Los Angeles: Univ. Southern California, 1957.

10. Guilford, J. P., Christensen, P. R., Frick, J. W., & Merrifield, P. R. The relations of creative-thinking aptitudes to non-aptitude personality traits. *Rep. psychol. Lab.*, No. 20. Los Angeles: Univ. Southern California, 1957.

11. Guilford, J. P., & Merrifield, P. R. The structure of intellect model: its uses and implications. *Rep. psychol. Lab.*, No. 24. Los Angeles: Univ. Southern California, 1960.

12. Hammer, E. F. *Creativity.* New York: Random House, 1961.

13. Hyman, H. *Some experiments in creativity.* New York: General Electric, Relations Services, 1960.

14. MacKinnon, D. What do we mean by talent and how do we use it? In *The search for talent.* New York: College Entrance Board, 1960.

15. Meadow, A., & Parnes, S. J. Evaluation of training in creative problem solving. *J. appl. Psychol.*, 1959, *43*, 189–194.

16. Meadow, A., Parnes, S. J., & Reese, H. Influence of brainstorming instructions and problem sequence on a creative problem solving test. *J. appl. Psychol.*, 1959, *43*, 413–416.

17. Merrifield, P. R., Guilford, J. P., Christensen, P. R., & Frick, J. W. A factor-analytical study of problem-solving abilities. *Rep. psychol. Lab.*, No. 22. Los Angeles: Univ. Southern California, 1960.

18. Osborn, A. F. *Applied imagination.* New York: Charles Scribner's Sons, 1953.

19. Osborn, A. F. *Development of creative education.* Buffalo, N. Y.: Creative Education Foundation, 1961.

20. Parnes, S. J., & Meadow, A. Evaluation of persistence of effects produced by a creative problem solving course. *Psychol. Reports*, 1960, 7, 357–361.

21. Taylor, C. W. (Ed.) *Research conference on the identification of creative scientific talent.* Salt Lake City, Utah: Univ. of Utah Press, 1956, 1958, 1959.

22. Taylor, D. W. Thinking and creativity. *Ann. N. Y. Acad. Sci.*, 1960, *91*, 108–127.

23. Taylor, D. W., Berry, P. C., & Block, C. H. Does group participation when using brainstorming facilitate or inhibit creative thinking? *Admin. Sci. Quart.*, 1958, *3*, 23–47.

24. Terman, L. M., & Miles, Catherine C. *Sex and personality.* New York: McGraw-Hill, 1936.

Creativity as a Character Trait:
An Expanding Concept
Leonard Steinberg

THE LITERATURE ON CREATIVITY HAS INCREASED ENORMOUSLY REFLECTING the urgency of cultural, social and educational concern about it. Educators have long been concerned with developing and nurturing creativity. Perhaps what is new is the growing realization that creative potential is not something confined to a gifted few and determined at birth. Increasingly, we are recognizing creativity as a normally distributed human potentiality. Evidence seems to support the view that no one is without creative potential; when we talk about creative behaviour we refer to every man rather than to the unique man.

If we are dealing with a universal characteristic which may be fostered in all children, what does the literature offer in helping us to understand this fascinating phenomenon?

It is the purpose of this paper to briefly review selected theory and research which emphasizes creativity as a character trait and to explore studies which attempt to discern some of the conditions that favor or thwart the emergence of this characteristic.

CREATIVITY—AN ATTITUDE OR AN APTITUDE?

The concept of creativity in recent years has been subjected to myriad interpretations. For many it has long been regarded as a special endowment bestowed upon a very few, a special talent that cannot be induced unless the proper genes and chromosomes are present. Traditionally, creativity has been associated with an act which eventuates in a novel construction or an observable product, considered outstanding by those deemed competent to judge.

Many authors have suggested, therefore, that creativity can best be studied through products. In the Committee Report on Criteria of Creativity (*13*), it is stated that the product of creative behavior should be the first object of study; after the product is judged "creative" the term can then be applied to the behavior which produced

REPRINTED by permission of the Author and *California Journal of Instructional Improvement*, 7:3–9, 1964.

it and also to the individual who produced it. Using this criterion, creativity may be defined as a characteristic with which a person is born; a talent, a unique capacity, an aptitude. And it is a phenomenon conditioned by certain social and economic circumstances which foster the developing of talent, and through study and practice.

From another perspective, creativity is viewed as an attitude rather than an aptitude; as a cognitive, stylistic or motivational mode of interacting with one's environment. In this case, the stress is on characterological qualities, on personality rather than achievement, on expressive or being qualities rather than on problem solving or product making qualities. Erich Fromm (*12*) suggests that creativity is shown if the individual has made something new and satisfying to himself or if he has related things in his experience not previously related and finds the product exciting and satisfying. In this context creativity is a character trait. It may become a style of life. It is an attitude every human being can achieve.

For those in education seeking a functional developmental understanding of creativity, there is provocative promise in the theories which deal with creativity as an attitude.

In his study of self actualizing people, those people who are making the fullest use of their potentialities, Abraham Maslow (*16*) differentiates between "special talent creativeness" and "self actualizing creativeness." He says, "This view discourages the either-or-none approach now so widespread and which amounts to a dichotomous separation of the creative from the noncreative; those who are, from those who are not." Maslow sees some degree of creativity in every person, even if only as a suppressed potential and asks: Why was it lost? How much is left? How much can be recovered? He further suggests that such a concept is stimulating for those who are interested in teaching. To be relieved of pointing to a tangible product when we talk about creativity is refreshing. The realization that we all have something to start with, if only from having once been children is encouraging.

WHAT IS THIS CREATIVE ATTITUDE?

One of the most striking characteristics of the creative person has been identified by various researchers as "openness to experience." Rollo May (*20*) defines creativity as "the encounter of the intensively conscious human being with his world." Increasingly, recent studies of highly creative individuals in a variety of fields emphasize the importance of being sensitive, of being open, aware of environmental stimuli; an openness which fosters a keen awareness of reality within and without. Carl Rogers (22) has expressed it in this fashion: "I find such a person to be sensitively open to all of his experience—sensitive to what is going on in his environment; sensitive to other individuals with whom he is in relationship and sensitive perhaps most of all, to the feeling, reactions and emergent meanings which he discovers in himself." Some authors have suggested that a basic goal of education must be the production of increased openness.

The attitude of openness is well illustrated by Theodore Geisel in one of his Dr. Seuss series, "On Beyond Zebra" (9). Here we find the following dialogue: "So now," says the first character, "I know everything anyone knows from beginning to end, from the start to the close, because Z is as far as the alphabet goes." His friend responds, "You can stop if you want with the Z because most people stop with the Z but not me . . . You'll be sort of surprised what there is to be found once you go beyond Z and start poking around." Many of us tend to be like the first person in this story, having restricted our ability to be aware and to respond.

CREATIVITY A UNIVERSAL CHARACTERISTIC

In recent years, more and more psychologists have been proposing the existence within each individual of an essentially biologically based inner nature propelling him toward growth, toward developing to the full stature of which one is capable. Abraham Maslow (18), one of the more eloquent proponents of this idea, has suggested that the need to know, the need to understand is profoundly rooted in man's biological nature. He identifies as forces which propel the individual toward greater knowledge and understanding, the satisfaction of sheer curiosity, sheer inquisitiveness, the craving for understanding. Inquiry appears to be a natural and rewarding activity for man.

There is considerable agreement among a number of writers too that everyone is born with a high endowment of awareness; the creative attitude seems to have been built into the species. The idea is repeatedly expressed that we are dealing with a fundamental characteristic inherent in human nature, a potentiality given to all or most human beings at birth but which often is lost or buried or inhibited as the person becomes enculturated. All of us have observed the eagerness with which happy and secure children start school—their curiosity, their capacity for wonder and puzzlement, their imagination; their sensitivity to and fascination with the world in which they live. One need but watch a group of kindergarten children in action to perceive the living proof of this. Apparently, it would seem, we all begin with the spontaneous, effortless, easy kind of freedom of perception and uninhibited expressiveness which are important ingredients of creativity. In the 1962 ASCD Yearbook (*4*) the authors state: "Creativity is in each of us . . . This idea is comforting in that it gives us a measure of hope as we work with individuals; it is disturbing in that it points up how much we have yet to learn about this intangible and illusive phenomenon."

Harold Anderson (*3*), in his book, *Creativity and Its Cultivation,* says: "In children, creativity is a universal; among adults it is almost nonexistent. The great question is: What has happened to this enormous and universal human resource? This is the question and the quest of our age."

Through research we are learning more about the experiences that dull curiosity and the freshness of approach which appears to be a universal attribute of all children. We are learning more about conditions which rigidify human experience and inhibit an individual's freedom to be and to express his deeper self. We are becoming more aware of the conditions restricting openness to experience, of circumstances which increase the individual's lack of trust in himself and discourage him from being different, from daring to change or to venture forth. We are learning what contributes to freedom from threat, to attitudes that value innovation and change, to a willingness *to be* and *to become*. Increasingly, research is beginning to provide some answers.

STUDIES FOCUSING ON COGNITIVE STYLE

Researches focused on cognitive style have led to fruitful observations. Individual differences in ways of perceiving have been a topic of study for some time but only since the second world war have we recognized that the perceptual style of an individual is closely related to his personality. Each of us through the vagaries of chance and the determining influence of personal experience develops a distinctive pattern of enduring dispositions to respond to people and to events in a characteristic way.

One researcher (*15*), investigating perceptual style, has identified a type of individual he calls a *leveler*. A leveler is one who holds tightly to his categories of perception, who tends to over generalize from past experience and to emit the same response when he perceives a new stimulus substantially equivalent to an earlier one. Having had experience with one dog, he reacts to encounters with other dogs in the same fashion. The leveler has difficulty judging new persons and new events independently of similarities to past encounters. This sort of person has been compared to another type referred to as the *sharpener*. The sharpener is more adventurous in coping with environmental data, is alert to change and responds to fine nuances and small differences. He tends to exaggerate change.

A related concept is suggested by another researcher (*21*) who distinguishes between the "percept-bound" and the "concept-bound" individual. The percept-bound individual tests theory against experience and revises theory to conform with experience for which theory does not account. The concept bound tests experience against his theory and rejects those experiences that do not fit the theory. This notion suggests that tendencies toward being concept-bound which exist within us may inhibit our ability to be open to unusual perceptions in what we see and thus may reduce our ability to be creative. Being percept-bound, on the other hand, implies openness; that is, a person who responds in an unstructured way before he tries to theorize or to interpret.

Still another writer (*10*) makes the distinction between *repressers* and *intellectualizers*. The former play safe by keeping strictly within the field and by excluding adventuresome perceptions and judgments. The latter are able to detach themselves from the field and make bolder judgments suited to the objective demands of the situation.

An elaborate series of experiments designed to explore the relationship between personality factors and perceptual processes has been conducted by H. A. Witkin and his associates (*31*). These experimenters designed a number of perceptual tasks on which they could measure their subjects' performance. Then perceptual performance was related to data from an array of personality tests.

The ingenious perceptual tasks designed for research involved, for the most part, problems of the relationship between the person and his perceptual field. The experimental subject was asked, for example, to sit in a gray room with walls outlined in white; while in this unstructured situation the subject's chair would be tilted or the whole room would be tilted. The subject was asked to judge when his body was upright by reacting to cues from his own body and ignoring the sometimes confusing visual cues. Another task involved the ability to see a figure that was embedded in another figure. The primary dimension of these perceptual performances was the subject's ability to respond to segments of the total perceptual experience rather than to the total perceptual field. As the result of these experiments, Witkin identified two perceptual styles: the *field dependent* subject who could not easily, for example, see the embedded figure or report accurately on his uprightness in a visually tilted world, and the *field independent* observer who could do so.

The field dependent perceiver and the field independent perceiver differed with respect to a number of personality variables. Among these were the following: field dependent perceivers tended to be more passive, dependent and submissive; field dependent subjects showed more fear of their own sexual and aggressive impulses as well as more anxiety in general; field dependent subjects also showed lower self esteem and less self acceptance.

Conducting similar experiments with children Witkin discovered that the organization of the personality of the field independent child is more complex. This child usually has a more definite sense of his role and status in the family. He tends to be more aware of his own needs and attributes and also of the needs and attributes of others. In terms of his age group he is usually able to function with greater independence in a variety of situations. The defenses and controls he has available to channel his impulses and direct his actions are generally better developed. More often than his field dependent contemporaries, he shows a desire and a capacity for active striving in dealing with his environment. His interests tend to be both wider and better developed.

One of the most concerted research efforts in the field of creativity is the work of a group of psychologists at the Institute for Personality Assessment and Research at the University of California (6). As part of their research they report that in the cognitive spheres the creative individuals studied tend to be more flexible and fluent; their perceptions and cognitions are unique; in approach to problems they are intuitive, empathic, perceptually open. They prefer complexity, that is, they have a strong desire to turn disorder into meaning, to accept innovation and the challenge presented by apparent imperfection.

STUDIES FOCUSING ON ATTITUDES

Social psychological research studies on attitude formation yield valuable insights about characteristics related to creativity. The actions of an individual are governed, to a large extent, by his attitudes. What the individual sees is influenced by what he takes for granted. Creativity requires the ability to make good observations. Unless one is aware of his assumptions he cannot be expected to make good observations or to interpret them correctly. He may, therefore, miss the clues that might lead to a new discovery. Since beliefs and attitudes play such a prominent and significant role it is essential that attitude formation be considered in an analysis of creative thinking.

An extensive study of the relation between attitudes and personality dynamics is the research on the "Authoritarian Personality" and the studies that followed it. The concept of the "Authoritarian Personality" has been most influentially developed by Adorno and his associates (1). During World War II, a group of investigators at the University of California at Berkeley attacked the problem of race prejudice believing that any answers which might be provided about its origins and social development would be useful in understanding some of the roots of antisemitism and Naziism. Their investigations of race prejudice, most particularly of prejudice against Jews and Negroes, led them to theories about personality that are much broader than the ideas of prejudice with which they began. Despite some methodological weaknesses the work on the Authoritarian Personality is an impressive achievement.

Highly prejudiced persons, it was found, share many characteristics in common. This combination of personality traits has been referred to as the "Authoritarian Personality," a personality syndrome which includes the following: rigidity and inflexibility, concreteness of thinking, an inability to handle abstractions easily; conforming and conventional behavior. The authoritarian person is generally unwilling to examine his own thoughts and is disinclined to be introspective; he places an extreme emphasis on masculinity and femininity; he is hostile and prejudiced toward groups other than his own; prefers absolutes—black and white, he does not like to deal with shades of gray; he cannot tolerate ambiguity; he tends to have a rigid conscience.

The evidence from this research reveals that a person who is insecure, distrustful of self—who feels threatened by life, or otherwise inadequate, tends to have a cognitive style which is rigid, concrete and acquiescent. By contrast, the more active, able, secure, relaxed individual is able to perceive and think in ways that are flexible and is on the whole better adapted to the objective demands of the situation in which he finds himself.

The characteristics of the authoritarian personality are the antithesis of the creative attitude we seek. Creative behavior is characterized by variety and richness of perception. Whatever produces narrowness and rigidity becomes an important factor in limiting creativity. Attitudes that characterize authoritarianism seem representative of a range of social beliefs and predispositions that children develop, beliefs that influence their behavior and are related to the development of the creative attitude.

Another contribution from the social-psychological literature is the research conducted by Richard Crutchfield (7) on conformity and character. Using an interesting research design, Crutchfield has identified individuals who reveal high conforming behavior and those whose behavior could be characterized as independent or nonconforming. Persons exhibiting extreme independence of behavior seem to have these characteristics: intellectual effectiveness, ego strength, leadership ability, maturity of social relations together with a conspicuous absence of inferiority feelings, rigid and excessive self control and authoritarian attitudes. They are self reliant, independent in judgment, and able to think for themselves. In sharp contrast to this picture of independent men is the following description of those high in conforming behavior: a narrow range of interests, submissiveness, compliance, overacceptance of authority, conformity, tendency to do the things that are prescribed, overcontrol of impulses, inhibitedness and needless delay or denial of gratification. Highly conforming individuals are unable to make decisions without vacillations or delay, become confused, disorganized and unadaptive under stress, are suggestible, overly responsive to other people's evaluations rather than their own and lack insight into their own motives and behavior.

These findings have interesting implications for those trying to understand the creative attitude. It is evident that conformity and creativity are essentially antithetical—what produces one tends to destroy the other. Conformity restricts freedom, experimentation, expression and facilitation.

Other relevant studies are those of Rokeach (*24*) and Frenkel-Brunswik (*11*). Rokeach reports his work in a volume entitled "The Open and Closed Mind." He suggests that closed mindedness is a general personality trait related to the ability to form new cognitive systems of various kinds—perceptual, conceptual, aesthetic. To measure this variable, he has developed a Dogmatism Scale as a measure of the extent to which the mind is an open or a closed one. Closed mindedness is said to be characterized by a high magnitude of rejection of opposing beliefs, a dogmatic orientation and a belief system closed to new ideas and resistant to change. The more closed the mind, the more cognitions depend upon irrelevant wants and external authority. Rokeach found that the open-minded group was significantly superior to the closed-minded group in the time required to solve certain problems requiring analysis and synthesis. The greater ability of persons with open minds to solve these problems appear to reflect a greater willingness to entertain novel and strange problems. Emotional rejection of the problem was found more frequently among the persons with closed minds.

Frenkel-Brunswik proposed that some people find it difficult to tolerate or manage ambiguities, inconsistencies or surprises. Such people have a generalized tendency to dichotomize the world; things and people are seen as all good or all bad; the world is black or white. When faced with an ambiguous situation, they quickly fix on one concrete interpretation. This way of managing ambiguous situations is found to characterize much of their behavior and their cognitions of persons and objects, their interpersonal relations and their ways of coping with problems. People who are intolerant of ambiguity are relatively "closed" to new information which would increase the richness of their intellectual resources. Their cognitive palette contains only blacks and whites. Intolerant of ambiguity, they seek simplified good-evil solutions to complex social, political and economic issues.

STUDIES FOCUSING ON EMOTIONAL-MOTIVATIONAL DISPOSITIONS

Another provocative source of data related to creativity as an attitude are the writings concerning the self concept and self theory. Knowledge about the self is now sufficient to indicate principles that have practical significance for an understanding of creative behavior.

One of the conditions that affects creativity is the individual's personal feelings about himself. Each of us has a mental picture of himself which governs much of his conduct and outlook. When one has confidence and pride in his self image, he feels free to be and to express himself. But when this image is a source of shame the tendency is to hide it rather than to express it and creative expression is blocked.

An increasing literature describes creative behavior as an emergent characteristic which matures as the individual attempts to realize his fullest potential through his interaction with his environment. Elizabeth Drews (*8*) has emphasized the similarities between the cultivation of the creative attitude and the process through which psychologists say mental health is achieved. The literature on the fully functioning personality (*23*), the self actualizing personality (*17*), the adequate personality (*5*), the mature personality (*2*), the highly effective individual (*19*) is congruent with the literature on the creative personality. Growth and ego psychologists, mental hygienists, personality theorists, philosophers and biologists have supplied detailed descriptions of the mature, emergent, psychologically healthy personality. The similarity in findings from such sources suggests a significant fusion of thought about the psychologically mature and the creative personality.

VALUES AND THE CREATIVE ATTITUDE

Moving from comment on factors within the individual it is interesting to review what is reported about aspects of the culture which foster or inhibit creativity. What social pressures serve as punishments or rewards? What character traits are socially valued? One writer reminds us of Plato's admonition "What is honored in a country will be cultivated there."

One of the more fruitful of these inquiries is a study of values. From this M. I. Stein (*28*) suggests that society encourages creativity to the extent that its value system includes a positive regard for change and novelty. It discourages creativity to the extent that social pressures for conformity are so intense that deviations are punished directly or indirectly through social ostracism. He observes too that a culture fosters creativity to the extent that it encourages openness to internal and to external experience. An important factor then is a value system that prizes openness.

George Spindler (*27*), an educational sociologist from Stanford University, collecting data from several hundred students, most of them in his professional education courses, has attempted to find out what features of social character these students value by requiring each student to write a brief paragraph describing his conception of the "Ideal American Boy." A sentence content analysis revealed features ranked in the following order from the highest number of mentions, to the lowest. The Ideal American Boy should be sociable, like people and get along well with them; he must be popular, be liked by others; he is to be well rounded, he can do many things quite well, but is not an expert in anything in particular; he should be athletic (but not a star); he should be healthy; he should be ambitious to succeed, and have clear goals, but these must be acceptable within limited norms; he must be considerate of others, ever sensitive to their feelings about him and about events; he should be clean cut, moral and respectful of God and parents; he should be patriotic and he should demonstrate average academic ability and average intellectual capacity. It is interesting that in this list such characteristics as leadership, independence, high intelligence, high academic ability, individuality, creativity are mentioned relatively infrequently.

Spindler summarizes these results by stating: "The implications are clear. The keynote of the character type regarded as most desirable, and therefore constituting a complex of values, is balance, outward orientedness, sociability and conformity for the sake of adjustment.

Individuality, creativity or even mere originality are not stressed in this conception of values. Introspective behavior is devaluated. Deviancy, it seems, is to be tolerated only within the narrow limits of sociability, of general outwardness, of conformity. The All American Boy is altogether adjusted."

A more recent study of a similar nature has been conducted by Dr. E. P. Torrance (*29*) of the University of Minnesota attempting to examine the features of social character most valued by teachers. In an article entitled "The Creative Personality and the Ideal Pupil" he points to the considerable evidence that creative personalities tend to be estranged by their teachers and are not liked by them. This finding is similar to that of Getzels and Jackson (*14*) who found that teachers preferred students with high IQ's but with less outstanding scores on tests of creative thinking to those with outstanding creativity scores but with less outstanding intelligence quotients. The indications concerning the dislike of teachers for creative personalities led Torrance to study the kinds of concepts teachers have of the ideal pupil, since it is assumed that teachers consciously and unconsciously reward pupils in terms of their own ideals and are less able to free the creative capacities of their pupils if their own values do not support creativeness.

In approaching the task of finding out what teachers consider an ideal pupil, Torrance used a list of sixty-two characteristics of creative personalities as described in fifty empirical studies comparing the personality characteristics of creative individuals in some fields with less creative individuals in the same field. Putting these into a checklist form he requested teachers to indicate by a single check the characteristics they thought should be encouraged and by a double check the five characteristics deemed most important.

Of the sixty-two characteristics listed, Torrance found that consideration of others was ranked first by teachers. This may suggest one reason why teachers apparently do not prefer highly creative pupils since such pupils are frequently lacking in this trait. Does placing this trait at the top of the hierarchy of values reflect an over-emphasis on conformity, an extreme which could work against freeing creative abilities? We need to ponder this ideal of the good pupil.

Recently language as an aspect of culture has been a subject of increasing inquiry. This variable in the past received relatively little attention in our efforts to understand behavior. Philosophers, linguists, anthropologists have long been interested in the question: Does the language of a person influence the way he comes to perceive and understand his world? More than one hundred years ago, Von Humboldt stated that the structure of the language of a society influences the peoples' conception of the world. E. Sapir (*26*) has restated these early ideas in his classic formulation of language and culture: "Human beings do not live in the objective world alone, nor alone in the world of social activity as ordinarily understood, but are very much at the mercy of the particular language which has become the medium of expression for their society . . . We see and hear and otherwise experience very largely as we do because of the language habits of our community which predispose certain choices of interpretation."

Benjamin Whorf (*30*) has similarly suggested the thesis that people in different cultures perceive the world in basically different ways. "We are thus introduced to the new principle of relativity, which holds that all observers are not led by the same physical evidence to the same picture of the universe unless their linguistic backgrounds are similar."

This thesis advanced by Sapir and Whorf has by no means received universal acceptance. It remains, however, an interesting and important question. Although linguistic patterns may not inescapably limit sensory perceptions and thought as Whorf suggests, the structure of language does, it would appear, serve to make salient for the individual certain objects and events in his world. Together with other cultural patterns, language may direct perceptions into certain habitual channels and may restrict or facilitate the individual's ability to see new relationships.

In this paper I have attempted to review some of the research literature which has contributed to our developing insights concerning the creative attitude. If we are born with a capacity to respond perceptively and in very original ways, if creativity is built into the species and is a manifestation of an innate orientation of the organism, how can we help this general human potentiality develop and express itself rather than atrophy? In the 1962 Yearbook of the ASCD (*4*) the authors suggest that "Man will become the best that he can when we have found the ways to set him free." In order to proceed toward this goal we must examine what goes on in the process of seeing and responding. What makes the difference between the creative and the noncreative attitude? Leo Rosten (*25*) in a recent article in the Teachers College Record has characterized the nature of this quest: "To unlock the awesome power of the atom was nothing in my judgment compared to what will happen when we mortal men unlock the power of the beauty, the bearing, the infinite imaginativeness which still resides in secret untapped places within the human spirit."

REFERENCES

1. Adorno, T. W., Frenkel-Brunswik, Else, Levinson, D. J. and Sanford, R. N. *The Authoritarian Personality*. New York: Harper and Row, 1950.
2. Allport, G. W. *Pattern and Growth in Personality*. New York: Holt, Rinehart and Winston, 1961, pp. 275–310.
3. Anderson, H. Ed. *Creativity and Its Cultivation*. New York: Harper and Row, 1959, p. xii.
4. Association for Supervision and Curriculum Development, *Perceiving, Behaving, Becoming*. Washington, D. C.: Association for Supervision and Curriculum Development, 1962, p. 142.
5. Combs, A. W. and Donald Snygg. *Individual Behavior*. New York: Harper and Row, 1959, pp. 237–264.
6. Crutchfield, Richard. *The Creative Process, In Proceedings of Conference on The Creative Person*. Institute of Personality Assessment and Research, University of California, Berkeley, California, 1961, p. VI–14.
7. Crutchfield, Richard. *Conformity and Character*. American Psychologist, 10:191–198, 1955.
8. Drews, E. M. *The Development of Talent*. Teachers College Record, 65, No. 3:210–219, December, 1963.
9. Dr. Seuss. *On Beyond Zebra*. New York: Random House, 1955.
10. Eriksen, C. W. *The Case for Perceptual Defense*. Psychological Review 61:175–182, 1954.
11. Frenkel-Brunswik, Else. *Intolerance of Ambiguity as an Emotional and Perceptual Variable*. J. of Personality, 18:108–143, 1949.
12. Fromm, Erich. *The Creative Attitude*. In H. Anderson (Ed.), Creativity and Its Cultivation. New York: Harper and Row, 1959, p. 44.
13. Gamble, A. O. *Suggestions for Future Research*. In C. Taylor (Ed.), The 1959 University of Utah Research Conference on the Identification of Creative Scientific Talent. Salt Lake City: University of Utah Press, 1959, pp. 292–297.
14. Getzels, J. W. and Jackson, P. W. *Creativity and Intelligence*. New York: John Wiley and Sons, 1962.
15. Klein, G. S. *The Personal World Through Perception*. In Blake, R. R. and Ramsey, G. V. (Eds.), Perception, An Approach to Personality, New York: Ronald Press, 1951, pp. 328–355.
16. Maslow, A. H. *Creativity in Self Actualizing People*. In H. Anderson (Ed.), Creativity and Its Cultivation, New York: Harper and Row, 1959, p. 94.
17. Maslow, A. H. *Self Actualizing People: A Study of Psychological Health*. In Moustakas, C. E. (Ed.), The Self. New York: Harper and Row, 1956, pp. 160–194.
18. Maslow, A. H. *Toward a Psychology of Being*. New Jersey: D. Van Nostrand Company, 1962, p. 21.
19. MacKinnon, D. W. *The Highly Effective Individual*. Teachers College Record 61:367–378, 1962.
20. May, Rollo. *The Nature of Creativity*. In H. Anderson (Ed.), Creativity and Its Cultivation. New York: Harper and Row, 1959, p. 68.
21. Pepinsky, H. B. *Cogito, ergo . . .* Journal of Counseling Psychology, 2:285–289, 1955.

22. Rogers, Carl. *Toward Becoming a Fully Functioning Person*. In Association for Supervision and Curriculum Development 1962 Yearbook, p. 31.
23. Rogers, Carl. *On Becoming a Person*. Cambridge, Massachusetts: The Riverside Press, 1961, pp. 183–199.
24. Rokeach, M. *The Open and Closed Mind*. New York: Basic Books, 1960.
25. Rosten, Leo. *The Creative Idea*. Teachers College Record :637–646, 1963.
26. Sapir, E. *The Status of Linguistics as a Science*. Language, 5:207–214, 1929.
27. Spindler, George. *Education in a Transforming American Culture*. In G. Spindler (Ed.), Education and Culture. New York: Holt, Rinehart and Winston, 1963, pp. 132–147.
28. Stein, M. I. *Creativity and Culture*. Journal of Psychology, 36:311–22, 1953.
29. Torrance, E. P. *The Creative Personality and the Ideal Pupil*. Teachers College Record, 63 (No. 3):220–226, December, 1963.
30. Whorf, Benjamin L. in J. B. Carrol (Ed.), *Language, Thought and Reality*. New York: John Wiley and Sons, 1956.
31. Witkin, H. A. et. al. *Personality Through Perception: An Experimental and Clinical Study*. New York: Harper and Row, 1954.

Give the "Devil" His Dues

E. Paul Torrance

RESEARCH HAS SHOWN REPEATEDLY THAT PEOPLE TEND TO LEARN AND develop along whatever lines they find rewarding. I had long been aware of the unfortunate consequences which occur in some schools where almost all of the rewards go to the talented athlete—or to the scholar, or to the lady's man. James Coleman's *Adolescent Society* (1961) has recently documented this observation.

It took the tragedy written into the imaginative stories of elementary school children to awaken me to the dangers of rewarding any one kind of talent, rather than rewarding a variety of talents. There was the story of the monkey that could fly but couldn't climb a tree. He was laughed at, ridiculed, and badgered because he couldn't climb, but no one gave him credit for his ability to fly. Great relief came to him when he was frightened out of his ability to fly—"people didn't call him names anymore." There was the tragic story of another flying monkey. He and his family were all ridiculed too, even though this flying monkey obtained all of the good bananas for the other monkeys. In desperation, he finally learned to hide his wings and refused to use them, except to get the best bananas for the other monkeys. For spite,

REPRINTED by permission of the Author and *Gifted Child Quarterly*, 5:115–8, Winter, 1961.

he refused to do even this, at times. Then there was the little lion, Ollie, who was regarded by his father as a complete failure because he could not roar; he could only purr. He could do many clever tricks, but he could never be the success that his loud-roaring brother, Leo, Jr. was.

The tragedy of rewarding only certain talents rather than a variety of equally valuable or more valuable ones has struck me with even greater force as I have received letters from hundreds of parents of creative children, high school students, and creative adults. There was the case of a boy who at four or five asked such mature and penetrating questions and gave such brilliant answers that he was frequently taken by strangers to be in the third or fourth grade. Now, at thirteen he is suspected of being mentally retarded. Some of the trouble started his first year in school when he wanted to change the drawings his teacher gave him to color or to add things like hats, boots, and the like to the teacher's drawings. A nursery schooler is in trouble now because he insisted on coloring his horse with stripes like the "Z-horse" he had seen at a zoo. All of the others had painted theirs brown, like a horse ought to be. There was the high school senior who wrote that during her first two years of high school she expressed her ideas, was contradicted, ridiculed, humiliated, and given poor grades. In her junior year, she decided to keep her mouth shut, stop thinking independently, and agree with the majority. Her junior and senior grades have been excellent but she is afraid that her grade-point average is still not high enough for admission to a good college. Thus, she feels that she has cheated herself and that she has been cheated.

WHAT TO DO ABOUT LITTLE BOYS

While the rewarding of a variety of talents might be useful in solving a number of different educational problems, I believe it is clearly involved in the perrenial problem, "what shall we do about the boys?" One educator (Maxwell, 1960) recently advocated that boys be kept out of school a year or two longer than girls. He supported his recommendation by the citation of evidence that girls are the superior of boys in practically every area of development until they are well in their teens, specifically mentioning handwriting, verbal expression, vocabulary, muscular control, reading, and written composition.

In spite of this gloomy picture for boys, my associates and I find that boys in the early school years are superior to girls in their development in some important ways. These differences are in the ability to think independently, constructively, creatively.

From first through third grade, boys become increasingly superior to girls in almost all of the creative thinking abilities for which we have devised measures. (These abilities include: ideational fluency, flexibility, originality, inventiveness, constructiveness, ability to ask questions, and ability to formulate hypotheses about consequences. Scores are based on a variety of tasks, both verbal and non-verbal.) By the fourth grade, however, boys begin losing their battle against conformity to behavioral norms and show a sharp measured decrement in most of these abilities.

These differences in favor of boys emerge even when stimuli inappropriate to the sex role of boys are used. For example, in one experiment three toys were used: a nurse's kit, a fire truck, and a dog. At the first grade level, girls produced more ideas than boys for improving the nurse's kit so that it would be "more fun to play with." Some of the boys stubbornly refused to think up any ideas for improving the nurse's kit, while others first changed it to a doctor's kit and then suggested improvements. Boys produced more ideas than girls for improving the fire truck and there was scant difference between boys and girls on the dog task. By the third grade, however, boys were clearly superior to girls on this task, both in the quantity and quality (flexibility, constructiveness, originality, etc.) of their ideas for improving all of the toys, including the nurse's kit.

One clue to the superiority of boys over girls on tasks of this kind is the greater manipulativeness of boys. It was found that the degree of manipulation exhibited during the test is related to the number and quality of the ideas produced. This tendency to manipulate, to explore, to experiment, appears also to be involved in invention and scientific discovery.

The superiority of boys over girls was also shown in a group task involving experimentation with science toys. Each group, composed of five members (two boys and three girls or vice versa), was confronted with the task of discovering in the first thirty minutes how many things these toys could be made to do and then in a second thirty-minute period to demonstrate and explain their discoveries. At almost every grade level from second through sixth boys demonstrated and explained more principles than girls. At the fifth grade level, girls initiated as many ideas as boys but explained significantly fewer principles than the boys.

At the same time that boys are becoming increasingly more inventive and curious between the first and third grades, peer pressures against boys with clever and original ideas are increasing. Girls appear to learn earlier than boys how to gain peer acceptance of their ideas and to avoid being labeled as having "silly" or "crazy" ideas. For example, highly creative boys received about four times as many peer nominations as girls on such criteria as: "Who in your class has the most silly or wild ideas? Who in your class has the most ideas for being naughty?" Highly creative boys also tend to have a reputation among their teachers for having "a lot of wild ideas" but highly creative girls do not gain such a reputation. This opinion may stem from the fact that highly creative boys exhibit more uniqueness, inventiveness, and originality in their drawings and other productions than do highly creative girls. Highly creative boys compared with highly creative girls also tend to be less accessible psychologically and to have more internal tension.

From the evidence accumulated in the Minnesota Studies of Creative Thinking in the Early School Years it seems that much in our present educational system tends to alienate boys, especially the highly creative ones, from their peers and teachers. Educators might do well to consider giving parallel treatment to the development of the thinking abilities (both creative and evaluative) along with the development of the memory and conformity to behavioral norms. This would involve, among other things, rewarding creative thinking. If boys in the early school years were rewarded for some of the things in which they appear to excel, they might possibly be more willing to master some of the language and other conforming skills about which there is concern. Why not give the "devil" his due?

Is it necessary to retard the mental development of boys by keeping them out of school a year or more longer until they can be coerced into greater conformity? Why not reward the creative thinking of both boys and girls and thereby encourage the healthy development of all of their mental abilities?

REWARDING CREATIVE THINKING

The problem of rewarding thinking is indeed a difficult one. I would like to suggest the following six principles which I believe that both parents and teachers can learn to apply.

Be Respectful of Unusual Questions. The first principle is: "Be respectful of unusual questions." Nothing is more rewarding to a child who asks questions than to find the answer to his questions. Questions reflect a "mind hunger" and this hunger must be satisfied lest the mind be starved. Although the need should be met immediately, there is much that we can do to enrich the period between the question and the answer. This means that we need to teach them the skills of inquiry.

Children need to learn how to sustain a question, to play with it, toss it back and forth, refine it, and accept the questioning mood without the need for ready-made answers from the teacher or parent.

The parent or teacher who sets out to be respectful of the questions children ask must be prepared for some shocks. Children will ask many questions which they cannot answer. This should be accepted as normal and desirable. Teachers and parents should not feel threatened and should find enjoyment in a mutual searching for solutions to the questions children raise. They should not be afraid to let children guess, but to let them guess and learn to test their guesses. This, however, calls for a second principle.

Be Respectful of the Unusual Ideas of Children. This second principle is: "Be respectful of the unusual ideas of children." Children who are stimulated by the creative approach will see many relationships and significances that their teachers miss. They will express ideas which their teachers will not be able to evaluate. Thus, it is extremely difficult for the teacher properly to reward such thinking and it is our more creatively talented youngsters who suffer most such unrewarded effort.

A workshop group recently criticized this principle, suggesting that it should be changed to read: "Stimulate unusual or original ideas." I would reiterate, however, that we should not stimulate such thinking unless we can be respectful of it. Certainly we shall not continue to elicit such thinking, if we do not respect it.

Show Children That Their Ideas Have Value. The third principle is: "Show children that their ideas have value." The trouble is that many teachers and other adults do not feel that children are capable of thinking of ideas that have value. Such individuals obviously will not be able to reward creative thinking in children. I would only suggest that such individuals be on the alert for a while to recognize new ideas among children. Children can be shown that their ideas have value, if we communicate them to proper groups or individuals, if we display them, if we give credit for them, and the like. There is also the matter of intrinsic rewards. We had said much about the role of reward and punishment in learning, but little about the lure of discovery and the role of curiosity and interest. This is the area where rewards have been neglected.

Provide Opportunities For Self-Initiated Learning and Give Credit For It. And old principle of learning is: "Excite and direct the self-activities of the learner, and tell him nothing that he can learn for himself." One mark of the highly creative individual is his self-starting ability. The strong curiosity of the child and his exploratory tendencies suggest that all or almost all children have this self-starting ability. The problem of parents and teachers is to keep it alive. It is hindered, however, by overly detailed supervision. It is quite possible that too much reliance is placed upon prescribed curriculum and that we need to make more effort to appraise and credit growth resulting from the student's own initiative.

Provide for Periods of Non-Evaluated Practice or Learning. We do not have to evaluate everything. There needs to be periods when the individual can learn without threats of being evaluated. External evaluation is always a threat and creates a need for defensiveness. This makes some portion of the individual's experiencing or sensing denied to awareness. Thus, there is lacking the openness which is so necessary in the production of new ideas. We have conducted experiments to try to validate this principle. We find consistent validation for it in the first, second, and third grades. In a one-hour laboratory-type task, however, we did not obtain the expected results in the fourth, fifth and sixth grades. It may be that by the time a child reaches the fourth grade, he is so conditioned to being evaluated and is so dependent upon external evaluation that he is not released by being told that the initial learning and exploratory phase is "off the records." I believe that it would have to be demonstrated to these older children that the practice really was "off the record," before they would respond to the non-evaluative condition.

CONCLUSION

In conclusion, I would like to remind you of a statement made long ago by that famous teacher, Plato: "WHAT IS HONORED IN A COUNTRY WILL BE CULTIVATED THERE." Thus, if children are to be challenged to learn and think creatively, we must honor this kind of achievement. A healthy society and a humane kind of education, however, requires that we honor all of those kinds of talent which contribute to our welfare.

REFERENCES

1. Coleman, J. S. *Adolescent Society.* New York: Free Press, 1961. 358p.
2. Maxwell, J. "What to do about the Boys?" *NEA Journal,* March, 1960.
3. Torrence, E. P. *Guiding Creative Talent.* Englewood Cliffs, N. J.: Prentice-Hall, in press.

Annotated Bibliography

Barron, F. "Creative Vision and Expression." (pp. 285–305) in *New Insights and the Curriculum.* 1963 Yearbook. (Edited by A. Frazier.) Washington, D. C.: Association for Supervision and Curriculum Development, a department of the National Education Association, 1963b.

Excerpts from Barron's book: In summary, the creative person is more comfortable with disorder, and more challenged to find a subtle way of reordering. He is also more independent in judgment. They are more troubled about the world and have more resources for dealing with their troubles. Last, creative writers and artists are moved by an intense commitment that impels them to seek for new forms of artistic vision.

Barron, F. "The Needs for Order and for Disorder as Motives in Creative Activity." (pp. 153–62) in Taylor, C. W., and Barron, F., editors. *Scientific Creativity: Its Recognition and Development.* New York: John Wiley and Sons, 1963a.

Creative people are more observant, they point to the unrecognized, they see and value things as others do not. Their world is more complex, they are healthier and have more available energy. They are more open to impulse and fantasy. They can "regress in the service of the ego."

Drews, Elizabeth, and Montgomery, Susan. "Creative and Academic Performance in Gifted Adolescents." *High School Journal* 48: 94–101; November 1964.

A description of creative and academic performance in various types of gifted adolescents. Gives scores of groups on omnibus personality inventory.

Drews, Elizabeth. "Profile of Creativity." *NEA Journal* 52: 1: 26–28; January 1963.

Reactions of a thousand students revealed that we need to accept and value creative behavior of students and supply them with challenging experiences.

Drevdahl, J. E. "Some Developmental and Environmental Factors in Creativity." (pp. 170–86) in Taylor, C. W., editor. *Widening Horizons in Creativity.* New York: John Wiley and Sons, 1964.

An investigation of creative vs. non-creative psychologists using Cattell's personality tests and biographical data. On the 16 P.F. questionnaire the creative group was lower on factors E, F, H and higher on G and N than the non-creative productive group; it was higher on H, O and 4 and lower on M than the non-creative, non-productive group.

Ehrenzweig, A. "The Creative Surrender." *American Imago* 14: 193–210; 1957.

The creative use of imagery depends on a flexible ego rhythm swinging between widely distant levels. Marion Milner (Joanna Field: *An Experiment in Leisure*) believes that the first stage in the creative process is a temporary giving up of discriminating ego which tries to see things objectively and rationally. Then the way to "oceanic undifferentiation" is open. Imagery loses its precise definition and sharp boundaries and "merges with other images into new symbolic equations." As the ego rhythm rebounds, the image recrystallizes and reassumes an independent existence. There is a distinctly manic quality to the creative surrender. 18 references.

Ghiselin, B., and others. "A Creative Process Check List: Its Development and Validation." (pp. 19–33) in Taylor, C. W., editor. *Widening Horizons in Creativity*. New York: John Wiley and Sons, 1964.

Describes development of a check list of attention and feeling on part of creative scientists, and appears to have validity.

Gowan, J. C., and Torrance, E. P. "An Intercultural Study of Nonverbal Ideational Fluency." Paper read at the Los Angeles Convention of the American Psychological Association, 1964.

Torrance nonverbal creativity tests were administered in English, Chinese, Malay and Tamil, and ideational fluency results are given by race, grade, stream, and vernacular. Students taught in English were less creative than others taught in their vernacular.

Herr, E. L., Moore, G. D. and Hansen, J. C. "Creativity Intelligence and Values: A Study of Relationships" (mimeo.) State University of New York at Buffalo, 1965.

Report of a test battery given to 60 talented high school juniors in a summer science institute found very few correlations of creativity measures with the Kuder Preference Record, Allport-Vernon Study of Values, Terman Concept Mastery Test, Watson-Glaser Critical Thinking Appraisal or Lorge-Thorndike. Guilford Ideational Fluency correlated .27 with Lorge-Thorndike. The AC Spark Plug Test of Creativity correlated .54 with the Lorge-Thorndike, .53 with the Terman Concept Mastery, and .24 with the Watson-Glaser. None of the creativity ratings correlated with teachers' estimates.

Holland, J. L. "Creative and Academic Performance Among Talented Adolescents." *Journal of Educational Psychology* 52: 136–47; 1961.

An exploration of the nature of academic achievement and creative behavior in adolescents and young adults. Academic performance appears to be the function of a personal syndrome characterized by: perserverance, self-control, good behavior, rigidity. Creative performance seems to be the outcome of a conscious conception of being original, actively participating in creative hobbies. Academic achievement involves different motives than does creative performance.

MacKinnon, D. W. "The Highly Effective Individual." *Teachers College Record* 61: 367–78; April 1960. (Cf. *Current Issues in Higher Education.* Washington, D. C.: National Education Association, 1961.)

The creative person is open to experience, often struggling to reconcile opposites in his nature, striving to tolerate increasingly large amounts of tension as he seeks solutions to problems he has set for himself.

MacKinnon, D. W. "What Makes a Person Creative?" *Saturday Review* 45: 15–17ff; February 10, 1962.

". . . it is high level of reflective intelligence, his openness to experience, his freedom from crippling restraints and impoverishing inhibitions, his esthetic sensitivity, his cognitive flexibility, his independence in thought and action, his high level of creative energy, his unquestioning commitment to creative endeavor, and his unceasing striving for solutions to ever more difficult problems. . . ."

Mackler, B. "Creativity and Life Style." Ed.D. thesis, Lawrence: University of Kansas, 1962. *Dissertation Abstracts* 24: 5571; 1964.

Five life style groups of 12 coeds (art majors, dance majors, visually disabled, physically disabled, and control) could be discriminated by Torrance Creativity Tests. Environmental manipulation also appeared to affect creativity.

Maw, W. H. and Ethel. *Personal and Social Variables Differentiating Children with High and Low Curiosity.* (Cooperative Research Project No. 1511). Newark, Del.: University of Delaware, 1965.

This booklet of 162 pages plus a 232 item bibliography represents the long awaited definitive report on curiosity by the Maws, who have for some time been interested in this subject. There are five sections to the report: (1) Purpose and Procedures, (2) Review of the Literature, (3) Measuring Instruments and Procedures, (4) Analysis of Results, and (5) Summary and Conclusions. The sample of children included about 200 girls and 200 boys with median IQ of 112 from the 5th grade of the Newark schools. The study sought the answer to the question: "Do high-curiosity children differ from low-curiosity children in personality, in social relations and in family backgrounds?"

Results indicated that high-curiosity children when compared with low-curiosity children (1) have a greater level of self-acceptance, (2) are more self sufficient, (3) tend to feel more secure, (4) tend to be more creative, flexible and consistent, (5) tend to be more dependable, (6) are more often identified as square-shooters, (7) show a higher level of group loyalty, (8) exhibit more healthy participation in group activities, (9) are more responsible for group welfare, and (10) show a better over-all social adjustment.

High-curiosity boys differ from high-curiosity girls on many personal and social variables. It appears that early environment is different and perhaps more important for boys than for girls.

High-curiosity boys when compared with low-curiosity boys (1) show a higer level of emotional maturity, and (2) a higher level of social skill. They feel that their discipline is more fair, and they are better in over-all social adjustment.

High-curiosity girls when compared with low-curiosity girls have a higher level of aspiration and a higher degree of responsibility.

Since it is evident that the development of curiosity in children is akin to training in divergent thinking and creativity, much interest has attached to the investigations of the Maws. It appears that the preservation of curiosity in children is a function of good child rearing practices which leave the child emotionally secure and well-adjusted socially; but it also seems that there are significant differences with respect to the rearing of girls and boys. It may well be that some of these differences stem from the opposite-sexed parent's relations with the child, a relationship which is often deeper between boys and their mothers than between girls and their fathers. It may also be that the good home performs other complex chores in making the child curiosity-oriented. Indeed, as the authors indicate, the study generates a number of questions which only future research can answer.

McGuire, C. *Creativity and Emotionality*. Report No. 12. Austin: University of Texas, Laboratory of Human Behavior, Department of Educational Psychology, 1962.

Eleven-page research on the relationship between creativity and emotionality. Ten "factors-in-persons" and three dimensions of personality are discussed.

McGuire, C. *Personality Correlates of Creativity*. Report No. 13. Austin: University of Texas, Laboratory of Human Behavior, Department of Educational Psychology, 1963.

Postulates that divergent thinking acts as catalyst to drive person to employ abilities, acquire new expectations, cope with pressures, produce creative or talented performances. Curiosity and need achievement are also catalysts. Three personality dimensions significant to mental health are (1) relaxed outgoing optimism, (2) creatively intelligent autonomy, (3) self-disciplined stability.

Myden, W. "Interpretation and Evaluation of Certain Personality Characteristics Involved in Creative Production." *Perceptual Motor Skills* 9: 139–58; 1959. (Cf. *Dissertation Abstracts* 17: 897–98; 1957.)

Rorschach protocols of 20 artists vs. 20 business leaders led to characterization of artist as a person of superior intelligence who functions close to his potential. He is intellectually oriented to the outer world, with a rich inner life. Results support Freud's notion that creative persons have easier access to primary process, less repression and more available psychological energy.

Newell, A., and others. "The Process of Creative Thinking." (pp. 63–119) in Gruber, H. E., et al., editors. *Contemporary Approaches to Creative Thinking.* New York: Atherton Press, 1963.

Creative activity appears to be a special case of problem solving characterized by novelty, unconventionality, persistence, and difficulty.

Discusses the logical heuristics of problem solving and planning applicable to computer functioning. This development is then used to elucidate (a) the use of imagery in problem solving, (b) the relation of unconventionality to creativity, and (c) the role of hindsight in the discovery of new heuristics.

Nydes, J. "Creativity and Psychotherapy." *Psychoanalytic Review* 49: 29–33; 1962.

"The truly creative seem to have the capacity to tolerate and override anxiety, to integrate and admit into awareness an unusual depth and intensity of conflicting reality without being overwhelmed by panic or losing touch with reality." Creativity may be both a constructive way of resolving inner conflict and a reaction against an unhappy, neurotic adjustment. The true creative artist achieves insulation from competitiveness by engaging in unconscious competition with an ego-ideal of his own choice.

Olshin, G. M. "The Relationship Among Selected Subject Variables and Level of Creativity." Unpublished Ed.D. thesis, Athens: University of Georgia, 1963. *Dissertation Abstracts* 24: 2365; 1964.

Analysis of relation of intelligence, age, and sex to creativity level finds the first two related, but not the third.

Pogue, Betty Caskey. *A Study to Determine Whether or Not There Is a Relationship between Creativity and Self-Image.* Unp. Ed.D. thesis. Muncie, Indiana: Ball State University, 1964.

Research concerned the relationship of creativity, self-esteem, and race, and their relationships to IQ, sex, socioeconomic status, and classroom performance. Tests given were the Incomplete Figures and Circles of the Minnesota Tests of Creative Thinking, the Draw-A-Person Test, and the Coopersmith Self-Esteem Inventory. A total of 263 students, half white, and half Negro, in grades four to six of a Muncie school were used as subjects.

Relationship was found between creativity and IQ, self-esteem, socioeconomic status, and the classroom experiences of students under different teachers. No relation was found between creativity and race, grade or sex.

Rutherford, J. M. "Personality Correlates of Creativity." *Dissertation Abstracts* 20: 4434; 1960.

Three characteristics of creativity are: (1) ability to differentiate various aspects of the problem, (2) openness of the self to experience, and (3) self-strength.

Spector, N. "Factorial Dimensions of Creativity." Unpublished Ed.D. thesis, Austin: University of Texas, 1963. *Dissertation Abstracts* 24: 2980; 1964.

Factor analyses on creative vs. non-creative 7th graders as measured by tests of divergent thinking established in 4 dimensions: (a) affective (ways of coping), (b) motivational (ways of achieving), (c) reputational (ways of being valued), (d) cognitive (ways of thinking).

Torrance, E. P. "Problems of Highly Creative Children." *Gifted Child Quarterly* 5: 31–34; 1961. (Cf. Education Digest 27: 40–42; November 1961.) (Also [pp. 240–45] in Crow, L. D., and Alice, *Educating the Academically Able: A Book of Readings*. New York: David McKay Co., 1963.)

Discusses the following factors regarding highly creative children:
1. Sanctions against divergency.
2. Creative children may not be well rounded.
3. Creative children prefer to learn on their own.
4. Creative children like to attempt difficult tasks.
5. Creative children are searching for a purpose.
6. Creative children search for their uniqueness.
7. The psychological estrangement of creative children.

Three characteristics of creative children show (a) they have reputation for having wild and silly ideas; (b) work characterized by its productivity of ideas off beaten track; (c) humor and playfulness.

Trembly, Dean. "Age and Sex Difference in Creative Thinking Potential" (mimeo) California State Polytechnic College, San Luis Obisbo, Calif., 1964.

An historical account of scientific interest in tests of imagination starting with British studies, with special attention to the efforts of Johnson O'Conner and the Human Engineering Laboratory.

Yamamoto, K. "A Further Analysis of the Role of Creative Thinking in High School Achievement." *Journal of Psychology* 58: 277–83, 1964.

When 54 high-creativity high school students were compared on Iowa tests of Educational Development with 54 low-creativity high school students, and the effects of intelligence fixed through covariance technique, it was found that the HC group outperformed the LC group on all subtests of the battery.

Yamamoto, K. "Evaluation of Some Creativity Measures in a High School with Peer Nomination Criteria." *Journal of Psychology* 58: 285–93, 1964.

When 428 high school students received creativity scores on flexibility, fluency and inventive level as a result of the Minnesota test of Imagination and the Ask-and-Guess Test, and these results were compared with peer nominations for creativity, validity coefficients ranging from −.18 to .65 were obtained, averaging around .25, which was barely significant.

Yamamoto, K. "Multiple Achievement Battery and Repeated Measurement: A Postscript to Three Studies on Creative Thinking," *Psychological Reports* 16: 367–375, 1965.

Data from the author's three earlier studies on interrelationships among creative thinking, intelligence, and school achievement were re-analyzed, applying the assumption of dependence among subtest scores. In three of four analyses the original findings held up even under this condition.

CHAPTER FOUR

Can Creativity be Increased by Practice?

Frontiers in Thinking That Teachers Should Know About

J. P. Guilford

THERE IS LITTLE DOUBT THAT THE TEACHER OF READING HAS A WEALTH of opportunities to teach the child to think. The teacher who has only the very general and rather vague objective of "teaching the child to think," however, is not likely to do justice to the task. In the past, the prevailing conception has probably been that thinking is a single kind of activity and that the ability to think is intelligence. Some relatively recent developments in research on the analysis of intelligence indicate that there are a great many different thinking abilities. If we look upon each of these thinking abilities as a distinct kind of thinking skill, and if we know what kind of skill it is, we have a much more definite objective at which to aim in teaching how to think.

COMPONENTS OF INTELLECT

During the past twenty years numerous investigations by the methods of factor analysis have brought to light some sixty different abilities having to do with intellectual activities. The large number is rather overwhelming to those who have been accustomed to the simple idea of one ability—intelligence—or at the most, a few primary mental abilities of Thurstone. Fortunately, it has been possible to find a definite system in which to organize the intellectual abilities, with some interesting new principles (1, 2). The system is known as the "structure of intellect." . . .

REPRINTED by permission of the Author and *The Reading Teacher*, 13:176–182, 1963.

There are five classes of abilities depending upon the basic kind of operation or activity involved. A group of cognitive abilities has to do with discovery or recognition of information. They are ways of understanding or comprehension. A parallel group has to do with retention of information. Two parallel groups are concerned with productive thinking. Given certain information, we not only understand it but we can generate from it some new information. An important new distinction is that between divergent production and convergent production. In divergent production the goal is to produce a variety of ideas, all of which are logically possible in view of the given information. In convergent production the conclusion is completely determined by the given information, or at least there is a recognized best or conventional conclusion. A fifth group has to do with evaluation, which, in more familiar ways of speaking, means critical thinking. We continually evaluate what we know, what we recall, and what we produce by way of conclusions.

A completely different classification of all the abilities cuts across the first. It is in terms of the kind of material in which the information comes. Some information is concrete, being in the form of things that we can see or hear. We may call this kind of material "figural." Other information is in abstract form, either in the form of symbols such as letters, words, and numbers, or in the form of the things for which they stand—meanings or ideas. The two categories are called "symbolic" and "semantic," respectively. A fourth content category, "behavioral," has been added on the basis of theory only, to take care of the obvious information that we have concerning the behavior of ourselves and of others: our thoughts, desires, and feelings, and intentions, and those of other individuals.

Still a third cross classification is concerned with products of information. These are forms in which the individual casts his information —units, classes, relations, systems, transformations, and implications. The technical meanings of these terms are so close to their common meanings that they will not be defined here. Their applications in connection with reading will be pointed out later.

One more word should be said on the "structure of intellect" as a system before taking the next important step in this discussion. When the three cross classifications are combined in the three-dimensional model, the intersection of a certain kind of operation, a certain kind of content, and a certain kind of product, is represented by a single cell. Each cell is expected to represent its own kind of ability, whose properties can be stated in terms of the three category concepts to which the ability belongs.

For example, there is an ability to cognize semantic units, which has been generally known as "verbal comprehension," and which is tested by means of a vocabulary test. It is the dominating ability represented in tests of verbal intelligence. Another ability can be described as the divergent production of semantic transformations. A simpler, prior term for the ability has been originality (in dealing with ideas). There are other such abilities for dealing with kinds of content other than semantic. Semantic originality can be tested by asking examinees to give a list of titles for a short story and by counting only the number of clever titles in scoring their work. To gain numbers of clever titles the examinee must have some drastic changes (transformations) of his conception of the story and in the meanings of words that he uses in titles.

There are 120 cells in the structure of intellect as now conceived, and at present we know only half as many intellectual abilities. It is expected that future research will bring to light others. The greatest doubt pertains to the behavioral category, for which no abilities have as yet been segregated. But it seems reasonable that "social intelligence," which the behavioral category no doubt represents, will break down into a number of different abilities and that this breakdown will be along the same lines that apply in the other content areas. At any rate, in later discussion this will be assumed.

COGNITIVE ABILITIES IN READING

Reading, when fully developed, is one of our most complex intellectual activities, involving many of the intellectual abilities, which we may also regard as intellectual functions. It does not begin that way in the young child. The preschool child has had considerable experience with visual forms, including letters, which he learns to discriminate. At this stage he is applying, and also perhaps developing, his ability to recognize visual figures, an ability that fits into the cell in the upper left corner of the structure of intellect. His readiness to start learning to read depends upon this basic ability.

In learning to recognize combinations of letters in syllables and words, the child depends upon and perhaps develops his ability to cognize symbolic units, the ability in the next cell to the right. Unusual reading difficulty may stem from a special weakness in this ability. The average IQ test should not be expected to predict progress in this particular respect, since this symbolic ability is not represented in the usual IQ test. Obtaining meaning from the printed symbolic unit involves abilities in the semantic column, first the meaning of single words, which is a matter of word recognition or recognition vocabulary. This is the aspect of reading development that is best predicted by an IQ test. But there is more to reading than recognition of word meaning. If we follow down the column of the semantic abilities in the cognitive category alone, we find a number of ways in which meaning can be enriched. There are relations to be understood, also class ideas. Sentences and paragraphs offer systems of ideas to be comprehended. Poetic and other literary writings, particularly, offer transformations of meanings and vague hints of implications that must be completed by the reader if he is to understand and enjoy his reading to the fullest.

READING AND PRODUCTIVE THINKING

Reading for understanding and enjoyment is a worthy objective and one that satisfies perhaps the great majority of those who read. There are multitudes of others, however, for whom reading is a means to other intellectual goals. The student who learns the material of his subject-matter courses largely from reading, and the scientist who enlightens himself about the discoveries of his fellow scientists, must go beyond comprehension. Even the reader who indulges for his own enjoyment, if he is at all philosophically inclined or if he enjoys making his own reactions to the thoughts of others, must do more than understand. All such individuals need to acquire skills in taking off from what they read into flights of thought of their own making.

Good teachers, of reading or of anything else intellectual, have always taken advantage of opportunities for the student to exercise his thinking equipment. Good teachers have felt their responsibility to contribute to the intellectual development of their pupils, whatever the subject matter. When we look upon the pupil's intellect as being an organized collection of distinguishable skills, each with certain properties, we are in a good position to decide what kinds of exercises are needed to develop those skills. These statements imply considerable faith in the possibility of developing intellectual abilities, including thinking abilities, through exercise. Until we learn something to the contrary, it is best for us as educators to proceed on that assumption.

From the learning theories that have been propounded by psychologists over the years, we have derived little in the way of substantial suggestions on the training of intellects. The prevailing model of behavior has been that of stimulus-response associations. The learner has been conceived as something on the order of a vending machine. You put in a certain coin and a certain thing comes out. Such a model has worked very well in instruction such as teaching the numerical operations. But even there, some added comprehension of the principles involved would be very desirable. Comprehension of principles is a matter of cognition and takes us at once beyond the stimulus-response model.

The major types of thinking, as indicated by the structure of intellect, are divergent production, convergent production, and evaluation. We shall now consider the possible relations of the thinking abilities to reading. In part, whether the reading material stimulates productive thinking on the part of the reader will depend upon the nature of the material. The teacher can therefore encourage pupils to think in response to their reading by selecting the more provocative materials. Does the material stir the imagination of the reader, and does it leave something for the reader to do? Does it open up alternative inviting avenues that would suggest divergent thinking? Does it, in other instances, carry the reader along step by step in logical sequences that point toward an inevitable conclusion? Such material should provide exercise in convergent thinking. Does still other material challenge belief and call for checking and testing of facts and arguments? Such material should automatically call for critical thinking or evaluation.

Even when the reading material does not itself obviously induce these types of thinking exercises, the alert teacher who is not a stranger to ingenuity will invent ways of turning that material to good use as the basis for thinking exercises. Skillful questioning should do the trick, as all good teachers know. Can the awareness of the abilities in the structure of intellect suggest types of questions that might be asked? Perhaps a survey of the possibilities represented in the semantic column, in connection with the two production categories and the evaluation category can suggest kinds of questions that may have been slighted. Let us consider a few examples.

SOME GENERALIZED THINKING TASKS

The examples to be given come directly from certain psychological tests that are known to indicate each ability, or from ideas of new tests that should be expected to indicate the ability if it is still unknown. In the latter case, we can readily suggest such tests by analogy to other tests for parallel abilities. In applying each task that is mentioned, the teacher will need to think of similar tasks and questions that can be utilized incident to the teaching of reading as a procedure for exercising each ability.

The divergent production of semantic units describes an ability more commonly known as "ideational fluency." This is the ability to produce a quantity of ideas in limited time in response to a specification of some kind. For example, we ask the examinee to name all the objects that he can think of that are white, hard, and edible, or we ask him to list all the uses he can think of for a common brick. In either case, the number of suitable responses given in a limited time is the score.

The ability to produce a variety of class ideas is indicated by a test called Unusual Uses. An item reads: "A newspaper is commonly used for reading. What other uses can you suggest for it?" The answers might be: "To swat flies," "To line shelves," "To wrap garbage," "To stuff packages," or "To make up a kidnap note." Notice that each response is in a quite different category.

The ability to produce a variety of responses involving relationships can be assessed by a test called Associational Fluency. The examinee is told to list as many words as he can which mean about the same as the word "high." In another test the examinee is given two words and is asked to state a number of different ways in which they are related, for example, the words "man" and "daughter."

The hypothetical factor of divergent production of systems has no known tests as yet, but it is expected that a test in which we give the examinee several facts and ask him to state a number of different problems that could be involved would apply. Another possible semantic system may be a story plot, in which case we might ask, given the same list of characters, what different story plots could reasonably apply.

As stated earlier, the divergent production of transformations means originality. This can be tested in a number of ways, one way having been mentioned earlier. In another test we ask the examinee to write "punch" lines for cartoons. In another we ask for clever interpretations of riddles. In still another we ask for simple symbols to represent meaningful words, such as "ring" and "bell," in the sentence "Ring the bell."

The divergent production of implications involves elaboration upon given information in different directions. One test presents the bare outlines of a plan (as for a school function) to which the examinee is to add as many details as he can. In another test we give a simple line or two, which the examinee is told to make into a familiar object. He is scored in both instances in terms of the number of additions he offers.

The convergent production area of abilities offers less exciting activities, but the development of carefully reasoned conclusions has always been recognized as an important objective in education. In each task that indicates abilities of this kind, we call for one right answer, or a best or most conventionally accepted answer. In the case of the production of semantic units we have an ability known as "abstraction naming." The examinee is presented with objects of a class, to name the class, or with two objects in relation, to name the relation.

A test of the ability to produce unique classes presents a list of perhaps a dozen words that the examinee must put into three classes, using all the words and putting no word in more than one class. This is in contrast to a test for divergent classification, in which the examinee must reclassify words in as many ways as he can, using each word as many times as he wishes.

Items of the following types indicate the ability to produce unique responses involving relationships: "What word means the exact opposite of *cold?*" "What is the wife of a king?" "Fish is to water as bird is to what?" In each case only one best answer is accepted.

The production of a unique system can be tested by calling for arrangement of given events in their most reasonable or optimal order. The events may be presented pictorially, as by using the scrambled pictures of a cartoon strip, or verbally, as in stating several steps involved in changing a tire, planting a new lawn, or building a dog house. Temporal order is one kind of system.

Transformations in the semantic area involve shifts of meanings or uses of objects. "Which of the following objects could be most reasonably used in making a needle: onion, book, fish, wheel, pansy?" The bone of a fish, when given an eye, would serve the purpose. "What more complex object could be made by combining a coil spring and a basketball?" This could most clearly be a punching bag. An object or part of an object must be redefined in order to use it in some new way.

Unique implications are fully determined conclusions. The item might be: "Frank is older than Jim and younger than Sam. Who is older, Jim or Sam?" Many readers who enjoy detective stories probably like to indulge in this kind of reasoning, and they probably want their stories to be logic-tight so that unique conclusions are possible.

In the evaluative or critical-thinking area we are less certain of the basic abilities, but most of them that are known are in the semantic column. In the case of figural or symbolic units we have two abilities that apparently have to do with deciding whether two given units are identical or not identical. One might give two proverbs, or a proverb and a non-proverb expression, the examinee to say whether they express the same idea. We are not sure, as yet, what kind of evaluation or standard may pertain to the judgment of classes.

The evaluation of semantic conclusions where relationships are concerned rather clearly involves the standard of logical consistency. Given a syllogism, with two statements of relationships and several alternative conclusions, one of which is determined by the premises, the examinee is to say which conclusion is sound.

In the evaluation of a system two criteria or standards are found to apply. One is whether the system is complete, and the other is whether the parts are internally consistent. In one test we show a simple picture, the examinee to say "What is wrong with this picture?" In one picture the doorstep is missing from the house, and the smoke from the chimney and the clothes on the line are flying in opposite directions.

The ability to evaluate transformations has often been called simply "judgment," or sometimes "commonsense judgment." Tests that seem most suitable for it involve decisions as to which improvisations are best. Workability seems to be the standard or criterion.

Evaluation of implications or evaluation involving implications represents a very interesting kind of ability. When first found, it was called "sensitivity to problems." One test asks the examinee to give two things that are wrong with such common devices as telephones, toasters, or refrigerators. Another asks what is wrong with social institutions such as tipping and divorce. Being sensitive to defects and deficiencies is the apparent quality involved. The sensitive person has evaluated unfavorably, and the person who sees no defects has evaluated positively the implication that things are all right as they are. The former feels problems still exist, while the latter feels they are solved.

In the short space of this article it has been impossible to bridge the gap between the kinds of exercises presented by tests of the semantic factors and teaching operations in the subject of reading. It is hoped, however, that a systematic exposition of the varieties of general thinking skills will be sufficient to extend the boundaries of conceptions of thinking activities and also to delineate each kind of thinking skill clearly enough to enable the average teacher to observe it and to help the student cultivate its development.

REFERENCES

1. Guilford, J. P. *Personality*. New York: McGraw-Hill, 1959.
2. Guilford, J. P. "Three Faces of Intellect." *American Psychologist*, 14 (1959), 469–79.

Can Teachers Encourage Creative Thinking?

R. E. Myers and E. Paul Torrance

"I WAS THRILLED TO THINK WE HAD FINALLY HIT ON A SUBJECT OF INTEREST to him."

"She's just a problem child and no matter what you do, it doesn't help."

"I was very interested in his ideas and encouraged the others to contribute."

"Ridiculous for children in second grade."

"This showed thinking on the students' part. They were not ready to accept someone else's ideas until more information was obtained."

"Our schedule is so full already."

"I passed no comment. I listened."

"I was just plain mad, mad, mad."

These pairs of contrasting statements were some of the comments made by teachers who were asked to write down what happened when they attempted to apply five principles for rewarding creative thinking in children. One hundred and fourteen teachers of children in public and private schools in 14 states recorded their experiences on questionnaires sent them by the University of Minnesota's Bureau of Educational Research. They were asked "to seek systematically and consciously to apply in a reasonable and appropriate way" the following principles:

1. Treat questions with respect.
2. Treat imaginative ideas with respect.
3. Show your pupils that their ideas have value.
4. Occasionally have pupils do something "for practice" without the threat of evaluation.
5. Tie in evaluation with causes and consequences.

Many of the teachers showed a thorough understanding of the principles by the manner in which they reported anecdotes illustrating their application. For example, a second grade teacher related the following incident in response to the invitation to describe an occasion

---

REPRINTED by permission of the Authors and *Educational Leadership* 19:156–9, Dec. 1961. (Copyright 1961 by the Association for Supervision and Curriculum Development.)

when she was able to communicate to one of her pupils that his ideas had value:

1. What was the occasion which provided the opportunity to show a pupil that his ideas are valuable? Who was the child? What did he do? How did he seem to feel about his idea(s)?

Science—Incident: Studying about the sun and how it affects the earth. Student's idea: "Some people must sleep while we are awake."

He examined the globe which was at his disposal to see which countries were actually having day. A large flashlight was also used to give half of the earth a shadow.

This same child went on with his intense interest to make a picture of the solar system to show the relation of the sun to the earth and the other planets.

2. What did you do to try to show him that his ideas are of value?

Set up a display letting him help to show the entire class how he had arrived at his conclusion.

Then a bulletin board was made with a huge sun and earth made by the class committees which were chosen. People who were awake were made and cut out, then placed on the board.

3. How did he react to what you did (immediate and/or long-range)?

Created a more intense interest toward the study of heavenly bodies and how they are affected by the sun.

He is now more aware of how space can affect us.

4. What was the reaction of the class, if observable?

Enthusiasm about and a very intense interest in what was being studied. Some were even beginning to display some small ideas which they wanted to develop further.

A mural was also drawn as a result of this type of study in science.

The response of the second grade pupils to their teacher's attitude of respect and encouragement was characteristic of the way youngsters of all ages were reported to have reacted when their teachers applied one of the principles.

On the other hand, quite a few teachers showed an inability either to interpret the meaning of a principle correctly or to cite an appropriate instance of its application. Contrast this report by another second grade teacher of the ideas-have-value principle with the preceding one.

1. What was the occasion which provided the opportunity to show a pupil that his ideas are valuable? Who was the child? What did he do? How did he seem to feel about his idea(s)?

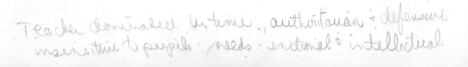

Little Jane who has a great many problems in class and few friends. She has a very poor family life as well as poor living qualities. She went to the grocery store and took a bag of candy and then came back to the class and told them, "If you will let me play I will give you some candy."

2. What did you do to try to show him that his ideas are of value?

I wanted to know where she got the candy, and she began to cry. I then tried to tell her that giving things does not win friends. The class all then participated and said that giving of nice things means you want to be friendly but that Jane should try to get along with them and then we'd all help her.

3. How did he react to what you did (immediate and/or long-range)?

I don't think that it did too much. It's just a problem child and no matter what you do it doesn't help.

4. What was the reaction of the class, if observable?

They were sincere and wanted to help her but it just didn't work.

A fourth grade teacher gave this anecdote as an illustration of the principle that imaginative ideas should be treated with respect. The superficial treatment accorded the questions was typical of the way many teachers from schools whose faculties participated *en masse* fulfilled their assignments.

1. What was the idea, who expressed it, and what were the general conditions under which the idea was suggested?

Wanted to play "rough" games while skating (ice). Don wanted to play high-jump.

2. What was your immediate reaction to the idea?

Asked if others thought it was safe.

3. What was the immediate reaction of the class, if observable?

Not safe.

4. In what way was respect shown for the idea?

Thought of other games we could play that would not be dangerous.

5. What, if any, were the observable effects (immediate and/or long-range)?

(No answer given.)

Many of the reports were indeed puzzling. In relating incidents in which they were supposed to have shown respect for children's questions and ideas, teachers told of their own evasive or derisive behavior.

Asked when they had been reassuring and accepting, they recited occasions when they had rebuffed their pupils. It is unlikely, however, that any of the teachers wanted to refute the principles which they had been urged to apply consciously in their classrooms—a discouragingly large number simply were unable to incorporate the principles into their teaching.

THE FORCES WITHIN

A majority of the incidents reported were faithful to the philosophy from which the five principles derive, and many contained important insights about teacher-pupil relationships. Nevertheless, those incidents which had little to do with the principles were perhaps more significant because they provided clues concerning *the forces within teachers which oppose innovation.* The increasing number of individuals and agencies whose aspirations include a complete or partial transformation of American education should look rather carefully into the motives of the teachers who must bring about their hoped-for changes.

The occurrence of a misinterpretation of one of the principles was taken seriously for two reasons. First, out of the innumerable interactions which took place between the teachers and their pupils during the two or three months when they were asked to be alert to opportunities to apply the principles, the teachers decided upon the incidents which were submitted. We can assume, therefore, that these incidents were either memorable or convenient when the teachers sat down to make their reports. Nearly all of the reports were candid and free from embellishment. Accordingly, the incidents cited were, in some ways, reflective of the values and attitudes of the teachers. Second, if a teacher does not prize creative thinking, it is difficult for him to cite examples of his encouraging children to express their individuality.[1]

Our guess is that the teachers who were unable to accept one or more of the five principles were prevented from doing so because of

---

[1] The reader may test the truth of this statement by asking several teachers to recall recent occasions when they encouraged their pupils to explore on their own, to experiment on their own, to hypothesize about their experiences, or to become more sensitive to their surroundings. Teachers whose teaching philosophy is goal-oriented or student-oriented will have no trouble in recounting many instances when they supported or instigated these activities. There will be other teachers, perhaps, who will be unable to cite more than one or two occasions when they actually fostered creative thinking and doing.

their predispositions or temperaments. It is difficult to imagine a classroom which could not offer an abundance of opportunities for the teacher to show respect for his pupils' questions and ideas, or for him to allow them to practice skills without being formally evaluated. Nevertheless, to be aware of such opportunities the teacher must be familiar enough with them to be able to identify them. Furthermore, even though the teacher possesses knowledge of the kinds of situations which can provide him with opportunities to show respect for creative thinking, he must be alert to the occurrence of these situations, which means he must be receptive to the ideas which define the situations. There are a number of personality traits which daily prevent teachers from being receptive to theories about encouraging young people to be imaginative or to trust in themselves, and these traits are closely associated with the values which many teachers have.

APPLYING SUPPORTING PRINCIPLES

At least ten characteristics were found to be present among the teachers who could not apply one or more of the accepting, supporting principles. Collectively they were authoritarian, defensive,[2] dominated by time, insensitive to their pupils' intellectual and emotional needs, lacking in energy, preoccupied with their information-giving functions, intellectually inert, disinterested in promoting initiative and self-reliance in their pupils, preoccupied with disciplinary matters, and unwilling to give much of themselves in the teaching-learning compact.[3]

The reports also revealed that, as a group, the teachers who could not accept the principles which were advocated placed a high value on the following concepts: time (but not timeliness), orderliness (but not necessarily logical thinking), respect for authority (but not respect for the potentialities of the individual), the child's responsibility to the group and to the teacher (but not especially the teacher's responsi-

[2] Robert M. Roth's definition of defensiveness may partially explain why some of the teachers unconsciously resisted the five principles: "Defensiveness has been defined as an attempt to maintain a concept of self. . . . The anticipation of an experience contrary to this tends to make the individual more adamant in his conception and hence more unrealistic." *Journal of Experimental Education* Vol. 27, No. 4; 1959. p. 275.

[3] "Resistance to change" is not listed among the personality characteristics of the rejecting teachers because it was not evident from the reports received that they were any more opposed to change than the teachers who apparently accepted the principles. However, it seems logical to suppose that they were in fact more conservative than the accepting teachers.

bility to the child or the group's responsibility to the child), the preservation of their self-image (but not the enhancement of their pupils' self-image), and the importance of information (but not the importance of information-getting skills).

Inasmuch as the impact of values upon the curriculum was the theme of the May 1961 issue of *Educational Leadership*, it is perhaps not necessary to echo here that which was so well expressed by Professor Wirth and others. Nevertheless, it is next to impossible to pay too much attention to our values in education, particularly during times such as these, when values are changing perceptibly. Ruth A. Willard's statement shows clearly why values must always be our major concern: ". . . whatever values are dominant for an individual at any one time determine his beliefs and actions and direct the use of his energies, skills and abilities." [4]

Actually, the only message which comes in loud and clear from these reports of incidents of rewarding creative thinking is that when we ask teachers to behave in certain ways we must take their values into consideration. We have devoted a tremendous amount of thought and energy to trying to understand the learner; it is time we begin, with as much care, to examine the teacher.

The Brainstorming Attitude

Marvin A. Rapp

IF MAN EVER FOUND A WAY TO REALIZE FULLY HUMAN CREATIVITY, IT would represent the greatest intellectual and artistic power source the world has ever known. How creativity generates or is generated, develops or is developed, expresses or is expressed, remains, and perhaps will remain, one of the mysteries of human phenomena. Much is known but so much more needs to be known of the human resources of creativity. Psychiatry, psychology, philosophy, chemistry, neurology, the work of Freud, Jung and others, have laid the foundations. Empirical and descriptive data have been compiled from individual and group analysis of the process of creativity. Each day our knowledge of creative action and human motivation enlarges.

[4] *Journal of Educational Research* 29:46; 1955.

REPRINTED by permission of the Author and *School Arts*, 59:5–8, June, 1960.

Because creativity is dynamic, and by its individual and group revelation and very nature, different, it probably follows no magic formula, no set sequence, no given method. Creativity probably knows no special time, no appointed place, no particular person or persons. All humans it would seem have some creativity. The range moves from extremely low power to almost immeasurable power. Some, many, never find it. Some find it and never use it. Some find it and abuse it. Fortunately, some find it and use it well. But the largest finds will always be rare. To tap the power lines of creativity would be to infuse civilization with its greatest renaissance of achievement.

Yet some discovered circumstances have seemed to prove fertile for creativity. Under certain intellectual and emotional climate with a certain individual attitude the process of creativity has seemed to flourish. When the proper group attitude exists with the proper individual attitude, brainstorming and other forms of stimulation can help to draw out and develop creative ideas. Whatever can be done any place, in schools, industries, offices, agencies, or the quiet of one's study to provide the proper atmosphere for nourishing creative imagination should be done forthwith. More than ever in the world's history the creative process is needed. Traditional ways in many areas of international affairs, space problems, personal problems, are not always and fully meeting the challenges of our individual lives, society or the world. The arts constantly cry for new imagination, presentation, interpretation. New outlooks, new ideas, creative imagination must be forthcoming to give us the new answers to our problems or the old answers related properly to meet the constantly changing needs of a rapidly changing society. As Brewster Ghilselin writes in *The Creative Process:* "For the creative order which is an extension of life is not an elaboration of the established but a movement beyond the established or at least a reorganization of it and often elements not included in it."

The conscious restricts through predetermination and the too rigid pattern of contemporary discipline the new that boils up out of the subconscious when the creative process is working. All, most especially educators, should strive to establish those conditions which release, not restrict, creativity so that the miracle of creativity may occur more frequently and more intensively.

Basic to our problem in education today is our inability, too often, to keep teaching and learning as a creative process. Our objective as teachers, as leaders of business and our communities, is to traffic freely and easily with ideas, to build new ones out of old ones, to catch the completely new ones, hold them, and express them soundly for others to keep and use and cherish. The classroom with a conducive climate can combine individual and group creativity. Here where illumination and inspiration, the one from within, the other from without, meet in harmony or conflict (and it matters not which) the new is born. Like humans, new ideas are born only with effort and labor.

Ideas cannot flow especially from the deep reaches of the subconscious unless all blocks and barriers, all inhibitions, emotional and intellectual, have been removed. It seems specious to argue individual creativity versus group creativity. Much of the world's greatest creative works come quietly to the artist when he works alone. Group creativity cannot be very productive unless individual creativity has taken place. Unless long and constant thinking has been given to the question at hand, the problem area, the mode of expression, group brainstorming cannot do as much toward the generation of new ideas as it can with proper and individual pre-preparation. So every individual should encourage in himself those rare creative moments and when they come he should exploit them to the fullest, developing the skill and craft necessary for their full expression.

Creative illumination can come to one alone—in the middle of the night, in a subway, in an airplane, any place. Inspiration can come casually—from chance remarks of friends at lunch, in formal situations, in bull sessions, in buzz sessions, or in a brainstorming session. Individual and group creativity, individual and group brainstorming, can help to unlock the subconscious sources of creativity.

Historically as society developed, as man began to move out of the woods into the tribal villages; as towns and cities developed; as men rubbed elbows, they also rubbed minds. The stimulation of human to human helped to create new ideas. Technological advancement is replete with the inventions of genius' working alone. But today many of the world's greatest discoveries are being developed by teams of experts working closely together developing and pooling their creativity. Group dynamics has helped to enliven the processes of politics, and to energize the processes of democracy.

Here is a personal profile of a creative moment which may outline in part the process of creativity. Several months ago I participated in a conference of students from the twenty two-year institutions of State University of New York. They came from all over the state. With other faculty people, we worked with the students for three days, listening, talking, attempting to guide them and to some extent be guided by them. Constantly in my mind was the desire to try to see the world as they saw it and to share with them whatever knowledge our experience and education could bring to their problems.

At times there was the feeling that we, the participating faculty members, were getting through to them; at other times, we were frustrated with our own failure to establish real contact with them.

At the closing banquet, I delivered a kind of valedictory address, "The Sense of the Conference and the Look Ahead." Again I felt myself reaching out for them, trying to develop the rapport so necessary for parent and child, student and teacher, one generation and another, to build the links that form the day by day chain of living; of civilization. As I talked to these students I thought also of my own son, thirteen years old, and my many attempts, too often failures, to see his problems as he sees them and to understand his world.

With the close of the banquet I was hurried to the airport and soon found myself winging back to my home in Albany. I sat quietly alone, turned off the seat light, closed my eyes, and relaxed after the three strenuous days of hard work and a rather exhausting effort to say something meaningful to these young people. Tired, but completely relaxed, I suddenly had a feeling of excitement, vague, rather hard to identify, as if something within me was trying to say something. Physically I felt a certain lift in the pit of my stomach—a lump in my throat. Mentally, whatever was occurring seemed rather indeterminate, suspenseful, a kind of muddling. I yielded to and enjoyed the uncertain feeling—that same kind of good feeling that comes with pleasant anticipation. There was a kind of surging chaos of something unexpressed. I was conscious that something seemed to be happening but I did not know what. It seemed dynamic and full of tension. Thoughts and words began to form. I did not immediately try to take control of the means or meaning of the experience. The substance of the thinking that I had been doing for the past three days on the relationship of the old to the young, the teacher to the student began to well up and come through. As it developed, slowly there also came an enhancement of certainty. I began consciously to take possession of these ideas, after I had surrendered to the feeling. The words fell into shape and order about the thoughts.

I pulled an envelope from my pocket. Quickly, without stopping, and as fast as I could, I wrote these words. Perhaps it is a poem. I do not really know nor care. Except for a change of one or two words the following morning, this is what I wrote:

The Young

You are of us, yet not of us
You are the more or less of us

Yet never the same as us
You are the new.

No matter the gnawing want or fervent wish
We cannot be of you
You cannot be of us
We are the old.

Though of us, womb and work,
Still even there not quite the one.
But though we cannot be, what cannot be
Can be at least approached,
In reaching out, in understanding out of love,
We touch.
Briefly hand in hand a bridge
Across what cannot be.
Different yet together, walking forward
Pushing our today into your morrow.
The old with wisdom and the slowing step.
The new with energy, the quickening step,
Side by side, hand in hand
Now together for a moment joined.

Then the young the coming goes ahead
And the old the going falls behind
And in between yet part of both,
A deep and yearning loneliness.

The world turns; begins again again
The coming and the going
The two, sometimes almost
But never quite, the one.

I had never written a poem before in my life. I never had any particular feeling or desire to use this type of expression. But at that moment something seemed to be alive in me and this is the form that it took. What is important to me is that had I had more skill expressing the creativity that came to me, the result might have been something truly beautiful and wonderful. For the gifted, that is what usually happens. For our purposes today, however, it does not matter whether it is poetry or whether it is good or bad. For me it was a creative experience which I enjoyed. In its analysis perhaps are hints on creativity that may be stimulating.

To cite a different experience of creativity, let me tell you the story of Charles Eagle Plume. An Indian tribe lived near the Sacramento River. So primitive were they that they did not even have a name.

They lived in miserable huts on marshy land. Because they lived at the lowest level of existence, other Indians referred to them simply and derisively as The Diggers. They had achieved none of the arts of the Cherokees or the Navajos, the skill of decorative baskets or the beautifully designed rugs. In 1851 a group of gold prospectors wiped out the entire tribe and every vestige of their lowly, primitive civilization—everything except one closely woven basket four inches in diameter. But this must truly have been one of the most beautiful creations one could imagine. This is the way Charles Eagle Plume described it:

"Imagine if you will," he said, "a native woman of this primitive tribe, a woman who had never had a single object of beauty in her whole life, either to see or to possess. What she had been taught of basket-weaving was only for utility, for the day-to-day needs of her household. Yet somewhere within her stirred an indefinable vague yearning, the awakening of a sense of awareness of beauty and loveliness, a craving to create something which would bring joy to her heart as she looked at it. And so in an almost miraculous way, she wove the basket. And when she had moments to herself, she trapped quail and pulled out the tufts of black on their heads. Or she sat patiently, hour after hour, completely motionless, holding a flower in her hands and waiting for a humming bird to come and feed. When it did, she closed her hands over it and plucked from its throat the tiny and downy red feathers. Or again, she searched along the marshy shore for the tiniest and most perfect of shells. All of these things she fashioned into her basket with no knowledge of design or craftsmanship, with nothing but this overwhelming urge to create."

As he spoke, Charles Eagle Plume held the tiny basket tenderly and lovingly in his hands. The perfectly matched shells were probably the tiniest that could be found. The black quail tufts, the woven reeds, the throat feathers of a humming bird, blended in a reddish cast of simple pattern. Here if ever was pure unalloyed creativity with no environmental influence or outside inspiration. Illumination within this woman brought it up out of her subconscious. From these two examples a number of conditions, a state of mind, or attitude, can be determined on which some creativity might be predicated.

For creativity there must be in the individual and in the group receptivity and sensitivity—the more finely developed the better. Both of these must be developed and constantly employed during the process of creativity. The mind must be free—permitted to soar into unchartered areas of the unknown. There must be keen awareness, efforted thinking, and energy to match both. Creativity needs enthusiasm and knowledge but discipline and predetermination must be avoided until the creative ideas have been permitted to come forth from the subconscious.

During the past year, I have had a hand in structuring, participating in, and evaluating two conferences of educators employing the brainstorming technique of creative education. The first was the Tenth Annual Faculty Conference of the two-year institutes of State University held at Alfred. The group addressed itself to these six problems: (1) How many ways can we think of to sharpen student's eagerness for personal participation in the learning process? (2) How many ways can we think of to evaluate our extracurricular programs most effectively? (3) How many ways can we think of to improve our faculty-personnel program? (4) How many ways can we think of to improve college-community relationships? (5) How many ways can we think of to improve intra-State University relationships? (6) How many ways can we think of to facilitate the acceptance of two-year transfer students by four-year institutions? Within a few minutes after the brainstorming groups had started, each had developed hundreds of raw ideas. These were later evaluated, recorded, and included in committee reports. Later with faculty and administrative approval many of these ideas will be implemented in the units of State University.

At a conference of teachers of textiles and clothing held in New York City, educators in this field concentrated on the problems and likewise within a few minutes of free thinking hundreds of ideas were developed. These were later put into a report and the demand has been so great that the committee has been forced to put a price on the document in order to defray the costs of printing and distribution.

I have described two experiences of individual creativity and two experiences of group creativity. They are, of course, related. In brainstorming, in fact in education any place, where man deals with ideas, one of the most important aspects of the process is attitude. If people do not want to learn there can be no learning. If people do not want to create, there cannot be any creativity. There must be the desire and love to learn and create before the miracle of creativity can occur. There must be freedom to let the mind reach deeply into the subconscious to stimulate the flow of the ideas that exist in the recesses of the soul of man. Superficialities, surface barriers, and inhibitions, must be removed. The person creating individually and in a group must have a feeling of release. The release and growth of ideas require the right climate of illumination and inspiration.

Many conditions should be present to stimulate individual and group creativity. Among them are: (1) Preparation—Pre-thinking of experience about the problem. (2) Mood or Posture—The right mental and physical attitude. (3) Open-mindedness—Release from pre-conceptions. (4) Receptivity—An awareness, a perceptiveness. (5) Enthusiasm —The joy of creating. (6) Stimulation—Mental and emotional excitement. (7) Concentration—Creativity and learning are the hardest work in the world. (8) Expression—Develop the skill and craft to best express the ideas.

Practice makes expression and creativity easier. If you would write, write; if you would speak, speak; if you would paint, paint; if you would create, create. Only by doing do we learn and by constantly doing, learn better. We must develop the skill and craft to express our creative ideas so that mankind can use them. Whatever helps us to release creativity will help us to release a force far more powerful than nuclear fusion or fission.

Clues to Creative Teaching:
The Creative Process and Education
C. W. Taylor

LAST MONTH WE DISCUSSED SEVERAL APPROACHES TO CREATIVITY, WITH the hope that teachers would try different approaches in an attempt to cultivate creativity in their students. Let us now look more deeply at the creative process approach. By understanding more about this complex internal process, we may get important clues about how to increase creativeness in our students.

A creative writer says that many early influences lead young children toward imitation rather than creativity. He feels that the great problem in teaching creative writing is to get them away from and beyond imitation into their own kind of literary production. The struggle between imitative and creative processes also appears in connection with historic events in art. Cézanne, through his own creative processes, was carrying a new living movement forward, while those who fought him and his ideas were actually mere imitators of a past no longer living.

Do we help our students to make use of creative and other thinking

REPRINTED by permission of the Author and *Instructor*, 73:4–5, Nov., 1963.

processes? Or do we too often require an almost uniform imitative process for all? Perhaps students should be told very clearly when we want them to imitate, and when we want them to put themselves into their work and express themselves, not someone else, in what they do and what they produce. Couldn't we select and design a sequence of tasks for students which would call for less and less imitation and for more and more creative production of their own?

It has been suggested that we develop and give to our students some take-home thinking problems, as a way to encourage the creative process. Then any time during the following few days or weeks that a student got an idea on his take-home task, he could jot it down, making an idea file on the problem. The teacher could take a few minutes every so often to refresh students' interest in the assignment, to spur their thinking along new lines about it, and to renew their involvement in it. This would counterbalance the short tasks which have simple solutions and can be rather easily wrapped up and returned as a completed package for the teacher to inspect at the end of the hour or the next day.

We could encourage our students to be more playful with ideas by providing time when they can be given full license to think freely, to play with given ideas (either specific or general), or with ideas of their own choice. We can let them create games and vary rules and restrictions, always watching to see what difference it makes in their thinking processes. Imposing dead seriousness all of the time on everyone may be suicidal as far as imaginative thinking and creating are concerned.

There is reason to think that much of the creative process is intuitive in nature, and that it entails a work of the mind prior to its arising to the conscious level and certainly also prior to its being in expressible form. It is most likely preconscious, nonverbal or preverbal, and it may involve a large, sweeping, scanning, deep, diffused, free, and powerful action of almost the whole mind.

Since we do not yet know to what extent the creative processes in children parallel the creative processes in adults, teachers can help discover what happens in their more creative students.

In adults, the first stage of the creative process is described as one of "mental labor." It entails something more than just rote memory or other accumulation of knowledge; it is a deeply involved, preparatory work that enables one to move through the next two crucial stages of the process. A most significant part of this preparatory effort may be a seemingly fruitless struggle of both the "outward and inward" mind in some vague out-of-the-way part of the problem.

The second stage is one of quiescence, so far as outward and even inward awareness is concerned. It has been described as an *incubation* or gestation period, out of which a new idea will hatch if the process is successful. Are there times in your class activities when you could tell your students, "Now that we've gone this far into the problem without seeing a solution, let's incubate it for a few hours or days, and see if a new idea will hatch for any of us."

The third stage is one of *illumination*, sometimes described as the "ah-ha" or "I've found it" experience, in which insight almost miraculously and unexpectedly breaks through.

The fourth stage is one of further labor and *deliberate effort*, including elaboration, revision, and verification.

How can we as teachers enter in during a student's incubation period to facilitate the creativeness of his processes? If we want to learn more about teaching for creativity, many of us should be attempting to generate good incubation processes in students, and then experimenting to see whether we can facilitate them. We could try leaving students alone; next we could try encouraging them with words, pointing positively to any signs of progress: then we could try challenges or deliberate probes.

For example, when a student is painting with watercolors, are there things the teacher can say or do which will loosen up the student so that he will paint more freely, and thereby keep up with the flow of the watercolor?

Again, in an idea-thinking situation, are there certain verbal or nonverbal communications that a teacher could use to spur the students' thinking so that ideas would come more easily and completely?

In the incubation period, attempts toward relaxation may prove more effective than deliberate attempts to force a new insight. Thinking aside, or thinking at right angles to the traditional thought stream, or even letting one's attention be more diffused and scanning rather than focused and concentrated, may facilitate the creative process.

A creative mind continually reaches toward new designs, new patterns, new insight; there is an almost endless freshness in its inexhaustible powers. One new design is replaced by another, and then still another. When our students reach what seems to be an end point, could we, after a brief breather, challenge them to leave that stopping place and try to move on to a greater understanding or better solution? At a certain stage of the process, can we add other pertinent information that upsets their conclusions, to see if their minds will take up the challenge anew?

One key notion underlying some of our current study of creativity is that a high degree of definiteness or focus of attention decreases the chances for any unexpected or new insights. Disorder, with some confusion, any obscurity, and dispersed attention, may be a favorable condition. Other favorable early conditions seem to be an ability to join together quite different and seemingly unrelated elements; vague wondering, and a free toying with ideas.

Can we teach such information directly to students? Can we keep alert for opportunities to illustrate when thinking at right angles might help? Can we recognize and acknowledge such thinking in our students instead of branding it as irrelevant or tangential?

All this discussion suggests that we may not have given sufficient attention to the crucial creative and other thinking processes that can occur in the minds of our students. As will be indicated in next month's article on knowledge and creativity, perhaps the thinking and learning processes in students may be as important as, or even more important than, the subject matter content which they are learning.

A classroom full of *thinking* students might be in sharp contrast to many classrooms today. What would you do if you saw a student in class leaning on his hand like Rodin's classic statue, "The Thinker," with that strange look on his face? You might say, "Johnny, what are you doing?" If Johnny were honest, he might answer, "Thinking." Some teachers might then be tempted to say, "Well, stop thinking, and listen to me!" What would you do?

Author's Note: My understandings of the creative process have come mainly from the excellent work of my colleague, Brewster Ghiselin (see *The Creative Process* by this author, a Mentor Book, 1955). See also his chapter 29 in *Scientific Creativity: Its Recognition and Development,* edited by Taylor and Barron (Wiley, 1963).

Creative Teaching Makes a Difference *

E. Paul Torrance

A FEW YEARS AGO, IT WAS COMMONLY THOUGHT THAT CREATIVITY, scientific discovery, the production of new ideas, inventions, and the like had to be left to chance. Indeed many people still think so. With

* The Florence S. Dunlop Memorial Lecture, Ontario Council for Exceptional Children, Point Credit, Ontario, Canada, October 30, 1964.

REPRINTED by permission of the Author and courtesy of Bureau of Educational Research, University of Minnesota, 1964.

today's accumulated knowledge, however, I do not see how any reasonable, well-informed person can still hold this view. The amazing record of inventions, scientific discoveries, and other creative achievements amassed through deliberate methods of creative problem-solving should convince even the most stubborn skeptic. Both laboratory and field experiments involving these deliberate methods of improving the level of creative behavior have also been rather convincing. In my own classes and seminars I have consistently found that these deliberate methods can be taught from the primary grades through the graduate school with the effect that students improve their ability to develop original and useful solutions to problems. The evidence is strong that creativity does not have to be left to chance.

I have similarly maintained that the development of the creative thinking abilities does not have to be left to chance. Here I find myself in a distinct minority. Indeed, some educators believe that it would be extremely dangerous to educate children to be creative while they are still children. They argue that the emphasis must be on obedience, conformity, discipline, and fundamentals like the three R's. One educator sought to clinch his argument by saying, "A child has to know the three R's in order to do anything! Isn't it enough that the schools teach him to read, write and figure? Let him dash off on his own errands later; let him specialize in college!" Such a statement, of course, reflects a gross misunderstanding of the nature of creative thinking. The development of the creative thinking abilities is at the very heart of the achievement of even the most fundamental educational objectives, even the acquisition of the three R's. It is certainly not a matter of specialization.

For years, students of creative development have observed that five-year olds lose much of their curiosity and excitement about learning, that nine-year olds become greatly concerned about conformity to peer pressures and give up many of their creative activities, that the beginning junior highs show a new kind of concern for conformity to behavioral norms with the consequences that their thinking becomes more obvious, commonplace, and safe. In 1930, Andrews published data to document the drops at about age five. Even earlier, the drops at about ages nine and thirteen had been documented and have been further supported in the Minnesota Studies of Creative Thinking (1962).

Those who have commented on the drops in creative thinking ability and creative behavior in general have almost always assumed that these were purely developmental phenomena. (For example, Wilt (1959) observed that creativity may all but take a holiday at about age nine or ten and returns only for a few after the crisis has passed. She concludes that about all that can be done is to keep open the gates for its return. Rarely, however, has anyone taken a contrary stand. One of these rare individuals, Susan Nichols Pulsifer (1960), has taken such a stand concerning the abandonment of creativity at about age five. She maintains that it is not a natural developmental change but is due to the sharp man-made change which confronts the five-year old and impels him by its rules and regulations.)

If our research at the University of Minnesota has contributed anything to thinking about this problem, it has come from my unwilingness to accept the assumption that the severe drops in measured creative thinking ability are purely developmental phenomena that must be accepted as unchangeable. As we entered into our longitudinal studies, it seemed obvious to me that many children needlessly sacrificed their creativity, especially in the fourth grade, and that many of them did not recover as they continued through school. It also seemed to me that many of our problems of school drop outs, delinquency, and mental illness have their roots in the same forces that cause these drops.

It will certainly take a great deal more research than we now have before very many people will be convinced about this matter. Personally, I consider the accumulated evidence rather convincing. One of the first positive bits of evidence came from my experiences in studying the creative development of two fourth-grade classes taught by teachers who are highly successful in establishing creative relationships with their pupils and who give them many opportunities to acquire information and skills in creative ways. There was no fourth-grade slump in these classes, either in measured creative thinking abilities or in participation in creative activities.

A somewhat more convincing line of evidence has come from our studies of the development of the creative thinking abilities in different cultures. As we have obtained results from the administration of our tests of creative thinking in diverse cultures, we have found that the developmental curve takes on a different shape in each culture and that the characteristics of the developmental curve can be explained in terms of the way the culture treats curiosity and creative needs.

For purposes of illustration, let us examine the developmental curve for non-verbal originality in the United States, Western Samoa, Australia, Germany, India, and in United States Negroes. There are no drops in the developmental curve for Samoan subjects. The level of originality begins in the first grade at the lowest level of any of the cultures studied but the growth is continuous from year to year.

The second greatest continuity in development is shown by the U. S. Negro sample, although some of the specific cultural groups in India show curves almost identical to those of the Samoan subjects. Through the fourth grade, German and Australian children seem to show about the same level and pattern of development. Pressures towards standardization and conformity apparently occur quite early and continue for the Australian child but not for the German child. The overall pattern of growth among the children in India is much the same as in the United States, especially in the mission schools and public schools.

What are some of the things which make a difference? This is the search in which my staff and I have engaged for the past five years. We have studied the development of the creative thinking abilities in a variety of schools in the United States and in other countries. We have tried to discover what are the factors in nature and society which influence this development. We have conducted both laboratory-type experiments and field experiments in an attempt to see what effect certain changes in teaching procedures will have. We have tried to create various kinds of instructional materials which will have built into them many of the principles which have been discovered through this research.

These and other experiences have left me with the firm conviction that teaching can indeed make a difference insofar as creative development is concerned. Methods, materials, attitudes, relationships with pupils, and other aspects of teaching have been shown to make a difference. Yesterday I stated that I believe creative needs and abilities are universal enough to make creative ways of learning useful for all children, though not an exclusive way of learning for any children. Yet I am convinced that some children who do not learn in other ways will learn if permitted or encouraged to learn in creative ways. In other words, for these children learning in creative ways truly *makes the difference!*

WHEN DOES CREATIVE LEARNING OCCUR?

You may be asking, "How can I tell that creative learning is taking place?" I do not believe this is difficult. This summer I asked 200 students in my class in "Creative Ways of Teaching" to list within a five-minute period all of the signs they could think of to tell whether creative learning is taking place. When I analyzed their lists, I found that altogether they had listed 230 different signs I would accept as valid indicators that creative learning is occurring in a classroom or other learning situation. Since a person can be creative in an infinite number of ways, it is not surprising that a list of 230 signs was produced within a five-minute period. You might be interested in some of these signs. I have them arranged alphabetically, so let us examine the A, B, C's of creative learning, remembering that there are also D, E, F's and so on.

Absorption—there is absorbed listening, absorbed watching, absorbed thinking, or absorbed doing—sometimes irritating but searching for the truth

Achievement—there is a feeling of moving forward towards goals, getting things done

Acceptance—of individual differences in preferred ways of learning, differences in learning rates, faults, etc.

Admission—of errors, mistakes, and failures

Alert—listening and observation, intense awareness of the environment

Aloneness respected—there are times when the best learning can be done outside of the group but with purpose

Animation—there is movement, aliveness and spirit in whatever is done

Analogizing—there is play with various kinds of analogies as ways of stating and solving problems

Arguments—differences are permitted and used to correct mistaken ideas and find more creative productive solutions

Art media are used to develop and elaborate ideas and to give them concreteness

Atmosphere is tingling with excitement and communication of ideas

Behavior problems rare

Bells frequently unheard or unnoticed

Bodily involvement in writing, speaking, thinking, etc.

Boldness of ideas, drawings, stories, etc.

Brainstorming possible

Bulletin boards contain pupils' ideas

Bursting out to complete the teacher's sentence or to communicate some new idea or discovery

Busy hum of activity

Change of pace and approaches to learning or problem-solving

Challenging of ideas

Charged atmosphere

Changes in plans to permit one thing to lead to another

Checking many sources of information and ideas

Choice making

Close observations possible

Colorful, bold art work

Communication of ideas and feelings

Comparisons and contrasts are made

Community used

Combination activities cutting across the curriculum

Composing own songs
Consideration of apparently unrelated ideas and showing relationships
Concentration on work, not easily distracted
Conflicting ideas leading to new ideas
Continuation of activities after the bell
Continuity of activities, one thing leading to another
Control freedom
Curiosity evident in questions, experimenting, manipulating, and reading
    to find out.

WHAT DIFFERENCE DOES CREATIVE TEACHING MAKE?

Even from this partial list of signs of creative learning, logical reasoning would lead us to expect that changes will occur in the lives of the children who participate in such learning. In our experimental work we have usually been concerned about some effect of creative teaching on classes, schools, or school systems. From these studies, we know that creative teaching seems to result in increased creative growth as measured by changes in performance on tests of creative thinking ability, creative writing, and the like; increased participation in creative activities on one's own; increased liking for school; and changed career aspirations. These experiments do not tell us what differences creative teaching makes in individual lives over extended periods of time.

To obtain some exploratory data to develop some clues about this matter, I asked my California students to recall instances in which they had allowed or encouraged children, young people, or adults to express themselves creatively and then observed that the experience made a difference in achievement and behavior. These students included teachers, administrators, and school psychologists at all levels of education from nursery school to college and adult education. Of the 165 students present when this request was made, 135 or 82 per cent were able to recall such instances.

Only a few of these respondents denied that creative teaching can make a difference. In these rare instances the denial seems to stem from the mistaken notion that all changes in behavior and achievement are of a developmental nature and independent of teacher influence. For example, one teacher wrote as follows:

"Right now, I can't really remember any particular child whom I've encouraged and where there has been a noticeable change. I have always felt that any change at the end of kindergarten year was due mainly to the natural development growth for the five-year old . . ."

This attitude is encountered frequently among teachers and developmental psychologists who have accepted the view that developmental processes are set, genetically determined, and unchangeable. I believe that this view results from a misinterpretation of developmental studies. These studies describe the developmental processes which occur when children experience only what the environment happens to provide. Recent studies are showing that the developmental processes can be quite different when children experience guided, planned experiences designed to lead to certain kinds of development.

Let us examine some of the changes mentioned most frequently by the 135 students who responded to my request to recall an incident in which creative teaching had made a difference:

From non-readers to average or superior readers
From vandalism, destructiveness and lack of school achievement to constructive behavior and improved achievement
From emotionally disturbed and unproductive behavior to productive behavior and even outstanding school achievement
From estrangement and lack of communication to good contact with reality and sensitive communication with others
From social isolation and rejection to social acceptance and productive group membership
From fighting and hostility to improved speech skills and lack of hostility
From bitter, hostile sarcasm to kindly, courteous, thoughtful behavior
From apathy and dislike of school to enthusiasm about learning
From lack of self-confidence and self-expression to adequate self-confidence and creative expression
From mediocrity of achievement among gifted pupils to outstanding performance
From diagnoses of mental retardation to diagnoses of normal or superior mental functioning
From a troublesome student to outstanding job performance

I was interested to note that some of these experienced teachers indicated that it was only a knowledge that teaching can make a difference that sustains them in their teaching roles.

Let us examine now a few examples which illustrate some of the different kinds of changes attributed to creative teaching.

From Non-reader to Reader. The most frequently mentioned type to change mentioned by the 135 respondents is from non-reader to reader, usually accompanied by improved behavior and achievement in general. Some of these changes occur in the primary grades, while others do not occur until the intermediate grades or the junior high school years. The following ancedote describes the occurrence of such a change during the second grade:

"In second grade we do lots of creative writing and I usually type the children's stories and let them illustrate them. John, a dreamy lad, artistic, sloppy, and a very slow reader, disturbed me by never getting more than a sentence or so written. Usually that was lost in the crumpled welter in his desk by the time the next chance to work on it came around. John was a "poor listener" and took offense over nothing. He often cried because he thought he was being slighted. (The sociogram showed him not so much rejected as ignored.)

"One day I let him dictate to me and I typed his story as he talked. He wanted to tell the story of the *Spider*—from a TV horror story. I was tempted to censor this, but fortunately kept my mouth shut. John's story was long. It was a problem to take the time to do it all, but I did, while the class carried on. His choice of words, sentence structure, use of suspense, etc. were very vivid, imaginative, mature. When I read the story to the class, the reaction was one of wild enthusiasm. John was starry-eyed. He learned to read the story, did many more, and learned to read other things. His behavior improved and he made friends."

From Destructive Behavior to Constructive Behavior. Destructive behavior on the part of a child or adolescent is especially disturbing to teachers, classmates, and administrative and custodial personnel. Students describing the consequences of creative teaching indicate that destructive behavior can be transformed into positive, creative energy and generally constructive behavior. The following is an account of one such instance:

"The principal, the janitor, the teachers all worked on the problem of John, the vandal. He was reported as being the culprit of many a weekend shambles at our school, but no one could prove anything. He couldn't stay still very long; his iron muscles semed to need to move every minute; he was as strong, at 12 years, as most grown men. He was almost a permanent fixture in the office because of undesirable behavior. He was skilled, a *natural,* in things mechanical. He liked to boss and was often swaggering and bully-like in his playground behavior. The consensus as a result of brainstorming, was that John did not feel he belonged. The problem was how to make him feel he *did* belong.

"He was appointed by the Student Council (in which he could never be an officer, because of their strict code of grades and behavior) to be a chairman of the Lunchroom Committee. He organized a team of boys; they spent half their noon recess cleaning, moving tables, helping the janitor. He began to notice the litter which collected in certain windy corners of the schoolyard. His 'gang' cleaned it up. He helped park cars for Back-to-School-Night. One woman ran her car into a deep ditch, when she did not wait for John to show her the way. The way he directed her, telling her how to cramp the wheels and when was a marvel. She would have had to have a tow-away, except for his know-how. He had organized the entire parking area without a hitch, where the drivers followed his directions, and all this done as well as an adult could have done it.

"Happily, as John became 'part' of the school, the vandalism became less and less. Reports came to us that he threatened (and coming from this boy that was no mean threat) others who tried to destroy school property. Happily, he began to take an interest in school work. His father told us that John had at last said, 'I like school.' He said John had learned to read things around the house, in the neighborhood, at the store, and on trips for the first time in his life. His art work (racing cars, car engines and antique cars) was excellent. We all hope some of this progress will continue when he leaves us this fall to go to junior high school."

From Trouble Maker to Star Learner and Teacher. In the case of John, ability for verbal learning is perhaps limited although his capacity for art, mechanics, and leadership may be outstanding. Thus, the development of his potentialities might take a direction quite different from that reported for David, a younger learner:

"David had been a problem in kindergarten. He knew it and acted it out in the first and second grades. He had thoroughly convinced everyone he was a problem by the time he entered my third grade.

"A thatch of yellow hair, crystal clear blue eyes—as he walked along the path to school all he needed was a fishing pole over his shoulder to be the perfect Huckleberry Finn! He intrigued me and interested me beyond words—there must be a key to David, and I must try to find it.

"I set the stage in every possible way so he would do a few things at least that we could praise—this was a shock to him and he didn't know quite what to do with praise! . . . By Christmas time we had arrived at the point of mutual respect for one another.

"At Christmas in our room we take a trip around the world and explore the Christmas customs of the children in our countries. This year we had decided to go by plane. We had a representative from the airlines as a guest speaker—telling about tickets, traveling by plane, and showing some slides of various countries.

"The day came when each child was to make his ticket for the country he wished to visit. I was surprised as I watched David—usually he was one of the last ones to start, but this time he was well on his way immediately. As I 'toured' the room, I noticed David's ticket would be for Sweden. This surprised me as he had brought many things from Mexico in for Sharing Time, and I had rather thought his ticket would be for Mexico. The 'Captain' for the trip arranged his 'passenger' list by countries. David was the only one for Sweden. This seemed to please him, and as time passed we were all amazed at the responsibility he assumed in finding things to present about 'his country.'

"We found that he had chosen this country because his favorite grandmother had come from Sweden. . . . He found it necessary to write five or six letters to her for various items of information. I was surprised at the neatness and the care with which he did the job—would that he had done many of his other papers in like manner!

"He wrote some wonderful factual stories about Sweden. His Swedish fairy tales were really something! He often found expression at the easel —and such vivid colors.

"The day when the class were his 'guests' in Sweden he told of the customs and even taught us a game the Swedish children play. He also taught us to make little 'goodie' baskets they hang on their Christmas trees.

"Our children come to school by bus, but the two weeks before Christmas David walked nearly every morning because he wanted to get there early so he could get extra painting or writing done. As he was telling me goodbye on the last day of school before the holidays, he said, 'Gee, Miss T., this is the neatest Christmas I've ever had—I feel like I've almost been to Sweden.'

"I had found my 'key' to David. He needed to find out things and tell them—sometimes do a bit of embroidery on them—sometimes do a bit of dreaming and make-believe on them. He liked his real world much better too.

"This did change David—he no longer needed to be the 'bad boy'—he adjusted to the praise and found it 'fun' (as he said) to write stories, draw pictures, etc. of his 'secret world.' He was so busy doing this he didn't have time to revert to the 'old' David."

From Estrangement and Retardation to Adjustment and Achievement. A number of the anecdotes related by the respondents involved children who seemed to be estranged and out of contact with reality and regarded as mentally retarded. The following account of Jamie at the time he was in the fifth grade falls into this category:

"Jamie lived on another planet. He seemed to feel no need to relate to the world around him. As he entered the fifth grade, the children thought of him as a 'dumb kid.' In a flexible individual reading program I was able to let him skip around in the book as the spirit moved him and report in the way he was able through drawings. He completed one fourth grade and two fifth grade readers during the year and I feel he is ready to face any sixth grade reading material.

"At the same time in a 'slow' math class he was exposed to an imaginative teacher. By allowing him to use his interest in motors to develop a math project he was able to show a real flair for teaching others and his classmates discovered that Jamie had brains!"

WHAT MADE THE DIFFERENCE?

The incidents I have just reported provide many provocative ideas about what makes a difference. In some ways, the teacher provided a responsive environment—one which involved a sensitive and alert kind of guidance and direction, the creation of an atmosphere of receptive listening, responding to children and young people as they are or might become rather than as they have been told that they are, fighting off ridicule and criticism, and making their efforts to learn worthwhile.

Now, I would like to give you a list of the factors mentioned most frequently by my students in "Creative Ways of Teaching."

Recognizing some heretofore unrecognized and unused potential
Respecting a child's need to work alone
Inhibiting the censorship role long enough for a creative response to occur
Allowing or encouraging a child to go ahead and achieve success in an
    area and in a way possible for him
Permitting the curriculum to be different for different pupils
Giving concrete embodiment to the creative ideas of children
Giving a chance to make a contribution to the welfare of the group
Encouraging or permitting self-initiated projects
Reducing pressure, providing a relatively non-punitive environment
Approval in one area to provide courage to try in others
Voicing the beauty of individual differences
Respecting the potential of low achievers
Enthusiasm of the teacher
Support of the teacher against peer pressures to conformity
Placing an unproductive child in contact with a productive, creative child
Using fantasy ability to establish contacts with reality
Capitalizing upon hobby and special interests and enthusiasms
Tolerance of complexity and disorder, at least for a period
Involvement
Not being afraid of bodily contact with children
Communicating that the teacher is "for" rather than "against" the child

PERMITTING CHILDREN TO WORK ALONE
AND IN THEIR OWN WAY

In learning and in doing creative work, many people are unable to function very well in a group. They seem to need to "march to a different drumbeat" and to work at their own pace. Much in established ways of teaching creates a set which makes this difficult. Even beginning teachers find it possible, however, to permit such divergency. The following story of Mark's report on Latin America illustrates this point and suggests a number of other ideas as well:

"Last year was my first year of teaching. I had a student, Mark, whom I immediately recognized as an extremely creative student, and someone for whom I had an enormous respect.

"The study of Latin America is a required part of our social studies curriculum for the sixth grade. I followed every step of what I had been taught in 'Teaching Social Studies in the Elementary School' . . . letting the class decide what you need to learn about a people and a country to understand them and their needs, and then a secretary wrote the names of the various Latin American countries on the board, so that the children could select the country's committee they would like to be on to prepare written reports. We decided that the major countries would need more on a committee . . . Ecuador came up, and two people volunteered and were given that country to research and do a project on. After all of the countries had been spoken for, I noticed that Mark had not made a choice.

"Talking with him, I learned that he had wanted Ecuador, as he had been reading Darwin's journals and was fascinated by the Galapagos Islands, but he hadn't wanted to work with anyone, so hadn't held up his hand. Well, I said that was all right, and that he could make up a separate report on the Galapagos Islands, which he agreed to do.

"Three weeks later, Mark had not begun his report, in the sense that he had nothing on paper. He was just too busy reading books, interviewing anthropologists at the University of California, and thinking. I tried very hard to help him get something on paper, but when I saw that he just was too interested in Darwin's discoveries and their implications and the evidence of it that remains to this day on the Islands, I decided Mark's assignment would be changed to an oral report. He reacted very favorably to this, delivering a magnificent account of what kind of person Darwin was, an account of the voyage of the *Beagle,* and then delivered a very instructive lecture on the various forms of a single species as they appear on the different islands, drawing pictures of the variants on the chalkboard, complete with describing the different environment a different island would offer and asking the other students in the class to guess what variant they would imagine would result!

"Mark got such a good feeling out of this experience, I was able, when the next report came up, to talk with him in terms of being able to operate in more than one manner and thus be prepared to be flexible and able to choose—I put it to him in terms of baseball; that a player might be a right-hander but it would be to his advantage to also learn to bat left-handed so that he could be a switch-hitter—that he decided he would prepare a written report, which he did—a very good one, and in on time and beautifully done, even as far as presentation—right down to the bibliography.

"The point is, I think, that in honoring his involvement at a particular time in research, he learned to respect me enough to consider the advantages when the next report came around of knowing how to prepare and get in on time a written report."

If we examine the teacher's report of this episode closely, we find several factors involved. It is likely that one of the more salient factors contributing to the success of the teacher in working with Mark was her willingness to change or bend her planned sequence of experiences to permit Mark to function in such a way to achieve his potentialities. He was able to function in terms of his abilities and interests, without actually upsetting the curriculum or the classroom organization. We find, however, that the teacher had already recognized Mark's creative potential and that she had an enormous respect for him. She recognized that she would be bucking a strong force to divert him at this time from his interest in the Galapagos Islands; furthermore, she saw how he might be able to contribute meaningfully to the curriculum for the entire class. She had not counted upon his absorption being so great that he could not find time to write his report. She remained open and flexible, however, and saw that he might contribute most by giving an oral report, a challenge which he met with unexpected skill. Having achieved success and having achieved respect for his teacher, he was then ready to learn some of the more conforming ways of behaving in the educational environment. In fact, he was even able to include a very proper bibliography documenting his report. He has learned adaptive and constructive ways of behaving which will doubtless stand him in good stead throughout his educational career.

A CONCLUDING SUGGESTION

My final suggestion is one created by J. H. Mohrman, one of my students, at the end of the course on "Creative Ways of Teaching." I shall present it to you just as he presented it to me—A Checklist for Creative Teaching:

"There is a story, common in the Navy and Merchant Marine, of the young third mate who had a great admiration for the Master of the ship in which he sailed. He was, however, puzzled about one of the Captain's habits. Quite occasionally while they were at sea, the Captain would take a dog-eared piece of paper from his pocket and study it intently for a few minutes. Following this ritual, the Captain was his usual picture of calm, self-assurance. Although he was never able to learn what was written on the paper, the Third Mate felt that it must contain the ultimate secret of the Captain's success as a seafarer. On one voyage the Captain died while they were at sea, and the Third Mate was given the task of inventorying and packing the Captain's belongings. He was in a high state of excitement as he went about this task knowing that, at last, he would discover the secret written on the slip of paper which the Captain had guarded so jealously. With trembling fingers, the Third Mate removed the paper from the Captain's jacket pocket and opened it to find this "secret" written inside: 'Starboard is Right—Port is Left.'

"We are all somewhat like the Sea Captain, and occasionally need some simple reminder of the elementary principles that we all 'know perfectly well.' For many reasons; partly because we all need a crutch for our courage from time to time, and a stiffner for our resolve, or perhaps more likely, simply a reminder of our good intentions, I have prepared a check-list to keep handy in my desk drawer to remind myself frequently of at least some aspects of the creative process. We all tend to be creatures of habit and to have our judgment beclouded by our ingrained prejudices and predelictions, particularly with regard to what the 'good' pupil or the 'good' classroom is like. Because of the many possibilities for conflict with our own personalities and the creative personality, or some aspect of the classroom where creative learning is taking place, I hope that this simple 'Starboard is Right—Port is Left' type of list will keep us closer to the creative course."

Don't be too "threatened" by the exceptional child—or the unexpected
    response.
Pay attention to the "atmosphere" of the room.
Don't be too concerned about a higher noise level—if it's a "busy hum."
Remember the creative need to communicate—maybe that whisper is all
    right.
Don't be blinded by "intelligence" test scores—they don't tell the *whole*
    story.
Don't be afraid to wander off your teaching schedule—stay flexible.
Encourage divergent ideas—too many of the "right" ideas are stifling.
Be accepting and forgiving of the "mistakes."
Remember, the "obnoxious" child may simply be escaping from the tedium
    of your class.
Don't let your pride get in the way of your teaching.
Different kinds of children learn in different ways.
Let them "test their limits."
Don't let the pressure for "evaluation" get the upper hand.
Give them a chance to "warm-up" to producing ideas.
Respect the privacy of their responses (especially the less successful ones).
Criticism is killing—use it carefully and in small doses.
How about those "Provocative Questions?"
Don't forget to define the problem.
Don't be afraid to try something different.

"This list could, of course, be added to indefinitely—and I intend to. Also these items won't 'translate' properly for everyone, but it's at least a start, and it will have served its purpose if it helps only me."

I would urge you to create your own list to fit yourself. Each teacher's way of teaching must ultimately be his own unique invention. I wish for you the very greatest success in perfecting your own invention—your way of teaching.

REFERENCES

Pulsifer, Susan Nichols. *Children Are Poets.* Cambridge, Mass.: Dresser, Chapman & Grimes, Inc., 1963.
Torrance, E. P. *Guiding Creative Talent.* Englewood Cliffs, N. J.: Prentice-Hall, Inc., 1962.
Wilt, Miriam E. *Creativity in the Elementary School.* New York: Appleton-Century-Crofts, 1959.

Annotated Bibliography

Bedmar, R. L. and Parker, C. A. "The Creative Development and Growth of Exceptional College Students." *Journal of Educational Research* 59: 133–136, Nov. 1965.
   Guilford tests administered to 90 students in an honors program at Brigham Young University revealed no significant relationship or growth during three years.

Eberle, R. F. *Experimentation in the Teaching of the Creative Thinking Processes.* Edwardsville Junior High School, Edwardsville, Illinois, June 1965.
   A research report which combines a search of the literature with a local study. Following a review of the literature the author reports that "aspects of creative thinking are learnable, and as such can be taught." Significant gains may take place in short periods and these are accompanied by personality changes. In the local study of 7 out of 16 cases significant differences on pre- and post-tests were obtained.

Lincoln, J. W. "Developing a Creativeness in People." (pp. 269–75) in Parnes, S. J., and Harding H. F. *A Source Book for Creative Thinking.* New York: Charles Scribner's Sons, 1962.
   The "Gordon technique" of synectics and its applications to operational creativity is discussed.

Maltzman, I. "On the Training of Originality." *Psychological Review* 67: 229–42; 1960.
   Reviews his work on training originality which he believes can be accomplished.

Mednick, Martha "Research Creativity in Psychology Graduate Students" *Journal of Consulting Psychology* 27:265–6, 1963.

The validity of the RAT (Remote Associates Test) was investigated by comparing ratings given individuals on a research creativity check list with the RAT. The correlation was .55 supporting the use of this test as a selection device for creativity.

Mednick, Martha, Sarnoff and Edward. "Incubation of Creative Performance and Specific Associate Priming." *Journal of Abnormal and Social Psychology* 69:84–88, July, 1964.

An investigation of the effect of associative priming on incubation of creative performance found that high scorers on the RAT (Remote Associates Test) performed better than low scorers and that the effect of specific priming was greater than no priming. Time relationship had no effect. Results support an associative interpretation of incubation.

Taylor, D. U., and others. "Does Group Participation When Using Brainstorming Facilitate or Inhibit Creative Thinking?" *Travail Humain* 24: 1–20; 1961.

In attempting to test high pressure creation of new ideas, 96 Yale students were tested singly and in groups of 4. There were significantly more ideas produced in groups, although 4 persons produced slightly less than twice the number produced by persons working alone.

Torrance, E. P. "Factors Affecting Creative Thinking in Children: An Interim Report." *Merrill-Palmer Quarterly* 7:171–80; 1961.

Discusses psychological factors affecting the creative thinking of young children.

Yee, G. F. *The Influences of Problem-Solving Instruction and Personal-Social Adjustment upon Creativity Test Scores of Twelfth Grade Students.* Unp. Ed. D. thesis, Pennsylvania State University, 1964. (*Dissertation Abstracts* 26:916, 1965.)

High-ability students showed significant increase in creativity scores after problem-solving instruction as compared with matched controls. Low-ability students did not. Creative high-ability students have greater sense of personal worth, and fewer anti-social tendencies than counterparts; creative low-ability students also differ in the same way from their less creative counterparts. There was no significant difference, however, in adjustment among high-ability students varying in creativity or in low-ability students varying in creativity.

CHAPTER FIVE

A Curriculum for Creativity

Frames of Reference for
Creative Behavior in the Arts [*]

J. P. Guilford

I<small>F MY INTERPRETATION OF THIS SITUATION IS CORRECT, WE HAVE GATHERED</small>
here a group of individuals representing the various arts, who desire
to further their understanding of what it means to be creative and
to give thought to procedures for investigating creative performance
in the arts. The title chosen for this conference, "Creative Behavior
in the Arts," by its appropriate emphasis on "behavior," implies that
many of the problems encountered in the pursuit of these objectives
lie in the realm of psychology. We have also in the gathering a group
of psychologists, and there is rather obvious expectation on the part
of organizers of the conference that there shall be fruitful intercom-
munication, cross fertilization of ideas, and, hopefully, some hybrid
offspring with superior qualities.

As a psychologist who has devoted quite a number of years to
investigations pertaining more or less directly to the potential understanding of creative behavior in general, I shall offer some suggestions
that I hope will be helpful. I have chosen to emphasize frames of
reference that I have found very useful in connection with the investigation of creative thinking and creative production. I shall speak first
of the needs for frames of reference and how they facilitate progress
in research. I shall describe two major frames of reference or theoretical models that I have found exceedingly useful and meaningful
and show how they are readily adaptable to investigations of creative
behavior in the arts.

---

[*] A paper presented to the Conference on "Creative Behavior in the Arts,"
sponsored by the University of California at Los Angeles, Feb. 18–20, 1965.

R<small>EPRINTED</small> by permission of the Author.

NEEDS FOR FRAMES OF REFERENCE

Whether or not anyone here decides to adopt the frames of reference that I shall describe, I should like to emphasize that any serious investigator, in basic science or in technology, will find a good frame of reference very helpful. A frame of reference may be as broad as a philosophical point of view or as circumscribed as a limited scientific theory. The kind that is close to a scientific theory is most useful to the investigator of some particular domain such as creative behavior. The advantages are the same as those of a scientific theory. Why do we need scientific theory?

Without scientific theory, the investigator has no major goals or directions; it is a case of the proverbial "ship without a rudder." It is not enough just to have a strong desire "to do research." Undirected effort is often futile. Such an investigator is likely to pick away at minor problems, here and there, as fancy of the moment dictates or as opportunity comes his way. Only more or less by chance is he likely to work on significant problems and to make a lucky strike, if he ever does.

A scientific theory is a source of significant problems, each problem a question, to which an answer is sought. Progress depends very much on being able to ask questions and to ask the right questions and the significant questions. Theory generates questions and also provides a basis for determining whether questions, however generated, are significant ones. Obtaining answers to questions by way of empirical testing, known as research, should be expected either to support the theory or not to support it. In the latter case, a change in theory may be called for. The need to change a theory is no disgrace. In research, one cannot afford to be afraid of making mistakes. Such fears put a damper on creative production. Correction of mistakes at least holds the prospect for real progress. Finding out what is not true is often as informing as finding what *is* true. And, very often, two alternative, positive, hypotheses can be tested, in which case either outcome is a positive gain.

REQUIREMENTS FOR A GOOD FRAME OF REFERENCE

A good frame of reference for an investigator's purpose has three important specifications; it should be comprehensive, it should be systematic, and it should be basic.

When I say that a frame of reference should be comprehensive, I do not mean that it should be of the broad, philosophical type. It should be sufficiently restricted to generate questions that can be answered by empirical tests by empirical procedures. But it should not be so circumscribed that one loses sight of the larger picture, for all phenomena have significant ramifications. Understanding one item in a complex of items depends in part upon knowing interrelationships. Keeping a broader view is needed to ensure that some item, perhaps an important one, if not a crucial one, may not be overlooked.

Some investigators, in their legitimate efforts to simplify things, in their dutiful application of the principle of parsimony, are likely to eliminate from possible view some of the phenomena that should come within the scope of their observations. Too many psychologists, at least, have overdone the urge to simplify, with the result that significant phenomena have been excluded from consideration. I urge you not to make the same mistake.

A good frame of reference is systematic. The only hope of human understanding of natural phenomena is the fact that there are regularities in nature. Such regularities are what we are seeking within the sphere of our investigations. They offer the possibilities of principles and scientific laws. Principles and laws provide a shorthand type of apprehending information, enlarging the scope of our understanding and our powers to operate with phenomena. In the pursuit of further simplification and at the same time larger grasps of information, model building becomes possible. Model building is theory construction.

It appears to be in the nature of human thinking to resort to one or more of a few standard types of models, which can be quickly pointed out. In the psychological development of children, Inhelder and Piaget (1964) point out that there is growth in conceptions of what they call "seriation." By seriation they mean the arrangement of items of information in linear order, each item related to the next in line in the same manner, e.g., larger than, harder than, or more beautiful than. In the adult, particularly the educated adult, thinking in terms of abstract dimensions becomes more or less natural. Thus, we have dimensional models, which are most widely applied in mathematics and in the physical sciences.

Inhelder and Piaget (1964) also point to a parallel development in the recognition of classes and of classes within classes, in other words, hierarchical systems or models. Such models have been relatively more common in the biological sciences, in the classification schemes of Linnaeus. They are not unknown in psychology and in psychiatry.

A third type of model, not nearly so well known, has been called "morpho-logical," by the astronomer, Zwicky (1957). Basically, this type of model is a cross classification of phenomena, in intersecting categories. The chemist's periodic table introduced by Mendeleev is a good example, in which the chemical elements are arranged in rows and columns, each row and each column representing a different category. It could also be referred to as a "logical matrix." An ordinary matrix, as in mathematics, has two dimensions. There is no reason for not extending the model to three or more dimensions, if necessary. I have advocated the use of the morphological type of model in psychology and later I shall give an example of a three-dimensional one.

A fourth type of model owes its origin most largely to the communication engineers and to the fields of cybernetics and computer technology. It is well-named as an "operational" type of model, for it conceives of events in terms of an interconnected series of transmissions of information. In the course of time, there have been some steps in this direction made by psychologists in attempting to account for sequences of events in behavior. But for the most part, the operational model utilized by psychologists has been an over-simplified one constituted of stimulus and response. Taking their cues from computer technology and the efforts to simulate human thinking and problem solving by means of computers, some psychologists are now proposing more complex and more descriptive operational models. I shall present an example of this kind of model.

When I say that a model should be basic, I am thinking in terms of basic science. Many of the problems with which art teachers are concerned are educational in nature and therefore technological rather than scientific in the basic sense. But the models of basic psychology should be relevant in educational investigations, just as chemical models are relevant in the studies of pharmacology or of petroleum engineering. There is no particular harm in developing models that may appear to represent phenomena more directly or more completely in a technological setting, but basic scientific models should carry the technological investigator a long way and serve certain of his purposes very well. In the present context, what I am suggesting is that the investigator into the realm of creativity in art could find certain psychological models quite useful; including their concepts and principles.

TWO PSYCHOLOGICAL FRAMES OF REFERENCE

I shall present for your consideration two psychological models, one in the operational category and the other morphological. They are not at all in the form of alternative models between which a choice has to be made. Being different in type, both can be applied and they are quite consistent with one another, in fact quite supplementary. They merely serve somewhat different purposes, they imply different kinds of problems and approaches, but share many of the same concepts and principles.

The model to be mentioned first is an operational one. The reason for mentioning it first is that it comes closer to a general description of psychological events with which all of you have had personal acquaintance. For the same reason, there has been some historical precedent. The model in question attempts to depict in very general form the events in problem solving. I might have said "events in *creative* problem solving," but that would be somewhat redundant. After a number of years of considering the relation of creative thinking to problem solving, I have come to the conclusion that wherever there is a genuine problem there is some novel behavior on the part of the problem solver, hence there is some degree of creativity. Thus, I am saying that all genuine problem solving is creative; I leave the question open as to whether all creative thinking is problem solving; it may be. At any rate, the relationship is so close that a problem-solving model is very relevant here.

The other model is more abstract but it is more basic and of greater consequence. It is of the morphological type. It arose out of some 20 years of efforts to analyze intelligence into its component abilities and is known as the "structure of intellect." Concepts arising out of the second model have been very serviceable in filling out the first, as we shall see.

The Problem-Solving Model. Three progenitors of the problem-solving model will be mentioned. One was designed to describe a quite general sequence of events in problem solving; one to present an outline of the steps in creative production; and one more specifically for the steps in an ordinary invention, such as comes to the attention of the patent office. John Dewey (1910) offered the first attempt of such a model, when he pointed out the following steps in typical problem solving (see Fig. 1): awareness that a problem or a difficulty exists; analysis of the problem, leading to understanding of its nature; suggestion of possible solutions; and testing the alternative solutions by a process of judgment and accepting or rejecting solutions.

Graham Wallas (1926) suggested four similar steps: preparation, which involves collecting information that may be needed; incubation, which means a temporary pause or relaxation of effort; inspiration, or the moment of insight or flash of genius; and evaluation, with elaboration of the created product.

Rossman (1931) considered what the typical inventor goes through in the total process of arriving at a new invention and concluded that there are seven steps: a need or difficulty is observed; the problem is formulated; available information is surveyed; solutions are formulated; solutions are critically examined; new ideas are formulated; and the new ideas are tested.

The Wallas steps in creative production

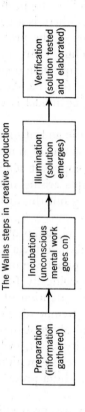

The Dewey steps in problem solving

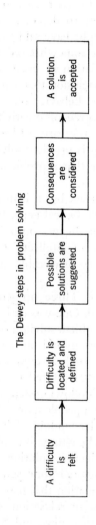

The Rossman steps in the course of a typical invention

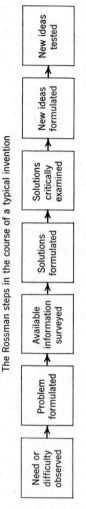

Figure 1. Three traditional conceptions of the sequence of events in creative production, problem solving, and invention.

Similarities among these three operational models, evidently developed independently, should be obvious, supporting the earlier assertion of the strong connection between problem solving and creative production, if, indeed, they are not one and the same. I should say that the major difference is the mention of incubation in the Wallas model. I consider this a logical error, for incubation is a state or condition rather than a psychological operation. This is not to deny the role of incubation, or to degrade it, but to place it in proper perspective.

The model for problem solving . . . was developed, taking into account the traditional models but also the structure-of-intellect theory and some of the more recent findings of neurology, experimental psychology, and communication theory. It is consequently somewhat elaborate, yet embodying simple principles. We are not concerned with all the detailed features of the model here. Those features most pertinent to our present needs will be explained.

In common with earlier models, the upper row of rectangles indicates a temporal sequence of events moving from left to right, with the sensing and understanding of the problem (cognition) being followed by generated solutions (production). The main difference is the addition of a repeated cycle of cognition and production, as suggested by the Rossman model. Such cycles could go on and on, of course, but one repeated cycle is sufficient to demonstrate the principle of repeated attempts at understanding and solution generation. Missing

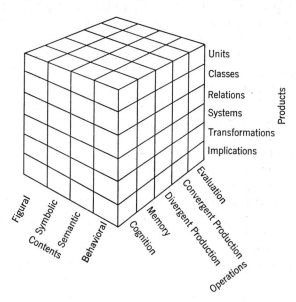

Figure 2. Theoretical model for the complete "structure of intellect."

from the direct sequence is the step of evaluation, which is put to one side (below the main stream), and which is repeated at every stage to indicate that there is continual self checking of behavior. Although evaluation may play its heaviest role after production, it can undoubtedly influence other operations at any time.

A novel addition is the memory-storage panel, placed at the bottom of the scheme to indicate that what happens at any moment along the course of problem solving can be and probably is influenced by what the thinker has in his memory storage. Most of the generated information in connection with production, also in connection with cognition and evaluation, comes from that source. New information that the thinker solicits and absorbs from his environment has at least a little time in memory storage before it is utilized. I shall ask you to put into your memory storage for use a bit later the fact that there are four major kinds of operation involved in the model—cognition, memory, production, and evaluation.[1]

The second important feature of the model that should engage our attention is the fact that there are four distinct kinds of information represented in memory storage, for this has far-reaching consequences. The four kinds of illustrated information are segregated for easy classification. First, at the extreme left we see some visual forms, having different visual properties of shape, size, and so on. Such information is concrete, much as we perceive it through the visual channel.

Next, to the right of the visual-figural information is a set of information called "symbolic," for the reason that when the individual processes information arising from stimuli such as letters, numbers, and musical notations, it is not the visual-figural properties with which he deals, but rather something for which those signs stand, as he has learned in his culture. The term "symbolic" here should not be extended too far. It does not include such things as Freudian symbols or national flags and the like. I shall give a different account of such symbolism later.

The third kind of information is touched off in our nervous systems by familiar objects or printed or spoken words that are meaningful to us. A printed word has a shape, which is a figural property; it is a certain sequential combination of letters, which is a symbolic unit; and it carries to the person who can read the word the communication of an idea, which is semantic. These three kinds of information are often distinguished by those who write about language and by others. The fourth kind of information, behavioral, is used by everybody

---

[1] Further details concerning the operations represented in this model may be found in . . . [Guilford (1964)].

every day but without the realization that it represents a distinct kind of information. It is information involved in the understanding of one person by another, often without the medium of verbal communication. The cues are in the form of facial expressions, bodily postures, tone of voice, and bodily movements. We implicitly recognize this kind of information when we say "Actions speak louder than words," or "It is not so much what you say as how you say it."

Information and Fields of Work. The four kinds of information were forced upon our attention in the Aptitudes Research Project at the University of Southern California, by findings concerning intellectual abilities. It has been demonstrated repeatedly that it takes quite different abilities to deal with or to process the four different kinds of information, even when performing the same operation—cognition, memory, production, or evaluation. There are parallel sets of abilities for dealing with the different kinds of information. But more of that later; here it is desirable to point out some of the consequences of all this for different kinds of work in everyday life, and more particularly in the various arts.

Figural information is the psychological meat of those whose occupation calls upon its members to deal with concrete problems. Of the non-artist groups, the mechanic, the athlete, the aircraft pilot (especially of small aircraft), and the inventor of gadgets come first to mind. Artists of various kinds are very much concerned with figural information of one kind or another. At this point we must bring in a new distinction, for concrete information can be of auditory or of kinesthetic origin as well as visual. The field of visual-figural abilities has been rather extensively explored, with almost no investigation of abilities in the auditory or the kinesthetic modes of information.

Obviously, among artists dependent upon visual-figural information are painters, sketchers, sculptors, designers, and all their variations. Artists dependent upon auditory-figural information are musical composers, arrangers, and musical performers. The poet should be mentioned, to the extent that rhymes and rhythms have auditory properties. Kinesthetic information is of significance for the choreographer and the dance performer, although visual information also plays a role for these groups.

Symbolic information is the meat of the mathematician, the modern logician, the cryptographer, the linguist, and the chemist. With symbolic information defined in the limited way that it is in connection with the problem-solving model, there is little to offer in the way of applications in fields of art.

Semantic information being so much connected with words, and words with communication, occupations that deal very much with verbal communication are heavier processors of semantic information —scientists, writers, speakers, lawyers, and teachers, for example. Among artists whose mode of expression is verbal are writers of various kinds of output—fiction, non-fiction, poetry, plays, librettos, and lyrics.

Behavioral information is of relatively great importance to people who deal directly with other people, who must understand them and possibly attempt to control them. Among such occupations we can list politicians, statesmen, salesmen, policemen, teachers, social workers, and psychiatrists. Among the artists who deal heavily with behavioral information are writers of psychological novels and dramas; directors of drama, and actors; cartoonists and portrait painters; and sculptors (such as Michaelangelo or Rodin).

I do not wish to leave the impression that any one artist or type of artist deals in only one kind of information. Many artists often process more than one kind of information in the pursuit of their creative productions. The painter or the composer or the sculptor or the choreographer may first conceive of his theme in semantic form, then proceed to translate it into figural form. Only the modern type of painter may entirely lack semantic information in his product.

The four kinds of information are like four different languages and there is the possibility of making translations from one to another. There are limitations to translating, however, for "vocabularies" are not complete and fully parallel in all four of the languages. Each artist may find it much easier to think in terms of one of the languages and may know another language so poorly that he cannot succeed in making the translation. Problems of translation must surely come into the sphere of investigation in the psychology of the arts.

The Structure-of-Intellect Model. Fig. 2 presents a view of the structure-of-intellect model, a three-dimensional matrix or morphological model; a cross-classification of human intellectual abilities, known and yet to be demonstrated. Each cell represents a unique kind of ability or intellectual skill, of which 120 are hypothesized by the theory and 70 have been demonstrated. When first conceived in this form, less than 50 such abilities had been demonstrated. The model has since served as the very useful source of suggestions as to where to look for new kinds of abilities, and further explorations are in progress. I mention this in support of an earlier statement about the advantages of having a productive theory or frame of reference.

In this model you will recognize the four kinds of information or content already discussed, also the four kinds of operations mentioned in connection with the problem-solving model. But here are represented *five* kinds of operations. The reason is that a distinction has to be made between two kinds of production abilities—*divergent* production and *convergent* production. Both have to do with the retrieval of information from memory storage, but convergent production occurs under severe restrictions. Starting with the given information, there is only one right or conventionally acceptable answer. The best examples of this kind of production are found in mathematics and logic. In divergent production, a variety of solutions or ideas is possible, under the freedom offered by the problem and the relaxed judgment of the thinker. The arts are notorious for such latitudes and they thus offer opportunities and challenges to the divergent thinker.

The entirely new concept in the structure-of-intellect model, not explicitly demonstrated in the problem-solving model (but actually illustrated there), is that of *products*. Psychological products are the special forms in which information is processed; as units, relations, classes, systems, transformations, and implications. Each and every separate item shown in memory storage . . . or, rather, the information that it stands for or implies, can be taken as a unit. A figural unit may be a letter, a geometric form, or the outline of a familiar object. A symbolic unit may be a familiar syllable or word, a bar of music, or a code letter or word. Concepts are semantic units; so are what are popularly called "ideas." Behavioral units are states of mind—perceptions, feelings, intentions, and the like. Examples of systems are the two theoretical models of which I have been speaking, although there are many simpler instances . . . when we analyze them to find the interrelationships among their parts. Examples of other kinds of products will come out in subsequent discussion.

Divergent-Production Abilities. Let us concentrate a while on the abilities in the divergent-production operation category, for it is believed that they play important roles in creative thinking. It should be kept in mind that the operation of production is a matter of generating items of information by retrieval or recall of those items from memory storage. The chances are that, to solve a new problem, those items of information must be recalled in new connections or in revised form, and this is where novelty comes in.

Before the divergent-production category of abilities was recognized, a number of abilities were found and described under the headings of fluency, flexibility, and elaboration. One test of fluency asks the examinee to produce items of information in response to given information as rapidly as he can. For example, in the verbal or semantic category, we ask him to list as many things as he can that are white, soft, and edible. For a parallel figural ability, we ask him to sketch simple objects or designs, each containing a circle or some other prescribed element. In these tests, units of information are being produced.

In another verbal-fluency test we ask the examinee to produce a list of four-word sentences. In such a task, the generation of a sentence means the organizing of production of a semantic system. In a parallel figural test, we give the examinee a set of elemental figures, such as a circle, a rectangle, a triangle, and a trapezoid, which he is to combine in various ways to produce more complex objects, in other words, figural systems.

In one verbal test for flexibility, we mention a very familiar object such as a newspaper, asking the examinee to suggest several unusual uses to which it can be adapted, all different. In a parallel figural test, we present a small set of figures that differ in several respects, each with some degree of complexity, asking him to form as many classes as he can, of three figures each. Similarities in terms of different attributes permit the regrouping of the figures in different ways. At first glance these two tests do not appear to be parallel, but psychologically they are; they both require the examinee to go from one class to another. Each unusual use of a newspaper (such as "to swat flies," "to light a fire," or "to wrap garbage") reclassifies it according to some particular property just as regrouping figures does in the other test. The product involved is that of class and the flexibility is shown in readily going from one class to another. You may have heard that one of the common diseases of the uncreative person is a "hardening of the categories."

For another kind of flexibility in the semantic context, we give a test called Plot Titles. Giving the examinee a very short story plot, we ask him to suggest alternative, appropriate titles. We may or may not instruct him to make the titles clever; some of them will be clever and some not. The number of clever answers is the score. Clever titles involve a playful shifting of views of the facts of the given story, in other words, revisions or transformations, which show up in titles in the form of puns, alliterations, and other literary tricks.

In the figural category of information, we give a Match Problems Test. This is based upon the familiar game that starts with a layout of adjacent squares or triangles, each side of which is a movable match. The examinee is told to remove a specified number of matches to leave a specified number of squares or triangles and to solve each problem in as many different ways as he can. Here, again, the examinee must be flexible. He must be able to take new looks at his problem and to strike off in new directions. The "new look" means a revision or a transformation. Being ready to transform given information and to revise our strategies accordingly is an important contribution to creative thinking. Transformations enable us to use information that is retrieved from memory storage in new ways, thus contributing to creative resourcefulness.

Ability to elaborate upon information has long been recognized as an important contributor to artistic production. The artist typically generates schema or systems first, to which he gives flesh and blood later. There are always finishing touches needed to round out the final product. We get at the elaboration ability in the semantic area in a test that calls for elaboration of a plan, for which only an outline of major steps is given. The number of detailed steps given in limited time is the score. In the structure-of-intellect theory, elaboration has been recognized as a matter of producing implications. That is, the details given to round out a scheme are implied by the scheme itself, and one added detail may lead to another. Where one item of information leads naturally to another, we have an implication. A more recently developed test of semantic elaboration is called Possible Jobs. Given is a relatively simple but realistic picture, such as a setting sun to which the examinee is to respond by listing occupations or groups of people for which the design may serve as a symbol. This test serves to measure the same ability as the Planning Elaboration test.

In the figural context, we offer simple lines or outlines of objects, asking the examinee to add lines of his own, as in our test called Decorations. Outlines of pieces of furniture and of clothing are presented and the number of appropriate additions is the score, where "appropriate" is given a very liberal interpretation. The same outline objects are presented twice, so there is added room for divergent production. As in the verbal tests, the lines are added by implication from what is given.

No examples were given for tests of divergent production involving symbolic information for the reason that this category of information is of little or no relevance for art. Remember that I ruled out of the symbolic category the kinds of symbolism that are so common in art. I now suggest that such symbolism really belongs under the heading of the product category of implications. The Possible Jobs test is an example. As in this test, symbolism in art often crosses the boundaries of information categories, hence involves the translation problem.

Nor were examples given for divergent production of *behavioral* information. At this point in time we are still in the hypothesis stage, for although the structure-of-intellect model predicts such abilities, we have only recently started research designed to test the hypothesized abilities. As a matter of fact, we have only recently demonstrated that there are *any* abilities for dealing with behavioral information at all. But a study testing the hypothesis that there are six abilities for cognition of behavioral information has just recently been successfully completed, giving strong faith in the expectation of other behavioral abilities, including those hypothesized for divergent production.

A word should be added regarding evaluation abilities, in view of the importance given to that concept in creative thinking and problem solving. I must confess that, although we have demonstrated a dozen evaluation factors, the rather limited kinds of tests that demonstrate those abilities suggest that only logical criteria are involved, for example, criteria such as identity and logical consistency. I am sure that the criteria of what is good and satisfying in art go well beyond those criteria. Psychologists have shied away from questions of value, but such problems must be faced, for, involving human behavior as they do, they should be challenges to the investigating psychologists as well as to investigating artists.[2]

SUMMARY

This paper has stressed the importance of having a frame of reference or theory as a source of significant problems in the conduct of research. It has suggested two psychological models that should serve the investigator in the area of creative artistic behavior; a model for the operations involved in problem solving, in which creative components are characteristic, and a model for the whole range of intellectual abilities, among which are many that are apparently relevant for success in creative artistic production. The concepts and principles offered by these models should be quite adaptable and serviceable in pursuing further understanding of the creative artist and his behavior.

REFERENCES

Dewey, J. *How we think*. Boston: D. C. Heath, 1910.
Guilford, J. P. Creative abilities in the arts. *Psychol. Rev.*, 1957, *64*, 110–118.
Guilford, J. P. Three faces of intellect. *Amer. Psychologist*, 1959, *14*, 469–479.
Guilford, J. P. The psychology of creativity. *Creative Crafts*, 1960, *1*, 5–8.
Guilford, J. P. Creativity in the visual arts. *Creative Crafts*, 1962, *3*, 2–5.
Guilford, J. P. Basic problems in teaching for creativity. Unpublished paper presented at the Conference on Creativity and Teaching Media, held at La Jolla, California, Aug. 31 through Sept. 3, 1964.
Guilford, J. P. and Hoepfner, R. Current summary of structure-of-intellect factors and suggested tests. *Rep. psychol. Lab.*, No. 30. Los Angeles: Univ. Southern California, 1963.

[2] Further information concerning the structure of intellect may be found elsewhere (Guilford, 1959; Guilford and Merrifield, 1960; Guilford and Hoepfner, 1963). For further thoughts on the psychology of creativity in the arts, see other sources (Guilford, 1957, 1960, 1962).

Guilford, J. P. and Merrifield, P. R. The structure of intellect model: its uses and implications. *Rep. psychol. Lab.*, No. 24. Los Angeles: Univ. Southern California, 1960.

Inhelder, B. and Piaget, J. *The early growth of logic in the child.* New York: Harper and Row, 1964. (Trans. by E. A. Lunzer and D. Papert.)

Rossman, J. *The psychology of the inventor.* Washington, D. C.: Inventors Publishing Co., 1931.

Wallas, G. *The art of thought.* London: C. A. Watts, 1926, 1945.

Zwicky, F. *Morphological analysis.* Berlin: Springer-Verlag, 1957.

Creativity and the Curriculum

Louis J. Rubin

"WHEN ONE CONSIDERS IN ITS LENGTH AND IN ITS BREADTH THE IMPORtance of this question of the education of the young, the broken lives, the defeated hopes, the national failures, which result from the frivolous inertia with which it is treated, it is difficult to restrain within oneself a savage rage."

Alfred North Whitehead made this observation some years ago in *The Aims of Education.* Until recently his words have been aptly descriptive of our educational scene.

In sharp contrast, the last decade has witnessed ferment and upheaval. Several deficiencies have been removed and a spectacular overhaul of the curriculum is in process. The transformation has consisted not of minor additions or deletions to content but of a deep-seated revolution in our approach to the selection of subject matter. The necessity for coping with increasingly untidy accumulations of knowledge, the recommendations of subject specialists, and a general reappraisal of learning theory have together been responsible for the change. The main postulate to be set forth here is that the arguments supporting the rebellion from traditional content must accord with the teaching implications of research on creativity. Efforts to invoke one necessarily call forth the other. In short, teaching which exploits the student's creative capacities also results in infinitely more effective learning.

Some contemporary learning theory stresses the learning impetus which young children derive from their innate tendency to explore unknown situations, to seek challenges which tax freshly won skills, and to deliberately find problem situations at the edge of their ca-

REPRINTED by permission of the Author and *Phi Delta Kappan,* 44:438–40, June, 1963.

pacities. This principle suggests that the mature student should similarly be involved in intellectual activities which animate his curiosity, which require him to deal with the challenging and the unknown, and that instead of carrying on his work in situations free from tension, he should purposely be thrust into a controlled study environment with built-in stress.

The crux of the method hinges upon the selection of questions for self-directed inquiry which demand a respectable degree of preliminary information and which require the student to employ a number of diverse intellectual skills in reaching his conclusion. It does not imply that the student must acquire all of his knowledge through discovery. It does imply that periodically the student ought to employ his aggregation of facts, however accumulated, in attacking problems which give meaning to his information and which shape both his conceptual understanding and his rational insights. Hence, implicit in the inquiry method is the belief that when the learner organizes available information to find an answer to his problem, he is able to capitalize on the function of knowledge and develop adeptness in self-directed learning. A benchmark of the new curriculum is thus an abundant provision for investigatory procedures, for experimentation with unknowns, and for the utilization of knowledge, at one level, as a catapult to additional knowledge at a higher level.

Inquiry, as a planned method of learning, is still in an exploratory stage. Devising a teaching strategy in which inquiry complements other useful methods of learning will require experimentation. If only because efficient inquiry requires a structure, the curriculum specialist must still find an efficacious way to select, organize, and present appropriate content. The prudent use of verbal explanation, expository discourse, drill, and memorization will continue to have a qualified place in the classroom.

Human achievement is as much a tribute to man's continuous escape from earlier error as it is to his invention of new truth. Lawrence Frank puts the problem succinctly:

"Until pupils are aware of their preconceptions, their customary assumptions and expectations, the folk-wisdom and traditional beliefs from earlier stages in the history of thought, the once valid common sense, they cannot learn the new, they are handicapped by these older concepts, these familiar ways of thinking. Here we should recognize a crucial problem for education today, namely the problem of *unlearning*, or if you prefer, re-learning. It seems clear that if a child (or an adolescent, or an adult) is to learn new concepts, new ways of perceiving and thinking about the world, he must first become aware of his preconceptions, recognize his familiar habitual patterns, what he has previously learned from his family and his neighbors, what has been built into his frame of references and so guides, directs, or even coercively controls what he learns. Without this cognitive self-awareness, he cannot ordinarily recognize that he must give up the old in order to learn the new." [1]

A separate facet of the current reorganization of the curriculum stems from the supposition that knowledge other than accepted facts, laws, and theories, is pertinent to the school's purpose. *What we do not know,* for example, also represents an important kind of knowledge. The student who receives a broad exposure to the nature of man's riddles, to the critical questions yet unsolved, and who is led to an appreciation of the historical evolution of a particular concept throughout each of its progressive stages, can begin to develop a flexible perception of the intellectual arena.

Combining the major provisions of the inquiry approach to learning with the assumptions underlying content reorganization, we can examine the parallel between curriculum innovation and the implications of creativity research. To restate, then, efforts to span sequentially the gamut of knowledge in a subject are giving way to an emphasis on significant concepts and their consequences. Information, once mastered, is put to use through engaging the student in investigatory learning—laboratory experimentation, formulation and verification of hypotheses, and theoretical reconstructions. The student develops skill in establishing crucial questions, in selecting relevant data, and in drawing conclusions which in turn suggest the formulation of new questions. In developing a competence to work with the different processes of learning he engages in diverse forms of thinking. The essence of the curriculum shifts from the mastery of content to the techniques for acquiring and using knowledge. The process of learning, in brief, becomes more important than what is to be learned. Because, to use Whitehead's notion, information keeps no better than fish.

CREATIVENESS AND CURRICULUM DESIGN

Of course the school should not seek to temper every student into an innovative genius. However, all humans have some creative potential whose release produces a measure of satisfaction. Therefore, a curriculum designed to encourage creativeness holds value for all students, not merely the creatively gifted minority.

Several preliminary observations are worthwhile. First, self-direction need not be unduly permissive; with proper caution even the relatively

[1] L. K. Frank, *The School as Agent for Cultural Renewal.* Harvard, 1960, p. 18.

inhibited student can function efficiently. Second, the intense satisfaction we take in having students reflect our cherished values has led our able students to be motivated by the conditions for reward—the exhibition of their knowledge in the preferred style. A successful student perceives that success stems not only from being knowledgeable but from being able to *appear* knowledgeable. Third, humans are strongly motivated by a desire to explain questions dealing with their milieu. The drive, unhappily, is as well satisfied by a false explanation as by a correct one. Our compulsion for omniscient instruction, providing answers for all questions, has resulted in an unwillingness to deal with unknowns, in a vast number of schooled individuals who espouse outdated convictions and in learning materials characterized by a deliberate misrepresentation of fact. The commercially successful textbook, for example, must necessarily be shorn of all irritants to all intellectual allergies.

Aside from its intellectual honesty, a willingness to introduce unknowns into the curriculum will offer the student a feeling for the creation of knowledge; when the answer to an important question is unknown to the teacher, the textbook, or to mankind, the student achieves a sensitivity to the importance of questing for information. If he is distinctively creative, both his inquisitiveness and his inventiveness may be stimulated. If he is relatively uncreative, his search for an answer can teach him much about the organization of knowledge and about efficient methods of finding solutions. Admittedly, it is sometimes difficult to lure the student into accepting the challenge of the enigma; when his curiosity is seduced, however, a truly sublime motivation is bred. The instructional technique of confronting unknowns opens the classroom for individual difference among students. It permits the able to attempt novel and difficult tasks; it places value on nonverbal achievement; it helps the inventive learner to clarify his own uniqueness, all of which offer profound nourishment to the creative.

While research has not yet yielded a generally accepted catalogue of the various forms of thinking, we can identify a number of different processes. Deductive thinking, for example, is easily contrasted with intuitive thinking. When one is endeavoring to find something out he will not think in the same way as when he is interested in interpreting something he already knows. Some problems require us to think analytically while others do not. If we can arrange the curriculum so that the student repetitively engages in as many kinds of thinking as possible, we will in all probability: (a) provide him with a basis for recognizing opportunities for transferring his learning; (b) expand his capacity for responding in several ways to a simple phenomenon; (c) improve his ability to select an effective way of thinking about a task; (d) provide him with cognitive alternatives he might otherwise have ignored.

One further example may be cited. The desire to solve a problem is a common point of departure in both creative effort and learning. Because the individual, through habit and conditioning, is "set" for a routine way of looking at a problem, he often fails to explore possibilities which might prove more efficacious. His susceptibility to habit, moreover, may cause him to labor excessively before he perceives that his usual approach is unworkable. Even in instances in which he is able ultimately to make his solution work, "set" frequently prevents him from discovering a more attractive method. It should be relatively simple to introduce various sorts of learning which stress skill in discriminating between procedures for attacking problems. Freedom from the restrictions of habitual response represents an obvious factor in creative thinking.

The examples given typify an astonishingly large number of situations in which creativity and education are enhanced by the same stimuli. Admittedly, the breadth of the school's responsibility requires that the nurture of creativity be an accessory gain rather than the chief target. As methods are refined for distinguishing the creative from the merely intelligent and from other forms of giftedness, considerable benefit may result from specialized training experiences for students with high capacity to produce original thought. As Toynbee has noted, a few creative minds can make an enormous difference to a civilization.

The Use of Questions as an Aspect of a Teacher's Behavior

Ben B. Strasser

ASKING QUESTIONS
1. A mutual self-dicipline and respect for each other's ideas must prevail.
    a. Welcome all ideas as valid contributions—teacher and children.
    b. In a class discussion, one person talks at a time and interruptions are out of order—teacher included.
    c. No experimentation, etc., when any discussion.
2. Probe beyond the answer to yes/no questions. Why, how, etc.

PRINTED by permission of the Author through the courtesy of the Los Angeles County Schools.

3. Consider your question; is it specific? Is the responsibility of the learner clearly evident? Does the learner know what is expected of him?
4. Will the questions asked clearly lead to development of the purpose(s) teacher had in using the question? E.g., to stimulate thinking, search for relationships, design experiments, make observations, etc?
5. Who summarizes or concludes? If teacher assumes this responsibility in every learning situation, the children will wait for it. How will they learn the complex skill of summarization if teacher continually assumes this role?
6. If teacher feels there is a value in children learning to pose questions, then teacher must respond to children's questions, as and when they arise, in some positive encouraging way.
   a. May stop teacher's direction and assume new direction implied by the child's question.
   b. Note the question for consideration some time in the near future.
7. Ask the question, then wait. If the children are to learn that the responsibility for thinking is theirs teacher must give them time to think and respond.
8. Are different kinds of questions posed to stimulate different kinds of purposes or objectives?

to predict:	"What do you think will happen when . . ."
to design an experiment:	"How might you work to test your idea?"
to validate data:	"Does it happen in the same way each time you try it?"
to interpret data:	"Now that we have some new data, do you have any new ideas, or do you feel your first ideas still work O.K.?"
to explore the child's vocabulary:	"Does anyone know what word is used to describe this event?"
etc., ad infinitum	

9. Regarding naming a child in the question "Billy, what is the . . ." This technique is certainly justifiable at times, but be aware of what happens in this case. It puts the pressure on the one individual, and others know, regardless of their thinking, that they will probably not be called upon to respond.
10. Are questions structured in a way that there is no one "correct" answer?

REACTING TO CHILDREN'S RESPONSES

Reaction to children's responses may take a variety of forms: a. accept; b. clarify; c. challenge; d. support.

Not only is the question you ask important, but your reaction to the answer is equally critical.

1. Is it really necessary to repeat the child's comments and/or ideas or should the child repeat them if all could not hear?
2. Do you react to all of the children's responses in a positive way?

3. Do you end up answering your own questions? If so, would it be better to "tell" when it's imperative the children know what you are thinking?
4. How would you react to a non-productive experiment proposed? Do you give children the chance to find out for themselves that their idea may be of little value?
5. How do you react to a right/wrong answer to your question?
6. Do you provide the time and opportunity for more than one child to respond, i.e., to go beyond the "correct" or "incorrect" answer?
7. What do you expect as an answer to your questions? a. a verbal response: recall; b. an idea: recalled or original; c. some overt behavior.
8. Do you react to the children's responses in a variety of ways in order not to present any subverbal cues?
   a. Do you continue to accept responses even after the "correct" answer is given by a child?
   b. Would you sometimes agree with a wrong answer and/or disagree with a correct one?
   c. Do you react only to "correct" or "incorrect" answers?
9. How are "correct" answers so determined? Is it always up to teacher to pass judgment?

REFERENCES

Aschner, M. J. McCue. "Asking Questions to Trigger Thinking," *The Reading Teacher*, September 1961.

CASCD. *Leadership for Science in the Elementary School*. Palo Alto, California: National Press, 1960.

Gross, R. E. (Ed.). *The Problems Approach and the Social Studies* (rev. ed.). National Council for the Social Studies. Washington: Curriculum Series No. 9.

Smith, Philip G., Associate Professor of Education, Indiana University. "The Art of Asking Questions," *NEA Journal*, September 1961.

Ten Ways of Helping Young Children Gifted in Creative Writing and Speech

E. Paul Torrance

CHILDREN SHOW THEIR GIFTEDNESS IN MANY WAYS—SOME IN ONE WAY and some in another. Many children show their giftedness first through creative writing and speech. If your child shows his giftedness in this

REPRINTED by permission of the Author and *Gifted Child Quarterly*, 6:121–7, Winter, 1962.

way, you may be fortunate in many ways. First, even very young children gifted in this respect provide themselves and others with much pleasure. Second, the exercise of this talent provides an excellent means for developing the creative thinking abilities and a variety of skills in creative problem-solving.

Most of our studies have been concerned with ways in which schools and colleges can foster creative growth of various kinds. I believe, however, that through these studies we can suggest some rather positive ways by which parents can help children who are gifted in creative writing and speech. In this article, I shall discuss ten of them.

1. PROVIDE MATERIALS WHICH DEVELOP IMAGINATION

Parents can do much to provide materials which help *develop* the imaginative powers of children. Some parents will argue that there is no need for this, that their problem is to keep their children from being too imaginative. It is tremendously important, however, that parents keep alive imagination and fanstasy until the child's intellectual development is such that he can engage in a sound type of creative thinking. I would like to place the emphasis upon the word *development*. Parents can use the child's natural inclination to engage in imaginative activity to bring about some of this development, and to bring it about in such a way that it will lead to this sound type of creative thinking which I have been talking about.

Perhaps I can best communicate what I have in mind by talking about some specific materials through books. One of my favorites is a series of books by an Italian artist and story-teller, Bruno Munari. They are now published in the United States by the World Publishing Company. An interesting one entitled, *Who's there? Open the Door?* is good for developing both the imagination and the evaluation of judgment abilities. The cover of the book is in the form of a big door with the eye of an animal peeking out. You can have the child guess all of the things he can think of that would be so big that it would take a room for them to stand up in. The child might guess an elephant, a camel, a giraffe, a pony and the like. You open the door and it's actually "Lucy the giraffe with a large crate come all of the way from Lisbon." It might also have been some of the other things guessed. You might accept such large ones as elephant, camel, and others. You might point out, however, that a pony would not take this much space. Next, the question becomes "What's in the crate?" Again, he might guess pony, bear, hippopotamus, pig, cow, and the like. It is actually "Peggy the zebra with a trunk come all the way from Paris." Again, other things similar in size to the zebra can be accepted and those larger and smaller can be eliminated. The game continues. We have Leo the lion with a valise come all the way from London. Next we have "Romeo the cat with a package wrapped in tissue paper, come all the way from Rome." In the package we have "Bertha, the blackbird, with a basket come all the way from Berlin." In the basket we have "Dick, the cricket, with a small parcel come all the way from Dublin." In the parcel we have "a little ant with a grain of wheat for the winter."

With such materials you are doing more than developing the imagination, you are developing the ability to think in terms of possibles, to make judgments about size, and to gain a more accurate picture of the world in which they live. Incidentally, they might on later occasions be stimulated in their curiosity to ask about the places from which these animals and insects have been shipped: Lisbon, Paris, London, Rome, Berlin, and Dublin.

Another of the Munari books that I like is *The Elephant's Wish.* The story begins: "The elephant is bored with being a big heavy animal. He wishes he could be something else. What do you think he would like to be?" This starts the guessing game. The child is asked to look into the mind of the elephant, to imaginatively put himself in the place of the elephant and think what he would want to do if he were to be tired of being an elephant. Then he is given a look into the elephant's mind by the artist and author. "He wishes he could be a little bird who flies and sings." The bird, however has his problems. "The little bird is bored with flying and singing. He is wishing too. What does he wish?" After some guessing on the part of the child, he can be given a look into the bird's mind. The bird "wishes he could be a fish and swim under water." But the fish is bored too. He is bored with swimming under water. What does he wish?" He wishes he could go on land. How tempting it must be to him to want to go on land! "He wishes he could be a lizard sitting on a stone in the sun." The story continues. The lizard wants to be a cow, a fat, lazy ox. The ox wants to be an elephant. Thus, we return to the place where we started. Everything wants to be something else. Our problem is to accept creatively our limitations and use our abilities and resources. If we do, we will not be bored. Life will always be exciting.

There are many others. One series is E. P. Dutton's *Imagination Books.* One is *Let's Imagine Thinking Up Things* by Janet Wolff and Bernard Owett. It is a kind of duplication of one of our tests of creative thinking. For example, the child is told, "Here is a circle. Let's imagine all the things a circle can be." The child can produce some either by drawing or in words. Some examples are given in the book.

I might add that the examples given are some of the most obvious and unoriginal ones: a face, the sun, the top of an ice cream cone, a ball, money, a clock, a hoop, and the like.

Other examples are Alastair Reid's *Just Suppose,* Lenore Klein's *What Would You Do, If . . .* and the monthly magazine, *Highlights for Children,* which you may have in your doctor's or dentist's office. *The Poetry-Drawing Book* by Cole and Colmore provides another innovation in children's books. It provides poems for children to illustrate and color by themselves. These materials have not been subjected to very much scientific testing, but on the basis of what we know I would assume that they provide rather sound approaches.

2. PROVIDE MATERIALS WHICH ENRICH IMAGERY

To go very far in really developing imagination or creative thinking, a child needs a rich store of imagery. This, I might add, is important not just in developing a background for writing and speaking creatively but in scientific discovery and invention, art, and the like. There are many ways of doing this. One way is through the use of the well-known classical fairy tales, folk stories, myths and fables. I still think that the Mother Goose stories; the folk stories and fables of Italy, Germany, France, India, and other countries; the Greek and Roman myths; and the like have a very important role in developing this kind of imagery. Of course, it is also hard to beat the fact book of nature— the models of creation we have in animal and plant life. It is from this source that so many of our modern inventions come (Gordon, 1961).

3. PERMIT TIME FOR THINKING AND DAYDREAMING

Many parents keep their children so busy that they don't have time to think, much less speak and write creatively. Certainly many families would find life much more exciting and would enjoy much better mental health, if they reduced the number of activities in their schedule and gave more time for creative development. We become very disturbed, however, if children want to be alone or if they are not *visibly* busy. It is almost illegal to be busy thinking. This condition must be changed, if you are to foster creative speaking and writing in children.

I always find it very rewarding to hear stories like the following one by a graduate student. His children had always made good grades and had found school work easy before coming to the Twin Cities. Early in the school year, he found his eight-year-old son crying over his homework. He had been assigned to make up a story about a picture and couldn't think of one. He had never been asked to make up a story before. He was an outstanding reader, but making up a story was something new to him. The father was disturbed by his son's new school difficulty and decided to do something about it. The family instituted a story-telling session during the evening meal. The four-year-old led the way with some of the most delightful stories, but the mother and father also joined in. The father attests that this greatly improved mental health conditions in the family and helped his son hurdle what appeared to be a difficult handicap.

We do many things which discourage children from speaking creatively—or at all, for that matter. Typical is the story of a mother who was shocked that her five-year-old daughter asked to be permitted to eat alone in her room when Mrs. Green came to lunch (Miller, 1961). The child explained that she didn't like to talk with Mrs. Green.

When asked to explain, the child said, "Oh you know. She talks to me in a baby voice—and keeps asking me things and never gives me time to answer."

Then the mother recalled that every remark Mrs. Green made to the child was some little question she obviously did not expect answered. "Where did you get that pretty dress? What have you been doing today? What makes Julie grow so fast?"

As a result, the child clammed up tight. Then, Mrs. Green made matters worse by adding, "My Julie is a shy one, isn't she? Are you bashful, honey? She doesn't talk much, does she?"

Many highly creative children appear to be either shy or show-offs. Shy children will talk freely with adults, if they are given time to answer questions—to take time to think and to find words to express their ideas. The show-offs will find that their acting up is unnecessary, if they are accepted as persons in conversations with adults.

4. ENCOURAGE CHILDREN TO RECORD THEIR IDEAS

Children's stories, poems, songs are valuable—they are charming and delightful and can give others great pleasure and insight. Children need encouragement, however to write down their ideas. They do not do so naturally. It is best done if some purpose is given to the writing. We found that children could be encouraged to do a great deal of writing on their own, through the use of a magazine in which we reproduced their stories, poems, inventions, opinions, drawings, and the like. Parents cannot easily provide such an outlet. They can, however, provide many good excuses for such productions—original greetings for birthdays, important family occasions, holidays, letters to friends and relatives, and so on. To encourage children to write poems or other creative productions whenever they have something to express, give them an attractive binder, folio, or the like in which to collect their writings. Forced writing will not help. The child needs to be warmed up to his creations whatever their nature might be. He needs only to feel free to do so when he has something to express. Such writings should be done to be read, heard, or used and not to be corrected or graded. They should be enjoyed.

5. GIVE CHILDREN'S WRITINGS SOME CONCRETE EMBODIMENT

In our work with children, I have learned that they are stimulated to greater heights in their creative thinking, if their ideas find embodiment in some concrete form. There is excitement in seeing one's ideas take form. Young children in kindergarten and first grade take great pride in the murals which they paint—and I have seen some wonderful ones done by them—the inventions which they contrive, the songs and poems they compose, and the stories they write. When children find that others value and do not disparage their productions, they take courage and are eager to keep building onto their ideas, improving them, creating new words, letting one thing lead to another.

Pre-school children have to tell their stories through drawings or by telling their stories and having someone else record them. In either case, their productions can be translated into some concrete form which will be appreciated. Their drawings can be placed in frames and given places of honor in the home. You can use attractive frames in which the pictures can be changed easily from time to time. These can give family and friends a great deal of enjoyment. Their drawings can also be used as designs in mother's ceramic work, sewing, and the like. I have a very treasured dinner plate which was designed by a four-year-old child. She drew a picture which she called "Snow Bubbles." Her aunt used it as the design for a set of dinner dishes for her family's Christmas gift. I liked it so much that she made a plate for me. The "Snow Bubble" title is a charming one and the dinner set is beautiful.

Children are natural story tellers and poets, and can compose charmingly and excitingly, if encouraged to do so. Seldom are these appreciated and given adequate treatment in publications. I would like to call to your attention two notable exceptions. One of these is an exciting little book by Susan Nichols Pulsifer entitled *Minute Magic* (1960). In this book, Mrs. Pulsifer presents a variety of poems by pre-school children and describes her experiences in getting children to compose poems and songs. Mrs. Pulsifer joins me in contending that the drop in creative behavior which occurs at about age five is not a natural developmental change. Instead, she contends that it is due to the influence of other children, group activities, the imposition of correct techniques and facts, rules and regulations. She believes, as I do, that with wisdom the home and school can do much to reduce this discontinuity in development and lessen this serious loss of creativity.

Another example is the work of Kathleen Wrenn and her son Robert (1949). When her son was about two years of age, Mrs. Wrenn discovered that he was responding much more readily to suggestions that were sung to him than he did when the same requests were spoken. Soon, she discovered that he was responding by singing and rapidly developed a sense of rhythm and a singing scale. When Bobby was about four years old, the idea of making a book of songs began taking shape. These were simple songs about everyday happenings—songs about the fireman, the milkman, the zoo, balloons, traffic signals, and the church bell.

With new experiences, Bobby would think of ideas for songs and work them out. On one occasion, his mother asked him to put some leaves over the tulips planted in the yard so they would not freeze. He came back with the following idea for a song:

Here comes the flowers out of the ground.
Spreading happiness all around.
Daffodils, hyacinths, tulips gay,
Oh, how I wish you were here to stay!

His mother suggested that "hyacinth" was a very difficult word for little children to sing and why not say "daisies" instead. His reply was, "I'm a little child aren't I and it's my word." (Yes, children dislike for others to tamper with their compositions and their reasons may be well-founded.)

One night Bobby lay for a long time listening to the sound of the rain on the roof. Then he called his mother to come quickly with a pencil and write down what he had been singing. This is what he was singing:

Pitter patter, pitter patter,
Hear the raindrops falling down.
Pitter patter, pitter patter,
Falling falling all around.

Dripping, dripping, dripping, dripping,
I can hear them overhead.
Dripping, dripping, dripping, dripping,
On the roof above my bed.

I would like to submit that the use of devices such as the ones used by Mrs. Pulsifer and Mrs. Wrenn might do much to reduce the discontinuity in creative development between the home and the school. It does not mean fixating development at a pre-school level of maturity. It could mean increasing maturity.

6. ACCEPT THE CHILD'S NATURAL TENDENCY TO TAKE A DIFFERENT LOOK

For some time I had been familiar with deliberate methods for increasing creativity by looking at something in a different way. Synectics (Gordon, 1961), for example, stresses the principle of making the unfamiliar, familiar or the familiar, unfamiliar. One idea was sparked when one member of the team tried to imagine himself as a drop of paint, struggling to get some kind of hold on a wall which had been painted and had not been scraped or cleaned. I noted, as I began to study the thinking of kindergartners, that children use the technique of synectics and of brainstorming spontaneously and naturally all of the time. This lesson was dramatized for me through a song composed by little Catherine Babcock, "Did You Ever Read a Clock Upside Down?" (with sound effects).

Did you ever read a clock upside down?
  Upside down!
Did you ever read a clock upside down?
It is very hard to do but I think you should
  Learn how to read a clock upside down.

Children think quite naturally in terms of analogy. They do not have to be *taught* the methods of synectics and bionics. Two interesting examples are given in a current advertisement of a new NBC program called "Exploring." A small boy is trying to tell us his foot has fallen asleep. He exclaimed, "Gee, my toes feel just like ginger ale!" Most people know exactly what he means. A little girl, discovering the woozy ribbons of color in a grease puddle, mournfully describes them as a "dead rainbow." Most people know exactly what she means, but do you know that many parents will "correct" such accurate and imaginative descriptions. If you take your cue from the amazing record of invention by the students of bionics and synectics you would do all you can to keep alive this habit of thinking by analogy. Fortunes are being made in this way!

7. PRIZE RATHER THAN PUNISH TRUE INDIVIDUALITY

Very early in our studies of creative thinking it became clear that children really prize their individuality. Just before Christmas I visited a class and admired their Santa Clauses. I commented quite informally that each one was so interesting, that no two were alike. Later in the year, they had prepared another exhibit of which they were very proud. Just as they had completed this, one little fellow said, "Dr. Torrance would like these. No two are alike!"

Not all kindergartners and first graders received this kind of encouragement for their individuality. One mother wrote me of her son's kindergarten troubles which arose over his desire to paint his dittoed horse striped like a "z-horse" instead of brown like all of the other children's. Another mother thinks that her son's learning problems began in the kindergarten over such a difficulty. Before he started to school, he was frequently mistaken for a third or fourth grader because of his penetrating questions and conclusions, his excitement in learning. In kindergarten, however, he began bringing home failing papers. To his teacher's dittoed drawing he would add cowboy boots and hats, or even change the teacher's drawings. Now, this boy's school performance is so apathetic that he is suspected of mental retardation.

Although such things, and worse, still occur in our schools, I believe and hope that they are becoming a rarity. If your child has a teacher who is a devotee of the dittoed drawing, as parents you may have to encourage original work, as Tommy's mother did. Tommy's story can be told through four drawings. Just before Easter, 1962, Tommy and his classmates were instructed to paint "nice" rabbits for their mothers. Tommy's coloring was not the smoothest possible, so the teacher was displeased and gave him another dittoed rabbit. Again, Tommy displeased the teacher who gave him another rabbit. By now, however, it was time to flit to another activity, so in desperation she told Tommy to take the rabbit home and paint it "nice" for his mother. When Tommy reached home he was almost in tears. How could he paint a rabbit "nice" for his mother! Quite wisely his mother gave him a blank sheet of paper and told him to draw whatever kind of rabbit he wanted. He drew a delightfully different rabbit which his mother loved.

8. BE CAUTIOUS ABOUT EDITING CHILDREN'S WRITINGS

Adults sometimes think they can improve the writings of children by editing them—"correcting them," they say. Sometimes we think we are improving them when we really do not. In fact, we may spoil some of their beauty and honesty and this disillusions children. We learned a very painful lesson on this score in one of our studies which involved the production of a weekly magazine of children's writings.

I had instructed the editor to be careful to maintain the integrity of the children's ideas but to correct spelling, punctuation, grammar, and the like—errors which might prove embarrassing to the children when it appeared in the magazine. This was not enough caution, however, and the fifth graders let us know about it in no uncertain terms. One of them wrote as follows:

Dear Editors:
"I don't think that you should change our poems, stories, etc. I know you are trying to make them better, but sometimes the way people write things—no matter whether it makes sense or not—is the way people want them.

"In poems this is especially true. Sometimes certain punctuation marks express an awful lot.

"Please try and understand the way we feel about it."

It was the following paragraph in another letter which really sobered me:

"Dr. Torrance, you told us that our ideas are important. The way our stories and poems have been changed around makes us wonder."

This doesn't mean that children aren't willing to proofread and polish their creative productions for publication. They are. Nevertheless, the experience has taught me how easy it is for adults unknowingly to communicate to children that their ideas are *not* really important.

9. ENCOURAGE CHILDREN TO PLAY WITH WORDS

Children and adults enjoy word games and there are a number of good ones on the market in a number of forms. Almost all of them involve the creation of new relationships. Since the ability to see or to create new relationships is at the very core of every creative act, this can be an important skill to develop in children. These make interesting family entertainment and provide one way in which parents can help. One delightful book about word play is Alastair Reid's *Ounce Dice Trice* (1958).

10. LOVE THEM AND LET THEM KNOW IT

Children will never reveal their intimate imaginings unless they feel that they are loved and respected. As I observed teachers and pupils during my first year of study, I was almost immediately impressed by the obvious importance of the feeling of affection between teacher and pupils and the development of what I have chosen to call the creative relationship. I like to call it the creative relationship because it operates so much like the creative thinking process. I think it works the same way with parents and children. The adult has to be willing to let one thing lead to another in this relationship, to embark with the child on an untraveled pathway, not knowing where the relationship will lead. It is something that a parent or a teacher can desire fervently and for which they can work hard. Then suddenly, it seems to "just happen," but the teacher or parent has to be willing to let it happen, just as the inventor or scientific discoverer does when the solution to his problem "just happens."

For some time I had observed that a certain teacher seemed to have such a relationship with almost all of her pupils, especially Brian. One day she showed me this picture that Brian had drawn of her one day when he became angry with her. He did not show the picture to her until several days later. When she asked him what were all of the scattered lines in the background, Brian explained, "That's your brains. I was so mad with you that day I thought your brains had fallen out." I felt that this was a good test of relationship. The teacher was not threatened by it. She knows that Brian loves her and Brian knows that she loves him.

REFERENCES

Babcock, Catherine Marly. *Did You Ever Read a Clock Upside Down?* Danbury, Conn.: Reeves Soundcraft Corp., 1962.

Cole, W. and Julia Colmore (Ed.) *The Poetry-Drawing Book.* New York: Simon & Schuster, 1960.

Gordon, W. J. J. *Synectics.* New York: Harper and Row, 1961.

Klein, Leonore. *What Would You Do If . . .* New York: William R. Scott, 1961.

Miller, Joyce. How to Talk to Children. *Home Life*, November 1961, *15(11)*, 13.

Munari, B. *Who's There? Open the Door!* Cleveland: World Publishing Company, 1957.

Pulsifer, Susan Nichols. *Minute Magic.* Boston: Chapman and Grimes, 1960.

Reid, A. *Ounce, Dice, Trice.* Boston: Little, Brown, 1958.

Reid, A. *Supposing.* Boston: Little, Brown, 1960.

Wolf, Janet and B. Owett: *Let's Imagine Thinking Up Things.* New York: E. P. Dutton, 1961.

Wrenn, B. and Kathleen Wren. *Fun For Everybody: Songs for Children.* Cincinnati, Ohio: Willis Music Company, 1949.

CHAPTER SIX

Guidance and Measurement
of Creativity

The Counselor and the Creative Child

John C. Gowan and George D. Demos

WHAT CAN A COUNSELOR DO TO HELP A CHILD BECOME MORE CREATIVE? As educators have grown more cognizant of and interested in creativity, this question has become more important. It has also become more obvious that creativity development and preservation is not purely a curriculum matter, but depends upon interpersonal relationships, and guidance can be a factor in promoting these. Although there has been little written upon the subject, we can learn a good deal by looking at the personality of the creative child, and then discovering what aspects can best be promoted by guidance.

The first point to note about the creative child is that he is usually well-adjusted, mature for his age, fully-functioning, and responsible. He is in this respect opposite of the delinquent. Dr. Paul Torrance, of the University of Minnesota, upon being asked, "What makes a child creative?" replied: "Anything that makes him *more* alive." This zest for living and acme of mental and physical health is often evident in bright, creative children. Whatever guidance can do to help a child to better mental health and maturity will aid what creativity he may possess.

It should, perhaps, be noted that in advocating guidance for children, we do not imply that guidance will produce creativity, but only that it will bring it out and make it manifest. It is probable that most of our educational aids to children merely *preserve* rather than *produce*

REPRINTED by permission of the Authors and *The Gifted Child Quarterly*, 9:184–186, Winter, 1965.

their creative functions. Children are naturally creative and only require the right atmosphere to manifest it.

A second point for the counselor is to help the child to value. A child needs to value himself and to have his ideas valued before he can value others or their ideas. Counselors should therefore help children build a consistent value system—the children's not the counselors. The values a creative child builds may flow from his divergent thinking, and hence he may not wish to emulate grown-up models. This includes the counselors' values, and as a result may cause problems, but it is important to remember that it is *his* values and *not ours* which are being built.

A third point that counselors need to remember is that creative thinking takes place only when other higher-priority systems have been satisfied. A child's basic needs come *before* the luxury of cognitive actualization. Body needs, safety, love, social-ego needs, and others in the Maslow hierarchy cannot be paramount in a child who is willing to risk "ego-capital" on creative effort. A child who is thinking about what others may think about him, or if his place with them is insecure enough to be of concern to him, cannot be expected to be creative. This implies that counselors need to help children "be themselves" (congruent) enough so that they can shut out their social anxieties long enough to be creative. Only a counselor who *values differences* rather than conformity in children can be supportive enough of these differences he finds to foster creativity.

Being creative is similar to "mining ore" from the subconscious. Yet many of us, children included, are afraid to "mine this lode" systematically for fear of some of the frightening or unpleasant things that may emerge. Counselors should give children, (1) the confidence to pull latent ideas from their preconscious minds, (2) the patience to examine each idea carefully, and (3) the ability to make the mind tranquil enough so that this kind of inner exploration can take place. Often the "ore comes out in an unpolished form," and the child may easily reject something, which with development and polishing could represent real value. Calm acceptance, understanding and positive reinforcement with the suspension of harsh evaluative processes at this time is exceedingly important for the successful experience and continuation of being creative. The child needs this experience, and he can best effect suspension of evaluation himself, when he is in the presence of a supportive, non-directive, non-evaluative person such as the effective counselor.

The fourth point for counselors to promote is the process of helping children channel their creative thrust and aggressiveness into con-

structive and not destructive channels. Creative children are going to be *nonconformists.* We can help them become constructive rather than nonconstructive noncomformists. The difference is often so subtle as to be imperceptible to many adult eyes, but whereas the constructive noncomformist is *situational* and *selective* in his aggressive attack on society and its ills, the nonconstructive, nonconformist is *compulsive* and *nondiscriminative* in attacking everybody and everything. As Sylvia Ashton Warner so well stated: "A child's mind is a twin fountain of creativeness and destructiveness, and the more open we keep the creative fountain, the more we help to close the destructive one." We need therefore to watch the ambivalence creative children have toward creativeness–destructiveness, and to help them channel their energy in the positive diastole into constructive action, and in the negative diastole into harmless outlets—like thrashing around and making splashes in a swimming pool. In the beginning, even creative children do not distinguish much between being creative and being destructive—both are an expression of sheer energy and libido. If the creative actions are not more rewarded than the destructive ones, it will be difficult for a wise counselor to untangle the child.

A fifth point for the counselor is to provide the emotional support for the child to become able to participate in peak experiences in the Maslovian sense. Peak experiences are often found in creative people, and they require a narrowing and constricting of attention so that a new perspective emerges. Such experiences also require psychological courage to give of oneself. They also produce a sense of strangeness, awe, and even a sense of the mystic in some people. These conditions require counseling support for many children. Just as oxygen may be required by the extended, perspiring athlete as well as the expiring invalid, so generous amounts of counseling may be necessary at the time of peak experiences as well as the removal of psychopathology.

The sixth point is there will be many times when the creative child finds himself either alone, neglected, ignored or unrewarded as a result of a creative response on his part. Both his peers and his adult acquaintances will on occasion fail to appreciate or even notice some of his creative actions, and at other times they may vociferously oppose them. In fact, many creative children have the experience of having their ideas turned down before examination, because the creative child in enunciating the idea sometimes engenders opposition to it by his manner or approach; whereas, the same idea may later be advocated by some more popular or high status member of the group and it will be readily adopted or rewarded. Thus, it is only natural that creative children may become somewhat embittered under these circumstances. They may wish to withdraw from the group, engage in passive resistance, or "reform" and conform for the sake of external reward. The counselor should talk with such children, and try to point out that to take any of these steps is to deny their gift. He can help them to reward themselves, to intrinsically value their own efforts, and learn to "market their different ideas." *Benjamin Franklin's Autobiography* contains a famous and helpful recital of his early difficulties in this regard. The counselor may not be able to improve the *external situation*, but he can aid the child in understanding the *internal* one; namely, his own feelings. This may be sufficient.

Finally, the seventh point, guidance for the creative involves the realization that counseling is not just the solving of problems, but a positive process promoting mental health. This is important for all students, but it is vital for creative children. We have found, in an institute for promoting creativity in children, that gifted children willingly sought and absorbed the counselor's efforts when on a $\frac{1}{25}$ counselor-client ratio, which is twelve times the concentration of guidance, ($\frac{1}{300}$ ratio), recommended by Dr. James Conant and others. In order to deal with more complex problems, to bring into concert and focus more kinds of abilities, in longer process sequences, for more constructive endeavors under conditions of less external reward, *the creative youth needs a higher level of mental health than the average youngster.* He needs it so that he can handle without disabling stress, keep in tension longer the problems which he can cope with, and the solutions which he alone can find. Like the diver whose oxygen supply enables him to stay under water longer, he is better equipped for the strange conditions under which he must labor. Thus, we *can* enhance the creativity of those who are highly able cognitively and highly sound emotionally—May we be more successful at this most important task.

REFERENCES

Conant, J. B. *The American High School Today.* New York: McGraw-Hill Co., 1959.

Damos, G. D. "Guidance and Counseling with the Ablest" (pp. 75–8) in Gowan, J. C. and Demos, G. D. Editors *The Guidance of Exceptional Children.* New York: David McKay Co., 1965.

Gowan, J. C. "The Organization of Guidance for Gifted Children" *Personnel and Guidance Journal* 39:275–279, Dec. 1960.

Gowan, J. C. and Demos, G. D. *The Education and Guidance of the Ablest.* Springfield, Ill.: Charles C Thomas, 1965.

Maslow, A. H. *Religions, Values and Peak Experiences.* Columbus: Ohio State University Press, 1964.

Schneider, D. E. *The Psychoanalyst and the Artist*. New York: Farrar, Straus & Giroux, 1950.

Torrance, E. P. *Guiding Creative Talent*. Englewood Cliffs, N. J.: Prentice-Hall Co., 1962.

Torrance, E. P. "Understanding Creativity in Talented Students" (pp. 86–94) in Gowan, J. C. and Demos, G. D. *The Guidance of Exceptional Children*. New York: David McKay Co., 1965.

Managing the "Post Partum" Depression in Creative Individuals

John C. Gowan and George D. Demos

THE PHENOMENON OF "POST-PARTUM DEPRESSION" IN BIOLOGICAL CREA-tivity is well-known, but little understood, and with less knowledge regarding its psychodynamics. A depressed period after childbirth is not rare in women. To be sure, this phenomenon is not always found, particularly in those in robust physical or mental health, but is more usually seen in cases where energies are lowered. Because an analogous situation seems to exist in persons who are mentally rather than "physically creative," we have called attention to this "post-partum" phenomenon together with some suggestions for its management. Numerous, similar reports in cases of artists, writers, musicians, actors, composers, and other creatives indicate that this problem is a general one. It has also been noted to occur after creative but more mundane occurrences such as giving a public address, cooking a meal success-fully, helping a client in psychotherapy, hosting a party, teaching a class, etc., and has also been found in adolescent students.

There is often a feeling at such a time that "the best has gone out of one." The word "spent" which also applies to the physical situation is apposite here; one feels "used up"; muscle tonus is flaccid and slack; one doubts that one can ever do anything else; there may even be a death wish, or a desire to punish oneself. Let us examine why this is so, and what may be done about it:

In the first place it should be pointed out that creativity is a gift from what Erikson (1950) calls the narcissistic or initiative period of life which occupies the child from age four to about seven. The positive side of this period is a thrusting initiative which carries the

REPRINTED by permission of the Authors.

child into various dimensions of discovery; the negative side is the immobilization of inner fear and outside prohibitions. Because the child at this stage discovers choice, he also discovers what Skinner (1965) refers to as aversive consequences. In the previous autonomy stage the child's failure to perform as society demands is a vice, for it is something (such as bladder accidents) which he cannot control—but now the child discovers that there are sins of commission, engendered by making the wrong choices, and this invests choice-making with special dangers. The joy and sheer delight (the German *Lust* is comparable) which the child finds in all kinds of new and creative discoveries is balanced by the guilt which society's sanctions against some of these efforts bring home to him in the form of myriad negative reinforcements (Skinner, 1965). Thus, we have a balance of initiative and joy on one side and immobilization and guilt on the other.

All children go through this state, but the creative child appears to get more out of it. Perhaps this is due to the affectional approach of the opposite sexed parent at this time, whose warmth puts a higher valence on creative activities, making available more preconscious areas in the reach of the ego. But at any rate, the *fantasy* of this period for most children is more of a *reality* for creative children. Whereas some children seem almost to have aborted this stage of development, the creative child seems to have "overstayed his leave in this kingdom," and its doors to fantasy are always "left slightly ajar." In a sense this is the opposite of regression, but it tends to throw the psychic energies slightly out of line. In particular the creative individual is apt to retain a super-abundance of initiative and joy in activity and discovery, only later to pay for this outburst of energy, by a slack time characterized by guilt and immobilization.

What can the counselor, teacher, psychologist or friend do to help the creative person who is in this depressed phase of such a cycle? A number of suggestions seem to be pertinent that can be ameliorative and therapeutic if not wholly regenerative:

1) An understanding and empathic discussion of the previous rationale may in itself be enough to help the client, who may come to see that this is part of a *normal not an abnormal process and does not signify a pathological condition.* A characteristic of cyclic or periodic processes is that conditions are certain to change. Frequently just being available for help is very therapeutic.

2) It is important for all to realize that descents from peak experiences (and creativity in any form is a peak experience) are apt to be disappointing. The frustration at the loss of pleasure is frequently associated

with the appearance of certain types of brain waves on the electro-encephalogram (EEG) as the individual vainly tries to maintain the pleasureable level. Whenever one's schedule of positive reinforcement or reward has been disturbed, it is apt to be somewhat distasteful. Moodiness is an interim method the ego utilizes in solving this loss of pleasure without an outburst of hostility.

3) The creative client needs to be made cognizant of the fact that *there is no evidence that creativity is limited or completely spent—once used;* on the contrary, all evidence points to the fact that it is like a well which soon refills when we dip water out of it; and that like most other powers, *it improves when fully functioning and actualized.*

4) The creative individual should know that while a pause and rest after a creative effort is natural and normal, *there is no evidence that it must be a depressive pause;* as a part of the natural rhythm it can be as refreshing as sleep after physical love.

5) *It can help to make the creative person aware that depression may be felt in part because the creative gift is not at first valued by others.* The creator may have been conditioned too much to expect his rewards extrinsically from society, and not enough to enjoy the intrinsic rewards of the creative act itself. *It is in action not accolade where we come to terms with our identity in full functioning* (This is, however, a high level form of functioning and may not be achieved but by a small number of self-actualized individuals).

6) *Creative people have need to be valued.* As a mother wishes her child to be appreciated, so creative people need valuation and love after their exertions. Those who are close to creative children, adolescents, and adults should remember to give them such valuing (unconditional positive regard—Rogers, 1961), during and following the time of creative activity. Otherwise the ego is thrown back on self reward and this may tend to make it a prey of depression on the down cycle.

Therapeutic aids of these sorts to creative people during and after creative performance may prevent them from developing neurotic symptoms which tend to represent a "dark valley" for some creative individuals. It is not necessary for creative youth to develop these patterns any more than it is a rule for all mothers to suffer "post-partum" depression. Some persons who *might otherwise be creative,* learn to control, permit to lie dormant or block it because of their fear of the guilt they experience afterward; others become too inhibited to use their full initiative in a joyful venturing forth. In any case, the world as well as the individual loses.

Thus, guidance which is important for all persons during their formative years is absolutely vital for the creatives (Gowan & Demos, 1964–65). For in order to deal with more complex aspects of problems and to bring into focus more kinds of abilities in longer process sequences, for more creative endeavors, under conditions of less external reward, the creative youth needs a higher level of mental health than the average. He needs this so that he can handle without disabling stress the problems he alone can cope with. *We can enhance creative performance in those who in addition to being highly able cognitively are highly sound emotionally.*

REFERENCES

Erikson, E. H. *Childhood and Society*, W. W. Norton & Co., New York, 1950.

Gowan, J. C. & Demos, G. D. *The Education and Guidance of the Ablest*, Charles C Thomas, Publisher, Springfield, Illinois, 1964.

Gowan, J. C. & Demos, G. D. "Counselor and the Creative Child," Mimeograph, California State College at Long Beach, Fall, 1965.

Rioch, M. J. in Farnsworth, P. R., Editor, *Annual Review of Psychology*, Annual Review, Inc., Palo Alto, California, 1965, pp. 193–96.

Rogers, C. R. *On Becoming a Person: A Therapist's View of Psychotherapy*, Houghton Mifflin Co., Boston, 1961.

Skinner, B. F. "Why Teachers Fail," *Saturday Review*, October 16, 1965, p. 80.

Identifying and Developing Creativity *

Donald W. MacKinnon

OUR TASK AS EDUCATORS IS NOT TO RECOGNIZE CREATIVE TALENT AFTER IT has come to expression, but either through our insight or through the use of validated predictors to discover talent when it is still potential and to provide that kind of educational climate and environment which will facilitate its development and expression.

It is, then, appropriate enough that we, as educators, should concern ourselves with the problem of identifying and developing creativity. And since I propose to comment about this problem, my first task, obviously, is to say what I think creativity is. I would suggest that true creativity fulfills at least three conditions. It involves a response

* This paper is an abbreviated and slightly modified version of a paper by the same title which was originally published in *Selection and Educational Differentiation*. Berkeley: Field Service Center and Center for the Study of Higher Education, University of California, Berkeley, 1960, pp. 75–89.

REPRINTED by permission of the Author and *Journal of Secondary Education*, 38:166–74, 1963.

a response that is novel or at least statistically infrequent. But novelty or originality of behavior while a necessary aspect of creativity is not sufficient.
If a response is to lay claim to being a part of the creative process, it
must to some extent be adaptive to reality. It must serve to solve a
problem, fit a situation, or in some sense correlate with reality. And,
thirdly, true creativity involves a sustaining of the original insight,
an evaluation of it, and elaboration, a sustaining and developing of it
to the full.

What I am suggesting is that creativity is a process which has a
time dimension, and which involves originality, adaptiveness, and
realization. It may be brief as in the jam session of a jazz band, or it
may involve a considerable span of years as was required for Einstein's
creation of the theory of relativity.

There are distinguishable stages or phases of creativity: (1) a period
of preparation during which one acquires the skills and techniques
and the elements of experience which make it possible for one to
pose a problem to oneself, (2) a period of concentrated effort to
solve the problem, which may be suddenly solved without much
delay or difficulty, but which perhaps more often involves so much
frustration and tension and discomfort that out of sheer self-protection
one is led to (3) a period of withdrawal from the problem, a
psychological going out of the field, a period of renunciation of the
problem or recession from it, (4) a period of insight accompanied
by the exhilaration, glow, and elation of the "aha" experience, and
(5) a period of verification, evaluation, and elaboration of the insight
which one has experienced.

The process of creativity is not easily come by nor are all of its
phases easy to endure. We should perhaps, then, be prepared to
discover that those who have high creative potential as well as those
who have demonstrated true creativity will show a disposition to
undertake problems where the degree of difficulty and frustration is
great, and the drive toward completion or accomplishment is persistently strong.

Whatever light I shall be able to shed upon the problem of
identifying and developing creativity comes in the main from findings
of researches carried on over the last few years in the Institute of
Personality Assessment and Research.

In our early studies we gave some attention to the personality
correlates of the independently rated or measured originality of our
subjects, who were, however, selected for study more because of
their over-all general effectiveness than because they were particularly

outstanding in their originality. They were graduating Ph.D.s in some fourteen different fields, young medical doctors, applicants for admission to medical school, Air Force officers, and the like. In our more recent investigations we have focused our attention upon individuals nominated by experts for their outstanding creativity in their respective fields of endeavor: writing, engineering, industrial research, mathematics, and architecture.

In these current investigations of creative work and creative workers in the arts, sciences, and professions, which are aided by a five-and-a-half year grant from the Carnegie Corporation of New York, we are seeking to discover those characteristics which differentiate highly creative individuals from less original and creative persons and which distinguish creative people in one field from those in others; investigating the processes whereby fresh insights arise, inventive solutions are achieved, and new media for artistic expression are discovered; and searching those aspects of the life situation or social and cultural milieu of individuals which facilitate or inhibit the appearance of creative thought and action.

TYPES OF CREATIVITY

In designing our several studies of creativity we made the simple and simplifying assumption that at least two types of creativity can be distinguished.

In the first of these the product of the creation is clearly an expression of the inner states, e.g., the needs, perceptions, evaluations, etc., of the creator. In this type of creativity, the creator externalizes something of himself into the public field. Examples of this kind of creativity would be found in the work of the expressionistic painter or sculptor, the poet, the novelist, the playwright, and the composer.

In the second type of creativity, the creative product is unrelated to the creator *as a person*, who in his creative work acts largely as a mediator between externally defined needs and goals. In this kind of creativity, the creator simply operates on some aspect of his environment in such a manner as to produce a novel and appropriate product, but he adds little of himself to the resultant. Examples of this kind of creativity would be found in the work of the research scientist in industry, the engineer, the mechanical inventor.

It would be an oversimplification to assert that the Type I creator creates a product or form made up of elements which did not exist before himself, while the Type II creator creates a novel product composed of already existing elements, but such a statement would probably not be far wrong.

However, let me hasten to add that there are domains of creativity which cut across these types, fields of endeavor in which the creative product is both an expression of the creator and thus a very personal product and at the same time an impersonal meeting of the demands of some external problem. One might, if one wished, call this Type III creativity. Examples of this third type of creative workers, revealing in their work characteristics of both Type I and Type II creativity, would be representational painters, scenario writers, musical arrangers and performers, and, perhaps most clearly of all, architects.

If all the data were in from these various studies and completely analyzed, I would be in an excellent position to speak with some competence on the identification and development of creativity. As it is, the most I can offer are first impressions, and tentative findings, and some hunches and guesses as to what our data mean for the identification and encouragement of creativity during the formative years.

RECONCILING ANTITHETICAL TRAITS

The first finding to which I would call your attention is one which we made in our first study of graduate students. This finding (Gough, 1953), repeatedly confirmed in subsequent studies of other groups, is that those individuals who are rated high on originality or score high on a composite measure of originality (Barron, 1955) reveal a characteristic pattern of scores on certain scales of the *Strong Vocational Interest Blank* (Strong, 1959). From sample to sample there has been some slight variation, but the general pattern is this: the more original subjects show relatively higher scores on such scales as psychologist, architect, author-journalist, and specialization level, and relatively lower scores on scales such as purchasing agent, office man, banker, farmer, carpenter, veterinarian, and understandably enough, policeman and mortician.

This pattern of relatively high and relatively low scores on the *Strong Vocational Interest Blank* suggests that the more original subjects are less interested in small detail, in facts as such, and more concerned with their meanings and implications, possessed of greater cognitive flexibility, and characterized by verbal skills and interest in as well as accuracy in communicating with others.

The Allport-Vernon-Lindzey *Study of Values* (1951) has been designed to measure in the individual the relative strengths of the six values of man as described by Edward Spranger—the theoretical, the economic, the aesthetic, the social, the political, and the religious. The profiles on the *Study of Values* of our creative architects, research scientists, and mathematicians show a high elevation on both theoretical and aesthetic values. The highest value for research scientists is theoretical (57.0) followed by aesthetic (47.5); for architects the aesthetic value is the highest (56.2) with the theoretical value in second place (50.8); while for creative mathematicians the two values, still well above average, are approximately equally high (aesthetic 52.9, theoretical 52.0).

There are slight variations in the strength of the other values from group to group, the political value in general being slightly below average, and the religious, social, and economic values falling considerably lower.

It may be that for many, perhaps for most, there is some conflict between theoretical and aesthetic values. If so, it would appear that the creative individual has the capacity to tolerate the tension created in him by opposing strong values, and in his life and work effects some reconciliation of them.

In another domain, in the realm of their sexual identifications and interests, our creative subjects appear to give more expression to the feminine side of their nature than do less creative persons. If one were to cast this into Jungian terms one would say that these creative persons are not so completely identified with their masculine *persona* roles as to blind themselves to or deny expression to the more feminine traits of the *anima*. For some the balance between masculine and feminine traits, interests, and identifications is a precarious one, and for several it would appear that their presently achieved reconciliation of these opposites of their nature has been barely achieved and only after considerable psychic stress and turmoil.

In this connection it may be noted that our creative subjects' mean scores on the eight clinical scales of the *Minnesota Multiphasic Personality Inventory* (Hathaway & McKinley, 1945) ranged from five to ten points above the general population's standard score of 50. While elevations of this magnitude are, in general, less suggestive of psychopathology than of good intellect, richness and complexity of personality, and a general lack of defensiveness, we must also note that there is in the *MMPI* profiles of some of our creative subjects rather clear evidence of psychopathology, but also evidence of adequate control mechanisms, as the success with which they live their productive lives testifies.

INTELLIGENCE AND CREATIVITY

Concerning intelligence as a predictor of creativity I have so far said nothing, for the simple reason that we all know from our experience that it is by no means the case that our most intelligent students are always the most creative. If they were, the selection of creative talent would be simple indeed.

And yet it is clear that there is some positive relation of intelligence to creativity over the whole range of intellective functioning. There were no feeble-minded subjects in our creative groups.

Our creative groups earn rather respectable mean total scores on the *Concept Mastery Test* (Terman, 1956), a test of verbal intelligence with a high ceiling. It is not surprising that on such a test creative writers out-strip all others. But we may note with interest that the group with the second highest mean score, the subjects in Terman's study of intellectually gifted, has not been distinguished by the creativity of its members.

One of the most creative of all our groups, the architects, shows an extremely wide range of scores, 39 to 179, with a mean of 113.15. And the correlation in this group between scores on the *Concept Mastery Test* and creativity in architecture as rated by a panel of five architects was not far different from the correlation in other creative groups, namely −.08.

LIFE HISTORIES

Turning to the life histories of our subjects there is little to report since there has not yet been time to examine them in detail and depth.

A first glance reveals that certainly not all of them had the kind of happy homes and favorable life circumstances so generally thought to be conducive to sound psychological development. Some underwent the most brutal treatment at the hands of sadistic fathers. These, to be sure, constitute the minority, but they appear today no less creative than those whose fathers offered them quite satisfactory male figures with whom easy identification could be made, though there is some evidence that they are not as effective or as successful in their profession as the others.

Settling upon their life careers came early for some, one of whom already at four had decided he wanted to be an architect. Others were slow in coming to a professional identity, not deciding until several years past college that architecture was what they wanted to practice.

In the case of several of these, the choice of a life profession was made the more difficult by virtue of the fact that they possessed so many skills and interests, providing them with the possibility of many quite different careers.

SCHOOL HISTORIES

But today our interest is upon their careers as students, and in this connection we may note that though the research scientists tended to be honor students in high school, they report having been unhappy during this period both at school and at home. In college their academic performance worsened; few of them were honor students and most earned no better than a "C+" to "B−" average. There is some hint that they were more interested in following their own interests and independently exploring problems of their own setting.

Our creative architects, on the other hand, performed somewhat better academically in college, averaging about a "B." But in their college work they were no less independent than the research scientists. In work and courses which caught their interest they could turn in an "A" performance, but in courses that failed to strike their imagination, they were quite willing to do little or no work at all. In general, their attitude in college appears to have been one of profound skepticism. They were unwilling to accept anything on the mere say-so of their instructors. Nothing was to be accepted on faith or because it had behind it the voice of authority. Such matters might be accepted, but only after the student on his own had demonstrated to himself their validity. In a sense, they were rebellious, but they did not run counter to the standards out of sheer rebelliousness. Rather, they were spirited in their disagreement, and one gets the impression that they learned most from those who were not easy with them. But clearly many of them were not easy to take. One of the most rebellious, but as it turned out, one of the most promising, was advised by the Dean of his school to quit because he had no talent; and another, failed in his design dissertation which attacked the stylism of the faculty, took his degree in the art department.

IDENTIFICATION OF CREATIVITY IN SCHOOL

And what, we may now ask, are the implications of our findings for the identification and development of creativity during school and college years?

First, it must be noted that we cannot be sure that the distinguishing

traits of creative workers observed several years after college characterized these same individuals when they were students. Nor can we be
certain that finding these same traits in high school students and college
undergraduates of today will identify those with creative potential.
Only empirical research can settle that question. But considering the
nature of the traits which best discriminate creatives from non-crea-
tives, I would venture to guess that most creative students as well as
students with creative potential will show profiles and patterns and
psychological preferences congruent with those of our creative subjects, though often with less extreme scale scores.

I must confess that my own worry is not so much that we shall find
creative students testing quite differently from mature creatives but
that the patterns of traits and dispositions and temperament and motivational structure which make for creativity or its opposite are set so
early in life that we shall not be able through experimental programs
and the creation of special educational atmospheres to effect the degree
of change which we so fervently desire.

What to me is most strongly suggested by our findings is that we
should seek to develop in our students a capacity for intuitive perception, an immediate concern for implications, and meanings, and significances, and possibilities beyond that which is presented to the
senses. This is not to suggest a slighting of facts, for there is a great
wealth of information which every educated person must possess.
Without a richness of experience, which may include a considerable
body of fact, intuitions may be original but they are not likely to be
very creative. But I would urge that in our instruction we never present a fact for its own sake, and that in our testing of our students'
knowledge we shun questions which require no more than identification of facts. I am convinced that we can measure information which
students have learned more reliably, more validly, and more economically by objective tests than by essay examinations. But it remains true,
I believe, that a student's preparation for and actual writing of an essay
examination forces him to exercise his intuitive perception.

On another occasion I said what I am now saying by reminding my
colleagues that "ledge, the second element in the word *knowledge*
means sport. Knowledge is the result of playing with what we know,
that is, with our facts. A knowledgeable person in science is not, as
we are often wont to think, merely one who has an accumulation of
facts, but rather one who has the capacity to have sport with what he
knows, giving creative rein to his fancy in changing his world of
phenomenal appearances into a world of scientific constructs." (Mac-
Kinnon, 1953) And so it is in all fields, not science alone.

While our data suggest that a rich development of intuitive powers facilitates creativity, they do not deny the necessity of accurate sense-perception. It is a matter of which gets emphasized.

THE TEACHER AND CREATIVITY

So, too, with the perceptive and judging attitudes, both of which each of us possesses but to different degrees. One must often enough judge and evaluate one's own experience, but it is important that one not pre-judge, thus excluding from perception large areas of experience. The danger in all instruction is that we criticize new ideas too soon and too often. Training of critical judgment is obviously important and so much emphasized I do not need to plead its case. Rather I would urge that an equal stress be placed on perceptive open-mindedness, discussing with students at least upon occasion the most fantastic of ideas. It is our duty as educators to profess what we have judged to be true, but it is no less our duty by example to encourage our students to be open to all ideas and especially to those which most challenge and threaten our own judgments.

I am impressed by the discrepancy between the scores our creative subjects earn on the achievement via independence and the achievement via conformance scales of the *California Psychological Inventory* (Gough, 1957). And I am also struck by the descriptions of their behaviors as students. These data are congruent with all our observations in assessment which suggest that these subjects are now and for a long time have been independent characters. It is an independence which manifests itself not in footless rebellion but in the accomplishment of goals which the individual sets himself and which he achieves in his own unique fashion. I would infer from this that if we are to encourage creativity in students we must give them a maximum of freedom in achieving their educational objectives.

It is our task as educators to set goals for the institutions in which we teach and for the individual courses also. The goals, I believe, should be set in only the most general fashion, but they must be set high enough to challenge the student and to involve him in the overcoming of obstacles.

Especially I would suggest that in higher education no course or seminar deserves a place in the curriculum unless it requires of the student the solution of some problem—a research project, a term paper, or the like. The requirement, stated in only the most general fashion, permits the student to determine what specifically his own problem will be. Thus he chooses, he sets the problem, and having done so, he might well be left to solve it in his own way. Thus we would provide the student with what I believe to be one of the necessary conditions for creative achievement: the undertaking of the solution of a problem where the degree of difficulty and frustration is great and the drive toward accomplishment is persistently strong.

If goals are set high enough, repeated periods of frustration will be experienced. It is at these times which I have called periods of withdrawal from the problem that the educational community, if it is a stimulating intellectual environment, can contribute importantly to the nourishment of creativity. For it is often in these periods of renunciation of the frustrating problem that those accidents which induce sudden insight and are thus not accidents at all, since one is set for them, occur.

This, as I see it, is the meaning of serendipity, the finding of valuable or agreeable things not sought for. If, when a student withdraws from a problem which has repeatedly frustrated his attempts at solution, he moves in an environment alive with ideas and stimulating conversation, the chances of the insight-inducing accident's occurring are maximized.

Finally, I think our data should remind us that our creative students may not always be to our liking. Almost certainly we will at times find them difficult to get along with. But if we recognize that some of their behavior which may be most irritating to us arises out of a struggling attempt to reconcile opposites in their nature and to tolerate large quantities of tension as they strive for a creative solution to difficult problems which they have set themselves, we may be in a better position to support and encourage them in their creative striving.

Understanding Creativity
in Talented Students

E. Paul Torrance

COUNSELING PROBLEMS OF
HIGHLY CREATIVE INDIVIDUALS

Isolation and Estrangement from Peers and Teachers. On the basis of information developed through our research with children in the early school years and by Getzels and Jackson in the high school years,

REPRINTED by permission of the Author and *The Guidance of Exceptional Children.*

I would suspect that a large share of the highly creative individual's personal problems are likely to be centered in his psychological isolation and estrangement from his peers and teachers. It will be no news to counselors that peer groups exercise rather severe sanctions against their most creative members. In no group thus far studied has the author failed to find relatively clear evidence of the operation of these pressures. Both sociometric studies and small-group experiments have thus far been used. Both types of study have yielded many clues for helping youngsters avoid some of the severity of peer sanctions without sacrificing their creativity. Since the results of the experimental study are simpler and more straightforward, only this study will be described.

In this study (Torrance, 1959), we formed groups of five children, and in each we placed one of the most creative children in the class, as identified by tests administered earlier. We then placed each group in a situation requiring creative thinking and involving competition among groups. This situation permitted the group to experiment for 25 minutes trying to discover all the things which could be done with a box of science toys and the principles whereby they worked. After a period of 5 minutes for planning demonstrations and explanations, each group was given 25 minutes in which to present their demonstrations and explanations. The focus of observation was upon the techniques used by the groups to control the most creative member and the strategies of the most creative member in coping with these pressures. Much of the behavior observed suggests that in many cases the highly creative individual may be responsible for his own woes.

At the second-grade level, the most highly creative individuals were generally quite unpleasant, showing little consideration for the group, little or no goal orientation, little or no identification with the group, and little or no heed to the leadership attempts of their less creative peers. In the third grade, the most creative subjects tended to work independently and were ignored for the most part. This tendency persisted into the fourth grade, where the most creative members assumed little responsibility for leadership and were given little credit in the final ratings for the important contributions which they actually made to the group's success. The highly creative subjects in the fifth grade manifested more leadership attempts and were more dominant than in the fourth grade but brought upon themselves open criticism and attack for "being too scientific," "being too greedy," and the like. These tendencies became more pronounced in the sixth-grade groups.

An examination of almost any of the many lists of personality characteristics of highly creative individuals suggests a number of quite valid reasons why such individuals alienate their peers and elders. In our studies it has certainly become quite obvious that many of the highly creative individuals are disturbing elements in classroom groups in elementary schools. The problem of teachers and guidance workers resolves itself into one of helping highly creative individuals maintain those characteristics which seem essential to the development of creative talent and at the same time helping them acquire skills for avoiding or reducing to a tolerable level the peer sanctions.

Stein (1956) has offered a set of interesting suggestions concerning the social role of the creative industrial researcher. If we translate Stein's principles to teachers and guidance workers, the objective in helping highly creative youngsters would run something like the following: Help the highly creative child to maintain his assertiveness without being hostile and aggressive. He must be aware of his superiors, peers, and subordinates as persons. He may work alone, but he must not be isolated, withdrawn, or uncommunicative. He must "know his place" without being timid, submissive, or acquiescent and must "speak his mind" without being domineering. As he tries to gain a point, he can be subtle but not cunning or manipulative. In all relationships, he must be sincere, honest, purposeful, and diplomatic but not unwilling to accept "short cuts." In the intellectual area, he must learn to be broad without spreading himself too thin, deep without being "bookish" or "too scientific," and "sharp" without being overcritical.

The model above obviously asks much of the child, but at least it provides a model which the highly creative child apparently needs to achieve, and it should challenge the imaginative counselor.

"Unrealistic" Career Choices. The career aspirations of highly creative students are sure to puzzle the counselor and to seem unrealistic. Getzels and Jackson's data throw some light upon this problem. When their highly intelligent and highly creative subjects were asked (Getzels and Jackson, 1959), on sentence-completion type questionnaires, to state the kinds of occupations they would like to have, the Creatives gave a significantly greater variety of occupations than did the highly intelligent group. When the occupations reported were divided into conventional and unconventional categories (e.g., doctor, engineer, businessman, etc., were classified as conventional; inventor, artist, spaceman, disk jockey, as unconventional), 18 per cent of the highly intelligent group gave unconventional career aspirations; 67 per cent of the high Creatives gave such aspirations.

I would also like to mention another problem regarding career choice, which has been discussed in detail by Anne Roe (1959). This problem concerns the highly creative and talented individual from the lower socioeconomic class. Even in the grade school, such an individual is likely to suffer as a consequence of the differences in the value structure of the home and those built into the educational career required for a full-fledged career as a creative scientist. Roe particularly emphasizes some of the hazards inherent in current national testing programs and efforts to urge talented youngsters to go to college and to prepare for careers in science. Counselors should be aware of the conflicts such youngsters are likely to experience. Both the lower and higher socioeconomic classes tend to devaluate scientific careers. She maintains that many scholarship students are likely to drop out in college because they do not become members of any in-group in college. She suggests that personnel workers give consideration to establishing the kinds of in-groups in which such individuals can obtain support.

Another career choice problem quite likely to exist among highly creative individuals concerns the choice made because it provides a technique for handling a particular personal problem. Their curiosity and their searching is for a solution to a personality problem. Roe (1959) maintains that in such cases all may go well as long as the individual is still climbing in his career and still has hopes of solving his problem. When the apex is reached, however, he may experience depression and become unproductive. Individuals so motivated in their career choices may be blocked in finding the solution to problems; they "just can't see the answer." Some such individuals are noted for their compulsive repetitions of experiments and inability to complete a task. Counselors could probably assist here by helping them to understand the nature of their creative processes and to seek psychotherapy. Successful psychotherapy is more likely to unlock greater powers of creativity than to destroy creative genius.

Values and Attitudes. The counselor should also recognize that the values and attitudes of the highly creative student are likely to be different from those of other students. The very fact that he is capable of divergent thinking, has unusual ideas, and is independent in his thinking in itself is likely to make his values and attitudes different from the norms of his group. Some of these differences are highlighted in the Getzels and Jackson (1959) study. They found that for the high IQ group, the rank-order correlation between the qualities they would like for themselves and the qualities making for adult success was .81; for the high Creativity group it was .10. Among the highly intelligent, the correlation between the qualities they desire and the qualities they believe teachers favor was .67; for the highly creative group, it was minus .25. In other words, the highly creative student desires personal qualities having little relationship to those which he believes make for adult success and which are in some ways the opposite of those he believes his teachers favor. Thus, counselors should recognize that the desire to emulate the teacher is absent or weak among creative students.

Getzels and Jackson (1959) also found a certain mocking attitude on the part of the Creatives toward what they call the "All-American Boy"—a theme almost totally lacking in the stories of the highly intelligent group. Again, this highlights the counselor's problem in helping the highly creative student to learn to be independent without being obnoxious.

HELPING TEACHERS UNDERSTAND
THE CREATIVE STUDENT

In closing, I would like to discuss briefly the problem of the counselor in helping teachers understand the highly creative student. In attempting to do this, the counselor should recognize that highly creative students think up many things which are difficult for teachers to cope with. Many of the most highly creative subjects in our studies in the early school years are almost famous for their skill in thinking up ideas for being naughty as well as for their wild or silly ideas. Few teachers are likely to respond as did one of the third-grade teachers in our study, who commented to me: "Even if you do not learn anything from the data you have collected, the study has changed the school and the way we teachers look at our students. For example, we no longer look upon them as being naughty but as creating ideas for being naughty." This difference at first glance might seem too subtle, but I think it is an important one.

As I have discussed the matter at length in another paper (1959), I shall only list what I think the counselor can do to help the teacher to understand the highly creative student and help him develop his creative thinking to its fullest degree. I believe that the counselor can help the teacher to:

1. Learn to value creative thinking and to forge an environment which places value on creative activity so that the highly creative student will not have to exist as a miserable deviate in the shadow of his more socially successful peers.
2. Find ways of assisting children to be more sensitive to environmental stimuli and to trust their own perception of reality.

3. Permit and encourage manipulation of objects and ideas.
4. Lead students to test systematically each new idea.
5. Develop tolerance of new ideas.
6. Beware of forcing a set pattern.
7. Develop a creative classroom atmosphere.
8. Teach the child to value his own creative thinking.
9. Teach skills for avoiding peer sanctions.
10. Understand the creative process and share this understanding with pupils.
11. Dispel the sense of awe of masterpieces.
12. Encourage and evaluate self-initiated learning.
13. Create "thorns in the flesh," to be sensitive to defects, to recognize the disturbing element.
14. Create necessities for creative thinking.
15. Provide for both active and quiet times for the production of ideas.
16. Make available resources for working out ideas.
17. Encourage the habit of working out the full implication of ideas.
18. Develop constructive criticism—not just criticism.
19. Encourage acquisition of knowledge in a variety of fields.
20. Become more adventurous-spirited.

SUMMARY

In summary, I would maintain that counselors and guidance workers should be concerned about understanding creativity in talented students. Such an understanding is important from the standpoint of personality development and mental health, the acquisition of knowledge and understanding, vocational success, and social welfare. A variety of materials are being developed and tested for identifying creative thinking at all educational levels and for guiding its fuller development. New directions have been toward the development of procedures for identifying creative talent at an early age and for understanding its development during the important early school years. The direction has been toward materials which can be manipulated and which yield such measures as Inventivlevel, Spontaneous Flexibility, and Constructiveness; materials which permit exploration through "asking" and "guessing" (formulating hypotheses) concerning the causes and consequences of behavior; and the like.

Both measures of IQ and measures of creativity appear to be essential in identifying giftedness. In spite of large differences in mean IQ (23 to 26 IQ points), elementary and secondary school pupils high on creativity but not high on IQ achieve as well as those high on IQ but not on creativity, as measured by standardized achievement tests.

Children high on measures of creativity appear to become alienated from peers and teachers and manifest behaviors which elicit pressures from their peers.

Counselors need to understand the special blockages to the development of creative thinking. Among those which appear most prominent and obvious are the following: premature attempts on the part of parents and teachers to eliminate fantasy, restrictions on manipulativeness and curiosity, overemphasis on prevention, overemphasis on sex roles, fear and timidity, emphasis in education on verbal skills, and limitations of resources for working out ideas.

Major counseling problems presented by the highly creative student are likely to center around his isolation and estrangement from his peers and teachers, what appear to be "unrealistic" career choices, divergent values and attitudes, and the like. Counselors can possibly do much by working with teachers to help them understand the creativity in talented students and to use procedures which will implement the greater development of creative thinking in all students.

Non-Test Ways of Identifying the Creatively Gifted

E. Paul Torrance

"HOW CAN I TELL, IF MERCEDES OR SAMUEL IS CREATIVELY GIFTED?" parents and teachers frequently ask. Is he a creative genius or is he out of his mind? Is he independent and creative or is he just unruly? Is his thinking creative or is it morbid and unhealthy? Although much progress (Getzels and Jackson, 1962; Torrance, 1962) has been made in the development of testing methods to identify the creatively gifted and to help answer questions like these, there is still much need for non-test ways of assessment.

In the first place, it will be some time before existing tests of creative thinking will be in common use in school systems and psychological clinics. Furthermore, Mercedes or Samuel might live in some remote area where there are no school psychologists or other persons qualified

REPRINTED by permission of the Author and *The Gifted Child Quarterly*, 6:71-5, 1962.

to use tests of creative thinking. Or, they might not be motivated to perform creatively on a test. There are also a number of inherent limitations of tests for eliciting creative behavior. Tests almost always have time limits, and creativity cannot always be hurried or forced. Some highly creative children, we find, have difficulty in writing down their ideas. Others are far more successful in writing down their ideas than they are in communicating them orally. The immediate testing conditions, personality disturbances, unfavorable reactions to time pressures, and the like may prevent some highly creative individuals from revealing their creative potential through tests.

NECESSITY FOR REDEFINING MEANING OF BEHAVIOR

Before parents or teachers can successfully identify, understand, and guide the creatively gifted individual, it may be necessary for them to redefine many kinds of behavior. Recently I asked two teachers of high achieving sixth graders to give me the names of five of the most and five of the least creative children in their classrooms. To help them in this redefinition process, we used Wallace and Ethel Maw's (1961) criteria of curiosity which are as follows:

1. Reacts positively to new, strange, incongruous, or mysterious elements in his environment by moving toward them, by exploring them, or manipulating them.
2. Exhibits a need or desire to know about himself and/or his environment.
3. Scans his surroundings, seeking new experiences, and
4. Persists in examining and exploring stimuli in order to know more about them.

After trying to apply these criteria, both of these teachers commented that they had never before thought of their pupils in this way and admitted with some discomfort that they were forced to place in the low group some of the children whom they valued most as pupils because they were so good in arithmetic computation, spelling, and the like. Incidentally, we obtained excellent differentiations on all of our measures of creativity between the two groups of children nominated as most and least curious. Almost all of those nominated among the more curious made higher scores on each of several tests of creative thinking than their equally intelligent but less curious classmates.

We first began examining the need for redefining many kinds of behavior soon after we had administered our first battery of creative thinking tests in our first school. A third grade teacher commented that the study had already helped the whole school, whether our research revealed anything or not. She said, "You have changed the entire way we look at children's behavior. For example, we no longer think of children as *being naughty* but as *creating ideas for being naughty*." As I began to think about the matter, I began to see what a difference it makes in the way teachers treat children, whether they see them as *being* naughty or as *creating ideas* for being naughty. Seeing children as *being* naughty is associated with a punitive approach to education; seeing children as *creating ideas for being naughty* is associated with a constructive, challenging approach.

What I mean by this is illustrated dramatically through the experience of one of my friends who teaches in the industrial arts field in college. He caught one of his students cheating on an examination near the middle of the course. The methods this student used in cheating were so clever and ingenious that this instructor recognized that he was dealing with an exceptionally talented individual. Suddenly the instructor realized that his assignments had called only for reproductive thinking and that he had done nothing to challenge this unusual talent. Instead of giving this cheater an automatic failing grade or expelling him from the class, he began thinking of more and more difficult problems calling for creative problem-solving and imagination. At the end of the course, this student's achievement was so far ahead of everyone else's that the instructor felt compelled in all fairness to award him a grade of "A." Many parents and teachers condemn this behavior of the teacher and call it immoral. I wonder which is more immoral: the failure to punish a student or failure to develop outstanding creative talent and to correct the deficiencies of one's teaching procedures?

Lying behavior in young children may need to be redefined in much the same way, as the industrial arts teacher redefined cheating behavior and transformed the abilities involved into productive creative responses. Leuba (1958), for example, contends that lying is frequently the first clear indicator of intellectual creativity. Lying may be a child's first creativity in the manipulation of symbols. "We may have failed to realize how commonplace creativity is," Leuba suggests, "because we have given that label only to socially desirable forms and they are rare." This does not mean that we should reward lying; it simply means that there are times when we need to recognize lying as an indication of creative talent which *can* be guided in positive, constructive directions.

SOME CREATIVE CHILDREN LEAD A DOUBLE LIFE

It may be difficult for parents or teachers to identify creatively gifted children because, some of the most creative ones live double lives. They behave quite creatively at home and quite non-creatively in school. Or, they may behave quite creatively at school and non-creatively at home. The first type is illustrated in the following excerpts from the letter of a mother whose son is apparently creatively gifted:

"He is now 13 years old and has had a steadily declining academic record that ended in his being retained in the seventh grade this year. . . . He has a burning main interest in electronics and rocks and believe me, his knowledge and interest in these two subjects is great.

"His teachers, principals, and counselors . . . all agree that he is very bright, very bored (day dreams in class constantly), and very withdrawn, though not rebellious. Two teachers have told me the school has destroyed his desire to learn. One teacher told me the school cannot help him because the only 'special cases' they are informed enough to help are the 'slow' children. Another teacher said to me, 'I'll make him work if I have to break his spirit to do it—and ridiculing and shaming him is the only way with children like him. . . .' Last spring the school counselor and principal decided that flunking him was the only way to make him 'buckle down or else.' He can't join the different types of science clubs because he doesn't have a B average—to which the principal urged that he take up football.

"Now, I will tell you of the boy *I* know, my son. . . . He is an irresponsible scatterbrain—he just can't harness his brain to such unimportant things as taking out the trash when he's hot on the trail of discovering perpetual motion. He *never* daydreams, *loves* to learn, and is *always* getting books from the library. He is a hard worker; many times he almost collapses trying to work and experiment late in the night. He has enough energy for ten people. He has an outgoing, bubbling personality and a terrific sense of humor. All this he is at home and in the rest of his world *until* he gets to school. . . ."

A youngster such as this thirteen-year old may or may not arise to the occasion when a test of creative thinking is administered. Much would depend upon the quality of the relationship established by the examiner, the adequacy of the warm-up process, and the challenge of the tasks presented.

SOME SUGGESTED REDEFINITIONS

What specific kinds of behaviors then can be used to identify the creatively gifted? I shall now present two tentative tests, one derived

from descriptions by parents of children whom they have identified
as creative and the other derived from the experiences of participants
in a creative thinking seminar I conducted recently.

Parents' Descriptions of Creative Children. I analyzed letters from 150
parents describing the behavior of their children whom they had identified as "creative." Most of the children described were having difficulty
in adjusting to school. Thus, the list derived from this source is likely
to include many of the kinds of behavior which might possibly call
for redefinition, not that the particular behavior is socially desirable,
but that it indicates special abilities which might be applied to achieve
socially desirable goals. The following is a list of behaviours most
frequently described in these 150 letters:

Overactive physically and/or mentally
Annoying curiosity
Forgetful and absentminded
Good sense of humor
Doesn't participate in class
Reads in room while friends (boys) roughhouse with sisters
Enjoys nature and outdoors
Won't join Scouts
Mind wanders too much
Friends think him slightly queer
Likes to work by himself
Imaginative; enjoys pretending
Sensitive
Likes color
Uncommunicative
Is a "what-if?" man
Daydreams; gets lost in thought
Feels left out of things
Spends time watching others
Loves to read
Good only in science; good only in art and music, etc.

Although these characteristics may be displayed by creative youngsters, it does not mean that such characteristics are necessary for creative behavior. Some of these characteristics are rather obviously
reactions to the way in which creative children are treated. Nevertheless, a checklist of characteristics might be helpful.

Indicators Listed By Teachers, Counselors, and Administrators. Eighty-
seven teachers, counselors and school administrators participating in a
Creative Thinking Seminar responded to my request to draw up a set

of five behavioral indicators of creative talent. Their responses were analyzed and summarized by Wilbur Kalinke, a Seminar participant. The most frequent categories of behavioral indicators are as follows:

Curiosity, inquisitiveness, investigativeness, penetrating questioning, etc. 66%

Originality in thinking and doing, unusual solutions, unusual answers, unusual approach to problem-solving, etc. 58%

Independent in thinking and behavior, individualistic, self-sufficient, etc. 38%

Imaginative, fantasy creating, story teller, etc. 35%

Non-Conforming, not bothered by acceptance of others, etc. 28%

Sees relationships, perceptive of relationships, etc. 17%

Full of ideas, verbal or conversational fluency, etc. 14%

Experimenter, tries new ideas, new products, etc. 14%

Flexibility of ideas and thoughts 12%

Persistent, perseverant, unwilling to give up, etc. 12%

Constructs, builds, or rebuilds 12%

Irritated and bored by routine and obvious, *prefers the complex,* copes with several ideas at the same time 12%

Daydreamer, preoccupied, etc. 10%

The following are examples of specific kinds of behaviors suggested as indicators of creative talent:

He can occupy his time without being stimulated.

He prefers to dress differently.

He goes beyond assigned tasks.

He is able to amuse himself with simple things in imaginative ways.

He may look like he's loafing or daydreaming when he's actually thinking.

He questions beyond the single "why" or "how."

He experiments with familiar objects to see if they will become something other than what they are intended to be.

He is a window watcher during class but keeps up with what's going on in class too.

He likes to make up games on the school yard.

He enjoys telling about his discoveries and inventions.

He comes up with ways of doing things that are different from the standard directions.

He finds unusual uses of toys other than the intended uses.

He is not afraid to try something new.

He draws designs and pictures on his notebook while the teacher is giving lecture or directions.

He draws elaborate pictures.

He goes further in his play with games than the directions accompanying them.

He doesn't mind consequences if he appears to be different.
He uses all of his senses in observing.

In summary, most of the behaviors listed by Seminar participants could be conceptualized in terms of the six kinds of thinking ability which Guilford and Merrifield (1960) now consider to be involved in creativity:

1. *Sensitivity to problems:* seeing defects, needs, deficiencies; seeing the odd, the unusual; seeing what must be done.
2. *Flexibility:* ability to shift from one approach to another, one line of thinking to another, to free oneself from a previous set.
3. *Fluency:* ability to produce a large number of ideas.
4. *Originality:* ability to produce remote, unusual, or new ideas or solutions.
5. *Elaboration:* ability to work out the details of a plan, idea, or outline; to "embroider" or elaborate.
6. *Redefinition:* ability to define or perceive in a way different from the usual, established, or intended way, use, etc.

Thus, if we are looking for a systematic way of redefining behaviors in such a way as to identify potential creative talent we can examine behavior in terms of these six kinds of thinking.

Procedures and Devices for Obtaining Non-Test Indicators. A variety of procedures have been reported by teachers, counselors, and school administrators in obtaining non-test indicators of creative talent. Several of these have been mentioned in the foregoing discussion: play activities, regular school activities such as examination, the use of a set of indicators such as the Maw and Maw (1961) curiosity criteria, various crisis situations or emergencies, and the like.

A number of more formal procedures might be considered. One of the most obvious of these is the use of school and home assignments which require creative behavior. Another obvious method is through the use of creative achievements in high school, in college, or in a profession. Holland (1961), for example, has reported the use of indicators of creative achievement in high school in the program of the National Merit Scholarship Corporation. Various kinds of checklists, life experience inventories, and reading questionnaires have also been used. I would like to discuss briefly two rarely mentioned but promising techniques: self-identification and descriptions of crisis experiences.

A number of programs for gifted students use some type of self-identification process. Brandwein's (1955) description of an apparently highly successful program for students gifted in the sciences constitutes an effective argument for self-identification. Many Honors programs make use of one kind of self-identification procedure in that students must apply for admission to the program. Recently I have designed a self-identification instrument which includes a 68-item check list composed of characteristics associated with the creative personality, items concerning test and learning preferences, self-ratings on the six kinds of abilities in the Guilford-Merrifield conceptualization of creative thinking, and a checklist of creative achievements. The value of such an instrument is yet to be demonstrated and will perhaps be most useful at the college and graduate school level.

Many teachers and counselors ask students to write descriptions of their most trying, most satisfying, or most embarrassing experience. Seldom do they use these as an aid in identifying the creatively gifted. An example from my wife's use of this technique in a course on interpersonal relations for freshman nursing students will illustrate the potential usefulness of this technique. Vast individual differences in creative thinking are reflected in these materials, ranging from the extremely obvious and commonplace experiences and solutions to highly imaginative, bold, and surprising ones. One which we particularly enjoyed involved a freshman girl who was suddenly confronted with the problem of exhibiting her older brother's prized calf at a cattle show. Her brother had given the calf little training and the calf absolutely refused to respond to all of the usual training procedures. In desperation, this freshman girl hooked the calf onto a tractor and pulled him along until he decided to walk. After this, the calf responded to training and the sister exhibited the calf with the highest of success. On a battery of creative thinking tests, this girl achieved one of the highest scores in a class of 100 students.

As imaginative teachers, counselors, principals, and parents come to understand creative behavior, they will be able to redefine many behaviors which they have usually labeled as socially undesirable and see in them a reflection of abilities which give promise of highly desirable talent. The next step should be an acceptance of the challenge to help individuals who possess such talents to apply these valuable abilities in productive, socially desirable achievements.

REFERENCES

Brandwein, P. F. *The Gifted Student as Future Scientist.* New York: Harcourt, Brace and World, 1955.

Getzels, J. W. and P. W. Jackson. *Creativity and Intelligence.* New York: John Wiley, 1962.

Guilford, J. P. and P. R. Merrifield. *The Structure of Intellect Model: Its Uses and Implications.* Los Angeles: Psychological Laboratory, University of Southern California, 1960.

Holland, J. L. Creative and Academic Performance among Talented Adolescents. *Journal of Educational Psychology*, 1961, *52*, 136–147.

Leuba, C. A New Look at Curiosity and Creativity. *Journal of Higher Education*, 1958, *29*, 132–140.

Maw, W., and Ethel W. Maw. Establishing Criterion Groups for Evaluating Measures of Curiosity. *Journal of Experimental Education*, 1961, *29*, 299–305.

Torrance, E. P. *Guilding Creative Talent.* Englewood Cliffs, N. J.: Prentice-Hall, 1962.

CHAPTER SEVEN
Teachers and Parents

Increasing Children's Creativity
through a Combination
of Teacher Training Approaches
Catherine B. Bruch

With current educational emphasis on releasing children's creativity as a national concern, a summer institute of four weeks was
designed for this specific purpose. This institute was held in August
of 1964 on the campus of San Fernando State College in Northridge,
California. The primary objective was that of training teachers for
encouraging children's creativity. An associated objective was the
release of creativity within gifted children.

A combination of multiple approaches to training teachers was the
unique feature of this program. Student trainees enrolled in the program were exposed not only to lectures concerned with theories of
creativity, but also to panel discussions by master teachers, observation and participation in classroom with gifted children, daily discussion groups, weekly seminars and informal meetings with staff members. Approximately forty trainees were programmed for observations
at their own choices of grade levels. They were also permitted freedom as to the degree of observation or participation preferred, according to their current experiences in teaching. Trainees ranged from
upper-classmen to graduate students with several years of teaching
experience.

Master teachers were free to concentrate upon teaching because
of the additional features of the total program. These included the

Reprinted by permission of the Author and *The Gifted Child Quarterly*,
9:24–8, Spring, 1965.

volunteer aides from the local San Fernando Valley Association for Gifted Children, and counselor trainees who facilitated communication between the special summer school, children and parents. Many clerical and routine tasks were performed by the volunteer aides, while the counselor trainees functioned in conferences with children and parents, and in leadership of the daily discussions with teacher trainees. The entire institute was a well-coordinated effort of cooperative staff, trainees, counselors and parent volunteers.

PROGRAM ORGANIZATION

Before the actual school program for gifted children, teacher trainees enrolled in the institute attended an hour of lectures by the institute director, Dr. John C. Gowan, or the assistant directors. Master teachers and counselors appeared as panel members at some of the later meetings to discuss practical applications of creativity from their own classrooms or counseling perspectives.

During the nine-to-twelve school morning, institute members observed and/or participated in two separate classroom settings, with their third hour scheduled for group discussions. Three groups of institute members were rotated so that the number of observers would not be too great in any classroom at a given hour. In the daily discussions these same group sections met, one group each hour. One counselor was assigned on a rotating basis to attend each discussion hour. Although the discussions were to some extent "leaderless," the counselor assigned could assume whatever leadership role seemed appropriate to the group process.

Organization of classrooms varied with different grade levels. Self-contained classrooms were maintained at the third and fourth grade levels. The fifth grade and the younger sixth grade classes were taught by an alternating team of two teachers, one specializing in mathematics and science, the other in language arts and social studies. Flexible scheduling was planned as needed between the two teachers. In the older sixth, the seventh and the eighth grades, teaching was departmentalized with language arts, mathematics and science as content areas.

Approximately 180 gifted children attended school only four mornings of the week, with Wednesday mornings between nine and twelve devoted to seminars for trainees. Each sectioned group of institute members rotated among seminars led by the director and the assistant directors, spending an hour with each. In addition to seminar emphases that varied between the directors, teacher trainees also experienced opportunities for taking and discussing results of creativity tests.

Informal meetings with staff were held, one group each week, after the seminars. Weekly informal staff meetings for constant evaluation and planning facilitated staff cooperation. Counselors, and sometimes parent group volunteers, also participated in these meetings.

STAFF

Master teachers were especially selected by the director on the basis of experience and concern with gifted children's creativity. The institute director, Dr. John C. Gowan, is a recognized authority on the gifted. He had led several previous special summer sessions for gifted children on the campus of Valley State College.

Assistant directors, both of whom taught as master teachers in the institute, were experienced in the areas of gifted and creativity. Dr. Juliana Gensley, Assistant Professor of Education at Long Beach State College, had also directed a special summer session for gifted children at Valley State College and courses for teachers of the gifted. The writer, a school psychologist, had been coordinator of the gifted program in the Lancaster Elementary School District, and had studied creativity intensively in preparation for a U.C.L.A. thesis.

FACILITIES

On the Valley State College campus, departmentalized classes were held in the Science Building, where some laboratory facilities were available for the science program. Other classes were held in bungalow classrooms on the original campus, where one classroom was equipped for observation. Surrounding lawns and areas under shade trees became locales for small group projects. College library cards for each gifted child were considered by the children as special privileges, as were visits to the data processing center, or other campus explorations. Some field trips were made off campus.

EVALUATION OF EFFECTS OF TEACHER TRAINING

As a means of continuous evaluation the director requested weekly that institute members complete brief evaluation questions. Tape recordings of the weekly seminars with the writer were made for future analysis, and for insights as to current program needs. Weekly staff meetings made possible flexible adaptation to the needs of the on-going

Table I.   Responses to Question Three—Ideas Received from the Institute Grouped into Areas of Major Concepts

I. *Self-perceptions of institute member and interpersonal relationships in creativity*

Self-evaluation	8
Interpersonal relationships	5
Affective domain	4
Teaching enthusiasm	4
Values of guidance and counseling	3
Classroom creativity as gradual (with "comfort")	3
Creativity as non-neurotic	3
Value of seminar, group discussions	2
Characteristics of creative teacher	1
Creative attitude as source of untapped energy	1
	34

II. *Creative classroom climate*

Incubation period	6
Respect for children's divergent thinking	5
Delayed evaluation	5
Creative climate	4
Productive thinking	4
Motivation of creativity	4
Flexible classroom procedures	2
Freedom to explore ideas	2
Brainstorming	2
	34

III. *Methods and materials for classroom creativity*

Various methods and materials	6
Discovery, inquiry, logic, problem solving	5
Creative writing, language arts methods	4
Asking divergent thinking questions	2
Re-evaluation of classroom control as learning	1
	18

IV. *Children's needs and interests*

Individualized learning	6
Children's needs and interests	4
Self-worth feelings of children	2
Group and committee work	2
Achievement	2
Responsibility of "Gifted" to society	1
	17

V. *Degree of classroom structure and creativity*

Structure	7
Classroom control	4
Absence of authoritarianism	2
	13

VI. *Knowledge of creativity*

Various aspects of creativity	6
I.Q. and creativity relationships	3
"Constructive" creativity	2
	11

VII. *Summary statement*

"Education courses can be interesting and informative"	1
Total ideas	128

program. Counselor trainees also provided in these meetings valuable feed-back for such adaptations. Although time has not permitted full analysis of the evaluation data collected, Table I would seem to represent synthesis of the effects of the institute upon the teacher trainees.

On the last weekly evaluation form institute members were asked to "Name three ideas you received from the institute." An initial frequency tabulation of these ideas was made. The ideas were then regrouped into areas of major concepts. This analysis is represented in Table I, with examples of categorized comments following.

EXAMPLES OF SPECIFIC COMMENTS
OF INSTITUTE MEMBERS

Self-Evaluation:
". . . to evaluate and re-evaluate as necessary and bounce back."
"Self-confidence—self-evaluation."
"A new self-satisfaction of using my own ideas by being more secure in what I am doing."
"Just a beginning of a new self-evaluation which will help me to be more relaxed in my teaching."

Interpersonal Relationships:
"Tremendous importance of inter-relationship between counselor and teacher in the approach and teaching of the gifted."
"Importance of sensitivity of teacher to students' responses and actions . . ."
"That a creative attitude in teaching, learning, and in all relationships is essential . . ."
"Real empathy between child and teacher."
"Idea of the creative relationship—it's gorgeous."

Affective Domain:
". . . most helpful to focus on the effective side of learning . . . I find it challenging and inspiring."
". . . affective domain—how enlightening."

Teaching Enthusiasm:
"Inspiration!"
"A new enthusiasm for teaching the gifted . . ."

Guidance and Counseling:
"Importance of individual guidance and counseling."

Gradual Classroom Creativity:
"To go slowly when you try out new methods to 'induce' creativity in our classrooms . . ."

"A learning as growth process . . . 'comfort'."

"Importance of slow steady progress in initiating creative thinking."

Creativity as Non-neurotic:

"That it is easier, better and more fun to use all of one's powers positively than to wallow in one's neuroses."

"Clarification of the personality difference between far-out constructive creativity vs. plain 'far-out'."

Incubation Period:

"The necessity of solitude in order to carry out the creative process."

"At last a sound reason why all children do not need to participate at all times. (Incubation period)

"Give creative child time to develop."

"Give ideas a chance to grow."

"Results may not be immediately obvious."

Respect for Children's Divergent Thinking:

"A child needs to feel worthy—that his ideas . . . should be respected."

"Value of each person's ideas and need to encourage development of his own creative characteristics."

"Importance of accepting unusual answers from students."

Delayed Evaluation:

"Value of evaluation without final judgment."

". . . creative in a very structured and strict situation: example—creative writing . . . free from . . . evaluation of spelling, punctuation, etc."

"Idea of withholding evaluation, of postponing . . . allow children to contribute without fear of being immediately judged."

Creative Climate:

". . . sensitivity of teacher . . . in order to implement the creation of a creative atmosphere."

"That a great deal more learning takes place by the children when they are given the opportunity and climate to participate at their interest and ability level."

Additional observations of the effectiveness of the institute program may be inferred from these informal examples. During the institute many trainees became involved to the extent of volunteering for self-initiated responsibilities. They seemed to view themselves as part of the total institute "team." They expressed personal concerns that others should be permitted to benefit, as they felt they did, from such an experience. One institute member described the total institute month as a "mountain-top experience." Another unpredicted result was the volunteer continuation of one of the institute groups in holding monthly meetings during the fall and winter for the purpose of discussing creativity.

EVALUATION AND EFFECTS
ON CHILDREN'S CREATIVITY

No organized data collection was attempted during this session as to specific effects of the school on children's creativity. It could be generalized, however, that parent comments were primarily favorable. In some instances parents made specific efforts to convey to school staff the increased motivation of their children for school. The degree of satisfaction on the part of parents and children may be reflected by the quantity of early enrollments already received for the summer school to be held in 1965, 175 by February, 1965.

The changes which may have taken place in the creativity of the children may only be evaluated in the next session in 1965, when creativity tests and observational data collected in 1964 can be compared. However, as an example of the interest of one sixth grade boy, when asked his ideas for the next summer school, he initiated and circulated a petition among his classmates to extend the length of the summer session program.

DISCUSSION OF PARTIAL EVALUATIONS

In reviewing Table I, the predominance of values perceived by institute members lie in their own self-perceptions in relationship to creativity, and in the understandings of characteristics of a creative classroom climate. Both of these areas would suggest implications that the teacher trainees were personally assimilating well the role of the teacher in facilitating a classroom climate conducive to children's creativity. It might be expected that this summer institute could have more than a temporary effect upon teachers' learning about creativity. The institute also may have modified attitudes so that teachers will apply in the future more creative classroom practices. That an understanding of what constitutes a creative classroom climate was more frequently acknowledged than the other conceptual categories would seem significantly related to the practical demonstrations institute members witnessed of creative characteristics and classroom conditions, as given by Torrance (1963), Parnes (1962), and Barron (1963).

Teacher trainees were exposed to a variety of examples of creative teaching, and creative and gifted children. The knowledges presented through lectures and readings were directly applied through observations, discussions, seminars, and some participation. Principles of creative teaching were applied in the organization and practices of the institute: freedom for each master teacher to plan and effect his own program; freedom for trainees to participate to the degree which was for them appropriate; freedom from the usual grading methods, such as tests upon content; highly satisfactory inter-personal group and staff relationships wherein each individual was respected as of worth; a composite of practices which represented both a complexity of inter-relationships and a vitally integrated total perspective (Barron, 1963).

SUMMARY

In that this attempt to improve the creativity of gifted children and to train teachers to do so was a beginning of an analysis of pertinent variables, no conclusive evidence can be offered as to the precise effectiveness of this experience. The total effect, from the majority of viewpoints which might be taken, was one of promise, of resourceful leads for continuing research. Tentatively, it could be said that a combination of the described methods of teacher training seems effective.

Further analyses of existing data from evaluation questionnaires, tape-recorded seminars, and creativity tests are anticipated. Follow-up procedures are being planned to determine whether there may be continued effects of the institute in actual teaching situations, and perhaps delayed effects in long-run attitudinal changes.

Continuing research in refining the variables present may lead to more effective means of training teachers for becoming more acceptant and encouraging of children's creativity. Specifically, the role of discussion and seminar groups in facilitating the understanding and application of creativity theories is apparently important, as are actual observations and experiences with gifted children. Whether the effect of such an integrated combination of training methods is superior to other single methods of presenting course content, or other combinations of methods, is yet to be investigated.

REFERENCES

Barron, Frank. *Creativity and Psychological Health*. Princeton, N. J.: D. Van Nostrand Co., Inc., 1963.

Bloom, B. S. *Taxonomy of Educational Objectives:* Cognitive Domain. New York: David McKay Co., 1956.

Bloom, B. S. *Taxonomy of Educational Objectives:* Affective Domain. New York: David McKay Co., 1964.

Gallagher, James J. *Teaching the Gifted Child*. Boston: Allyn & Bacon, 1964.

Guilford, J. P., and Merrifield, P. R. "The Structure of Intellect Model: Its Uses and Implications." *Reports from the Psychological Laboratory*, No. 24. Los Angeles: University of Southern California, 1960.

Maslow, A. H. "Cognition of Being in the Peak Experiences." *Journal of Genetic Psychology*, 94:43–66, 1959.

Parnes, Sidney J., and Harding, Harold F. *A Source Book for Creative Thinking.* New York: Charles Scribner's Sons, 1962.

Torrance, E. Paul. *Education and the Creative Potential.* Minneapolis: University of Minnesota Press, 1963.

Torrance, E. Paul. *Guiding Creative Talent.* Englewood Cliffs, N. J.: Prentice-Hall, Inc., 1962.

A Preliminary Report on Analyses
of Classroom Interaction *

James J. Gallagher and Mary Jane Aschner

THE INTRODUCTION OF MANY INNOVATIONS IN CURRICULUM AND METHODS has changed the face of American education and has increased interest in methods of evaluation of educational programming. The purpose of the present article is to present a new approach—one involving analysis of classroom interaction—which may be useful in arriving at such an evaluation.

The educational literature teems with examples of past evaluations of educational programs, most of them focused primarily upon the *product.* The measure of the success of a given program was the standing of the child at the end of a period of a kind of educational treatment, or the amount of change the child achieved over a given period of time. Such methods of evaluation have been especially common in research evaluating the usefulness of ability grouping or acceleration. Methods of teaching reading have also been frequent objects of evaluation. In a comparison of reading-method X with reading-method Y, one common procedure has been to obtain two groups of children, presumably comparable on important variables, with one group being placed in a classroom where they would receive reading-method X, and the other group where they would receive reading-method Y. The children would be tested on reading skills both at the beginning and at the end of the experiment. Such a procedure has been curiously

* This research has been supported by the Elizabeth McCormick Fund and the Cooperative Research Branch of the U. S. Office of Education.

REPRINTED by permission of the Senior Author and *Merrill Palmer Quarterly*, 9:183–94, 1963.

sterile in producing improvements in reading programs and other areas of educational curriculum and planning as well. Why?

Let us suppose that the group mentioned above, who received reading-method *Y*, obtained scores on reading ability that were superior to those of the group who underwent reading-method *X*. We may then conclude that there were certain variables at work in the total environment provided by reading-method *Y* which were superior to those operative in the environment in which reading-method *X* was applied. The problem confounding the educator lies in the multitude of possible factors that could have been responsible for the resulting differences in the experimental and control group test scores. Was it the organization of content that brought about the improvement? Was it a superior teacher, or his enthusiasm for the new method? Or was the change due to one small part of the total instructional method rather than to the whole? Could not the same benefits be obtained perhaps, merely by adopting only one part of program *Y*?

Yet faced with such results, the educational administrator must often limit his decision to either accepting or rejecting method *Y*. This, in short, is the basic defect in attempts that have been made to use the product of the program—or the children's achievement gain—as the criterion for the effectiveness of programming.

An alternative method of evaluation consists in analysis of the teaching process as it goes on in the classroom. Such analyses can be accomplished in the examination of teacher-pupil interaction and of the developmental processes of learning. In analyzing these interaction sequences, it is possible to identify—and to describe—fruitful or fruitless teaching procedures in a way that has not been possible under the conventional "pre-post test" type of study.

PRIOR INTEREST IN SEQUENCE ANALYSIS

Interest in the process of verbal interaction is not new; the present study has profited from the experiences of two different lines of investigation. Rogers (1951) and Snyder (1947) pioneered a series of investigations into the process of psychotherapy through the classification of the verbal interactions of client and counselor relationships. Rogers has commented, "Let it be said at the very outset that in the present stage of our knowledge we do not really know what is the essential process of therapy." Practically all counselors and therapists believe that there is a flow and sequence in the process of counseling itself, but it has not been thoroughly investigated.

In a more specifically educational setting, Aschner (1961) using in-class analysis techniques, has discovered certain conventions and ground rules that tend to shape the course and contexts of classroom operation. Smith (1961) has investigated classroom interaction in an attempt to identify the logical dimensions of the teaching process. Smith points out the importance of studying both teacher and pupil behavior, as well as their mutual interaction. His view of the present state of knowledge of the teaching process is quite similar to that expressed by Rogers.

"Our knowledge of the act of teaching as well as that of taking instruction is meager. Neither of these acts has been investigated sufficiently to justify from a scientific standpoint fundamental changes in teaching. . . . The act of teaching has received far less attention than its central role in pedagogy would seem to require" (pp. 93–94).

There are two major prerequisites to an efficient analysis of the teaching process: (a) some type of classification system which enables the investigator to label teacher-pupil and pupil-pupil interactions, and (b) a theoretical structure which provides a basis for evaluating teacher behaviors in terms of their effectiveness. By using a particular frame of reference or theoretical structure, the investigator can evaluate a given instance of teacher-pupil interaction or a sequence of such interactions to see how closely the observed sample of behavior approximates the theoretical ideal or goal. Other investigators have adopted similar approaches in the study of the classroom or of a particular type of educational program (Flanders, 1960; Spaulding, 1962; and Suchman, 1961).

A RESEARCH PROJECT ON PRODUCTIVE THINKING

The present research is investigating productive thought processes in gifted children, as these are evidenced within the context of classroom verbal interaction. The definition of productive thinking used in this study is similar to that formulated in the theoretical structure developed by Guilford (1956). We define "productive thinking" as consisting in those divergent, convergent and evaluative operations whereby the individual draws upon available past and present acts, ideas, associations and observations in order to bring forth *new* facts, ideas and conclusions. Productive thinking, so defined, includes both the creative and critical-analytic dimensions of reasoning. The basic data for the present study of verbal interaction were obtained through tape recording five consecutive classroom sessions in 12 classes of intellectually superior children of junior high school age, in a variety of subject matters: Social Studies, Mathematics, Science and English.

THE GUILFORD CLASSIFICATION SYSTEM

Guilford's *Structure of Intellect*, (1956), was developed through a series of studies using factor analytic methodology. The parameters of this theoretical structure consist in the *operations* of thinking, the *content* within which these operations are performed and the *products* which result from the performance of these operations upon the content. Guilford has identified four types of content in his theoretical structure: *figural, symbolic, semantic* and *behavioral*. Figural content is represented by geometric patterns and designs which convey no intrinsic meaning. Symbolic content is made up of signs and signals which convey meaning by representing other things, such as numbers or formulae. Semantic content represents meaning as conveyed in spoken and written language. Behavioral content is identified as the physical actions and social behaviors of the individual. The present research concentrates primarily upon the areas of symbolic and semantic content, since these are emphasized in a school setting.

As products of thinking, Guilford lists *units, classes, relations, systems, transformations* and *implications*. For example: The apple (*unit*) is a tree-grown fruit (*class*). If the wind blows much harder, the roof will be torn off our house (*implications*). A brick has little in common with an ordinary book (*association*), but I could use it for a book-end (*transformation*). The more people there are who want something, the higher the price will be (*system*). The last three of these product categories represent, in reality, more complex combinations of the first three, placed in various relationships with one another.

The present category system was constructed primarily on the operations of intellect as Guilford has described them. Five primary categories have been developed. These are: cognitive memory (*C-M*), convergent thinking (*CT*), divergent thinking (*DT*), evaluative thinking (*ET*), and routine (*R*). The routine category consists in the familiar and conventional interpersonal maneuverings of speakers in the management activities of the classroom setting, and in a number of categories defining behaviors—verbal and otherwise—expressing affect and feeling tone.

In addition to the tape recordings of the classroom proceedings, two observers were present in the classroom during each recorded session, and took extensive notes on the classroom activities. They noted, for example, such things as blackboard diagrams and written material, textbook references, charts, and demonstration apparatus materials. In addition, they tried to identify the more obvious attitudinal dimensions of interaction between teacher and class, such as censure, praise, frustration, humor, etc. Each transcribed classroom session has been classified, unit by unit, by trained judges working with the scoring manual developed for this purpose (Aschner, Gallagher, *et al.*, 1962). These codings are then transferred to a flow chart for more extensive analysis. In order that the reader have some idea of the dimensions of each of these areas of cognitive behavior in the classroom, a brief description is given below.

Cognitive-memory operations represent the simple reproduction of facts, formulae, or other items of remembered content through use of such processes as recognition, rote memory and selective recall. Some examples of cognitive-memory performance would be seen in the following:

T: Will you tell us what is the first question on the guidesheet?
Bill: What is the "spoils system"?
T: What were some of the main points covered in our discussion about mercantilism?
Mary: One of the things we learned was that there was an attempt to keep a favorable balance of trade.
T: Does anybody remember who was the sixteenth President of the United States?
Bob: Abraham Lincoln.

All of the above are examples of teacher-student interchanges that do not require the student to integrate or associate facts; the questions dealt with are all of the kind that can be handled by direct reference to the memory bank. The sole duty of the student is to select the appropriate response from his store of remembered items. While factual information is clearly indispensable to the development of higher thought processes, it is also obvious that it would be a sterile and uninteresting class that dealt exclusively with this type of question, never moving into the challenge and excitement of more complex operations.

Convergent thinking represents the analysis and integration of given or remembered data. It leads to one expected end-result or answer because of the tightly structured framework through which the individual must respond. Some examples of convergent thinking follow:

T: If I had six apples and gave John two, how many apples would I have left?
Bob: Four.

T: Can you sum up in one sentence what you think was the main idea in Paton's novel, *Cry The Beloved Country?*

Pete: That the problem of the blacks and the whites in Africa can only be solved by brotherly love; there is no other way.

Thus, convergent thinking may be involved in the solving of a problem, in the summarizing of a body of material, or in the establishment of a logical sequence of ideas or premises—as, for example, in reporting the way in which a machine works, or in describing the sequence of steps by which the passage of a bill through Congress is accomplished.

Divergent thinking represents intellectual operations wherein the individual is free to generate independently his own data within a data-poor situation, or to take a new direction or perspective on a given topic. Some examples of divergent thinking would be:

T: Suppose Spain had not been defeated when the Armada was destroyed in 1588 but that, instead, Spain had conquered England. What would the world be like today if that had happened?

Sam: Well, we would all be speaking Spanish.

Peg: We might have fought a revolutionary war against Spain instead of England.

Tom: We might have a state religion in this country.

These examples represent teacher-stimulated divergent thinking, but it need not always be teacher-generated. In a regular discussion of the "spoils system," a student may come up with the following:

"Well, sure, the spoils system might be a good thing when a political party is getting started, but what about when there's no party system— like in the United Nations?"

Here the student reveals his ability to take off from an established fact or facts and see further implications or unique associations that have not been requested or perhaps even thought of by the teacher. Instances of this type of self-initiated student behavior would also fall under the general category of divergent thinking.

Evaluative thinking deals with matters of judgment, value and choice, and is characterized by its judgmental quality. For example:

T: What do you think of Captain Ahab as a heroic figure in Moby Dick?

Bob: Well, he was sure brave, but I think he was kind of mean the way he drove the men just because he had this crazy notion of getting back at Moby Dick.

T: Is it likely that we will have a hard winter?

Mary: Well, I think that the pattern of high pressure areas suggests that we will.

T: Who was the stronger President, Jackson or Adams?
Mike: Adams.

In the first of the above examples, the student is asked to construct a value dimension of his own in terms of what he considers "heroic," and then to make a judgment as to where on this value dimension he would place Captain Ahab. In the second response, the student is asked to make an estimate or to give a speculative opinion or assessment or probability. A third possibility involves entering a qualification or disagreement, wherein the respondent would offer a modification of a prior judgment of another student; or he may state a counter-judgment, in which he declares direct opposition to the statement of the previous speaker.

The final category, routine, contains a large number of miscellaneous classroom activities. Included here are the attitudinal dimensions of praise and censure of others and of self. Also present are dimensions of *structuring*, a kind of prefatory remark, telling in advance what the speaker intends to say or do, or what he expects someone else to say or do. Other characteristic occurrences, such as humor, as well as the ordinary, "routine" classroom management behaviors—even to requests to close the door or asking what time it is—are included in this primary category.

The excerpt given below represents about one and a half minutes of recorded classroom activity in a science class. The discussion concerned the relationship between gravitational attraction and the weight of a body in space.

[1] Doug: All right, then, so that if you weighed one-fourth as much as 10 lbs. you'd weigh 2.5 lbs., and since you go 4,000 miles from—and every time to weigh one-fourth as much, you would go 4,000 miles further than 12,000 miles, and that is 16,000.

T: At this point, I weigh 10 lbs., 16,000 miles out from the center of the earth.

[2] Doug: You said from the surface.

T: No, it is measured from the center of the earth. 12,000 miles from the surface would be 16,000 miles from the earth.

Doug: Oh.

[3] T. Are you with me now?

Doug: I thought you said to double the distance. . . . (remainder of Doug's comment unclear.)

T: No, you've got to double that distance every time. So, for example, in order to find out where I would weigh one-quarter as much as I do on the earth, I've got to double that distance. In order to find out where I weigh one-quarter as much as I weigh here, I've got to double that entire distance. So it's . . . . 20 . . . . 32,000 miles from the center of the earth or it's 28,000 miles from the earth's surface. Now, can you see that if I keep on doing this, and you can see that as I keep on doing this, I'll never, never, ever—Don—as you see that I keep on doing this, I'll never get to a point where I'll weigh nothing. [4] It would always be one-quarter of something. It would always be a small number. I can go out there forever and there will still be a small, a small fraction of an ounce that I would weigh. In other words, the gravitational attraction of any object never stops. It just keeps on going out. It gets less very rapidly but it never gets to nothing. Peter?

[5] Peter: Well, it's just like the rabbit who was being chased by the hound and the hound caught up by half as much each time and he never got there but he kept gaining more and more, half as much each time—closer.

[6] T: (Addressing the class) You all understand that problem?/[7] If I'm chasing one of you and every five minutes I get half the distance to you, I'll never reach you. I'll keep getting half the distance to you, but I'll never get there, because there will always be something—some distance between us.

The numbered remarks above represent typical features of teacher-student interaction behavior. These merit a closer consideration:

1. In this instance, Doug is giving a typical example of convergent thinking; he is spelling out the steps that he is following to obtain a solution to the problem.
2. Here, Doug is making a request for clarification, and is also actually questioning the correctness of the teacher's approach. This is a type of response that is usually observed only in the more self-assured students —youngsters who do not hesitate to express their doubts about the correctness of the teacher's position.
3. This type of teacher behavior is classified in the routine category and is called "monitoring-feedback." It is one type of teacher behavior in which the teacher attempts to ascertain whether or not the student or the class as a whole understands the point that he is trying to make.
4. In this instance, the teacher—after a long clarifying explanation—sets forth the general rule or principle underlying the phenomenon that they are discussing. Depending upon one's philosophy, one might suggest, in this instance, that it might have been better for the teacher to elicit the general rule from the students rather than to state it himself.

These are the sorts of points that can be brought under discussion through the use of tapescripts. In this way an experienced teacher, or a teacher-in-training, has the opportunity to examine his own performance and that of the students in the cool and quiet aftermath of the class session. Using tapescripts in this way is not unlike using motion pictures of football games to view on the day after the game, in order to find out why certain plays were successful while others were not. The teacher can profit greatly from a close study of the responses of his students to the ways in which he carries on instruction.

5. Despite the fact that this class sequence centers upon convergent thinking processes, some students, Peter for instance, are irrepressible; such students can be counted upon to come up with unique or unusual associations, as Peter does here by bringing in a highly appropriate analogy. This type of divergent thinking performance is far from commonplace, even among groups of highly talented students.

6. This is an example of teacher clarifying behavior in which he restates the analogy that Peter presented, thus to make sure that the students all grasped the point that Peter was trying to make.

7. The diagonal line between the first and second sentences of the teacher's remarks represent the division between thought units on the tapescript. In addition to being a promising tool for research in classroom inter-action, the tapescript also provides, as we have said, an opportunity for the teacher to look over both his own performances and those of his students, in order to detect weak points in his own presentation, and to discover particular student problems that escaped him in the swift moment-by-moment pace of the classroom session itself.

Table 1 shows the total thought units classified in one social studies classroom over five consecutive 56-minute sessions. In this class, the boys seemed to be consistently more fluent verbally, and in the flow of ideas in all expressive areas. Using the Mann-Whitney U test, this difference between boys and girls was significant at the .10 level in the area of divergent thinking and total production, and approximated that level in the three other areas. Despite these differences in production, the proportion of the different thought processes used was quite similar in boys and girls. The interpretation to be applied to these proportions must await further analyses and comparisons with other classroom groups and other teachers.

The teacher's proportion of total thought productions (questions and statements) was rather similar to the students. She produced a higher percentage of cognitive-memory and evaluative responses, but a lower proportion in convergent and divergent thinking. Many of the teacher's cognitive-memory responses represented attempts to clarify and add to student statements, rather than a mere doling out of facts.

The low percentage of teacher divergent questions in comparison with student responses is described in more detail in Fig. 1. Figure 1 indicates the relationship of the thought processes expressed by the students to the types of teacher questions posed during the five class sessions.

Table 1. Sex Differences in Expressed Thoughts in Social Studies Class for Gifted Children

		Expressed Thought Processes (Five Consecutive Class Sessions)				
		Cognitive Memory	Convergent Thinking	Divergent Thinking	Evaluative Thinking	Total
Boys (N = 10)	Mean	12.8	7.7	8.9	5.6	35.0
	Percent of Total	36	22	25	16	
Girls (N = 9)	Mean	8.0	5.1	4.1	3.1	20.3
	Percent of Total	39	25	20	15	
Teacher	Total	262	100	31	107	500
	Percent of Total	52	20	6	22	
Boys vs. Girls * Mann Whitney U		25.5	28.0	24.0	28.5	24.0

* A U of 24 significant at .10 level.

Although divergent production is presented in this figure, similar graphs can be made for each area of cognitive operation. It can be noted that 17 per cent of the teacher's total question-asking activities was done in divergent thinking in class session I, as opposed to 4 per cent in class session II, and 11 per cent in class session III, etc. It is interesting to note that the profile of the divergent production of both girls and boys, follows the same general pattern as that of the teacher. In those sessions during which the teacher asks for more divergent production, the percentages of responses in this area are correspondingly high. When the amount of divergent production requested stays below 5 per cent, the decrease in divergent production by the students is marked.

It may be noted however, that only a slight increase in the teacher's percentage of divergent questions brings forth a large increase in divergent production in the students. This results from the fact that a single question, such as "What would happen if the United States were colonized from the West coast to the East instead of vice versa?", can bring forth as many as fifteen or twenty responses, each related to divergent production on the part of these gifted students.

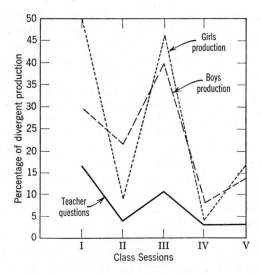

Figure 1. Relation of teacher questions to student divergent thinking production.

While the boys produced more divergent responses than the girls, the ratio of their total responses to the divergent area was about the same, as seen in Fig. 1. In addition to capturing much of the general flavor of the varieties of intellectual operations that occur in the classroom context, it is also possible to trace profiles of individual children, and to determine whether certain students may have problems in expressing themselves in a given area of intellectual operation. Further analyses will also deal more directly with the sequential patterns of teacher-student interaction, as distinguished from that quantification of total, over-all results, as indicated in Table 1 and Fig. 1.

The long range goals of the present research include:

1. The construction of a reliable classification system by means of which the verbal interaction of teachers and pupils can be analyzed in any classroom, regardless of subject matter content or student ability level. It may be possible eventually to investigate the question of whether there are fundamental differences in expected intellectual operations from one subject matter to another—for example, from science to social studies, or from mathematics to English. Such differences might explain, in part, the reason why some students are able to perform quite well in one subject area and yet perform poorly, or in a mediocre way, in other areas.

2. It is hoped that through an analysis of classroom interaction it will be possible to identify examples of certain kinds of highly desirable intellectual performance. It should then be feasible, working backward from these criterion cases, to see what types of teacher behavior or pupil behavior preceded and hence may have stimulated these desirable outcomes. In this manner it may be possible to gain insight into effective methods of teaching for higher conceptual performance, and thus to lay the groundwork for experimental studies in which teachers could—through the strategic use of certain kinds of behavior—seek to raise the level of intellectual productivity of gifted children and, indeed, of children at all levels of ability.

3. Attempts will be made to relate the in-class performances of the children in this study to a wide variety of measures of intellectual aptitude and personality characteristics, measures which were administered to them prior to tape recording their classroom sessions.

4. Measures of family attitudes and behavior will also be related to individual in-class performances through family interviews and questionnaires designed by the sociologist on the project staff.

The eventual goal of the project is to arrive at a description of the intellectual processes that occur in the classroom and, through this, to acquire not only a greater understanding of the teacher process itself, but also to work out more effective ways of training teachers for the stimulation of productive thought processes.

REFERENCES

Aschner, Mary Jane. The language of teaching. In Smith, B. O. and Ennis, R. H. (Eds.), *Language and concepts in education*. Chicago: Rand McNally, 1961.

Aschner, Mary Jane, Gallagher, J. J., Jenne, W. C., Perry, Joyce, Farr, Helen, & Afsar, Sibel. A system for classifying thought processes in the context of classroom verbal interaction. (Mimeographed, Institute for Research on Exceptional Children, University of Illinois, 1962.)

Flanders, N. A. *Teacher influence, pupil attitudes and achievement*. Minneapolis: U. of Minnesota Press, 1960 (Final report, Cooperative Research Project No. 397).

Guilford, J. P. The structure of intellect. *Psychol. Bull.*, 1956, *53*, 267–293.

Rogers, C. R. *Client-centered therapy*. Boston: Houghton Mifflin, 1951.

Smith, B. O. A concept of teaching. In Smith, B. O. and Ennis, R. H. (Eds.), *Language and concepts in education*. Chicago: Rand McNally, 1961.

Spaulding, R. L. Some correlates of classroom teacher behavior in elementary schools. Address given at A.E.R.A. meeting, Atlantic City, New Jersey, February 20, 1962.

Snyder, W. U. *A casebook of non-directive counseling*. Boston: Houghton Mifflin, 1947.

Suchman, J. R. Inquiry training: building skills for autonomous discovery. In Morse, W. C. and Wingo, G. M., *Psychology and teaching*. Glenville, Ill.: Scott Foresman, 1961.

Relationships between Creativity
and Teacher Variability
Judith L. McElvain, L. N. Fretwell, R. B. Lewis

OF CURRENT INTEREST TO PSYCHOLOGISTS IS THE CONCEPT OF CREATIVITY
as a component of personality that needs explanation. Several attempts
have been made to identify it and to actually test its complex nature.
One such instrument (Torrance, *et al.*, 1960; Yamamoto, 1962) was
used in this study to find a relation between creativity and teaching
competency as well as to find other common characteristics of teachers
in comparison to levels of creativity.

A total of 209 teachers were secured for creativity testing from the
summer school population at Eastern Washington State College in
1962. Personal data were gathered concerning sex, age, number of
years of teaching experience, number of years of college education,
and teaching level. Letters were sent to the teachers' principals asking
them to rate on a 5-point scale the over-all effectiveness of the teacher
in the classroom. There was over a 90% return of these ratings.

Six hypotheses were tested. The major hypothesis of the relationship
between creativity test scores and principals' ratings was supported
with a Pearson product-moment correlation of $-.22$ ($p < .01$). A
product-moment correlation of $-.14$ between creativity and age of
the teachers was significant ($p = .05$). No significant differences were
found between creativity test scores and sex, number of years of
teaching experience, number of years of college education, or teaching
level. The point-biserial correlation of .02 suggested there were no
significant sex differences on creativity scores. The product-moment
correlation of $-.12$ indicated there was no significant difference
between creativity scores and number of years of teaching experience.
The non-significant χ^2 of 4.39 indicated there was no significant
relationship between creativity scores and number of years of college
education and the biserial correlation of .05 indicated there was no
significant difference between creativity scores and teaching level.
(All *rs* were considered for significance from a .00 point.)

Results suggest that, for the selected adult population, creativity
may be a fairly stable trait since all variables but age were non-

REPRINTED by permission of the Author and *Psychological Reports*, 13:186, 1963.

significant and correlated so close to zero. The evidence reported here that school administrators tend to give lower ratings to the highly creative teachers gives direction to other topics for research. There may be inherent within creativity, as it is measured, personality characteristics that are not valued in teachers.

REFERENCES

Torrance, E. P., Yamamoto, K., Schenetzki, D., Palamutlu, N., & Luther, B. *Assessing the creative thinking abilities of children*. Minneapolis: Bur. of Educ. Res., 1960.

Yamamoto, K. *Revised Scoring Manual for Tests of Creative Thinking (Forms VA and NVA)*. Minneapolis: Univ. of Minnesota, 1962.

Suggestions for Mothering the Gifted to Encourage Curiosity, Learning, and Creativity

Alison Thorne

To put it mildly, my husband and I were startled when our two oldest children became National Merit finalists.

I am a non-working mother—odd phrase, that denotes the fact that I don't earn money. For years in what spare time I could muster I have been studying housewives' values, a little explored field. Our civilization has spent more effort on improving kitchen efficiency than in scrutinizing philosophy of homemaking. Middle-class values for years judged as excellent the woman who was a good cook and perfect housekeeper, but times are changing fast and in discussing values with other mothers I can see this cake of custom crumbling.

Neither Perfect Housekeeping nor House Beautiful dominates our home. We live in a university town in a high, square, old-fashioned house. The upstairs bathroom contains an immense closet with wide shelves for quilts and blankets, but we don't keep our extra bedding there. Instead we keep stacks of *National Geographics*, all the art

REPRINTED by permission of the Author and *Gifted Child Quarterly*, 7:47–50, Summer, 1963.

work and notebooks which our five children have lugged home from school and wanted saved, lots of maps, and a stack of very large envelopes containing pictures and clippings about American history, English history, Renaissance art, religion, plants, animals, etc.

A child comes home from school and says, "We're studying Abraham Lincoln. What've we got?" So we retire to the bathroom to emerge presently with one magazine article, several pictures, and a yellowed replica of the newspaper telling of Lincoln's assassination, this latter a souvenir saved from a trip to Washington, D. C. The shelves also hold scrapbooks on art, space, elementary French, a year spent in Tennessee, a collection of bookmarks, etc.

Precariously stacked on the very top shelf are rolled-up, homemade charts, mostly on shelf paper. One chart shows the relative size of the planets. Another lists famous persons of history, arranged by civilization and chronology. Another is a rough drawing of the world with small pictures of fruits, vegetables, and flowers pasted onto the area of origin. There is also a chart showing routes our great-great-grandparents took from Europe to America and on across to the far West. These and others have each at some time been pinned to the dining room or kitchen wallpaper. We live with pin-pricked wallpaper, just as we live with shredded upholstery where the cat sharpens her claws.

By the way of further inventory let us consider the kitchen cupboards. The glassed-in shelves intended for lovely china and glassware are filled instead with games, puzzles, stamp collections, two decorated cans which contain embroidery floss and half-completed dishtowels, two sets of knitting progress—I think they are to be bedroom slippers. My silverware box does not contain silverware; it has been subdivided for a sea shell collection which has overflowed into Christmas card boxes. There are tennis and badminton rackets and three cameras.

Scattered in various other places are scratch paper, type paper, pencils, crayons, scissors, water colors in small jars, three kinds of glue, chalk, compass, rulers, three kinds of tape, balls of string, and ink. At this very moment two children are at the kitchen table writing with a pheasant feather and ink, just to see how it might have felt to be a scribe in colonial days.

As for books, we have them on stars, birds, trees, flowers, shells, history, and the usual childhood classics. Our history books include one of our local valley, telling of ancient Lake Bonneville which once covered the entire valley floor and reached into the canyons of our mountains. The two older children brought home their geology texts from Cal Tech and Stanford, and the local geology professor gave us an excellent sourcebook written for elementary and secondary schools. Our nearby canyons are Paleozoic and we find such books valuable.

We also own, as a traveling companion, the WPA guidebook for our state. We studied about the fallen ghost town of Silver Reef as we walked over its rocks and picked up rusty square nails and bits of bottles turned violet in the desert sun. Nails and glass now lie in the drawer of my dressing table after several excursions to school to be "shared." •

We take the *Scientific American*. Its advertising has magnificent pictures of rockets, satellites and other matters dear to the heart of the young devotee of space. Its articles need translation for the small fry but often the puzzle pages are entrancing. We did the Chinese tangrams and wrestled with the Japanese art of paper folding.

My theory is this: Helping children to love learning involves first, creative materials. I have named some, but the last thing on earth that we ever call them is creative materials. They are "stuff."

Second: Love of learning requires enthusiasm. If parents are enthusiastic their offspring will pick it up by contagion. In fact the offspring will spring off in directions where their parents can only stumble, music, in our case. Four-dimensional geometry, another case, and thereby hangs a tale. The tale I am about to tell concerns a third requisite, sustained attention, and how four-dimensional geometry was its climax.

When our oldest son was about four years old, he brought into the kitchen a brown paper sack of clods. He had seen his father collect soil samples in brown paper sacks, so he had invaded a vacant lot and gathered his own sample. Then he asked me to get out our food chopper, an affair of cast metal, and he began to grind up the clods. It was hard work but he stayed with it to the end. Our kitchen looked like the Oklahoma dust bowl and the blade of my chopper was ruined forever.

The years went by and he reached age seventeen. I had tried to teach him and his sisters and brother that when you are pursuing an interest, throw everything you have into it and let the chips fall where they may. You can pick up the chips after the project is complete. (Here I must confess sadly that I never adequately trained them to pick up their chips because by then I was in the midst of some private project of my own, or helping someone else on a project, and couldn't stop to supervise a thorough chip-picking-up. Consequently we seem to dwell perpetually in chips.)

The Science Talent search was on. Our high school senior chose four-dimensional geometry as a project. He cut coat hangers into short strips and hung the corners together with modeling clay. The device which he created was large, angular, and occupied all the top of his desk. This meant his books moved to the floor. Scraps of paper with penciled mathematics lay scattered everywhere in the room. His clothes hung on the floor; his bed was perpetually unmade. Any real tidying-up was impossible for work was in progress, let the chips fall where they may. Just as he completed his paper two days before the deadline, he rushed downstairs, gave it to me and said, "Type this for me, will you Mom?" and hurried out the door to join his friends on an overnight hike. Well, I typed it. He can type—all our children can type—but I make the fewest mistakes. There were seven pages. I understood the first two; his father understood the first four; I still wonder if the judges understood all seven. Anyway it won a placing.

Our household usually looks chaotic because of works in progress and it was a real pleasure for me to read Frank Barron's statement that creative people can stand more chaos than ordinary people. Barron was not speaking of housekeeping but I think the principle applies.

Barron also states that creative persons are more independent in judgment than other people. Years before we ever read Frank Barron or Solomon Asch we had been trying to teach our children to think for themselves and not to conform blindly to groups.

"But all my friends are going to this movie," wails a youngster bent on attending a horror film.

"We don't live like everyone else. We have our own ideas about how to live, and that's a lousy movie," I reply firmly.

But judgment about when to conform and when to rebel comes slowly. In his enthusiasm for individuality, our oldest wore a beard for weeks and a pair of bilious yellow trousers. At the time I could not make him understand that rebellion in dress is a waste of time and energy; one should save one's rebellion for more worthwhile causes. I think he understands this now.

In contrast to the episode of the bilious pants we have a daughter who at five years insisted on more and prettier Sunday school dresses.

"But clothes are not the most important thing in life," I said.

"What is then?" she asked.

"Well," I said slowly as my mind went into high gear, "Knowing things and loving people."

Thousands of pages have been written on philosophy of values and I have struggled with a good many of them. But when you tell a five-year-old about values you do not invoke Kant's categorical imperative.

Knowing things and loving people imply the Truth and Goodness of the ancient Greeks. Beauty; the third of the famous trio, might possibly refer to more beautiful Sunday school dresses, but I think not.

Loving people is a tremendous ideal. We taught the children not to hurt the feelings of others. Their own tears over personal hurt feelings always exceeded the quantity of tears shed from physical pain, and they early learned that other people have feelings too. We taught them that teachers are people and that teachers can get tired and cross just as parents do. It is hard work to be a teacher and they should help her where possible.

Then pride reared its ugly head. "I'm the best in the room," a child would boast.

"Yes but you don't boast about it," we said. "You are fortunate to have good ability, but he who receives much must give much. It is your obligation to help smooth the way for other people. There are many things that need doing in this world and you must help do them."

Humility about one's gifts combined with the ideal of service to others will prevent snobbery, and it is the home which must take first responsibility in teaching these matters.

Because there is so much talk of giftedness these days, children of ability are likely to become self conscious and feel set apart from their friends. I say that all children are gifted; each child must be able to excel at something for his own satisfaction.

But what of the child who is superb at everything? If he is truly a member of his own neighborhood, the other children are not going to judge him as being apart. Around here our children and the neighbor children play marbles together in the living room, make popcorn in the kitchen, and roller skate in the basement. Nobody pays any attention to who is bright in school and who isn't.

I am a cub scout den mother to my young son and seven of his contemporaries. I am a 4-H leader to my young daughters and their crowd. For some reason my relatives chortle at the idea of my teaching girls how to cook, but I can follow directions as well as anyone and our club did win a blue ribbon at the county fair. We can turn out perfect products when we want to but we have flexible standards. When other matters are more important it doesn't hurt our conscience to let housekeeping and cooking go to pot.

Actually, I'm no professional at teaching children. I'm a mother struggling along, trying to strew creative materials and enthusiasm and affection as I go.

Has it occurred to anyone that it might be possible to evolve some suggestions for mothering that would encourage curiosity and learning and creativity among youngsters at home? Homemakers have been deluged for years with recipes, budgeting suggestions, and sewing patterns. But this is something else entirely.

And furthermore, has it occurred to anyone that many of today's gifted girls will be mothers of a good many of tomorrow's gifted children? If heredity causes giftedness, they have the genes. If climate of the home causes giftedness, they will have the opportunity. From the curriculum chosen by today's gifted girls, what can they adapt for use in their future mothering of the gifted? Or will they play it by ear, as mothers have been doing for generations.

The Search for the Creative Teacher

Frank E. Williams

How to identify and nurture creativity at all levels of the educational process is one of the most pressing problems of our time. As our complex society tries to assimilate burgeoning new knowledge, we need creative people who can accept and adapt new methods and new relationships.

But this clear objective of education presupposes that the teacher understands the elements of creativity, knows how to promote it, and is skilled in the use of suitable means for determining the success of his techniques. This supposition in many cases is not true. Most teachers need to develop appropriate procedures for the development and evaluation of creativity.

The problems of nurturing creative thinking in education are particularly difficult, since we are only beginning to discover the frontiers of this field. We cannot expect to gain much from a study of creativity unless we know what is being done and where the research will direct us. I shall attempt here to describe some current studies from which we may begin to form hypotheses.

Curricular practices have too often involved what the teacher does

Reprinted by permission of the Author and *California Teachers' Association Journal*, 60:1:14–16, January 1964.

with methods and materials and what subject matter the teacher imparts to the student. We need to know more about how the student learns. Laboratory research on learning and concept formation has made it possible for us to identify a large number of intellectual processes, each of which the student should know how to use while simultaneously acquiring the subject matter content.

Research in learning to date has been a feast of investigations in factual learning, attitude change, and perceptual-motor learning; a famine of investigations in what we now call "the higher mental processes." (See Fig. 1.) I should like to limit my comment to the divergent process as creative-productive thinking and the evaluative process as decision-making operations of the intellect.

One may seriously question what the teacher does when the student strives for a better answer or a different question than either the text or the teacher has given him. The answer is, of course, variable. I am sure that in many institutions the student feels disapproval for seeking a better answer. In others, students receive approbation for digging into things, for producing imaginative responses, for questioning what the teacher or the book has told him, and for forming his own hypotheses and wishing to try them out. The latter is found at the university graduate level and it is beginning to creep into the early curriculum of the elementary school. But what is happening in the junior high school, the high school, and the undergraduate college years of the student?

Many experiences must be provided to allow the student intellectual persistence in the manipulation of ideas and objects, to let him resist premature closure in reaching conclusions, and in making generalizations and solving problems while gaining an emotional involvement in the process of subject-matter learning. Students must be able to use a wide variety of the higher mental processes. Teaching a concept creatively implies the teacher's readiness to modify techniques which acquaint students with facts in favor of stimulating the student to think and to do something with the facts.

An interaction analysis in classrooms over a long period of time attempted to show the teachers' spontaneous verbal behavior and resultant student reaction. Such studies show the teachers' most frequent behavior is telling the pupil what to do (from one quarter to one half of total class time). Almost another quarter of classroom time is spent in providing information, a great deal of it administrative. Reinforcement of classroom responses occurred in only five per cent of the time. In only 1½ per cent of the time did teachers delegate the decision-making function to the pupils. Time for question-asking reached a maximum of 15 per cent.

In another study the majority of seventh grade classroom activity was devoted to retrieval of information. The mental processes of identifying, recalling, and comparing were thus called into play but inferring, exploring, evaluating, inventing, and synthesizing were either completely lacking or in a minority.

How to include these missing mental abilities in classroom activity, to treat pupils as thinkers rather than only as information receivers and retrievers, is the major task. Teachers must modify teaching methods to include the productive thinking operations of the intellect.

By changing the percentages of time spent in routine tasks calling for retrieval of information to those involving cognition, divergent thinking, and evaluation, one researcher produced a broad range of thought processes with assimilation of subject matter. In his seventh grade class, there were greater achievement gains in lower and middle intelligence groups. An experimental group which received a wide variety of thinking experiences achieved much better than a control group which was subjected to the traditional method of information transmission and retrieval. We know a lot about how to teach subject matter. Now we need to teach subject matter effectively as we lead students to use and think in these unaccustomed categories.

One teacher found he could train his students effectively in fluency, flexibility, and originality. Achievement test scores for the trained class indicated no loss in academic learning.

These illustrations answer the complaint of the teacher who says, "All this is fine, but where do we find time to teach creative thinking in an already overcrowded curriculum?" By sacrificing routine tasks, teachers can seek and develop the creative thinking abilities of students with as much or more subject matter achievement.

Over the past several years I have trained some 350 California teachers in what we now call creative and productive thinking processes. Each was asked to comment on his reaction to using the processes and materials in his classroom. Eight per cent thought they were creative teachers and the in-service training helped them identify what they were doing. Another 32 per cent wanted to know how to use creativity in the classroom, with applicability to subject matter. The largest group, 60 per cent, said they always wanted to experiment in this area but were apprehensive because they thought time would be lost and administrators might not accept the new idea. We have indicated the need and significance of change in classroom procedures, integrating established methods with existing knowledge of the thinking process.

Teachers may ask what childhood activities, early life experiences, and family environment contribute to creativity in the lives of young

Figure 1.   Classification of Creative Activities and Experiences into the Higher Mental Processes

I. *Cognitive ability:* discovery, recognition, comprehension, awareness, understanding.

   Activities that: generate curiosity, provide rediscovery, require comprehension, cause awareness.

II. *Memory:* storage and retention of knowledge—what has been cognized; ability to recall information when needed.

III. *Convergent thinking:* redefinition, transformations, recognized best or conventional solution, improvisations.

   Activities that: transform, redefine, improvise; ability to pick best of choice of several alternatives.

IV. *Divergent thinking:* scanning stored information, searching for many possible solutions, thinking in different directions, ability to go off in new and untested directions, deferred judgment.

   A. Fluency: quantitative—emphasize rate within classes.
      1. Ideational fluency—generation of a quantity of IDEAS, words, titles, responses, phrases, sentences, uses, consequences, productions (drawings, pictures, designs, or other sense stimuli).
      2. Associational fluency—completion of relationships—production of relations; generation of synonyms, analogies, similarities, problems of likeness.
      3. Expressional fluency—new ideas to fit a system or structure organization into systems or logical theories; sentences, verbal ideas, question responses.

   B. Flexibility: quantitative—variety.
      1. Spontaneous flexibility—variance of kinds of responses into classes; number of considerations of properties, attributes, or inherent characteristics of problem or product; number of shifts of category responses, versatility.
      2. Adaptive flexibility—number of detours, freedom to make changes, number of approaches or strategies used in seeking solutions; number of changes of interpretations, changes in direction of thinking.

   C. Originality: qualitative—unusual, remote, clever, uncommon, infrequent, remote associations.
      verbal, figural, symbolic transformations as uncommon objective unusualness—statistically infrequent—subjective choice as clever, far-fetched, novel, different from standard or norm.

   D. Elaboration: production of detailed steps, variety of implications and consequences; quantitative measure.

Figure 1 (*Continued*)

V. *Evaluative ability:* goodness, suitability, adequacy, determination of fit, ability to determine if produced solution fits the problem (search model).

Activities that: produce conceptual foresight, raise pertinent questions, cause sensitiveness to problems, require curiosity, noticing defects or changes, seek improvements to social customs, institutions, behavior, noting defects in objects or ideas, evaluating implications, observations of imperfections or inadequacies, constructive discontent, flexibility of critical-mindedness, purposeful judgment.

(Memory, item II, is normally operable in all individuals; all other abilities listed are those used by all *creative* individuals.)

---

people. One study has shown that creativity may be developed during the very early life of the child through attitudes of both parents and teachers. Factors found in the study included environmental factors in the home, parental tolerance for expressiveness without domination, acceptance by parents of regression in children, and lack of dependency of each parent on the other. The influence of parents in pre-school years is perhaps greater than that of teachers in the years to follow. Training teachers to understand and use creativity in the classroom may even be too late.

We have only begun to form the questions; we have very few final answers on the nature and the application of creativity in education. Some of the questions which keep recurring include: How can we determine whether future teachers will be creative? How can we predict the success of a creative teacher? What is the relationship between manipulative and verbal type tasks in distinguishing creative behavior among children? Are there genetic or nutritional factors which will produce the high energy, vast output, and perseverance known to be characteristic of creative persons?

While we are seeking the answers to these questions and many more like them, we might ask: What is the status of creativity in education? We must admit that it has the status of a freshman at Harvard. It must prove itself. In terms of acceptable educational policy, creative education has not yet arrived. Yet the need for creatives who think to and beyond the frontiers of knowledge is now recognizable in our society. It seems logical that the shortest route to a creative society will lie through the education and development of teachers who think and teach creatively.

Annotated Bibliography

Bates, C. O. "A Study of Creativity Potential as Found in Elementary Student Teachers." Unpublished Ed. D. thesis, Muncie, Ind.: Ball State Teachers College, 1963. *Dissertation Abstracts* 24:4561; 1964.

   High creatives exceeded lows on MMPI M-F, Purdue Placement Test in English, need for precision and self-reliance, total score on SCAT, writing, history, and social studies scores on the STEP, high school rank and college GPA. No difference found on SVIB or MTAI.

Brecher, Ruth, and E. "Creative Ability—What Is It? Who Has It? What Makes It Flourish?" *Parents Magazine;* November 1960.

   Deplores fact that the older children grow and the longer they are exposed to our care and education, the less creative and original most become. Poses the question: What can we, as teachers and parents, do to keep creativity alive while they are: (1) learning to behave by "our" standards; (2) playing their proper role in a group; (3) learning the facts and skills they need; (4) being judged, disciplined, and jointly approved by teachers and parents. Proposes six ways to increase creativity.

Bruch, Catherine. An Analysis of Characteristics and Classroom Behaviors of Effectively Creative Teachers. (Unp. Ed. D. thesis, in progress, 1965) U. C. L. A.

Burkhart, R. C. "The Interrelationship of Separate Criteria for Creativity in Art and Student Teaching to Four Personality Factors." *Studies in Art Education* 3:18–38; Fall 1961.

   Problem posed is to identify the attributes of creative behavior and personality structure in art and student teaching. In the art area, criteria was determined by a judgment of the art products' "spontaneity" or "deliberateness"; in the teaching area, by an objective count of the "divergency" or "convergency" of the student-teachers' questions to the pupils. Concluded by determining four attributes of creativity in personality structure that are applicable to both creativity in teaching and in art, as well as the fact that both are significantly related to the same Creativity-Personality Dimensions. The differences are between divergent and relative values, and factual and absolute values, in that a pronounced lack of creativity is the correlate of the latter, while creativity is related to the former.

Castelli, C. D. "An Exploration of the Relationship between Teacher Creative Ability and Teacher Pupil Classroom Behavior" (Unp. Ed. D. thesis) State University of New York at Buffalo, 1964.

Teachers with creative ability were identified by scores on N or the intuition scale of the Myer Briggs Type Indicator. Teacher-pupil classroom behavior was measured by the OScAR technique of Medley and Mitzel ($N = 61$). Teachers high on tests of divergent thinking tended to be more supportive. The creative teachers also had a wider dispersion of rewarding and punishing behavior; they smiled more and frowned more than controls did.

Lagemann, J. K. "How We Discourage Creative Children." *Redbook* 120:44; March 1963. (Cf. *Reader's Digest;* May 1963.)

Quotes Torrance that: "I.Q. tests do not measure creativity; by depending on them, we miss 70% of our most creative youngsters." Torrance's findings, after studying over 15,000 boys and girls from nursery school to 6th grade, show that most children start life with a variable, creative spark and that most of them have it knocked out of them by the time they reach the 4th grade. He observes that "it is not that parents and teachers deliberately squelch creativity; rather, they fail to recognize it."

Pointed up in the article are: (1) how creativity differs from the kind of mental ability measured by I.Q. tests; (2) signs to look for in detecting creativity; and (3) what parents and teachers can do to eliminate or mitigate the pressures that make children give up their creative work.

Stewart, Evelyn Seeley. "The Big Question of Creativity." *Parents Magazine* 38:62–64; June 1963.

What is it? Who has it? Can it be acquired? The author cites Dr. D. W. McKinnon's (U. C. Berkeley) definition of true creativity as involving: (1) response to an idea that is novel; (2) ability to adapt this idea to reality; (3) sustaining the original "insight," evaluating and elaborating it. She then reviews Dr. E. Paul Torrance's long list of characteristics of creativeness. Stressed is: the need for parents and teachers to learn how to foster creativity when and where it is. As he sees it, creativity can be developed. Everyone possesses to some degree, (a) the ability to be creative, depending on the way children are treated; and (b) the provision made possible in home and school for experiences and guidance which will free them to develop and function fully.

Thorne, Alison. "Mothering the Gifted to Encourage Curiosity, Learning, and Creativity." *Gifted Child Quarterly* 7:47–50; Summer 1963.

Contains practical hints about ways to stimulate gifted children from parental point of view.

Tonn, Martin "Parents Are Your Children Creative?" *Gifted Child Quarterly* 9:142–5, Autumn, 1965.

> Hints for parents with creative children. This issue also contains other short articles of interest to parents.

Uraneck, W. O. *Creative Thinking Workbook.* Massachusetts: 56 Turmag Road, Lexington 73, 1963.

U. S. Department of Health, Education, and Welfare, Office of Education. *New Dimensions in Higher Education.* No. 8:2–11; 1961. Washington, D. C.: Office of Education. (Cf. [pp. 302–10] in French, J. L. *Educating the Gifted, A Book of Readings.* New York: Holt, Rinehart and Winston, 1964.)

> A review of the Advanced Placement Program.

CHAPTER EIGHT

Research and Summary

A Taxonomy of Creativity and Giftedness

John Curtis Gowan

0: CREATIVITY

0.0 *Non-educational aspects*
.01 Art and music
.02 Business, advertising, sales promotion, public relations
.03 Creative writing, drama
.04 Hobbies, sports, recreation
.05 Leadership, group dynamics, government, conformity
.06 Management, industrial research
.07 Mental and physical health, medicine, psychology
.08 Science: physical and biological, mathematicians, architects
.09 Supernatural and religious; hypnotic drugs
0.1 *General Works* (see under 1 for subdivisions)
0.2 *Theory and Policy re Creativity*
.20 General theory
.21 Structure of Intellect and factor theory
.22 Concept-formation, problem-solving, mediating strategies
.23 Psychological, non-cognitive, affect and other theories
.24 Transactional theories
.25 Imagination, intuition, insight
.26 Originality, complexity
.27 Motivational theories
0.3 *Characteristics of Creative People*
.30 General
.31 Genetic
.32 Developmental and early environmental
.33 Environmental, cultural and parental factors

EXCERPTED from *Bibliography of Creativity and Giftedness*, San Fernando Valley State College Foundation, 1965.

.34 Effects of Stress, anxiety, authoritarianism on creativity
.35 Differences by race, class, sex, etc.
.36 Personal and social
.37 College and adult studies
.38 Attitudes, sets, reactions of and toward creative persons
.39 The highly creative
0.4 *Practice: Can Creativity Be Increased by Training?*
.40 General
.41 Surveys
.42 Brainstorming studies
.43 Classroom methods
.44 Pupil creativity as a function of teacher behavior and training
.45 General advice to teachers
.46 Miscellaneous methods to increase creativity
0.5 *Curriculum for Creativity*
.50 General works
.51 Elementary
.52 Secondary
.53 Language arts
.54 Creative writing
.55 Library
.56 Social studies
.57 Mathematics
.58 Science
.59 Art and music
0.6 *Guidance and Measurement of Creativity*
.60 General
.61 Counseling for Creativity
.62 Identification
.63 Tests of Creativity: Reliability and Validity studies
.64 Tests of Creativity: Factor-analytic studies
.65 Creativity vs. I. Q. studies
.66 Guilford Structure of Intellect Studies
.67 Torrance Minnesota Tests of Creativity Studies
.68 Miscellaneous Test Studies
.69 Non-test assessments and ratings
0.7 *Administration for Creativity* (see subdivisions under 7)
0.8 *Research and Development* (see subdivisions under 8)

1: GIFTED CHILDREN: GENERAL

1.0 General material
1.1 Integrated works (books covering whole of subject)
1.2 Readings and compilations

1.3 General articles and pamphlets
1.4 Definitions and assumptions
1.5 Foreign practice
1.6 Public attitudes toward the able
1.7 Manpower demand and talent supply; talent preservation
1.8 History
1.9 Miscellaneous

2: THEORY AND POLICY

2.0 General
2.1 Philosophy and principles
2.2 Policy and objectives
2.3 Critical thinking objective
2.4 Social leadership objective
2.5 Productivity objective
2.6 Scientific orientation objective
2.7 Motivation objective

3: CHARACTERISTICS

3.0 General
3.1 Genetic
3.2 Physical and early developmental
3.3 Longitudinal
3.4 Case studies
3.5 Differences in intelligence by race, class, sex and family
3.6 Personal and social
3.7 College and adult studies
3.8 Reactions of and toward gifted persons
3.9 The highly gifted: genius

4: PRACTICE

4.0 General
4.1 Surveys
4.2 Elementary
4.3 Secondary
4.4 Integrated systems
4.5 College and entrance into college
4.6 Enrichment
4.7 Grouping
4.8 Acceleration
4.9 Special and summer school

5 : CURRICULUM

5.0 General
5.1 Elementary
5.2 Secondary
5.3 English
5.4 Reading, writing and spelling
5.5 Library
5.6 Social studies
5.7 Math
5.8 Science
5.9 Art and music

6 : GUIDANCE

6.0 Organization and general
6.1 Counseling needs
6.2 Identification
6.3 Vocational and college guidance: scholarships
6.4 Controlled guidance studies
6.5 Achievement and underachievement
6.6 Statistical identification of achievement
6.7 Personality studies of underachievers
6.8 Counseling underachievers
6.9 Emotionally disturbed gifted children

7 : ADMINISTRATION

7.0 General
7.1 Organization
7.2 Films
7.3 Material
7.4 Costs and budget, staffing, scheduling
7.5 Brochures, explanations for parents and public, public relations
7.6 Starting a program
7.7 Teachers, qualifications; preservice and inservice training
7.8 Parents
7.9 Community and public aspects

8 : RESEARCH, EVALUATION AND DEVELOPMENT

8.0 General
8.1 Agencies and organizations
8.2 Conference reports
8.3 Surveys

Different Predictors, Criteria, and Routes to Criteria

E. Paul Torrance

DURING THE PAST FIFTEEN YEARS THERE HAVE BEEN NUMEROUS CRITIQUES of the criteria that college admissions officers and graduate departments have been attempting to predict. I have been more keenly aware of the ones that have emanated in the United States and Great Britain, but I know that there have been similar ones in other countries such as Japan, Italy, Australia, and India. One of the most compelling arguments to me has been the one that the criteria we have been trying to predict do not themselves predict important criteria in the world outside college and university campuses. Such arguments, usually with data to support them, have been presented by Guilford in 1950, Thurstone in 1952, Calvin Taylor in 1959, Getzels in 1960, Liam Hudson in 1962 and 1964, Carl Rogers in 1964, and others. In general, these arguments and the data that have supported them have been ignored by college personnel workers. Within recent months, however, there have appeared what impress me as rather irrational attacks on these heretical ideas by such stalwarts as McNemar (1964), P. C. Vernon (1964), and others. I am glad that the Commission on Testing and Prediction of Academic Success of The American College Personnel Association saw fit to entertain the question, "Prediction for What?"

I was at first asked to deal with "Creative Aspects of College Behavior." As I continued to receive interpretations and suggestions concerning my 20-minute presentation, I decided that I might contribute most by trying to show something of how changes in ways

REPRINTED by permission of the Author from a paper delivered at the Annual Meeting of the American College Personnel Association, Minneapolis, April 14, 1965.

of measuring achievement bring about changes in how predictors operate and how changes in methods of instruction result in changes in the operation of predictors, using the same criteria. In my opinion, we shall continue to amass confusing research findings until we recognize that the problem is at least this complex.

A failure to recognize this degree of complexity and an attempt to oversimplify the problem is causing a great deal of difficulty in the area of investigation related to the creative thinking abilities, creative imagination, divergent thinking abilities, or whatever term you prefer to use. Dozens of investigators have published articles attempting to discredit these measures by showing that they do not correlate significantly with measures of school achievement or that they correlate negatively. The problem is simply too complex for claims of validity or invalidity to rest on such bases. The nature of the measure of achievement and the teaching method are two minimal factors that must be considered.

Let us examine first some rather simple statistics that involve two types of predictors and several types of criteria in one of the courses that I teach, an Educational Psychology course in Personality Development and Mental Health. The predictors were scores on the Miller Analogies Test, taken as a part of a battery required for admission to candidacy for the master's degree, and a composite score derived from a 40-minute battery of creative thinking tests. This composite score was the sum of the fluency, flexibility, originality, and elaboration scores on one form of the Ask-and-Guess Test, the Product Improvement Test, the Unusual Test, and the Circles Test. (Since that time I have stopped working with composite scores, but I still believe that there are times when one is justified in obtaining a composite score from these tests.) Four types of examinations were given in the course: (1) a rather traditional multiple-choice test requiring recognition of a correct answer, (2) a completion and short-answer test requiring recall, (3) a test of creative applications requiring divergent productions, and (4) a decision-making test requiring evaluation and judgment.

In a class of 110 students, Bentley (1961) obtained the following set of coefficients of correlation from these data:

Achievement Measure	Creativity	Miller's
Recognition	.03	.47
Memory	.11	.41
Productive Thinking	.53	.37
Evaluation and Judgment	.38	.27

In addition to the course examination, students were required to develop an original idea. Judges evaluated these original idea papers according to two sets of criteria. First, they were evaluated in terms of how well they described the idea, the process by which it occurred to them, the psychological rationale behind the idea, how the idea could be tested, and what consequence the idea might have should it be found valid. This was called the Convergent Rating. The second evaluation was based on criteria very similar to those used by the United States Patent Office: (1) the extent to which it is a step forward, (2) its potential usefulness, (3) the creative intellectual energy required to produce and develop it, (4) its surprisingness, and (5) its newness. This was called the Divergent or Inventive level Rating. The Convergent Rating tended to correlate more highly with the Miller Analogies Test score than with the Creative Thinking score (.33 and .16), while the Inventivlevel Rating tended to correlate more highly with the Creative Thinking score than with the Miller Analogies score (.25 and .19).

Well, there is really nothing very puzzling about these findings. Many college instructors are certainly aware of the fact that a relatively different group of students will receive A's if they grade on a multiple-choice test than will receive A's if they grade on an essay examination, a term paper, or a similar type of production. What has been puzzling to some investigators in recent months is that some researchers have found significant positive relationships between traditional kinds of measures of achievement and measures of creative thinking ability (Torrance, 1962; Bisch, 1964; Bowers, 1965), while others have found no significant relationships or significant negative relationships between the same predictors and the same criteria. If one examines closely the research concerning the interaction between different kinds of abilities and different methods of instruction, these results need not be puzzling (McConnell, 1934; Stolurow, 1962; Gotkin and Massa, 1963; Hutchinson, 1963; MacDonald and Raths, 1964). To support this position, I shall have to rely upon studies involving secondary and elementary school subjects, since I am unaware of appropriate studies at the college level.

In general these studies indicate that when knowledge is obtained by authority (i.e., receptive reading, listening, etc.), traditional measures of intelligence, scholastic aptitude, and the like are better predictors of achievement than measures of originality, fluency, elaboration, and the like. When knowledge is obtained in what I have called creative ways (discovery, experimentation, and the like), the measures of originality, fluency, elaboration, and the like appear to be better predictors than the intelligence and scholastic aptitude tests.

A careful study reported by McConnell in 1934 can serve as a convenient starting point for reviewing some of the studies relevant to this problem. The study involved 653 pupils in 15 different schools and lasted for seven months. One group was taught by what McConnell termed "authoritative identification"; the other, by "discovery." McConnell was puzzled by his finding that mental age as measured by the Pintner-Cunningham Test was a better predictor of post-training achievement on the seven criteria used under authoritative identification than under discovery methods. The difference was greatest for the criterion on which pupils under the discovery method were most superior to those under authoritative identification (r's of .401 and .177, with a critical ratio of 3.61).

Today, these results do not seem puzzling. What McConnell did not recognize then was that the abilities involved in the predictor represent only a small sampling of the abilities involved in learning and that the particular abilities tapped by the predictor are more useful in learning by authority than by discovery. A variety of recent studies throws considerable light on this problem.

Hutchinson's 1963 study involving learning in junior high school social studies parallels McConnell's study in a number of ways and answers some of the questions that McConnell's study could not answer. Hutchinson employed both measures of intelligence and measures of divergent thinking abilities. Hutchinson also found that under traditional authoritarian teaching, there is a statistically significant positive correlation between mental age and achievement but not between measures of divergent thinking and achievement. In the experimental conditions where there are considerable opportunities for learning in creative ways the reverse was true. In another 1963 study involving fifth grade children using programmed instruction in language arts, Gotkin and Massa found significant negative relationships between measures of creative thinking and achievement. A year earlier, Stolurow (1962) had found higher positive correlations between measures of originality and post-training achievement than between mental age and achievement with programmed materials in mathematics and statistics. The difference was that Gotkin and Massa used programmed materials that permitted only tiny mental leaps and gave little opportunity for making, identifying, and correcting errors, while Stolurow's programmed materials emphasized the trouble-shooting or hypothesizing approach that builds specific but multiple associations to a stimulus.

MacDonald and Raths (1964) found that highly creative children as identified by a battery of the Minnesota Tests of Creative Thinking are more productive on frustrating tasks than are less creative children. Furthermore, they enjoyed such tasks more than their less creative peers. The least creative children were less productive in open tasks and the most creative ones react less favorably to closed tasks. Thus, pupils of varying levels of creative thinking ability react differently to different kinds of curriculum tasks or assignments and are possibly best taught by varying procedures.

Here, we have what to me has been the most exciting insight that has come from recent research. Children learn best when given opportunities to learn in ways best suited to their motivations and abilities. Whenever teachers change their ways of teaching in significant ways, a different group of learners become the stars or high achievers. Thus, even if we insist on retaining the same criteria we have been trying to predict, this means that we have clues that should enable us to educate a larger number of people to a higher level than we have been doing. If we add to this the further almost obvious insight that changing the criteria (even if we stick to examinations as a basis for grading), we have an even more optimistic picture. Somewhere, however, we need to reassess our objectives and determine what criteria we *should* be interested in predicting. This would probably lead to a recognition that we need multiple criteria and that we should value a variety of different kinds of achievement.

REFERENCES

Bentley, J. C. "The Creative Thinking Abilities and Different Kinds of Achievement." M. A. research paper. Minneapolis: University of Minnesota, 1961.

Bisch, Gertrude. "A Study of the Relationships of Intelligence, Achievement, Creativity, Anxiety, and Confidence among Intermediate Grade Pupils in a Suburban Area Elementary School." Doctoral dissertation. Washington, D. C.: The George Washington University, 1964.

Bowers, J. E. "A Factor-Analytic Study of Creative Thinking Abilities, Achievement, and Intelligence." Unpublished manuscript, University of Minnesota, Minneapolis, 1965.

Getzels, J. W. "Non-IQ Intellectual and Other Factors in College Admission." In K. E. Anderson (Ed.) *The Coming Crisis in the Selection of Students for College Entrance.* Washington, D. C.: National Education Association, 1960.

Gotkin, L. G. and N. Massa. *Programmed Instruction and the Academically Gifted: The Effects of Creativity and Teacher Behavior on Programmed Instruction with Young Learners.* New York: The Center for Programmed Instruction, 1963.

Guilford, J. P. Creativity. *American Psychologist,* 1950, *5,* 444–454.

Hudson, L. "Intelligence, Divergence and Potential Originality." *Nature,* 1962, *196,* 601.

Hudson, L. "Academic Sheep and Research Goats." *New Society*, October 22, 1964.

Hutchinson, W. L. "Creative and Productive Thinking in the Classroom." Doctoral Dissertation, University of Utah, Salt Lake City, 1963.

McConnell, T. R. "Discovery vs. Authoritative Identification in the Learning of Children." *University of Iowa Studies in Education*, 1934, *9(5)*, 13–62.

MacDonald, J. B., and J. D. Raths. "Should We Group by Creative Abilities?" *Elementary School Journal*, 1964, *65*, 137–142.

McNemar, Q. "Lost: Our Intelligence? Why?" *American Psychologist*, 1964, *19*, 871–882.

Rogers, C. R. "Graduate Education in Psychology: A Passionate Statement." Unpublished paper, Western Behavioral Research Center, LaJolla, California, 1964.

Stolurow, L. M. "Social Impact of Programmed Instruction: Aptitudes and Abilities Revisited." Paper presented at the American Psychological Association Annual Convention, St. Louis, Mo., September 2, 1962.

Taylor, C. W. "Identifying the Creative Individual." In E. P. Torrance (Ed.) *Creativity: Proceedings of the Second Minnesota Conference on Gifted Children*. Minneapolis: Center for Continuation Study, 1959. Pp. 3–21.

Thurstone, L. L. "Creative Talent." In L. L. Thurstone (Ed.) *Applications of Psychology*. New York: Harper and Row, 1952.

Torrance, E. P. *Guiding Creative Talent*. Englewood Cliffs, N. J.: Prentice-Hall, Inc., 1962.

Torrance, E. P. *Rewarding Creative Behavior: Experiments in Classroom Creativity*. Englewood Cliffs, N. J.: Prentice-Hall, Inc., 1965.

Vernon, P. C. "Creativity and Intelligence." *Educational Research*, 1964, *6*, 163–169.

Creativity and High School Climate
(Abstract and Summary)
W. J. Walker

ABSTRACT

THE PROBLEM

THIS STUDY WAS DESIGNED TO EXAMINE PSYCHOLOGICAL CLIMATE, teacher personality, teaching methodology, student attitudes, and student creativity in schools judged to be the type that promote the development of creativity as compared with schools not considered outstanding in this regard. Five hypotheses were tested: In "high creative" schools, as compared with "traditional" schools, (1) the psychological environment will be characterized by factors usually considered conducive to the development of creativity, such as high intellectual climate and high student dignity; (2) the teachers will be less authoritarian and more rational; (3) there will be more evidence of originality, initiative, and inventiveness in the classroom learning situations; (4) the attitudes of highly creative students toward their school experience will be more positive; and (5) students will perform better on tests designed to measure aptitudes believed important for creativity.

PROCEDURES

Four high schools judged to be comparable with regard to socioeconomic level and student ability level were involved in the study. Two of the four schools were judged to be the type in which originality and invention were encouraged ("high creative" schools). The other two schools were not considered outstanding in this regard but were judged to have excellent traditional programs ("traditional"

REPRINTED by permission of the Author and exerpted from a doctoral thesis (Syracuse University, 1964).

schools). In each of the four schools, (1) the High School Characteristics Index, a measure of environmental press, was administered to
sixty students; (2) the Inventory of Beliefs, a measure of authoritarianism, was administered to thirty teachers; (3) twenty periods of instruction were observed; (4) fifteen students rated as highly creative
wrote essays about their experiences of education; and (5) a battery
of tests of factors considered important for creativity was administered
to sixty students.

FINDINGS

In comparison with the traditional schools, the high creative schools
(1) were found to have psychological environments characterized
by high aspiration level, high intellectual climate, high student dignity,
high academic climate, low academic achievement, low group life,
low academic organization, low social form, and low vocational
climate. (2) The teachers were less authoritarian, but not less rational.
(3) In the classroom, teachers exhibited more stimulating-original
behavior; students exhibited more initiating behavior; and there was
more evidence of activities of a creative nature. (4) The attitudes of
highly creative students toward their school experience were not significantly more positive. (5) The students did not perform better on
tests of factors believed important for creativity.

IMPLICATIONS

Although the present study raised more questions than it answered,
it did serve to provide clues concerning the environmental characteristics of schools in which creativity is likely to find a favorable climate
for development. Among the values and implications suggested by the
findings are the following: (1) The descriptions of schools judged to
be high creative provide a basis for comparison and self-analysis for
other schools interested in improving the climate for creativity. (2)
The personality dimension of authoritarianism seems to be relevant
to a consideration of factors contributing to a creative environment.
(3) The classroom observation instruments employed in the present
study are useful in assessing classroom behaviors believed related to
the development of creativity. (4) Attempts to discover efficient ways
to encourage teachers to teach more creatively should pay valuable
dividends. (5) As employed in the present study, paper and pencil

tests of creativity do not appear to differentiate students in high creative schools from students in traditional schools. (6) An extension of the present study might include provisions for comparing creative student productivity. (7) There would appear to be a need among educators for a greater understanding of the nature of creativity and of the relationship of the school environment to its development.

SUMMARY, DISCUSSION, AND IMPLICATIONS

The present study was designed to obtain information related to the question: What are the environmental characteristics of schools judged to be the type that foster the development of creativity as compared wih schools not considered outstanding in this regard? A number of hypotheses were made regarding expected trends as revealed by measures of environmental press, teacher personality, classroom performance, student attitudes, and student creativity. In comparison with traditional schools, high creative schools were found to have psychological environments characterized by high aspiration level, high intellectual climate, high student dignity, high academic climate, low academic achievement, low group life, low academic organization, low social form, and low vocational climate. The teachers were found to be less authoritarian, but not significantly less rational. In the classroom, teachers were more stimulating and original; students were more initiating. There were more evidences of activities believed to promote creativity. The attitudes of highly creative students toward their school experience were not significantly more positive. On the tests of factors believed important for creativity, the students did not perform better; in fact, on the factor of spontaneous flexibility the scores of students from one of the high creative schools were lower than the scores of students from the other three schools.

In the following paragraphs a discussion of each of the five hypotheses of the study will be presented, together with the implications suggested by the findings. A number of questions, problems, and proposals for further research suggested by the present study will be listed.

The first hypothesis concerned both environmental press scale scores and factor scores. The findings confirmed the hypothesis with regard to factors to a greater extent than with regard to scales, due probably to the more complete definitions made possible as a result of factor analysis. For this reason, the factor data, rather than the scale data, will be discussed.

Hypothesis 1 stated that high creative schools would score high on such factors as aspiration level, academic achievement, self-expression, academic climate, and student dignity; and low on such factors as academic organization and vocational climate. With the exception of the factors of academic achievement and self-expression, hypothesis 1 was generally supported. An examination of the academic achievement factor reveals that schools high in this factor set high standards of achievement for their students and that course work, examinations, honors, and similar devices are employed for this purpose. Because a case could be made that an overemphasis upon extrinsic means of motivation—such as formal examinations or honors—might tend to inhibit creativity, the findings with regard to academic achievement are not surprising. Quite likely, a high creative school would tend to de-emphasize external means of motivation.

It is difficult to explain the findings with regard to the factor of self-expression. This factor is concerned with the opportunities offered to the student for the development of leadership and self-assurance. One certainly would expect a high creative school to score high on this dimension. Although one of the high creative schools did receive the highest score, it was not significantly higher than the two traditional schools; the second high creative school scored significantly lower than two of the other three schools. Since it is difficult to account for this finding, further investigation would seem warranted.

Certain implications with regard to the psychological environments of high creative schools are suggested. Assuming that the high creative schools do, in fact, promote the development of creativity, we have available from the present study extensive descriptions of the environmental press of this type of school. These descriptions can be useful in a number of ways.

Pace and Stern (1958) have suggested that one potential value of the psychological approach to the measurement of environment is that of self-analysis. A study of student responses to the test items should reveal something useful about the dynamics of the school environment. The environmental press should have some clear relationship to the purposes of the school. The following statements about colleges are appropriate for high schools as well. "The objectives of a college are formal or explicit statements of intent: they indicate the directions in which a college means to influence the behavior of students. They find expression in curricula, practices, services, policies, and other aspects of the college environment. The press . . . constitute

. . . an operational definition of objectives, or implicit influence of the environment upon the students. Implicit press and explicit objectives should reinforce one another, for an institution should operate in reality the way it means to operate in theory" (Pace and Stern, 1958, p. 276). Thus it would appear that a high school that has the development of creativity as one of its purposes would profit from a comparison of its own High School Characteristics Index profile with that of the high creative schools of the present study. Discrepancies might suggest directions for change.

Some aspects of the psychological environment can be changed more readily than others. The Index "provides some direct indications of the psychological implications of the various policies and practices. Roughly, one-fourth to one-third of the items in the Index state specific practices which an administration or faculty could more or less easily change if they did not like the implications. For example, being able to drop a course in which one is having difficulty, or to substitute another course for one which has been failed, is associated with counteraction; insisting that students reports or papers be neat, or giving students an assigned seat in class, or taking attendance regularly, is associated with order. As the relationships among press variables and between these variables and institutional objectives as well as personal needs are established, the significance of such specific practices will become clarified. Other items in the Index are more indirect in their implications about the effect of various policies or practices. But the clues can be investigated and can thus be the starting point for serious discussions about the impact of the environment on the student and the relation of this impact to the intended objectives" (Pace and Stern, 1958, p. 276). For example, a school purporting to foster creativity but which scores low on the factors of intellectual climate or student dignity would profit from an examination of the reasons for the low score. An examination of specific test items might suggest specific changes that would improve the climate for creativity.

Hypothesis 2 stated that teachers in the high creative schools would be less stereopathic and more rational than teachers in the more traditional schools. The findings confirmed the first part of the hypothesis, but not the second part; the teachers in the high creative school were less stereopathic, but not significantly more rational. Since the sample of teachers in all four schools included highly educated individuals who would be expected to be reasonably rational and consistent in their beliefs, the findings with regard to the rational-irrational dimension are not particularly surprising. The most crucial part of the hypothesis was that concerning the stereopathic dimension, and that part of the hypothesis was confirmed. Teachers in the high creative schools tended to be more adaptive, flexible, outgoing, permissive, and nurturant.

These findings suggest that teacher personality is an important variable in the school environment. Any institution attempting to move in the direction of making greater provisions for the development of creativity would need to take into account the influence of teacher personality upon the over-all climate. The findings of the present study would suggest that non-stereopathic teachers would contribute in a positive way to a high creative school climate. In staffing a school, considerations of this aspect of teacher personality would seem reasonable. Although it is difficult to change existing attitudes, effort expended to this effect might pay valuable dividends in situations where one must work with an existing faculty.

Hypothesis 3 stated that classroom learning situations in high creative schools would contain more of the features expected of an educational program that encourages creativity. There would be evidence that originality, initiative, and invention were encouraged. The teachers would be more stimulating and original; the students would be more initiating. This hypothesis was generally confirmed.

The findings suggest that the classroom observation instruments employed in the present study (the Observation Schedule and Record and the Classroom Observation Record) are useful in evaluating classroom activities and behaviors considered important for creativity. Instruments such as these should prove useful in experimental studies in which deliberate attempts to influence classroom behavior are made. For example, observations made before and after a period of teacher in-service training might indicate whether or not expected changes in classroom behavior had occurred.

Hypothesis 4 stated that highly creative students in high creative schools would exhibit more positive attitudes toward their school experience than would highly creative students in traditional schools. This hypothesis was not substantiated. It would appear that whether or not a school environment contains characteristics considered important for the development of creativity makes little difference with respect to attitudes toward the school of the highly creative students.

A number of explanations might account for this finding. Possibly the personality characteristics of highly creative students (independence, for example) enable them to function well in situations which would appear to stifle creativity. Since they are more resourceful and self-confident than the average student, highly creative students might be better equipped to function in creative ways even in restricted environment. One student at the most traditional of the four schools of the present study stated that even with the large number of restrictions at the school, he felt he had the freedom necessary to do what he felt was important to do.

Another possible explanation might be that students are not aware of the short-comings of their school experience. A number of essays written by students at the most distinctively high creative school who had previously attended traditional schools describe the startling difference in school atmosphere at the high creative school. It would be interesting to investigate changes in attitudes of students in traditional schools if they had the opportunity to spend some time at a high creative school. How would the students of Thornton react if they were placed in the Dover setting, and vice-versa? Quite likely, the Dover students would be extremely unhappy at Thornton, and the Thornton students quite uneasy at Dover—at least at first. However, it would be expected that after a time at Dover, the Thornton students would be less satisfied with the educational program at Thornton. It would probably be discovered that highly creative students moving from high creative schools to traditional schools would experience extreme discontent, whereas highly creative students from traditional schools would at first be uneasy in high creative schools, but soon would adapt to the freer situation and be reluctant to return to the traditional program.

Hypothesis 5 stated that students in the high creative schools would perform better on tests of factors considered important for creativity. This hypothesis was not confirmed. In fact, there was a tendency for one of the traditional schools to perform better on these tests and for one of the high creative schools to perform less well. On the factor of spontaneous flexibility, the high creative school having the greatest number of characteristics considered essential to a high creative school environment (Dover) scored significantly lower than the other three schools. It is difficult to account for this finding, especially since most of the other evidence would tend to indicate that Dover had many of the environmental characteristics considered important for developing creativity.

A number of possible explanations for this finding are presented. (1) There is still uncertainty about the degree of validity of the creativity tests of the present study. (2) There was some evidence that the particular group of students at Thornton High School was atypical, the class being considered by a number of teachers to include a greater number of highly creative youngsters than usual. Although there was little evidence to the effect, it is possible that the students at Dover might have been atypical in the opposite direction, that is, the sample might have included students who were less creative than the typical Dover student. The only suggestion in this regard was the fact that the sample at Dover included a number of students under psychiatric treatment for emotional problems. During one testing session a number of students behaved in a disruptive manner. One teacher said he thought this particular group contained a number of individuals who might have perceived the testing situation as threatening to themselves. (3) The testing situation itself might have adversely influenced the effort the students put forth in taking the tests. At Dover the students had not been previously notified that they would be tested at the particular time agreed upon by the principal and the investigator. A number of students resented losing their study period. About ten percent of the group refused to take the test, and went to the library. It is possible that the students who remained to take the tests had a negative "set" toward the activity, and put forth less than their best efforts. (4) Some students at Dover seemed to resent testing in general, expressing the opinion that they were tested too much as it was. In addition, a hostile feeling toward evaluation of any kind was in evidence at the school. (5) The fact that the tests were timed might have bothered some of the students. It was noted that some students seemed disturbed when time was called and they had to move on to a different part of the test.

(6) Another observation that might have some bearing on the test performance was that there seemed to be a difference in the way students responded to direction in the public schools as compared with the private schools. (It is noted that students in the public schools tended to perform better on the creativity tests than did students in the private schools, although not significantly so.) The private school students were considered by the investigator to be less cooperative, more autonomous, and more independent than the public school students. They wanted to know whether or not they were required to take the tests and why they were taking them. A number of students at Dover and Elmwood refused to participate. At the public schools (Thornton and Waverly), on the other hand, there were few questions asked. The students responded to the tests very well; they seemed to put forth a great deal of effort. Although some were curious about the tests, no one asked to be excused from taking them. The cooperation was nearly perfect, with close to one hundred percent participation in both schools. It is possible that the attitudes of the students toward taking the tests in the different schools affected the performance on the tests. The public school students appeared to be accustomed to doing what they were told to the best of their ability. The private

school students were not accustomed to doing things just because they were requested to do so, especially when an "outsider" was involved and when the activity was not a part of the regular school program.

Since the tests of factors considered important for creativity used in the present study were selected from the tests developed by Guilford and his associates, a number of implications for education of the structure of intellect are examined. Guilford (1959) stated that the most fundamental implication is that we must change our conception of the learner and of the learning process. At the present time the learner is considered to be a kind of stimulus-response device, similar to a vending machine. A coin is placed in the machine and something comes out. The machine learns the proper reaction when it receives a certain coin. We must change our conception and begin to think of the learner as an agent for dealing with information in a way similar in many respects to an electronic computer. A computer is fed information; the information is stored; the information is used, in either a divergent or convergent manner; and the results are evaluated. The human learner has the advantage of being able to seek and discover new information from sources outside itself and of being able to program itself. This conception of learning leads to the idea that learning is discovery of information rather than the formulation of stimulus-response connections. "If we take our cue from factor theory, however, we recognize that most learning probably has both specific and general aspects or components. The general aspects may be along the lines of the factors of intellect. This is not to say that the individual's status in each factor is entirely determined by learning. We do not know to what extent each factor is determined by heredity and to what extent by learning. The best position for educators to take is that possibly every intellectual factor can be developed in individuals at least to some extent by learning" (Guilford, 1959, p. 478).

Guilford believes that if education has the general objective of developing the intellects of students, we might consider each intellectual factor as providing a particular educational objective. "Defined by a certain combination of content, operation, and product, each goal ability then calls for certain kinds of practice in order to achieve improvement in it. This implies choice of curriculum and the choice or invention of teaching methods that will most likely accomplish the desired results" (p. 478). We need to ask whether general intellectual skills are now being neglected and whether appropriate balances are being maintained. It is possible that we need a better balance of training in the divergent thinking category and the transformation category as compared with training in convergent thinking, critical thinking, or evaluation.

A model such as the structure of intellect serves to provide a specific framework for considering the dimensions of intellect. Even though it is tentative and imperfect, it provides a concrete model based on sound theory and sound basic research methodology. Assuming that training and experience are related to the development of thinking skills, it is important not only to understand the skills but also to plan procedures for their development through education. A model such as the structure of intellect could be used in helping teachers and students understand the nature of intellectual skills.

Once an understanding of intellectual skills important for creativity is obtained, it is possible to develop improved methods for observing and evaluating classroom activities designed to exercise these skills. Assuming that it is possible to judge classroom behavior, advances could be made in pointing out ways for improving school programs. For example, an instrument might be used which spells out in detail various behaviors considered to facilitate the development of certain intellectual skills. The teachers observed might be involved in discussing the particular observations made in their own classrooms. The feasibility of including certain types of classroom activities might be examined. This would assist teachers in learning how to develop in their students skills important for creativity. This might lead to a reexamination of existing units of instruction to discover whether or not they include a reasonable balance between provisions for learning creativity as well as provisions for learning by authority. It might be helpful deliberately to revise a traditional unit so that it includes provisions for creative learning.

Listed below are a number of questions, problems, observations, and proposals related to the present study or suggested by it. Included in these questions are ideas related to implications for education of existing research knowledge on creativity.

1. Research indicates that in-service programs designed to encourage creative teaching have not been particularly effective (Torrance, 1964). The present study furnished a number of descriptions of creative learning situations. In the judgment of the investigator, there could and should be considerably greater provisions for developing creativity than exist in the "high creative" schools of the present study. The problem would seem to be to discover effective ways to teach teachers how to initiate creative activities. A knowledge of techniques does not seem to be the answer. Possible attempts to change teacher attitudes in directions considered desirable for creativity would prove

helpful. What would be the effect upon the climate for creativity of changes in teacher personality in the direction of becoming less authoritarian, and therefore more flexible and adaptive? What techniques are most effective in changing teacher attitudes? Longitudinal studies might be planned which record the development of student creativity through different levels of education in a school system in which deliberated attempts are made to create a more favorable school environment for creativity.

2. At Dover High School, the most distinctively high creative school, the scores on the environmental press scales of deference, narcissism, and order were markedly low. On the narcissism scale, for example, whereas the raw score values for most schools tended to be high, the raw score at Dover was only 3.52, and the stanine score was 0.17, the lowest standard score for any of the schools on any of the scales. This would indicate that at Dover, in comparison with most schools, students do not take a great deal of pride in their personal appearance; looking and acting "right" is not very important to teachers and students; students who are not neatly dressed are not likely to have this called to their attention; students seldom receive compliments when they come to school with new clothing, a new haircut, or a new hairdo; making a good impression is not important; and teachers are not always carefully dressed and neatly groomed. Further investigation into the causes and implications of these findings would seem warranted. Does the lack of concern for personal appearance, for example, provide clues to a pattern of values that has a bearing upon the climate for creativity?

3. A number of questions are suggested by the finding that teachers in high creative schools tend to be more flexible and adaptive than teachers in traditional schools. Do flexible teachers have needs that are best met in a relatively freer school environment? In what ways does this dimension of teacher personality influence the climate for creativity? How crucial is this dimension of personality for creative teaching? What techniques are effective in helping teachers become more flexible and adaptive? Should in-service programs focus on attempting to change teacher attitudes before attempting to provide specific techniques of creative teaching?

4. What advantages would accrue if students had the opportunity to select the type of learning experience they preferred, that is, if students could choose between a course with provisions for creative learning versus a course taught mainly by traditional methods, or if students could choose between teachers who teach in creative ways versus teachers who teach mainly in traditional ways?

5. What differences in student creativity would result from deliberate attempts to change certain features of the psychological environment of the school? Many of the characteristics measured by the High School Characteristics Index could be changed if the change seemed desirable. For example, if the administration and faculty at Elmwood desired to improve the intellectual climate at the school, they might attempt to change policies and activities that contribute to the intellectual climate factor. The score on the press scale of reflectiveness, which contributes to the factor of intellectual climate, was somewhat low at Elmwood. To change this value, the faculty and administration might encourage students to read books and attend movies dealing with psychological problems, promote an interest in modern art and music, the basic meaning of religion, personal values, and a philosophy of life; and encourage and reward imaginative writing, the expression of individual ideas, and serious discussion.

6. A study similar to the present one might be conducted at the elementary school level. An Elementary School Characteristics Index might be developed which would provide a measure of elementary school climate. Because of the many differences between elementary and secondary schools, such as those relating to departmentalization, the greater exposure of the children to a single teacher, the potential for greater program flexibility, and the size of the school, a study at that level should suggest interesting implications of some of the differences between the elementary and secondary level.

7. Would the differences in performance on the test of spontaneous flexibility which appeared in the present study appear in other similar situations? If so, what might account for the differences?

8. Using the structure of intellect as a model, an instrument might be devised which would make it possible for an observer to discover which of the factors of intellect are being exercised in a learning situation. The instrument would include descriptions of all the known factors. The observer would tabulate whether or not provisions in the learning situation were available for exercising the factor and to what extent. For example, activities which would encourage originality might be tabulated and described.

9. The present study would have been strengthened if it had been possible to include a consideration of the creative productivity of the students of the four schools. If it had been possible, for example, to assess actual creative achievement in science, literature, mathematics, the social studies, and art, considerably greater confidence could be placed in the findings. To some extent this was done in an informal fashion. It would be obvious even to the casual observer, for example,

that the creative productivity in art at Dover far surpassed that of the other three schools. Several individuals who had read the student essays of the present study commented that the treatment of the topic was more imaginative and the writing more creative in those essays written by students from the high creative schools. An extension of the present study might include the use of some type of evaluation instruments for judging the creative production of the students.

10. The present study provides considerable evidence to substantiate the judgments of the individuals involved in nominating high creative schools. The selection was confirmed by the findings of the High School Characteristics Index, the Inventory of Beliefs, and the classroom observations. In addition, it is felt that the student essays contain data which would have provided additional confirmation had the essays been subjected to content analysis. It is suggested that the essays from the high creative schools not only describe learning environments that are essentially more favorable to the development of creativity but that they are more creatively written as well. The essays themselves might be considered samples of student creative productivity. For these and for other reasons, an analysis of the content of the essays quite likely would yield additional valuable information.

Although the present study raised more questions than it answered, it did serve to provide data related to the central question of the investigation: What are the environmental characteristics of schools judged to be the type in which creativity finds a favorable climate for development? Tentative descriptions of the psychological environments of high creative schools are presented, together with information about teacher personality, classroom behavior, student attitudes, and student creativity. The extremely complex nature of creativity becomes evident from an attempt such as this to examine it in actual school situations. Since there is a need among educators for a greater understanding of the nature of creativity and how its development is promoted, studies of this type, which attempt to relate recent research and theory to classroom situations serve a useful function in suggesting directions for further effort in this important area.

Creative Thinking:
Some Thoughts on Research
Kaoru Yamamoto

A RECENT SURVEY OF RESEARCH LITERATURE IN THE AREA OF CREATIVE thinking (Torrance, 1962a) made it clear that, although sporadic reports can be found on this topic dated as early as 1898, sustained efforts by numerous research workers are of quite recent origin. Guilford, in his 1950 Presidential Address to the American Psychological Association (1950), pointed to the appalling neglect of this subject by psychologists and called their attention to this important area of investigation. According to him, less than two-thousandths of about 121,000 titles listed in the *Psychological Abstracts* over the period of 23 years preceding 1950 could be regarded as definitely bearing on the subject of creativity.

Fortunately, the picture has been changing rapidly since 1950, possibly because of Guilford's plea, or because of the nationally felt need for mobilization of talents, or even because of "a culturally acceptable rationalization of our own fear of loss of Self" (Henry, 1959, p. 266). The swing of the pendulum has, in fact, made the word "creativity" surprisingly popular. "It is more than a word today, it is an incantation. It is a kind of psychic wonder drug, powerful and presumably painless; and everyone wants a prescription" (Gardner, 1962, p. 8).

The field is effervescent and it is not easy to achieve a well-balanced perspective of what is really happening and what is lacking in our research efforts. Without, therefore, trying to be comprehensive, this paper examines some of the problems and possibilities presented by studies in creative thinking.

DEFINITION AND ASSUMPTIONS

The word "creativity" has been used in myriad ways by people in different walks of life and, accordingly, no single definition will cover all the meanings ever attached to it. Rhodes (1961) reported that, out

REPRINTED by permission of the Author and *Exceptional Children*, 30:403–10, May, 1964.

of approximately fifty definitions collected, he could roughly discriminate four strands in terms of (a) person, (b) process, (c) press (interaction between human beings and their environment), and (d) products as embodiment of ideas. It is easily seen that various investigators could be studying quite different aspects of human behavior according to the specific definition of the term employed. Definitions by MacKinnon (1962) and Torrance (1962a), for example, seem to belong to the second category, process, while Rogers (1961) seems to prefer a definition in terms of the fourth category, products, in conjunction with the third, press. In the future research, then, it is of utmost importance for a research worker to define the term explicitly and to try to deduce his hypotheses from this definition. There is no absolute need for everyone to agree on a single, universal meaning of "creativity," but at least investigators should be clear about what they mean by this word. "If we can get people to be precise . . . we can learn to live with any discovered disagreement" (Sprecher, 1963, p. 77).

When a complete taxonomy of creativity is achieved through descriptive methods, including the "critical incident" approach, we will be in a better position to discriminate precisely among such terms as "spontaneity," "originality," "imaginativeness," "ingenuity," "inventiveness," "inquisitiveness," and "productivity," but for the moment, "creativity" would seem to be used as a generic word to cover these and other relevant aspects of human behavior. In this paper, "creative thinking" or "creativity" is defined, after Torrance, as "the process of forming new ideas or hypotheses, testing these ideas or hypotheses, and communicating the results." The definition is necessarily a broad one but the emphasis is on the searching, exploring aspect (what Guilford calls "divergent thinking") of the *process* of hypothesis-forming, testing, and result communication.

There are several rather basic assumptions seemingly taken for granted in many studies. First, after Wilson (1958), it seems to be generally assumed that the abilities involved in being creative are universal and that these abilities can be cultivated by adequate procedures. Secondly, it seems assumed that such abilities are expressed in our daily life through invention, discovery, curiosity, imagination, experimentation, exploration, and the like, as well as by their final products such as scientific inventions, theories, improved products, novels, poems, designs, paintings, drama, and the like. The third assumption would seem to be that such abilities can be observed and/or measured reliably by various instruments of observation and/or assessment. As we accumulate enough evidences through our studies, some of these and other assumptions undoubtedly will be re-examined and re-structured. Meanwhile, it is desirable to remember that many investigations are based upon unstated and untested assumptions.

CRITERION OF EVALUATION

Evaluation of creative thinking involves a difficult problem of criterion. Maslow (1943), for example, believes that we may expect the clear emergence of self-actualization needs and, hence, of the fullest and healthiest creativeness only from "basically satisfied people" whose physiological, safety, love, and esteem needs are satisfied. This reasoning raises several interesting topics for discussion.

The first is about the nature of the criterion. When Maslow talks of the fullest and healthiest creativeness, he seems to be using the individual as his own criterion. Since, in Maslow's system, satisfaction of the basic needs leads to the highest needs of self-actualization, one's creativeness is measured, more or less, in terms of what he can do or what he has as potential. In his logic, needs to be creative could be expressed, so to speak, as "what a man *can do,* he *must do.*" In our society, however, this is not the only criterion used in judging man's creativeness. If something or some idea is *new to the society,* we call it imaginative, ingenious, or perhaps even wild regardless of the degree of self-actualization for the people involved.

Difficulties arise from the fact that these two sets of criteria (individual and social) do not always agree with each other. Desperate efforts of a poor but brilliant painter could lead and really have led, as historical fact, to a masterpiece which outlives him for many centuries to come. Did he "actualize himself?" The answer is, yes and no. Socially speaking, he expressed himself and his talent to the fullest under the circumstances the society could provide him. He was a creative painter. But he might have been a case of failure in his "becoming" process from the individual criterion. He did not "live" to the fullest extent possible, and hence he did not develop what he had to its bloom. With his basic needs unfulfilled and being driven by financial demands, the poor painter tried his best, but surely he did not do all that he could have done. Vincent van Gogh, Robert Schumann, and other similar examples tell us that society can accept as creative those products of very "unhealthy" creativeness.

As pointed out by Wilson (1958), we face the same difficulty in our appraisal of creative thinking in children and adolescents. In judging adult creativity, we usually resort to a social criterion, and the evaluation of newness is based on the concept of new to our society or at least new to the group doing the evaluation. In evaluating creativity in children, on the other hand, an individual criterion is more customarily adopted in which major emphasis is placed on the newness of an idea or object to the individual child who produced it. It is merely on an assumption that we are basing our efforts to cultivate creativity in children, an assumption that activities promoting self-expression in children will eventually produce adults who will be regarded creative in the social sense of the term. This assumption has not, however, been examined empirically by longitudinal studies. In passing, it should also be pointed out that we need studies, possibly after that of Sprecher (1963), to find out what behavior patterns characterize creative individuals in children's minds. Contrasts in interpretation between adults and children, and their longitudinal vicissitudes, would cast much light upon the problem facing us today.

Another feature of socially determined evaluation is its inevitable value-centeredness. Schumann's musical pieces and van Gogh's paintings are deemed highly creative, while the most ingenious method of by-passing a bank alarm system is condemned by society. Even though these two modes of evaluation are closely intertwined with each other, we have to choose one of them as the criterion in our research. The difficulty in this choice might be partially obviated by shifting our attention from the end *products* of creativeness to the *process* of creative activity. Naturally, we must start from products to discriminate original activities from unoriginal ones (note, incidentally, the value connotations in these adjectives), but if we concentrate upon the process, we could work with less difficulty.

First we exclude the goodness-badness judgment of the product and pay our attention to newness, imaginativeness, and originality of the idea. Then we explore the process by paying particular attention to certain common features among the creative workers. We must depend mostly upon verbal behavior and other expressive movement of organism to explore such a process. For example, a photographic record of the many intermediate stages of Picasso's paintings and concurrent observation, plus his own report, could give us certain clues in this regard. Protocols of counseling process could be analyzed from such a viewpoint too. A similar approach was suggested by Flanagan (1963) as the first step toward measurement of creativity. Our anchoring points are still stimulus situations and products, but in spite of the long-standing behavioristic taboo, we must infer to the process within the organism to fully understand the phenomenon. Sooner or later, we need in our research something of an equivalent to Hull's theory of learning, if we should go beyond mere description.

Still another point might be made: Maslow's hierarchical interpretation of creativeness of man gives a misleading impression in that he deals with this aspect of our behavior as if it were something culminant, something which adds to already well-functioning personality and not as something essential in our "existing" or lower-order living. The fact would seem, however, that it takes creativeness for any man merely to be alive in the threatening world; therefore, this could very well be an indispensable aspect of human existence and behavior. It would be useful to observe how differently people deal with their dissatisfied needs at different levels of creativity. In a sense, a person's current personality is as much a product of his creative abilities as of his motives, habits, and values, and his characteristic ways of handling successive new situations are the best indicator of his creativeness. Again the *process*, not the *product*.

Our preferred approach to the problem, therefore, might be something like this: we explore three sets of variables, (a) external demands for an organism to be creative, (b) basic needs of the organism which call for creative behavior, and (c) the organism's potential to be creative. In the flux of these three, we find an organism behaving creatively under a given situation. We pay our full attention to the process and, finally, check our "process diagnosis" against the final products.

INSTRUMENTS OF MEASUREMENT

Most of the present instruments for measurement of creative thinking are developed after Guilford's suggestions (Guilford, Wilson, Christensen, 1952) which are, in turn, based upon his factor analytic model of human intellect (Guilford, 1959). Seemingly, almost all of these instruments are of the assessment type in which tests are based upon assumptions about and knowledge of the nature and structure of creative abilities; therefore, our test items should be representative of these abilities to be valid. So far as the factor-analytic model of creative thinking abilities satisfactorily explains those high on these traits and those low on them, and so far as our items are representative samples of these basic traits, our instruments should serve as good assessment. These two fundamental conditions, and hence, content validity of our tests are more or less assumed at present rather than proven.

On the other hand, if we would deal with these tests as predictors to find either concurrent or predictive validity against some external criterion, a troublesome situation also arises. It is quite difficult to obtain reliable and valid criteria at present. A committee report on criteria of creativity (Harmon, 1956) presented an outline of the general evaluation procedure. This is the procedure of working backward from an ultimate criterion, a measure of individual scientists' total creative scientific accomplishment based upon panel assessment by fellow scientists, to some more immediate and "feasible" working criterion, such as their papers, patents, rate of achievement, and still further to their present performance. At the final stage, we pass from criterion behavior to test behavior, or predictors.

A difficulty in this very reasonable procedure is that it is almost impossible to find a criterion which is not contaminated by other features of human traits and behavior, especially by intelligence. In school situations, such "feasible" criteria as honor point ratio and achievement test results are apparently quite poor for our specific purpose. Teacher nominations have been found inadequate by Holland (1959) and peer nominations also present some problems (Getzels and Jackson, 1962; Torrance, 1962a; Yamamoto, in press, a). Quite often, judges do not know what to look for in appraising creative thinking abilities, and strong halo effects are observable.

Even when a single criterion is selected, there still remains a difficult question of whether various tests of creativity are, in fact, measuring the same quality of mind. As Thorndike (1963) aptly pointed out, there is some doubt as to the presence of "any common characteristic running through these tests to which the common term 'creativity' may legitimately be applied" (p. 422). Low correlations, even with the confounding effects of a common general ability factor, would seem to suggest that a modest common core, if any, plays only a minor role so far as success on any given test is concerned. In the worst case, some of these subtests might not, in fact, be measuring anything over and beyond simple response variability.

This directs our attention to one of the most urgent needs in this area of study—namely, for more basic studies to obtain information on reliability and validity of these tests, on relationships of these tests with other kinds of cognitive and conative measurements, and on normative characteristics of scores on these tests among various populations. Before every single investigator runs away with his imagination and before we thus get thousands of unrelated and often private tests of creativity, we have to stop and take stock of what we now have and find out more about the already existing instruments, their strengths and weaknesses. First of all, we need publicly accessible scoring manuals, and then, we need studies on several kinds of reliability and of validity. In addition, inter-relationships both among the current tests of creativity and between these and other measures of human behavior should be intensively investigated to weave a nomological net to support this old, but new, concept. Finally, we must have studies on normative distribution of creative quality of mind based upon representative populations so that "highly creative" subjects in a local group, for example, will not in fact correspond to "low creative" subjects in another group.

In measurement and discussion of creativity, it is perhaps wise to distinguish among true, measured, and effective ability to reduce possible confusion. These are, respectively, "the true ability or the life space which is being measured; second, the actual measurement itself or the metric which is an approximation of the life space, and third, the effectiveness of the person or the manifestation of the ability in the life situation which may differ from both the hypothetical true capacity or the measurement which approximates it" (Anderson, 1960, p. 17). Our hope is that measured creativity is a good approximation of true creativity (potential) and also that effective creativity (achievement) has some, and wishfully, simple relation to true and to measured creativity. We should not, however, expect perfect relations among these three, partly because of imperfections in measurement and partly because adjustment in the life situation involves factors, both psychological (intellectual and nonintellectual) and sociological, other than creativity itself.

It should also be remembered that a time element is often absent from our short-period test, while actual creative process tends to involve a longer time perspective (Anderson, 1960). "What seems to appear is that deep concern with a problem over a period of time on the part of an able person results in a creative output. Our tests of ability measure the level of ability, not whether the person will be deeply concerned" (Anderson, 1960, p. 19). This aspect of the phenomenon, corresponding to what Sprecher called "work habits" (Sprecher, 1963) deserves careful attention in our future studies.

UNEXPLORED FRONTIERS

When public interests in a topic are intense, it is particularly difficult for research workers not to be carried away in overgeneralization of their results which are, at best, merely suggestive. To be quite honest and fair, we do not yet know so much about creative thinking, its nature and nurture, that we may prescribe some magic formulae to suit every individual in every situation. In fact, we see unsolved problems every place we turn.

For example, it has been suggested (Meadow and Parnes, 1959; Osborn, 1957) that participation in a certain type of group preparation and discussion tends to increase scores both on quantity and quality of ideas. The case has not, however, been closed at all since there are reports to the contrary (Dunnette, Campbell, and Jaastad, 1963; Taylor, Berry, and Block, 1957) and because, accordingly, we do not know specifically the why, how, when, what, and what for of rein-forcement of creative responses (or rather, response variability). We do not, likewise, know whether expression of creativity is general or specific to stimulus situations, and we have not investigated transfer of training concerning this kind of behavior. It is obviously premature to declare that "we interpret these results as demonstrating a lasting effect on certain types of creative ability produced by the creative problem-solving course" (Parnes and Meadow, 1963, p. 315).

Another area left wide open at the moment is anthropology and sociology of creative thinking. Some exploratory attempts have been reported (Pepinsky, 1961; Torrance, 1962b; Torrance, 1962c) but there is much room for more studies on, for example, cultural deter-minants of creativity, including sex stereotyping, group reaction to original members, and familial and social-class variables affecting de-velopment of a child's imaginativeness. In classrooms and in homes, it might be questioned whether American "buddy-daddying" or "af-fectionate-mothering" (Henry, 1959) is the only requirement and means for cultivation of creative talents.

School environment provides thousands of research topics. Although there seems to be a fair amount of consensus among research workers (Taylor and Holland, 1962; Torrance, 1962a; Yamamoto, 1961) on the possible relationships between intelligence and creativity, we need to explore further and deeper to establish qualifications and limitations which are to be placed on such a general statement as "correlation be-tween measures of creative thinking and those of intelligence is low (.20-.40) in the general, unselected population and practically zero in selected (high ability) populations, and correlation seems to be slightly higher for girls than for boys."

The interesting concept of "threshold of intelligence" in the relation-ships between creative thinking abilities and school achievement, first proposed by Anderson (1960) and explored further (Torrance, 1962a; Yamamoto, in press, b) deserves additional investigation. According to Anderson (1960, p. 25), "We can think of ability level in terms of thresholds and ask questions as to the amount necessary to carry on a task and then consider the factors that determine function beyond this threshold. There are cut-off points or levels above which the demon-stration of ability in relation to environmental demands is determined by the presence of other factors." In other words, creative thinking abilities might show their really differential effects only beyond a certain minimum level of intelligence.

In pursuance of this line of study, it is well to employ multiple approaches to the problem including correlational and regressional methods. The now-traditional arbitrary group classification (Getzels and Jackson, 1962; Torrance, 1962a) might result in a serious loss of information because of the exclusion of subgroups of considerable size and interest (de Mille and Merrifield, 1962).

Another task is to examine the so-called school atmosphere and teacher behavior in the classroom which either facilitate or hinder the development of creative thinking abilities in pupils. Torrance, in his preliminary analysis (1960) of the evaluative thinking of teachers, gave data collected from 163 teachers from grades six through 12 by achievement tests, aptitude tests, and daily logs recorded and submitted by teachers themselves. The results, though tentative, suggest that the most effective teachers do more "thinking" activities (convergent, divergent, and evaluative thinking) than the least effective ones, while the former tend to report fewer cognitive and memory activities compared to the latter. In addition, the most effective teachers, when they evaluate, make a "trouble-shooting" or hypothesis-making kind of evaluation rather than straight-forward positive or negative evaluation. The phenomenon under investigation here is obviously quite complex and does not allow a simple, common-sense conclusion (Yamamoto, 1963) but some leads and hunches are already available for exploration by willing workers (Torrance, 1962d; Yamamoto, 1963).

Along this general line, Flanders, Anderson, and Amidon (1960) reported a study on dependence-proneness responses in the classroom by a 45 item pencil-and-paper test. They suggest that students showing low dependence-proneness might show a stronger tendency toward creativity and, at the same time, be less restricted by teacher influence. Investigation of dynamic interaction processes will add much to our understanding of human personality.

Studies on school environment as a determinant of creative growth are obviously needed to explore the impact of school climate on students. A study by Thistlethwaite (1963), for example, suggested that college environment conducive to productivity in science might show characteristics quite different from those of another environment conducive to productivity in arts, humanities, and social sciences. Thistlethwaite, together with many professionals, believes that our graduate programs should be critically examined in terms of both student and faculty creativity and productivity. Similar studies in the lower levels would also be informative.

As our demands on teachers keep on expanding in number and in scope, it becomes imperative for us to find the way, first, to prepare teachers better for their job and, second, to protect them from personal frustrations and tensions in dealing with creative, often wild, children. We cannot and should not overemphasize the importance of this aspect of human intellect at the cost of teachers' mental health. Similar remarks could be made in regard to school counselors, and thus the task is squarely put on applied psychologists and teacher-counselor educators to come up with a balanced preparation program for teachers and counselors.

Further, we must carefully analyze our educational objectives and our curriculum to see what kinds of mental functions are aimed at and developed in our education. Whether the "inquiry-type" curricula suggested by Suchman (1961) or Rubin (1963) are the answer is not to be determined rashly because, as elaborated elsewhere (Yamamoto, 1963), this inescapably involves a thorough re-examination of our fundamental values. If, however, our purpose is really "the full, rounded, and continuing development of the person," as stated in the report of the President's Commission on Higher Education (1947, p. 9), we must make certain that all aspects of mental functioning are equally well cultivated through our fundamental education.

REFERENCES

Anderson, J. E. The nature of abilities. In E. P. Torrance (Editor), *Education and talent.* Minneapolis: University of Minesota, 1960. Pp. 9–31.

de Mille, R., and Merrifield, P. R. Book review of *Creativity and intelligence* by J. W. Getzels and P. W. Jackson. *Educational and Psychological Measurement,* 1962, *22,* 803–808.

Dunnette, M. D., Campbell, J., and Jaastad, Kay. The effect of group participation on brainstorming effectiveness for two industrial samples. *Journal of Applied Psychology,* 1963, *47,* 30–37.

Flanagan, J. C. The definition and measurement of ingenuity. In C. W. Taylor and F. Barron (Editors), *Scientific creativity.* New York: John Wiley & Sons, 1963. Pp. 89–98.

Flanders, N. A., Anderson, J. P., and Amidon, E. J. *Measuring dependence proneness in the classroom.* Minneapolis: Bureau of Educational Research, University of Minnesota, 1960.

Gardner, J. W. Renewal in societies and men. *Annual report of Carnegie Corporation,* 1962. Pp. 3–13.

Getzels, J. W., and Jackson, P. W. *Creativity and intelligence.* New York: John Wiley & Sons, 1962.

Guilford, J. P. Creativity. *American Psychologist,* 1950, *5,* 444–454.

Guilford, J. P. Three faces of intellect. *American Psychologist,* 1959, *14,* 469–479.

Guilford, J. P., Wilson, R. C., and Christensen, P. R. *A factor-analytic study of creative thinking: II. Administration of tests and analysis of results.* Los Angeles: Psychology Laboratory, University of Southern California, 1952.

Harmon, L. R. Criterion committee report. In C. W. Taylor (Editor), *The first University of Utah research conference on the identification of creative scientific talent.* Salt Lake City: University of Utah Press, 1956. Pp. 251–259.

Henry, J. Spontaneity, initiative, and creativity in suburban classrooms. *American Journal of Orthopsychiatry,* 1959, *29,* 266–279.

Holland, J. L. Some limitations of teacher ratings as predictors of creativity. *Journal of Educational Psychology,* 1959, *50,* 219–223.

MacKinnon, D. W. The nature and nurture of creative talent. *American Psychologist,* 1962, *17,* 484–495.

Maslow, A. H. A theory of human motivation. *Psychological Review,* 1943, *50,* 370–396.

Meadow, A., and Parnes, S. J. Evaluation of training in creative problem solving. *Journal of Applied Psychology,* 1959, *43,* 189–194.

Osborn, A. F. *Applied imagination.* (Revised edition.) New York: Charles Scribner's Sons, 1957.

Parnes, S. J., and Meadow, A. Development of individual creative talent. In C. W. Taylor and F. Barron (Editors), *Scientific creativity.* New York: John Wiley & Sons, 1963. Pp. 311–320.

Pepinsky, Pauline N. The social dialectic of productive non-conformity. *Merrill-Palmer Quarterly of Behavior and Development,* 1961, 7, 128–137.

President's Commission on Higher Education. *Higher education for American democracy.* Volume 1. *Establishing goals.* New York: Harper and Row, 1947.

Rhodes, M. An analysis of creativity. *Phi Delta Kappan,* 1961, *42,* 305–310.

Rogers, C. R. Toward a theory of creativity. In C. R. Rogers (Editor), *On becoming a person.* Boston: Houghton Mifflin, 1961. Pp. 347–359.

Rubin, L. J. Creativity and the curriculum. *Phi Delta Kappan,* 1963, *44,* 438–440.

Sprecher, T. B. A proposal for identifying the meaning of creativity. In C. W. Taylor and F. Barron (Editors), *Scientific creativity.* New York: John Wiley & Sons, 1963. Pp. 77–88.

Suchman, J. R. The University of Illinois studies in inquiry training. In E. P. Torrance (Editor), *Creativity: third conference on gifted children.* Minneapolis: Center for Continuation Study, University of Minnesota, 1961. Pp. 67–84.

Taylor, C. W., and Holland, J. L. Development and application of tests of creativity. *Review of Educational Research,* 1962, *32,* 91–102.

Taylor, D. W., Berry, P. C., and Block, C. H. *Does group participation when using brainstorming facilitate or inhibit creative thinking?* New Haven: Department of Psychology, Yale University, 1957.

Thistlethwaite, D. L. The college environment as a determinant of research potentiality. In C. W. Taylor and F. Barron (Editors), *Scientific creativity,* New York: John Wiley & Sons, 1963. Pp. 265–277.

Thorndike, R. L. The measurement of creativity. *Teachers College Record,* 1963, *64,* 422–424.

Torrance, E. P. *A preliminary analysis of the evaluative thinking of effective and ineffective teachers of experimental mathematics courses.* Minneapolis: Bureau of Educational Research, University of Minnesota, 1960.

Torrance, E. P. *Guiding creative talent.* Englewood Cliffs, New Jersey: Prentice-Hall, 1962. (a)

Torrance, E. P. The creative personality and teachers' concepts of the ideal pupil. Paper read at National Association for Gifted Children, Chicago, April, 1962. (b)

Torrance, E. P. Cultural discontinuities and the development of originality of thinking. *Exceptional Children,* 1962, *29,* 2–13. (c)

Torrance, E. P. Who is the underachiever? *NEA Journal,* 1962, *51* (8), 14–17. (d)

Wilson, R. C. Creativity. In N. B. Henry (Editor), Education for the gifted. *Yearbook of National Society for the Study of Education,* 1958, *57,* Part II. Pp. 108–126.

Yamamoto, K. Creativity and intellect: review of current research and projection. Paper read at Minnesota Psychological Association, Minneapolis, April, 1961.

Yamamoto, K. Relationships between creative thinking abilities of teachers and achievement and adjustment of pupils. *Journal of Experimental Education,* 1963, *32,* 3–25.

Yamamoto, K. Creativity and sociometric choice among adolescents. *Journal of Social Psychology,* in press. (a)

Yamamoto, K. Threshold of intelligence in academic achievement of highly creative students. *Journal of Experimental Education,* in press. (b)

Epilogue: Creativity in American Education, 1865–1965

E. Paul Torrance

IN A SENSE, "CREATIVITY" HAS ALWAYS BEEN AN ISSUE IN EDUCATION. Certainly it has been an issue in American education throughout the century from 1865–1965. Interest in creativity in American education, however, has waxed and waned during this period and has been discussed under a variety of names. At different periods educators have used different ways of describing the status and role of creativity in education. See if you can guess the period in which the following description was published:

"A boy of good ability has just completed his high school course. In a conversation with a friend the question is raised about going to college. 'A man is a fool to go to college after he has had a good high school education. Haven't we learned everything there is any use of knowing? We have had astronomy and geology, chemistry and physics, botany and zoology, physiology, psychology and political economy, and a great many

REPRINTED by permission of the Author and adapted from an address presented at the Symposium on Creative America: 1865–1965, Clarke College, Dubuque, Iowa, March 13, 1965.

more, and I don't see as there is anything more to learn. And if we forget something, why, there are our books: we can learn it over again!

"But suppose a youth in this condition be advised or constrained to go to a university and continue, if we may so designate the process, studies. . . . His instructor asks him for an account of the work he has done along the line he proposes to follow. Our student names over a number of books and courses he has taken. Very well. The professor next asks him whether he is especially interested in any particular problem that he wishes to solve. He evidently does not understand the question, and the professor puts it more plainly. Is there not some particular point in this whole field which you are conscious that you do not know and have not been able to find in books, and that you think may be worth your time and labor to investigate? No, he does not think of any such point. He has never been taught to look at the subject with a view of doing anything about it himself. . . .

"Finally the instructor shoulders the man bodily, gives him a problem that he is anxious to have worked out, gets all the material and apparatus ready to his hand and tells him to go to work. Next day he calls at the man's laboratory and finds him reading a book. Asks him what he has done? What observations he has made? What experiments he has tried? And finds that he has made no observations, done nothing, but has found a 'very interesting book.' "

Actually, this is a quotation from an article by C. F. Hodge and published in a 1900 issue of *Pedagogical Seminary*. In what ways are college students today different from the one described by Hodge? If I can judge by the college students that I know, the ones that my colleagues describe, and the ones described in the educational literature of 1965, they have much in common. Today's high school student would not say that "A man is a fool to go to college after he has had a good high school education." He realizes that he must go to college in order to get along in life and succeed in a vocation. He may believe that he has already learned everything there is any use of knowing, because apparently most high school students are still being taught as though knowledge is complete. The textbooks they have studied present knowledge in this way, as though all truths in the field are known. We do have new curricular materials that treat fields like physics, chemistry, biology, mathematics, and even social studies as incomplete and as ways of thinking. In Minnesota, for example, only 12 percent of the high schools use the newer curricular materials in physics and less than 15 percent use any of the newer curricular materials in chemistry (Kleeman, 1965). These newer curricular materials have now been available for several years.

Our entering college student would *not* be expected to answer the questions that Hodge in 1900 expected him to answer about choosing a problem for investigation. We college professors have long ago given up such expectations. We have even given up such expectations of graduate students until they pass their preliminary doctoral examinations. It is then that we start asking students the questions that Hodge's professor asked his entering freshman. It is then that we usually receive the same answers that Hodge's professor received.

It is not that high school graduates are incapable of meeting this expectation. They are. This has been abundantly demonstrated by the work of such men as Jablonski (1964) at the University of Pittsburgh. Jablonski first discovered the potential of high-school students participating in National Science Foundation Summer Science Programs. He encouraged his summer proteges to continue their research work the year round and solicited the help of personnel in Pittsburgh schools. Some of their experiments have been published in regular professional journals against the competition of mature and experienced scientists. Jablonski estimates that 25 percent of his high-school researchers are producing publishable material.

Jablonski wanted next to begin working with younger students. His colleagues told him that this was really getting ridiculous, but nevertheless he went ahead with projects with fourth-, fifth-, and sixth-grade students. Jablonski admits that he had grossly underestimated the readiness of these children to do research. Groups of them have joined him in cancer research. They asked the meaning of words and soon mastered the technical language just as if they were learning English. As a result, these youngsters produced useful research ideas and discoveries.

EDUCATIONAL EXPERIMENTATION

It is interesting to examine the ups and down of educational research and the experimental testing of creative ideas in education. Let us examine the following quotation from *Education*, a journal that has been published continuously from 1880 to the present time:

"Our incessant experiments in educational reform serve only to interrupt the traditions, and therefore to lessen the prestige of our culture; they perplex teachers, scholars, and parents alike; they lead to doubt and hesitancy, and must all end in a simple return to the old system" (Marble, 1880, p. 176).

Although these words were written by A. P. Marble in 1880, they are words that have been shouted during every period in American education since 1865. In fact, they have been shouted so loudly and so effectively that one might wonder if Marble's prediction is not accurate—that is, that we continually return to the old system. Certainly, this is a loud and powerful voice in America today.

It has not mattered that the experimental methods, materials, or procedures frequently have been able to demonstrate their superiority to the "old system." For example, let us examine what happened to the curriculum that Francis Parker, one of the Progressive Educators, established at Quincy, Massachusetts, between 1875 and 1880. As the fame of Parker's methods spread, the attackers arose. They so disturbed the patrons of the Quincy schools that they demanded an evaluation. The children were then tested by the old tests, not by tests that would have assessed the objectives of the new curriculum. Nevertheless, the pupils in Parker's school came out ahead of pupils taught by the old methods, even on the old tests (Atkinson and Maleski, 1962).

These same loud cries are heard today. One reads that we do not know enough about creativity to increase the chances that creative behavior will occur, that anything learned in a creative way is superficial and of no value, that children who learn in creative ways will neglect the three R's, that the best way to produce creative individuals is to be rough with them and make school as unpleasant for them as possible. When we conduct controlled experiments to see what would happen, if we were to teach various kinds of subject matter creatively, these claims simply do not hold up. In one carefully-controlled and thrice replicated study, for example, Sommers (1961) in a technical course found that students who learned in creative ways not only showed more signs of creative growth but also did better on the old tests than did their controls who learned under the old methods.

Have we achieved a more creative kind of education from 1865 to 1965? Let us examine in broad perspective the pulsations, the educational reforms, the innovations and experiments of the past 100 years and see what progress we have made and perhaps out of this re-evaluation we may be able to avoid some of the mistakes of the future and not have to "return to the old system."

STAGES OF AMERICAN EDUCATIONAL THOUGHT

Frederick Mayer (1964) maintains that American educational thought has passed through four identifiable periods. The first was dominated by Puritan ideas, authoritarianism, stress on the limitations of man, and the view of man as a sinner filled with evil. It made of the teacher a punitive disciplinarian. All dissenters were persecuted.

During the second period, we find a spirit of enlightenment and freedom. This is the period that gave us the Constitution and the Bill of Rights. Thinkers such as Franklin and Jefferson stressed creativity and the possibilities and freedom of man. Franklin said, "When a man ceases to be creative, he ceases to really live."

The year 1865 finds American educational thought moving into a third period. It was the time of Emerson, a thorough-going individualist, who believed in intellectual independence, the inadequacy of the scientific method, and the importance of intuition. He believed that though books can both stimulate and hinder man in the search for truth that there was too much conformity and too much respect in the United States for the printed word. He believed that one must be creative even to read well. He believed that the learner should be free and brave. Emerson's ideas, however, were ridiculed and ignored. They had little impact on the educators of his day.

Here and there, however, we find records that a few courageous and imaginative educators were trying to translate Emerson's ideas into educational methods and materials. For example, in 1865, Professor S. S. Greene at a meeting of the National Teachers Association reported on an innovation called "Object-Teaching." He is quoted as follows:

"Object-teaching is that which takes into account the whole realm of nature and art, so far as the child has examined it, and assumes as known only what the child knows, and works from the well known to the obscurely known, and onward and upward till the learner can enter the fields of science, or of abstract thought. . . . It is that which makes the school a place where the child comes in contact with realities, just such as appeal to his common-sense when he roams at pleasure in the fields. It is that which relieves the child's school task by making it intelligent and possible. It bids him examine for himself, discriminate for himself, and express for himself, while the teacher stands to give hints and suggestions, not to relieve the labor" (Calkins, 1880, p. 170).

He describes something that comes quite close to what I have called the "responsive" or "creative" environment, a kind of teaching that stresses self-initiated learning and discovery but which combines with it the most sensitive and alert kind of guidance and direction—a kind of teaching that involved an absorbed kind of listening, fighting off criticism and disparagement, and making all sincere efforts to learn rewarding enough to keep up the zest and excitement of learning. Teachers often ask what they can do to stimulate creativity in the class-room and it is quite natural that teachers imbued with a stimulus-response psychology would count upon a stimulating environment to bring about creative growth. As a matter of fact, probably nothing could do more to discourage creative behavior than to stimulate original ideas, searching questions, invention, and the like and then not be respectful of these ideas, questions, and inventions.

The fourth period, known as the era of pragmatism, was represented by such eloquent spokesmen as William James, John Dewey, William Heard Kilpatrick, Francis Parker, Boyd Bode, George Counts, and others. This was the era of Progressive Education which centered on the interests of the child, emphasized democratic ways of behaving, made group standards important, and used problem-centered inquiry. Educational psychologists such as G. Stanley Hall and William James may be said to have supplied the educators of this period with many of their ideas, ideas which were disbelieved then and are still disbelieved rather widely but many of which are being tested today and found to be accurate. For example, G. Stanley Hall (Mayer, 1964, p. 287) who stressed creativity placed emotions above intellect and intuition above reason. He believed, however, that too much analysis into the creative processes would destroy spontaneity and creativity and that we should not ask too many impertinent "how's" and "why's." Hall (1905) believed in the potentiality of man and that too much time is wasted in school training for orderliness in going, standing, and sitting and that teachers erred by helping children over difficulties instead of spurring them on to self-activity.

William James (1900), too, believed in potentiality. He recognized and respected individual differences, although he did not have a very clear idea about mental abilities and how different kinds of mental abilities are called into play by different ways of learning and by different kinds of tests. In his *Talks to Teachers* in 1900, he cautioned:

"Be patient, then, and sympathetic with the type of mind that cuts a poor figure in examinations. It may, in the long examination which life sets us, come out in the end in better shape than the glib and ready reproducer, its passions being deeper, its purposes more worthy, its combining power less commonplace, and its total mental output consequently more important."

In general, however, history indicates that teachers have not been patient with this creative type of mind. In a study of over 400 eminent men and women, Goertzel and Goertzel (1962) estimated that at least 60 percent of them had serious difficulties in schools. Many of them did not make good grades on the examinations and many of them dropped out of school, at least for a time.

Francis Parker (1905) reacted against the Puritan tradition in education. He believed in man's goodness and potentiality. To the Puritan, education must be authoritarian; to Parker, education has to be democratic. In Puritan education, the supernatural was all important; in Parker's curriculum, nature was the guide. To the Puritan, truth is absolute; to Parker, truth is discovered in the relativity of experience. He assigned roles of importance to curiosity, fantasy and imagination, intellectual courage, and observation. He believed in planning learning activities, methods, and materials in the light of information about developmental stages. He maintained, however, that there is no perfect method.

William Heard Kilpatrick (Van Till, 1963), is generally recognized as the leader of that wing of the Progressive Education movement that sought answers in the potential of the individual learner. He emphasized purposeful activity, intrinsic motivation, planning, open-mindedness, rigor, honesty, group action, and child-centeredness.

John Dewey, however, was one of the most prolific writers and thinkers associated with the Progressive Education movement. He was a spokesman of the rebellion against authority and showed how the scientific method can be applied to all realms of inquiry. He believed that the knowledge of the future must be functional, experimental, and subjected to the rigorous tests of laboratory methods. In *My Pedagogic Creed* in 1900, he stressed the importance of developmental processes, interests, and learning as an active rather than as a passive process.

According to Cremin (1961) and others, Progressive Education died in 1957 when the *Journal of Progressive Education* ceased publication two years after the Progressive Education Association had passed out of existence. Many say that it was dead long before this. Others point out that the issues raised by the leaders of progressive education have not died and that many of the ideas developed by them will never die. Progressive Education aroused so much controversy and still engenders such strong negative reactions that the label of Progressive Education is still used to damn educational innovations. Many of those who attack ideas directed to a more creative kind of education are trying to attach to them the label of "Progressive Education" as a way of damning them.

LOOKING TO THE FUTURE

Let us examine the major precepts of Progressive Education and see if what we have learned during the ten years since the dissolution of the Progressive Education Association in 1955 places us any nearer the achievement of the creative kind of education that will help us realize the American dream of a kind of education that will give every child a chance to grow and to achieve his potentialities. It is perhaps an oversimplification but it may be said that Progressive Education rested its case on the following six chief precepts:

1. Individual differences among children must be recognized.
2. We learn best by doing and by having a vital interest in what we are doing.
3. Education is a continuous reconstruction of living experience that goes beyond the four walls of the classroom.
4. The classroom should be a laboratory for democracy.
5. Social goals, as well as intellectual goals, are important.
6. A child must be taught to think critically rather than to accept blindly (Atkinson and Maleska, 1962, p. 78).

On the basis of what we have learned during the past ten years about the human mind and its functioning, mental abilities and their development, and the interaction of mental abilities and ways of learning and teaching, it would appear that all of these precepts are good as far as they go but that they do not go far enough. For example, examine the precept that "individual differences among children must be recognized." This precept cannot help us a great deal unless we know what individual differences are important in individualizing instruction and what individual differences in mental functioning, motivation, and personality are brought into play in various ways of learning. What we have learned during the past ten years has enabled us to remove much of the puzzlement experienced by educational researchers of the 1920's and 1930's.

We need no longer be puzzled by McConnell's finding in 1934 that mental age as measured by an intelligence test is more highly related to achievement in second grade arithmetic when taught by authoritative identification than when taught by the methods of discovery advocated by many of the Progressive Educators. Hutchinson in 1963 in a study involving learning in junior high school social studies also found that under traditional, authoritarian teaching, there is a statistically significant correlation between mental age and achievement but not between measures of creative thinking and achievement. In the experimental conditions where there was considerable opportunity for learning in creative ways the reverse was true. In another 1963 study involving fifth grade children using programmed instruction in language arts, Gotkin and Massa found significant negative relationships between measures of creative thinking and achievement. A year earlier, Stolurow (1962) had found higher correlations between measures of originality and achievement than between mental age and achievement with programmed materials in mathematics and statistics. The difference was that Gotkin and Massa used programmed materials that permitted only tiny mental leaps and gave no opportunity for making, identifying, and correcting errors, while Stolurow's programmed materials emphasize a trouble-shooting or hypothesis-making-and-testing approach that builds specific but multiple associations to a stimulus. MacDonald and Raths (1964) found that highly creative children are more productive on frustrating tasks than are less creative children. Furthermore, they enjoy such tasks more than do their less creative peers. The least creative children are less productive in open tasks and the most creative ones react less favorably to closed tasks. Thus, pupils of varying levels of creative thinking ability react differently to different kinds of curriculum tasks and are possibly best taught by varying procedures.

Perhaps the most exciting insight that has come from our research (Torrance, 1962, 1963, 1965) is that different kinds of children learn best when given opportunities to learn in ways best suited to their motivations and abilities. Whenever teachers change their ways of teaching in significant ways, a different group of learners become the stars or high achievers. This has far-reaching implications for educating a larger number of people to a higher level and for achieveing a higher level of dignity and mental health in our society.

Regarding the second precept that "we learn best by doing and by having a vital interest in what we are doing," we recognize now that people do not learn automatically by doing. This type of learning requires the most sensitive and alert type of guidance and direction. Children must be taught the skills of inquiry and research—the spirit and skills of historiography, the concepts and skills of descriptive and experimental research. Curiosity and creative needs are strong enough and universal enough to make creative ways of learning useful for all individuals. Creative ways of learning should not be regarded as an exclusive way of learning for all children nor for any single child, even though he may prefer learning in creative ways and learn little when we insist that he learn exclusively by authority.

I see no real quarrel with the third precept that "education is a continuous reconstruction of living experience that goes beyond the four walls of the classroom." From an understanding of the creative process, we recognize that one thing must be permitted to lead to another. To accept such a precept requires a great deal of courage on the part of the teacher. Both teachers and pupils have to learn to think in terms of possible consequences. Too frequently, the educational system is unwilling to accept the consequences of this "continuous reconstruction of living experiences beyond the four walls of the classroom." To illustrate what I mean I would like to cite a couple of examples, since they also identify the potency of the threats that arise when schools accept the fourth and fifth precepts that the classroom should be a laboratory for democracy and that social goals, as well as intellectual goals, are important.

The first illustration (Courtis, 1964) involves a beginning fourth grade teacher who had received a directive to put aside the regular work of the day and devote time with the children to plan what they might do to make their city more beautiful. After some hesitation, one pupil reported that his alley was full of ashes and wondered if cleaning out the ashes in the alley would do. This struck a responsive chord and soon the children were inspecting the condition regarding ashes in 35 blocks around the school. Every child found that not only the alleys were full of ashes but that yards were overflowing with metal baskets, barrels, and ashes. From what their parents had said the children knew that the city should have collected the ashes. They asked why the ashes had not been collected and decided that it was probably because the city did not have enough money. One girl said that her father worked in city hall and thought she could find out. Her father found that the city had appropriated $30,000 for the purpose. Now, the children were really excited and made their reports to their parents. A day or two later, the principal of the school received a telephone call from the head of the Department of Public Works. He asked, "What are you doing up there? Your business is to teach reading, writing, and arithmetic. Lay off meddling in city affairs." Thus, the city beautiful project came to a sudden halt.

The second illustration (Courtis, 1964) was in the classroom of an able and experienced teacher. One of her brightest pupils reported from a local newspaper clipping that half of the people in their city live in substandard houses. They wanted to know what is a standard house and if they lived in one. No one knew what a standard house was and the teacher confessed that she did not know either. The quotation was from the State Commissioner of Housing so they wrote letters to him, using models found in their textbooks. The next day letters were passed from one to another and judged until the best one was selected. The Commissioner replied promptly. The material that he sent was studied avidly without any assignment from the teacher. Applying the criteria of a standard house to their own homes, the entire class reported that they all lived in standard houses. The teacher explained that they were fortunate people, but they insisted that they wanted to see some substandard houses. Together they planned, with some suggestions from the teacher, an extensive survey. They discovered a long strip of the city where the houses were mere shacks, with only one source of water, a small pipe coming out of the ground, outdoor privies, and a wide ditch that was an open sewer. They were indignant.

The father of one of the boys was so affected by his son's excitement that he went to the city hall to verify his son's statement. The city engineer showed him a map with well laid out streets and sewers, and laughed at the statement. The man was embarrassed and took his son to task for telling him such a story. The boy stood his ground and demanded that his father come with him and see for himself. After his visit he was more incensed than his son. The next day he gathered together a group of important citizens and took them along the entire length of the open sewer. The indignation of these men led to investigations that revealed much graft and dishonesty that had escaped public notice. Eventually, new elections were held and the grafters removed from office and the slum district uncovered by the class was greatly improved. Almost daily the class read the newspapers and covered the classroom board with clippings, feeling that they had had a part in the reforms. They read avidly in school and library books about civics, city management, etc. The teacher had never had a class so active in planning their own learning activities and asking for help when they ran into new problems.

From these illustrations, it seems clear that when these precepts are accepted, learning becomes alive, plenty of creative behavior occurs, there is cooperation with parents and action by them. It is also clear that the acceptance of these precepts can be very threatening to the security of the teacher and call not only for courage but for skills in group dynamics, creative problem-solving, and strategies for coping with change and stress. We have now accumulated enough knowledge about group dynamics, creative problem-solving, and strategies for coping with change in stress to make these precepts meaningful. Even now, however, it is still a struggle to get such information into the textbooks and curricula of teacher education. Knowledge in these areas, however, has the potentialities of permitting us to stand on the shoulders of the Deweys and Kilpatricks and see further than they were able to see.

We are also beginning to understand the inadequacies of the sixth precept that "a child must be taught to think critically rather than to accept blindly." We know now through creativity research that it is not enough to be able to criticize the ideas of others. It is necessary that students be able to produce ideas of their own, to be critical of their own ideas, and to use tests that keep them from deceiving themselves. Furthermore, we have learned that in the production of ideas it may be necessary to suspend judgment temporarily to avoid unduly putting the brakes on our thinking (Osborn, 1963). After ideas have been accumulated, it is then necessary to formulate criteria for use in judging these ideas and making decisions. If knowledge is to be used constructively in solving problems creatively, the learner must have a constructive, though not uncritical, attitude towards information. He must be willing to entertain and test the possibility that the information may be true and useful. In two different experiments, I (1965) found that students who assumed a constructive rather than a critical attitude toward available information were able to produce a larger number of creative solutions and more original ones. One of these experiments involved the reading of research articles and a second, textbook material. In both, one group was asked to read material with a critical attitude, identifying defects; and the other was asked to read material with a creative or constructive attitude, thinking of other possibilities, applications and the like.

In a presentation of this type, it is possible to review only a very small percentage of the ideas and research information that has the potentiality of moving us ahead and of adding to the precepts of Progressive Education many of the missing elements required in the education demanded by our day. I would not venture to say whether or not education today is more creative than it was in 1865. I do believe that we have made enough advances in educational thinking to make possible a more creative kind of education. The big questions are: "Will we choose to use these advances in knowledge and thinking and will we choose in time?"

It seems to me that we have reached a stage in history when we *must* make such a choice. In the past, we have been able to survive with static goals and concepts. Things are changing so rapidly that we can no longer survive, if we insist on thinking and living in static terms. It seems to me that we cannot afford to return to the old ways. We must accept the creative challenge.

REFERENCES

Atkinson, Carroll and E. T. Maleska. *The Story of Education.* Philadelphia: Chilton Books, 1962.

Calkins, N. A. "Object Teaching: Its Purpose and Province." *Education,* 1880, *1,* 165–172.

Courtis, S. A. "How to Shift from Teaching to Serving." *Forward Look in Education,* 1964, Vol. 1, No. 5.

Cremin, L. A. *The Transformation of the School: Progressivism in American Education.* New York: Alfred A. Knopf, 1961.

Dewey, J. *The Child and the Curriculum.* Chicago: University of Chicago Press, 1902.

Goertzel, V. and Mildred G. Goertzel. *Crades of Eminence.* Boston: Little, Brown, 1962.

Gotkin, L. G. and N. Massa. *Programmed Instruction and the Academically Gifted: The Effects of Creativity and Teacher Behavior on Programmed Instruction with Young Learners.* New York: Center for Programmed Instruction, Inc., 1963.

Hall, G. S. *Aspects of Child Life and Education.* Boston: Ginn and Co., 1907.

Hall, G. S. "A German Criticism of American Schools." *Pedagogical Seminary,* 1905, *12,* 508–512.

Hodge, C. F. "Foundations of Nature Study." *Pedagogical Seminary,* 1900, 7, 95–110.

Hutchinson, W. L. "Creative and Productive Thinking in the Classroom." Doctoral dissertation, University of Utah, Salt Lake City, 1963.

Jablonski, J. R. "Developing Creative Research Performance in Public School Children." In C. W. Taylor (Ed.) *Widening Horizons in Creativity.* New York: John Wiley & Sons, Inc., 1964. Pp. 203–219.

James, W. *Talks to Teachers on Psychology.* New York: Holt, Rinehart and Winston, 1900.

Kilpatrick, W. H. *Education for a Changing Civilization.* New York: Macmillan Co., 1926.

Kleeman, R. P. "Survey Finds Most Schools Don't Teach Modern Science." *Minneapolis Tribune,* February 2, 1965, p. 15.

McConnell, T. R. "Discovery vs. Authoritative Identification in the Learning of Children." *University of Iowa Studies in Education,* 1934, *9(5),* 13–62.

MacDonald, J. B. and J. D. Raths. "Should We Group by Creative Abilities?" *Elementary School Journal,* 1964, *65,* 137–142.

McNemar, Q. "Lost: Our Intelligence? Why?" *American Psychologist,* 1964, *19,* 871–882.

Marble, A. P. "Learning or Training: Which?" *Education,* 1880, *1,* 173–176.

Mayer, F. *American Ideas and Education.* Columbus, Ohio: Charles E. Merrill Books, 1964.

Parker, F. W. *How to Study Geography.* New York: Appleton-Century, 1905. (Copyright 1899)

Osborn, A. F. *Creative Imagination.* (Third Revised Edition) New York: Charles Scribner's Sons, 1963.

Sommers, W. S. "The Influence of Selected Teaching Methods on the Development of Creative Thinking." Doctoral dissertation, University of Minnesota, Minneapolis, 1961.

Stolurow, L. M. "Social Impact of Programmed Instruction: Aptitudes and Abilities Revisited." Paper presented at the American Psychological Association Annual Convention, St. Louis, Mo., September 2, 1962.

Thayer, V. T. *The Role of the School in American Society*. New York: Dodd, Mead and Co., 1960.

Torrance, E. P. *Guiding Creative Talent*. Englewood Cliffs, N. J.: Prentice-Hall, Inc., 1962.

Torrance, E. P. *Education and the Creative Potential*. Minneapolis: University of Minnesota Press, 1953.

Torrance, E. P. *Rewarding Creative Behavior: Experiments in Classroom Creativity*. Englewood Cliffs, N. J.: Prentice-Hall, Inc., 1965.

Van Till, W. "Is Progressive Education Obsolete?" In P. Woodring and J. Scanlon (Eds.) *American Education Today*. New York: McGraw-Hill Book Co., 1963.

Author Index

(Names appearing in capitals refer to the principal authors of articles, with the article beginning on the page followed by an asterisk. Names with initials refer to annotated bibliographic citations at the end of chapters. Names without initials refer to sources cited in the readings. Names of junior authors are followed by reference to the senior author of the article.)